I0868023

WAYANG & Its DOUBLES

WAYANG & Its DOUBLES

Javanese Puppet Theatre, Television and the Internet

Jan Mrázek

NUS PRESS
SINGAPORE

© 2019 Jan Mrázek

Published by:

NUS Press
National University of Singapore
AS3-01-02
3 Arts Link
Singapore 117569

Fax: (65) 6774-0652
E-mail: nusbooks@nus.edu.sg
Website: http://nuspress.nus.edu.sg

All rights reserved. This book, or parts thereof, may not be reproduced in any form or by any means, electronic or mechanical, including photocopying, recording or any information storage and retrieval system now known or to be invented, without written permission from the Publisher.

ISBN 978-981-4722-95-7 (paper)

National Library Board, Singapore Cataloguing in Publication Data

Name(s): Mrázek, Jan.
Title: Wayang & its doubles : Javanese puppet theatre, television and the internet / Jan Mrázek.
Description: Singapore : NUS Press, [2019] | Includes bibliographical references and index.
Identifier(s): OCN 1089242429 | ISBN 978-981-47-2295-7 (paperback)
Subject(s): LCSH: Wayang. | Shadow shows--Indonesia--Java. | Puppets--Indonesia--Java.
Classification: DDC 791.53095982--dc23

Cover image: "Cah Ayu" wayang puppet from *Hidden Violence: Contemporary Wayang Performace* (2009) © Eko Nugroho

Designed by: Nur Nelani Jinadasa
Printed by: Mainland Press Pte Ltd

To Javanese puppet masters,
in admiration.

Contents

List of Illustrations

(Photos are by the author unless otherwise indicated.)

Acknowledgements

This book was researched and written, intermittently, over a period of twenty years. The final product is a small trace of much solitude and great many encounters and experiences, in Indonesia and other countries—while watching *wayang* and/or television, chatting at performances, in coffee shops, on buses, in people's houses and offices. I have been given time, attention, thoughts, stories, information, assistance, access, many scary motorcycle rides, food and drink, and writings and recordings. People have shared with me something of themselves, their anger and bitterness, as well as enthusiasm and happiness. Puppeteers, musicians, television crew, producers, and executives, wayang and television audiences, netizens, students, colleagues, friends, people sitting next to me on buses or in coffee shops, *becak* and taxi drivers ... most of their names do not appear in the Acknowledgements; as I reminisce, I feel thankful to all of them. I feel special gratitude for many brief, fleeting encounters, when people gave selflessly, namelessly, to a stranger.

The initial questions about the interaction between wayang and other media began to form already at the time of my dissertation research in the 1990s. As always, I thank my teachers, each of whom has shaped my thinking: my main puppetry teacher Ki Naryocarito in Kertosuro, the late Alton "Pete" Becker at the University of Michigan, Stan O'Connor, Jim Siegel, Marty Hatch and John Wolff at Cornell University, and Sumarsam from Wesleyan University.

The idea to write a book about wayang and television (the internet came later) came to me in panic when I found in my mailbox, one day after the application deadline, a torn, cramped piece of paper (courtesy of Jim Siegel) with an advertisement for a postdoctoral research position at the Verbal Arts in Audio-Visual Media in Indonesia (VA|VAVMI) study group at Leiden University. There I first researched the topic in a focused way for three and half years (1998–2001). I am grateful to Ben Arps, the leader of VA|AVMI, for his support, guidance, and inspiration, at that time and in later years. I remember fondly my fellow VA|AVMIers, Theresa Birks, Edwin Jurriëns, Klarijn Loven, and Suryadi.

At various later stages in researching and writing the book, I have received encouragement, help, and ideas from (I succumb to alphabetical order) Bambang Murtiyoso, Matthew Cohen, Didik Yulianto, Kathryn Emerson, Eri Kusmeri, Miguel Escobar Vallera, Ki Faizal Noor Singgih, Hanggar Budi Prasetya, Irving Chan Johnson, Ki Manteb Soedarsono, Nunuk Sri Rahayu, Marc Perlman, Preciosa de Joya, Priyambudi Sulistiyanto, Raharja, Roosmala Endah, Sri Hartati, Laurie Sears, Suratno, Thow Xin Wei, Ki Tristuti Rachmadi, Wakidi Dwidjomartono, Ki Warseno Slenk, Philip Yampolsky, Yayang Naza ... among many others. Some of them, and many others, are mentioned and often quoted in this book, always with gratitude.

For my parents, this book is just another attempt: *v komoře je*

Last but not least, I would like to thank Paul Kratoska, Peter Schoppert, and copy editor, Lindsay Davis, at NUS Press, for the care and thoughtfulness with which they have taken the book through the publication process.

Introduction

Wayang in the Age of Television: An Event

> *It was warm and bright on the roof. The summer afternoon was drowsy with the hum of passing helicopters; and the deeper drone of the rocket-planes hastening, invisible, through the bright sky five or six miles overhead was like a caress on the soft air.*
>
> —Aldous Huxley, *Brave New World*

In a town in East Java, at the courtyard of the local army headquarters, preparations were being made for a *wayang kulit* (shadow puppet theatre) performance. A spacious stage and a large tent without walls were set up, like at a pop music concert—except for the *wayang* screen, a white translucent cloth stretched in a wooden frame, somewhat like an oversized widescreen television. (*Voice-over: These sorts of similes and semantic slippages, in which traditional theatre and modern technology/entertainment/media are juxtaposed, compared, even conflated, allowed to clash and blend, summarize this book's exploration.*) In front of the screen, the instruments of a large gamelan ensemble were arranged on the stage—the metal parts (the dozens of gongs of different sizes and the metal keys of metallophones) all polished and shining with the colour of bronze, beamed with pride and wealth like a new Mercedes. Later, during the performance, the *dhalang* (puppeteer) would sit facing the middle of the screen. A strong electric lamp (with a halogen bulb, which provides sharper, high-definition shadows) was attached to the wooden frame in the centre of the screen so that it would hang above the puppeteer's head and illuminate the screen and the flat, perforated puppets, which would project shadows, rather like when film is projected on a screen in a movie theatre. Two banana tree trunks were attached horizontally to the lower edge of the frame, so that the puppeteer could stick the sharp ends of the puppets' central manipulating sticks into them when he wanted the puppets to remain on the screen. To the puppeteer's left was a large wooden puppet box, which he would use to produce sound effects by striking it with a beater and by sounding an attached set of metal plates with his foot. On the box, as well as to the puppeteer's right, were large trays stacked with puppets. Throughout the performance, the puppeteer, with a large microphone attached to his chest and the electric lamp above his head, would sit in the centre of this sophisticated apparatus, rather like a pilot in the cockpit of an airplane, directing his crew and every aspect of the performance. Chairs for spectators and sofas for VIPs were set up on the side of the screen where people could see the gamelan instruments, the puppeteer, and the puppets. A small space was left on the other side of the screen, where people could watch the black and white version: the shadows of the puppets. The amplification system was installed with massive speakers arranged around the performance area. Numerous mikes on stands were visible on the stage, next to the instruments, almost like in a recording studio. Hawkers slowly began to gather just outside the courtyard, preparing to sell food and drinks. This kind of preparation, like much of the performance that would follow, was no different from other wayang performances, which are typically part of all-night communal celebrations (weddings, anniversaries, and such), where people not only watch wayang, but also socialize and enjoy the festive atmosphere. More like when watching television than watching conventional Western theatre, people move around freely, come and leave, and talking, drinking, eating and smoking are part of the enjoyment of the performance. When the puppeteer makes mythological characters come alive in the present, makes old stories speak to people's experiences, and comments more or less directly on local, national, and international current affairs, the people watch, laugh, gossip, and freely chat. In wayang, rather like on television or the internet, they find news, education, art, entertainment, violence.

0.1 The wayang event televised by Indosiar described in this Introduction. It is illuminated by strong television lights. The puppeteer (*dhalang*), Ki Anom Suroto, sits at the centre of the screen. Kediri, June 2000.

0.2 The wayang screen with puppets during a performance. The puppeteer is visible sitting under a lamp (*blencong*) which illuminates the screen and the puppets. While most people usually watch from this side, some people may watch the shadows on the other side of the screen.

The possibility of wayang's resemblance to its doubles, to television and related, earlier and later electronic media, has haunted wayang performances and people's imaginations. In a play of identification and othering, in an endless, disorienting search for its self and its image, in a struggle with and about its self, wayang has both been becoming and resisted becoming, more like television—growing into something like a modern, electronic mass medium and a popular commercial entertainment—since even before its first encounter with it.

This event was among the small minority of wayang performances covered by television. The crew of the large Indosiar television company arrived from Jakarta—some 16 hours by car—together with a mobile recording studio (resembling a large bus), a generator, cameras, lights, and cables. While the performers were preparing instruments, the wayang screen, the puppets, and the whole wayang machinery, the television crew was setting up cameras at the margins of the stage, powerful television lights, and cables. Everything was arranged so that, while the television hardware would be immediately noticed by people present at the performance—it shared the stage, literally and figuratively, with the wayang hardware—it would not be visible for people watching the event on television. There seemed to be no communication

0.3 Setting up television lights and cameras (on office desks), as well as the wayang screen frame and musical instruments, for the performance described in this Introduction.

between the wayang crew and the television crew—they were working independently, both during the preparations and throughout the performance, as if following parallel trajectories not destined to come together. As if ... and yet, the actions of the television crew had to follow and respond to the performance, while the performance was influenced by and infused with television.

Most of the expenses for the event were covered by the sponsor, a local army chief. He paid for the puppeteer and his troupe, for renting the tent, chairs, and other equipment, and for food for guests—as would be the case in most wayang performances—but he also paid a large sum to Indosiar, and provided lodging and food for the television crew.

To make the event even more spectacular, the sponsor rented two special vans with large projection screens and projectors on their roofs, which were originally donated by the Japanese government to promote family planning. On these screens in the outer performance area, as well as on a television monitor inside the house, people could watch the output from the television cameras.

The event's sponsor approached the television producer, asking him to broadcast not only the wayang performance, but also a speech. The producer recorded the speech but it was never broadcast, which

0.4 On the margins of the same performance, people watch wayang simulcast (in this case, the output from the Indosiar mobile studio), projected on the screens attached to the top of vans, which had been donated by "Japan" for the promotion of family planning.

made the sponsor complain later, as the producer told me. The producer was annoyed by what he saw as the sponsor's audacity; the sponsor by the producer's.

The producer asked the puppeteer to keep the performance short—four or five hours. The puppeteer, showing that he wouldn't be ordered around, and probably irritated, went on for about seven hours, which upset the producer.

The recording of the performance was edited: cut to about half of the original length, with long parts—that the producer, but not necessarily the puppeteer, considered unessential, uninteresting or inappropriate—deleted. It was broadcast several weeks later, late on a Saturday night. I was then watching "it" again—its spectre, its double, the same performance yet not the same—alone in the quiet of a home in the city of Solo, several hundred kilometres away, in a very different atmosphere from the original lively event. Many others would be watching like me, alone or with a few friends. Quite likely, the recording was rebroadcast over the next few years. If not this particular performance then other Indosiar broadcasts very much like it would be "pirated" and sold on VCDs (video compact discs) in markets, and eventually, in a later but not so distant era, uploaded on YouTube and watched by thousands of wayang fans on their laptops, office computers and, especially, smartphones.

A Coffee Shop

Television and wayang are two media/technologies/institutions and modes of being/communicating/seeing/imagining/fantasizing. (Among different genres and regional variations of wayang theatre, I focus primarily but not exclusively on Javanese wayang kulit, just as I focus on television among related audio-visual media.) In this book, I explore how they meet/coexist/invade/haunt each other.

Tele-vision is, among other things, a powerful kind of visibility (pervading, in more or less new modes, also the internet), and much of what happens revolves around seeing that overcomes place and distance; around the seductive, transformative power of the tele-gaze; around light and speed; around people's desires for their own and wayang's tele-visibility; and around their attempts to manage (their) images.

Being, seeing, place and distance are at stake, in a world conjured and haunted by wayang, television and other media. To try to understand the encounters and interpenetration of the media means to learn about multiple, clashing and changing ways of being in the world, and ways of handling and fantasizing continuities and change. One is lead beyond thinking in terms like modernization and globalization, to feeling the clashing rhythms and tempos, the incoherent situations, contradictory developments, and the diversity of people's positions, views, emotions, dreams and nightmares.

This book is inspired, disturbed, irritated, haunted by Javanese discussions, texts, performances, and media, as well as works of authors such as Martin Heidegger (especially his late texts on art and technology), Maurice Merleau-Ponty (on perception, the body and space), Jacques Derrida (on spectrality and media), Paul Virilio (on speed, light and exposure), Samuel Weber (on media), James Siegel (on language, technology and space), and others. I do not apply their theories or methods, but rather shamelessly localize their thoughts and gather them into one coffee shop, so to speak, with those of Javanese practitioners, wayang audiences, and theorists, as well as with my observations and reflections. I open this metaphorical coffee shop as near as possible to the places where wayang and television happen, and let the actuality of wayang and television invade, interrupt and check the discussion.

One could see my and others' interest in the interaction between wayang and the electronic media in the context of developments in wayang scholarship: studying wayang, less as a timeless cultural object, and more as a lively form of theatre, entertainment, and social event intensely involved in contemporary world.[1] One can also situate the book in television studies. When I began thinking about wayang and television in the 1990s, the mainstream literature on television was focusing predominantly on Europe and America, and often construed television and its problems as universal. Scholars studying television beyond Europe and the United States were few, but their work challenged then-dominant notions about television and the media. It suggested that television had to be studied in each place to some extent all over again, through the thickness of local situations and experiences, as an extended, multiplying, and changing family of phenomena, histories, fantasies.

Writings on Indonesian television and related media demonstrate the fruitfulness of thinking about the media locally.[2] Many of them were published in the first decade of the millennium, yet I believe I "haven't missed the funeral" (to paraphrase a Czech saying). Rather, this book hopes to take advantage of a long-term view of the interaction between wayang and television, and as the last chapter should demonstrate, television (in various manifestations), rather than being simply replaced, continues to figure in the wayang world in interesting ways today, alongside, as well as on, the internet.

The internet figures prominently only in the last episode of this book's narrative. Yet, just as I will try to show that something of the interaction and mutual haunting of wayang and television had been foreshadowed in pre-televisual times, so the story of the Net in Indonesia today is in many ways continuous with, or haunted by, the adventures of older media, in a ghostly play of doubles across ages. Not only have television and tele-visibility been in some ways reborn and continue to thrive on the Net; but a sense of the long-term interplay between wayang on the one hand, and electronic media/entertainments such as the radio, television, and audio(visual) recordings, on the other, a sense of the net of old and new media as it has been developing and changing over time, and a sense of how people have been forever caught in the net of mediation, local and global, make for a richer understanding of current Indonesian mediascapes, including the workings and hauntings of the Net today.

All thinking and all presence is mediated: by technologies and media in the broadest sense; by language and images; by the thoughts and gestures of others, living and dead; by my own imagination, fantasies, dreams, and body; and by things both absent and present that are always between me and the world, between me and other people, between me and me. There is no simple equivalent of Javanese wayang in Singapore or Europe, for example, but—or because of that—one can reflect on parallels: how television and other earlier and later media have affected the rhythm and speed of people's lives, how people experience place and distance, acquire knowledge, think, enjoy themselves, and socialize. One can think about how media shape what people do in the evenings, what children talk about with their friends, how the forms and functions of storytelling have (and have not) changed, or how the role and experience of older media, such as books or theatre, have been affected. These questions are behind many academic and popular debates about television and the internet, but the particularity of the Javanese case twists familiar questions in thought-provoking ways. When people in Java speak about wayang, television, and the Net, one often feels that they are talking about problems familiar and relevant beyond Java; one feels that we are all caught in the same net; that "we are all wandering in the same storm".[3]

This is also true about wayang scholars, myself included, who like and unlike television producers, represent wayang—record it, frame it, zoom in on details that they deem interesting and zoom out to show wayang in a larger picture, revealing and concealing and managing its image and, in the process, their own. Scholarly representations, including this book, intersect those of television and the internet. I have suggested elsewhere, with particular reference to art history, that scholarship works somewhat like television[4], and in the concluding part of this book I discuss how especially in the age of the internet, we can recognize anew how puppeteers and wayang scholars are wandering in the same storm. This work then, as a scholarly representation, reflects on phenomena that are not simply out there, outside this book. It looks—are not books endowed with the power of vision? like puppets? like cameras?—it looks at wayang, television, the internet, and especially their interaction, as one looks at a fellow wanderer in whom one recognizes something of oneself; as one looks in the mirror; as one one looks—with fascination, sympathy and/or horror—at one's double.

Behind this book is a desire to enjoy an episode in the human comedy; getting lost in it, rather than presenting "findings" or an "argument". Imagine that coffee shop I mentioned earlier, set up at a wayang performance. Imagine yourself sitting in it, listening to the conversations—about wayang, television, VCDs, or the internet, and, indivisibly, life; a net of discussions with many knots and many loose ends, with no single argument, moving easily from gossip to philosophical and mystical ruminations, from personal anecdotes to historical reflections, from observations on what is happening at this particular wayang event to what someone read in a book about wayang, with reflections and observations interwoven somewhat like the voices in the many-layered texture of Javanese gamelan music. It is an exchange that strives to understand life as much as to be entertained by it. Don't assume that this Javanese coffee shop is so Other from a café frequented by French philosophers.

The Marriage of Wayang and Television

In September 1996, less than a year after Indosiar had begun to broadcast wayang on a weekly basis, an Indonesian newspaper article about wayang on television commented:

> The "marriage" of traditional art with electronic mass media cannot be evaded any more. In the beginning, this "marriage" happened between traditional arts—specifically performing arts—with radio and cassette technologies. Now, it is between traditional arts and television.[5]

This "marriage", according to another newspaper from the following year, is a matter of "cultural collision [*tabrakan budaya*] between the art of our traditional culture with the art of {*modern-global*}[6] culture represented by *sinetron*"[7] (short for *sinema elektronik*, "electronic cinema": Indonesian television drama or soap opera). The "stumbling" of wayang on television, the article explains, comes from the fact that television and wayang have different "principles", and wayang is stumbling as it tries to adjust to the principles of the television medium. To get over the stumbling, wayang "has to be ready to accept various eliminations and additions of artistic-technical principles".[8] Another writer speaks in similar terms about combining Javanese and Western music: it is, he writes, "a marriage full of conflict".[9]

The above distinctions and assumptions are frequently encountered in Indonesian discussions of the interaction between wayang and television: wayang represents "our traditional culture" while television stands for "modern-global culture"—also often said to be international and/or Western—and the interaction of the media, both a marriage and a collision, is also an interaction of cultures. The marriage, according to the quotation above, started even before wayang encountered television, for it is construed as the same marriage that took place earlier, between wayang and other modern mass media.

One could doubt the usefulness of dichotomies like "traditional" and "modern", or "Javanese" and "Western", for bringing out the fluid complexity of Indonesian life: "People are dancing to different beats, and terms like *modern* and *postmodern*, while helpfully vague, are insufficiently elastic to encompass such variety."[10] One could point to the extent to which wayang today is a (post)modern electronic mass medium, and Indonesian television is often very Indonesian and/or Javanese.

And yet, these basic conceptualizations used by Indonesian practitioners and observers foreground something important. What makes the interaction between wayang and television so resonant with larger issues, so charged with passionate aspirations, conflicts and tensions that reflect forces in Indonesian society, is that the two media and the people who work with them are involved with "cultures". In the interaction of the two media, cultures meet. This book is about this "marriage", its persistence and its stumbling; a disorienting love-hate relationship which involves intercourse as well as collisions between people (wayang performers, TV producers, patrons, audiences, Jakartans, Chinese, Javanese) and, inseparably from that, between media and the ways they represent the world, work with space and time, and make people see, think, and be in the world in particular ways.

One can think of the philosophical notion of "technological system" (and I am attracted to how the language of the definition clashes with my image of shadow puppet theatre): "the complex of hardware (possibly plants and animals), knowledge, inventors, operators, repair people, consumers, marketers, advertisers, government administrators, and others involved with technology".[11] People think, work, communicate, socialize, enjoy themselves, and acquire knowledge in the context of technological systems. Our case suggests that a particular culture (I think of bacterial cultures in yoghurt, alive, fermenting, spreading) permeates the (unsystematic) "technological system". I do not mean culture characterized mainly by being "Javanese" or "Western" (though these Javanese perceptions matter and are part of the cultures)—thus, not culture in the common anthropological sense, connected to an ethnic group—but rather the culture of a technology.

Neil Postman notes in his book on television, drawing on Barthes' notion of myth: "There is no more disturbing consequence of the electronic and graphic revolution than this: that the world as given to us through television seems natural, not bizarre."[12] Technologies are not fully controlled by people. Salman Rushdie: "If a man created god then he could uncreate him too. Or was it possible for a creation to escape the power of the creator? Could a god, once created, become impossible to destroy? Did such fictions acquire an autonomy of the will that made them immortal?"[13] Wayang and television, too, have a degree of "autonomy of the will". Such will is not just the sum of the intentions and dreams of producers or performers, but something that to some extent controls, affects, or infects people. Wayang and television have their own agency, predilections, creative powers, and the power to resistance.

As media—as something in between people and the world through which people see the world, think, communicate—wayang and television are especially deeply part of human lives. They overcome or expand the limits of human faculties, and stimulate imagination and fantasies about seeing, knowing, representing and socializing in new ways. Much of the interaction between wayang and television with which this book is concerned happens in that zone where fantasy and reality meet and, as with doubles, the distinction is in doubt.

0.5 "Parabola antenna, paranormal antenna": evidence of kinship between supernatural forces and modern technology. A cartoon from a Javanese magazine.

I have been writing about wayang and television as if they were two things of the same kind (technologies, audio-visual media), which they are, and are not. It is like when a Javanese author writes that the magic power inherent in a *keris* (a kind of dagger) works like radio broadcasting:

> Incense indeed facilitates the contact [*kontak*] between a person and a keris. So, when we use the analogy of the mechanism of radio, keris is the object that broadcasts the vibration [*vibrasi*], and, with the help of the incense (as the antenna [*antena*]), the human can receive the vibration. At the same time, the human, a radio {*receiver*}, is also the broadcaster. That is because in a certain manner, the human can also broadcast vibration which can be recorded on the keris.[14]

In the same vein, in Indonesian texts it is common to use terms usually applied to television (and adopted from Western languages) to describe wayang as well, such as "wayang media", "wayang technology", or "the dhalang's crew" (*media wayang, teknologi wayang, kru dhalang*). Magical weapons and powers in wayang are commonly compared to the latest American weapon and medical technology, often with the implication that something like the equivalents—doubles—of these apparently recent inventions had been in fact known in Java since ancient times.

Comparisons of radio and the keris, or wayang and television, cross boundaries between what might appear to be incomparable realms, between modern technology and magic, between science and mythology. This free mobility of imagination is key to the interaction between wayang and television. It allows wayang to be seen/fantasized about/feared almost as a kind of television, and television as a kind of wayang, even as their otherness is thus brought into play along with their sameness. Between their sameness and otherness, the desires and anxieties concerning wayang's relationship to its double are played out, all as part of wayang's ego-formation and survival. (Hearing the last words, Sigmund Freud, who happens to be sitting in our coffee shop, looks up with a terrified expression, as if he saw his ghostly, ghastly double.)

We will see throughout this book how people think about the differences between the two media, but for now—more in the spirit of poetic associations than scholarly generalisation—we could relate the question to the late writings of Martin Heidegger. There, art and modern technology,—sitting with *Mbah*[15] Martin in the coffee shop, we may playfully substitute wayang and television—each is a mode of revealing, of truth, but each involves a different way of being in the world. Javanese interpretations of wayang in that the latter tend to treat wayang as a "symbol of human life in this world",[16] and one is told to watch wayang to understand how the world works. Glimpses of such revelations are searched in hidden clues (*sasmita*) that both reveal and conceal, like the shadow as conceived by Heidegger, "a manifest, though impenetrable, testimony to the concealed emitting of light".[17] If one thinks, for a moment, along the lines of Heidegger's thought and Javanese commentaries on wayang, then what is at stake is truth, not any specific truth, but "the unconcealedness of beings as a whole".[18] This thinking does not come anywhere close to capturing what is wayang, what is television, or what is the multiplex interaction between the two, but it might suggest one reason why the "marriage" is of serious concern to people.

What wayang screens is real, imaginary, and symbolic in a way that crosses distinctions between fiction and reality, and between sign and the referent. In ritual wayang performances, the sponsor's family members become characters in the story, as wayang gods and demons visit the village where the wayang takes place. The villagers and the gods, demons, and spirits all meet on the wayang screen, greet each other and negotiate terms of peaceful coexistence. One Javanese said that wayang characters are real for people who believe in supernatural beings and forces (and, she said, most Javanese do) because both the real (*nyata*) Javanese world and the world shown in wayang are full of spirits and invisible forces, so the two worlds are not sharply separate. Even in non-ritual performances, there is a sense that the world evoked in wayang is not simply watched. Stories are chosen in such a way that they are auspicious for the particular occasion, for example, a story about a royal marriage for a wedding. Certain stories, such as those about deaths of powerful heroes, are either avoided or require protective offerings, for again what happens on the wayang screen is not safely separate or distinct from reality—in a somewhat different way than in the case of television. It is telling that most puppeteers do not allow ritual performances to be televised or recorded on video: there are times that technology must respect the silences of wayang and the darkness of the night. This side of wayang sometimes dominates its reductive representations. It is felt in some performances more than others. Even special, magically potent and ritual wayang performances include lively, often rowdy entertainment. Still, part of what wayang is, is its involvement with mysterious, invisible forces, which wayang screens—reveals and conceals.

Television is a different mode of revealing. When a television crew arrives at a wayang performance, strong television lights are set up. One of the developments in wayang that has brought it closer to television has been the increase in electric light, which transforms the space and the theatre: everything is made clearly visible, clean, neatly ordered, and tidy, the visual representation more direct, and more realistic, and language simpler and easier to understand. Thanks to television, the performance becomes visible "everywhere". The world as a whole is (un)concealed, screened differently.

In making a comparison or in opposing two things, one tends to reify and essentialize—the paragraphs above are a case in point. Wayang performances in Java are in many ways different from each other. There are many televisions in Java—different channels, programmes, different spatial and social settings for watching television, there is television on the internet, and so on. Like wayang, Indonesian television is always changing, as is clear from Philip Kitley's work: it "is complexly articulated with a range of historical tensions and political and cultural policy issues that attract interest and comment from advocates representing widely differing views".[19] It has been imagined and fantasized about by many people. To make it meaningful to use the words "wayang" and "television" in a way that respects this variety and variability, we may think about these different wayang and televisions—welcoming Ludwig Wittgenstein into the coffee shop—as "families". In our case, the families are marked by "intermarriage" between wayang(s) and television(s), and during the wayang programme (and not just then), one is watching both wayang and television.

How is wayang Javanese? People in Java as well as foreign scholars commonly focus on wayang as a key to understanding Javanese life-philosophy. Much has been said about how wayang reflects basic values of Javanese culture, how it can be understood as a "Javanese religion",[20] and how wayang as a social event "dramatizes" Javanese social relationships and styles of social interaction.[21] To understand the significance of this study, the "much ado" about the interaction of wayang and television that this book reveals and perpetuates, the desire to bring the two media together and the strength of the opinions and conflicts involved in the process, one needs to keep in mind that wayang is felt by many people to be the matrix of the Javanese worldview, the event is a central ritual embodying Javanese cultural values, and many people are strongly attached to it, feeling that it is an important source of their identity. Assertions of wayang's cultural centrality, and certain ideas about the ethical and mystical meanings of wayang, have been common in various political discourses since at least colonial times, they have been recycled or rethought in a variety of texts and contexts (it is telling, for example, how many books on Javanese philosophy—perhaps most—have wayang figures on their covers), and they remain a topic of lively coffee-shop debates and the object of genuine feelings. All this, alongside and never quite separately from, the continued popularity and liveliness of wayang performances, and—how to put it into words?—the warmth, intimacy, homeliness, the deep-inside emotion of experiencing the wayang event with others (to my mother I would say: like listening to Smetana), is somehow part of wayang's rootedness in the Javanese world, even as this world is changing, alive with tensions, contradictions, and myths (also in Barthes' sense).

How is television "Western" or "international" or "global", particularly the television that we are concerned with here—as it broadcasts wayang on Javanese nights, as it stimulates imagination and fantasy in a Javanese world, as it is watched in Javanese spaces by Javanese people? How is *this* television a Western vision and practice? Just as wayang is not reducible to being "Javanese", television is in many ways as intensely, though differently, part of Javanese lives and nights as wayang. And yet, it would be a hasty oversimplification to say that Indonesian observers are wrong when they claim that television is Western, global, or modern.

Television is different in different places and different times, and during different programmes. This book is about specific instances of television, and to the extent that it reveals something about television in general, it does so through reflections on specific cases. That said, there are certain elements of television which are often important or practically always present—electricity, a flow of programming, certain dominant kinds of framing shots and editing, audio-visuality, certain ways of seeing and relating to the world.

Television grew out of a specific historical situation and worldview. As a family of phenomena and dreams, *that* television was part of Western culture rather like wayang is part of Javanese culture and society, and television shares many "family resemblances" with other Western visions and technologies. Television's mode of representation, for example, is part of the same family history as the realisms of Western painting and the impersonal, objective, scientific representation dominating Western knowledge. In a programme such as the coverage of an event, the screen of television, which separates what is seen from the seer and helps to abolish experienced distance, is a relative of the lenses in scientific instruments as well as the window-like surface of an oil painting, just like the frame of television is a relative of the frame in Western painting and the proscenium stage.[22] Raymond Williams and others have shown how television as a social institution has grown from the specific social conditions of the Western world at a particular time.[23]

How does television, as a technological-cultural complex that is so ingrained in a certain historical time and space, move transculturally, to Java? Similar questions have been central in Southeast Asian studies—one thinks especially of Oliver Wolters' notion of localization.[24] Something radical happens that involves not only the transfer of an idea, technology, and its re-contextualisation (and thus changes in function and meaning), but a deep, internal transformation and reconfiguration of the technological system or cultural complex called television. It involves intercourse—interpenetration, merging, clashing—between cultures, ways of seeing, ways of being. Nothing remains quite the same in the process. And television is merely a drop in a sea with many currents.

Television's claim of objective representation (again I am thinking here primarily about television in the case of wayang/event coverage) creates an illusion of universality that transcends place and culture. The illusion, as illusion, affects how television travels, *as if* being perfectly translatable, *as if* being, like modern objective vision, unaffected by place and distance. In the spirit of coffee shop conversations, we may recall that other powerful ideas and technologies adopted in Southeast Asia in the past had also something universalist about them. Wolters discusses the purported universality of Indian knowledge in early Southeast Asia, and the new, attractive idea that knowledge can be universally applicable rather than local. This follows his discussion of "the single ocean" with its "fundamental unity of communications",[25] whose influence, like in the case of television, derives—to evoke James Siegel's writing on modernity and modern technology— not from the content of transmitted messages, but from connecting people and places: "a middle point that produces cultural effects".[26] The world religions Islam and Christianity, in their claimed universal applicability and transferability, and even in the God's placeless, distance-less point of view and universal knowledge, also have something of the claimed universality of television. Curious connections, which suggest that from a Southeast Asian perspective, the case of television may not be entirely new. Fried banana, anyone?

The introduction of television culture into Java from outside is an ongoing process. Technologies, programmes, techniques, and fashions from Japan, China, Korea, Mexico, the United States, Europe and elsewhere—what Javanese often see as the global or international culture—continue to flow into Indonesia. On the other hand, television is now part of the Indonesian and Javanese worlds, and Javanese and Indonesian culture is part of Indonesian television. In Indonesian television, cultures mix, and as Kitley puts it, it is "'the same but different' from television in Western democratic countries"[27], or, we could add, from television anywhere.

During my research, especially during what I will call the Indosiar era (about 1995–2005), I often felt that despite all the intimacies and interpenetration, wayang and television lead separate lives: one day, I interviewed a village dhalang in his bamboo house with dirt floor, and the other day the executives of Indosiar in the high-rise buildings of

Jakarta's business district, in luxurious offices decorated with Chinese vases from the Ming dynasty, an occasional antique wayang puppet in an elegant glass vitrine, and a widescreen digital television with a few video recordings of German *lied* performances next to it.

At some moments, wayang performers and television people work in very different worlds, yet, at other moments, their worlds overlap and merge, in an unstable, ever-changing love-hate relationship of varying intensity.

As wayang is changed by its co-existence with television, television, as it presents wayang, is a curiously wayang-ised kind of television, a medium haunted, perhaps even possessed, by the spectre of wayang, and watched by many spectators who see wayang even as their eyes are glued to the television medium.

Especially in the realm of experiments and dreams, a fusion of the two media may go quite far. For example, Dr Primadi Tabrani, who was involved in making a "*wayang golek* soap opera" (wayang golek is a form of wayang popular in West Java) that attempted to fuse wayang and television, told me: "It will be a new art. It's not open-air wayang, and it is not television, but it is actually a new art!" (See Chapter Four.) But somehow these attempts never get very far. The dreams grow from unsatisfied desires and remain dreams, or ghosts.

Wayang and television do not meet on a level plane or as equals. When a wayang performance is shown on television, television "brings" (*menayangkan*, from *tayang*) the wayang medium to the audience, and wayang becomes a television programme and is incorporated into the flow of television programming. Television handles, manipulates, appropriates wayang. *Tayangan*, the Indonesian word most commonly used for the "presentation/broadcast" of wayang, also means "something held in the palms", and the verb *menayang* means not only to broadcast/screen but, in the poetry of dictionaries, to "carry something resting on one's palms".[28]

Television, a powerful reality, works with reality and its semblances, pretending that "this is reality", inducing "suspension of disbelief", and redefining the real; or (my/our Heidegger-puppet says) television replaces wayang with its image or representation, conceals wayang's original being, and enframes, orders and harnesses wayang; or (my/our Marx-puppet adjoins) in many cases the television station transforms the transient performance, the labour of the performers, into an object (a recording is the most obvious manifestation) which it can own, stock, manipulate, and exploit (for example, through multiple broadcasts).

But that is not the whole story. Television's claim, articulated by producers of the mainstream wayang programmes, that people see on television an authentic wayang performance unaffected by television, is challenged by puppeteers and audiences who are aware of the agency of television, and of how it makes people see wayang very differently than when they are present at a live performance. Indeed, wayang fights back, often through humour and masquerade—sometimes it seems that wayang *menayang(kan)* television, that wayang holds television in hand like a puppet and plays with it. The struggle and the play is, in part, about truth.

There are conflicts and there is power struggle, but often—at some times more than others—there is the kind of lack of understanding that results when two people, who think that they speak about the same thing, in fact talk about something quite different. In a play of mistaken identities, the different players in the interaction between wayang and television have something spectral about them. The interaction involves a kind of hide-and-seek play with reality, and an interplay between wayang in actuality and semblances of wayang (saying either that the two are different, or that they are same, would be an oversimplification). Involved in this play are people with different backgrounds, lives, aspirations, ways of talking. They are all real and they are all imagined, both people and spectres; they try to communicate, argue, and/or fail to understand each other, with their different and often conflicting perceptions and fantasies of what wayang and television are, and with their individual or institutional ambitions. They are self-motivated individuals, and yet they are also puppets, and what they see, think and do is shaped by something larger than them—by their backgrounds, cultures, ways of seeing, and not least by the cultures and "norms" of the media themselves; by multiple forces pushing and pulling people in different directions.

A television producer may try to make a good television programme and a puppeteer may try to perform a good wayang (or vice versa—often the producer tries to tell the puppeteer what is good wayang). Television uses wayang to television's own ends, while wayang uses television to wayang's own ends—their aims and visions only partly overlap. And people, often frustrated by the hard edges of actuality, or by the impossibility of swimming against the current, talk about how things should be and imagine ideal productions of wayang on televisions, which, when occasionally realized, often turn out to be disappointing.

Perspectives and Experiences: The Present, Historical Narratives and Tense

This was the dominant feeling especially during the "boom" of wayang on national, Jakarta-based television, for about a decade after 1995. Then and even before, the two worlds would sometimes blend. Especially more recently, in some cases at least, wayang and television seem to have become more part of the same world—a telling case is Jogja TV where the producer in charge of wayang is still a puppeteer outside of his TV job, as I discuss in the last chapter. But then, in the earliest day of wayang on Indonesian television, in Yogyakarta in the early 1970s, there seemed to have been similar closeness, to an extent at least. While I hesitate to draw conclusions about any linear development (for example, about the gradual integration of wayang and television), certainly the dynamics of this marriage have been changing over time, as have wayang performances, as has our vantage point. In the light of recent developments, certain underlying factors of the conflicts in the "boom" years come into sharper focus. For example, because of the contrast with local television stations, one sees how the cultural distance and friction between Jakarta (as a symbolic centre of the *modern-global*) on the one hand, and, most visibly, Central Java on the other, was key to the conflict between the media. Jakarta-based Indosiar wayang dramatized this cultural dynamic.

Maurice Merleau-Ponty writes:

> The historian who is not engaged in the battle and who sees it from all angles, who brings together a mass of evidence, and who knows what the result was, thinks he has grasped it in its essential truth. But what he gives us is no more

> than a representation; he does not bring before us the battle itself since the issue was, at that time, contingent, and is no longer so when the historian recounts it, since the deeper causes of defeat and the fortuitous incidents which brought them into play were, in that singular event called Waterloo, equally determining factors, and since the historian assigns to the said historical event its place in the general process of the decline of the Empire.[29]

And the philosopher comments in a footnote: "It would therefore seem that history should be written in the present tense."

From the distance of time, the decade after the television station Indosiar began in 1995 its weekly broadcast of wayang, stands out as a time of "boom" of wayang on television (as the well-known dhalang Ki Purbo Asmoro called it in retrospect, in 2017). Wayang had been shown on television for decades before Indosiar, but it was in those years that the interaction between wayang and television felt to be especially intense, as were the debates that revolved around it. I, too, was drawn into these debates and controversies, as I watched wayang with others, or as people shared with me their excitement and anger, loves and hates, dreams and despair, ambitions and jealousies, as they tried to make me take a side and see the other party through their eyes; and I couldn't help but to do that, although I have kept changing sides, have been pushed and pulled in all directions, crossed between opposing camps. Ideas, theories, observations, and (hi)stories were indivisibly part of, and gained significance and intensity from, the passionately held positions, allegiances, and the back-and-forth of debates. I felt then that blind spots and silences characterized each perspective, each passionately engaged view, but it is only in retrospect that I realize how much I experienced and thought the "battle" from within, and at the same time how my vision was what it was because I could not see into the future, and did not see those times as they now figure in the light of later history, as a part of the longer history of wayang, television, and the internet, as well as later political, social, and technological developments.

To an extent, the first three chapters think of wayang and television from within this time, from within the battle, overwhelmed by the present rather than contemplating it from the distance of time. Present tense in those chapters—and in earlier parts of this Introduction—should be read as referring loosely, fluidly, primarily but not exclusively, to the present of those boom years. Writing from the perspective of that present best captures how I experienced those years, and it was then, in that present, that I began to write down my observations and ideas. To translate those experiences into the past tense, and to enframe moments and events in a historical tele-perspective, would mean to lose something important, particularly since I believe that a strength of this book is to let the reader feel how people felt and thought in particular situations and at particular moments. I speak here about emphasis or tendency, not a historiographical dogma. After reflecting that perhaps "history should be written in the present tense", Merleau-Ponty suggests that thinking from within the battle does not entirely preclude thinking of the structure of the event: "There is a way of thinking, in contact with the event, which seeks its concrete structure. A revolution ... can be thought as well as lived."[30]

Paul Ricoeur argues that "our confused, unformed, and at the limit mute temporal experience" is (re)configured by "the plots we invent".[31] He writes: "time becomes human time to the extent that it is organized after the manner of a narrative; narrative, in turn, is meaningful to the extent that it portrays the features of temporal experience".[32] Different narratives, historiographies, and languages plot and make sense of time differently. Not all but much of what was said and what was going on with wayang and television 15 or 20 years ago still applies or still happens today. Things past persist and sometimes gain new life in the present, to different degrees and in different manners—one example is the way that Javanese internet today is pervaded by television, radio and wayang, including (through "live chat") coffee-shop wayang discussions. "Past" and "present", as concepts employed to plot history, must be thought as fluid categories or constructs, if they are to be helpful in understanding lived temporality. Sometimes the interaction between wayang and television is best narrated in ways that do not insist on too rigid a distinction between "past" and "present", which in English I feel is often accomplished by using relatively unmarked (in the linguistic sense) and more temporarily neutral present tense. (At times I wish I were writing in Javanese or Indonesian, where one is free of tense and the distinction between past and present, when one so chooses.)

Complementing this view from within the "battle" of the boom years, the last two chapters examine the developments in the interaction between wayang and television over several decades before and after, and give a sense of the multiplicity of cases and perspectives. This allows the reader to form a larger picture of continuities, discontinuities and change from 1970s to the second decade of the 21st century, and situate the boom years in that development. This is not to say that a conclusive view is reached; instead, one could think of it as a filmic montage consisting of glances of particular moments and situations, which may aspire to a broader view of history, but which—and this is true also of the resulting montage— is never final and conclusive. As Merleau-Ponty writes:

> My hold on the past and future is precarious, and my possession of my own time is always postponed until a stage I may fully understand it, yet this stage can never be reached, since it would be one more moment, bounded by the horizon of its future, and requiring in its turn further developments in order to be understood.[33]

This describes well what I feel I have learned from thinking about wayang and television not only from within the battle of the late 1990s, but also from later times, including the present moment. If there can be no definite conclusions, our thinking can benefit from doubts and questions that emerge from our present perspective, and the awareness that it is inconclusive. It was already clear at the time of the "boom" that the intensity and character of the interaction grew from particular constellation of factors, which brought out certain characteristics of wayang and television. Puppeteers, television producers, and scholars were imagining other possibilities. Then, however, those other possibilities were in the realm of imagination, supported at most by experiments that could not compete with mainstream wayang. What was actually happening then had to be taken seriously. Now, the interaction between wayang and television has changed (even as there are many continuities), and other possibilities—not necessarily those envisioned before—have become reality and command our attention. The passions of the boom years had then the monumentality of the inevitable (not casual inevitability, but in the way that the present is inevitable as something that one has to face), even a kind of timelessness that occurs when one is fully engaged with the present. Now that battle feels more like an episode in a series, which could have been scripted differently. None of this, I believe, makes the views held in those times, the views from within the battle, incorrect or somehow false; rather, our new perspective, from the distance of time, underlies what was clear enough then but was easily forgotten in the heat of the battle—that all views are bound by their horizons.

History: A Preview

Wayang was broadcast on radio, first in 1934, and beginning in 1936, in regular monthly programmes.[34] By 1962, when television began broadcasting in Indonesia, increasingly frequent radio wayang broadcasts and since the 1970s also recordings of wayang on cassettes, have become an important force in the wayang world.

After its introduction in 1962, television's role in Indonesian society grew only slowly and gradually, becoming more common and influential only in the late 1970s and 1980s.[35] In the world of wayang, where radio and cassettes had been well established, before the mid-1990s televised wayang did not play a prominent role. Starting in the early 1970s, TVRI Yogyakarta (a local branch of the state television) organized 30-minute and 1-hour wayang broadcasts. Since then, different TVRI (state television) stations have been broadcasting wayang in different ways, from brief performances specially commissioned for television, to (later) live coverage of all night wayang events. In 1995, Indosiar, a new, Jakarta-based commercial television station, began to broadcast wayang regularly every Saturday night. In addition to Indosiar and TVRI, other commercial television stations aired occasional performances or short-lasting wayang series, but for a decade Indosiar continued to be the television station most strongly associated with wayang: its Saturday night broadcasts attracted many viewers and sparked sometimes heated debates about wayang on television, probably more than at any time before or since. While this book is not limited to this historical period—about 1995–2005—the events and controversies of this time are at its centre.

By this time, a television set was found in almost every household in Java. A dominant institution in the world of media and popular culture, television had probably even stronger presence in people's lives and in imagination of modernity than it does now, in the age of internet-based media and portable devices, although, as the last chapter shows, television continues to be an important medium, and wayang continues to be broadcast on a number of television channels, in some cases on a daily basis.

While modern media and popular culture have been part of the Javanese world since the colonial period and there is a degree of continuity, the actual development of wayang on television began during the New Order (1966–1998) under President Soeharto. Before the New Order, especially in the later years of the Soekarno era, the influx of Western popular culture was comparatively restrained, in part because of Soekarno's resistance to cultural imperialism and neocolonialism. In contrast, Soeharto's pro-"free market" New Order was a time of intense involvement with Western commercial popular culture and entertainment. At the same time, traditional arts and culture gained a particular kind of visibility under Soeharto: cleaned up, peaceful and orderly, they were put on show, as if on pedestal, as if on television, to create a positive image of the nation under the New Order, and their tamed spirit was meant to pervade Indonesian society. However, this never worked perfectly. The spectacular late New Order wayang performances, often sponsored by government and army officials or by the Soeharto's ruling party (GOLKAR), and often broadcast on television, were exciting and popular events full of lively contradictions. In any case, this double emphasis—on modern commercial popular culture, and on local traditional culture—characterizes the larger political context of the interaction between wayang and television, and the discussions of tradition and modernity, especially in the early "boom" years—even as it needs to be kept in mind that these New Order dynamics were merely one episode in a long history of debates, negotiations, and conflicts concerning tradition versus modernity, or our/Indonesian versus foreign/Western culture. This New Order sociopolitical setting is also relevant here because of the direct involvement of Soeharto's family and associates in commercial television business, as well as the frequent directives to puppeteers coming from "above", often through official puppeteer organizations, that actively attempted to shape wayang.

The economic and political crisis around 1998, the year of Soeharto's downfall, lead only gradually, and in no simple way, to changes in the overall political and cultural setting, and in the interaction between wayang and television—old issues and problems, loves and hates, persisted alongside new ones: there was much truth to how the "new" era was sometimes called in Indonesia: "new New Order" (*Orde Baru baru*); and then there was also the SARS epidemic, short for *Sindrom Amat Rindu Soeharto*—"Very Much Missing Soeharto Syndrom". Wayang on Indosiar, and the debates and conflicts surrounding it, did not stop or significantly change in 1998. The event described at the outset of this chapter took place in June 2000, but is fairly typical for, at least, the whole Indosiar era—even as there were other kinds of wayang events; and even as there would be nothing surprising about seeing a fairly similar event today, 19 years later, including the sponsorship by local or regional government or army officers. A major development has been the gradual decentralization of political power and greater regional autonomy, but even this process has been in no way simple. For example, starting in 2005, a number of local television stations emerged, which were committed to local programming and audiences. However, these have been seen as business opportunities for, and are often controlled by, those same business groups that previously controlled national television stations.[36] Nonetheless, the existence of local television stations has important implications for our case. Some of them have begun to broadcast wayang regularly, and new wayang programmes appeared on other commercial and state television stations, even as Indosiar's dominance of television wayang gradually waned.[37] At around the same time, wayang began to be uploaded and watched on YouTube, and some years later, live-streamed, even as it continues to be watched on television, listened to on radio, and experienced directly at celebrations. Wayang spectators and performers have been creatively and enthusiastically taking advantage of the various new possibilities offered by the internet. On the other hand, there are many continuities between wayang on television and wayang on the internet (most obviously perhaps, a substantial number of the thousands of performances on YouTube comes originally from older media), and some of the new, creative and playful uses of the internet in some ways allow people to return to older but still-current ways of watching wayang – on television, radio and directly at celebrations. As in earlier years, there are also moments of irritation and critical resistance to the powers and illusions of the Net.

While this book is meant to be read loosely against the backdrop of the history of cultural politics in Indonesia, it aims to give a sense of the particular multiple, diverse, and often contradictory experiences, moments, sensations and thoughts, and through them evoke a feeling of how wayang and television, people's pasts and people's dreams—and, some may insist, modernization and globalization—figure in the particularity of human lives.

The Chapters

Chapter One shows how wayang has been becoming more like television, both as a result of interaction between the two media, and, more broadly, because of its involvement in the modern world. Puppeteers seek (tele)visibility and the power that comes with it, by trying to make wayang look good on television. Wayang has been becoming a modern, electronic mass medium, disconnected (or freed) from a particular place of performance, audio-visible across Indonesia. A new kind of visibility has been introduced into wayang. Also, I consider how wayang has had intercourse with other media and technologies, with television's relatives, at the time of and before its marriage with television; and how the marriage is but one knot in a vast net linking people, media, and ways of seeing across generations, foreshadowing and later entangling the Net.

Chapter Two focuses on the production of the mainstream wayang television programme, and discusses resistance to the developments described in the first chapter, as well as the (non)interaction and power struggle between performers and television producers. I discuss how television tries to control and exploit wayang: for example, how it appropriates wayang's image, selling it as "authentic" wayang and as "cure for nostalgia", and how it dispossesses puppeteers of their work and objectifies and appropriates performances by turning them into products/recordings, even as these are then reappropriated by "pirates" and screened at traditional celebrations. Much of the struggle/collaboration among performers, television producers, wayang sponsors and various institutions, concerns everyone's "good image".

In Chapter Three I focus on audience experience, and reflect on what viewers, performers, and television producers say about watching wayang directly and on television. They emphasize the physical, multisensory, collective immersion in the festive wayang event, and contrast it to the experience of watching wayang on television. The spectators' observations show from a different angle both the success and the failure of the "marriage".

Whereas chapters one to three speak about wayang on television rather generally and focus on the mainstream forms of televised wayang in about 1995–2005, Chapter Four attempts to give a sense of the variety and history of different versions of televised wayang, before and during the era of Indosiar wayang. It reviews individual cases that differ from the mainstream, as well as performers' and producers' unrealized ideas, fantasies, and plans.

Chapter Five is an account of later developments, from after the age of Indosiar to the "present" (2019). I examine the emergence of local private television stations and the interaction between wayang and the internet—both change and continuities with the past, as older media and experiences, as well as old and old-new loves, hates, and fears continue to figure in the contemporary world, and persist as they interact with newer media. Against the background of a long view of Indonesian history of image-making and localization, starting with prehistoric cave paintings, I conclude with a reflection on the entanglement of scholars and performers at the age of the internet and IT—how we and our media are all caught in the same net.

1

Bright, Fast, Funny, and Sexy: Wayang in a World with Television

"We just move what is there to the viewers' homes—that's all," says Mr Handoko, the president of the Indosiar television station, a clever man who knows about the power of appearances. We sit in his spacious, posh, truly presidential office, decorated with enormous painted Chinese vases. A large window allows us to survey a slum area far below, punctuated by high-rise buildings and sliced by highways. I feel we are very far from, high above, the world in which I usually watch wayang. President Handoko continues: Indosiar presents "authentic [*asli*] *wayang*".

I frequently hear similar statements from Indosiar producers. The claim of authenticity is an important rhetorical gesture of television. In Chapter Two, we will question it with reference to the implication that wayang is "just" moved from a particular site to people's homes and remains unchanged in the process. However, the "that's all" also conceals something of the (omni)presence of television in the world, because the allegedly asli (authentic, original) wayang—the "live performance", televised or not—is always already influenced by the presence of television and other media.

Most wayang events are not televised. When a performance is covered by television, it may be more or less affected, but its general structure and appearance remains to a large extent the same. Most televised performances do not exist in a world apart from other wayang shows. This situation supports the appearance of authenticity of wayang on television. But this also means that performance practices motivated by television easily penetrate into all performances, because there are no clear borders and no definite limits to television's influence on wayang, and changes inspired by television are not clearly distinct from other developments. (Shouts Baudrillard, banging on the table in our coffee shop: "Such a blending, such a viral, endemic, chronic, alarming presence of the medium, without the possibility of isolating the effects [...] dissolution of TV in life, dissolution of life in TV—indiscernible chemical solution: we are [...] doomed not to invasion, to pressure, to violence and blackmail by the media and the models, but to their induction, to their infiltration, to their illegible violence.")[1] Those puppeteers who do not perform on television imitate televised performances, and so live wayang is in some ways an image, a double, of televised wayang. Untelevised wayang performances cannot be simply posed as something original, virginal, untelevised; or when they are so presented (as when Indosiar people claim that they are "asli"), their originality, in this context, is an effect of television, the real being preceded (Jean Baudrillard)[2] or haunted (Jacques Derrida)[3] by its simulacrum, its spectral double, its own image and its imagined potential.

Performers and audiences watch and think about television as an entertainment comparable to wayang, and the performers see the success of television and look for what they can learn from it. Television images, technologies, aesthetics, values, ways of organizing a show, and sense of time, space, and distance, all penetrate wayang. Beyond its direct encounter with television, wayang is affected by something of which television is a part: the web of practices, technologies, and mentalities that one can think of as Indonesian modernity. At the same time, there are moments of critical awareness of what is happening, or resistance, or failure, or just discomfort, there is a sense of loss and anger, and these are signs that the dissolution is not as perfect as Baudrillard would have it, or as is suggested by some scholarship on the media that insists that there is no ontological distinction between "mediatized" and "live" performances;[4] Derrida's images of haunting are more open to the complexity, inconclusiveness, and unpredictability of what happens.

If the aim of this book might be compared to describing the relationship between two people (wayang and television) and the ways in which they are transformed by it, then this chapter focuses on the less direct and less obvious aspects of their interaction (and aside from the image of the difficult marriage of the media, one can also think of the haunting relationship between the doubles): How is a person affected by catching a glimpse of or overhearing someone else, by meeting someone else's acquaintances or mother-in-law, or just by being in the same world? How is one affected by another person's glance, by trying to see oneself through the eyes of another, by seeing and fantasizing one's own image? How is an encounter between two people shaped by their relationships to others, living and dead?

For wayang it is often a deeply disorienting struggle about and with itself, its split self. All of a sudden, I see E.T.A. Hoffmann (or his spectre?) sitting across the table in the coffee shop. His (anti-)hero reflects on encountering, seemingly (but not really) killing, and appearing as, his double: "My own I had become the cruel play of whimsical coincidence and was swimming unceasingly in a sea of events which were breaking over me like raging waves—I could not find my self again! [...] I am what I seem to be, yet do not seem to be what I am; even to myself an insoluble riddle, I am divided [*entzweit*] from my I."[5]

Our case speaks to a more general phenomenon: how the life-world, "live" world, is never entirely free of image-making and tele-technologies, how we are in the world through our body but at the same time through languages, images, texts, media, technologies, how the self and its images, reality and appearance, dissolve into each other. In an interview on the media, Derrida emphasizes that before we start thinking about modern tele-technologies, we need to remember actuality's "artifactuality" and "actuvirtuality":

> [Actuality] is not given but actively produced, sifted, invested, performatively interpreted by numerous apparatuses which are factitious or artificial, hierarchizing and selective, always in the service of forces and interests to which "subjects" and agents (producers and consumers of actuality [...]) are never sensitive enough.[6]

The specificity of modern tele-technologies, "whatever it may be, does not all of a sudden substitute the prosthesis, teletechnology, etc., for immediate or natural speech. These machines have always been there, even when we wrote by hand, even during so-called live conversation."[7] Marshall McLuhan—strange to see him sitting there like that, next to

Derrida—chips in that "the 'content' of any medium is always another medium", which has related implications.[8]

Moreover, as Derrida emphasizes, the present time is "out of joint" with itself, it is invaded by things from "beyond the living present".[9] Our questions intersect other questions, since

> the question of the specter [...] crosses those of repetition, of mourning, of inheritance, of the event, and of messianicity, of everything that exceeds the ontological oppositions between absence and presence, the visible and the invisible, the living and the dead, and thus, above all, the question of the prosthesis as "phantom member", the question of technics of the teletechnological simulacrum, of the computer generated image, of virtual space, etc.—again we encounter the themes [...] of artifactuality and of virtuoactuality.[10]

Wayang lives with and is inspired and haunted by televised, virtual wayang performances, which are in the nature of spectres in that they are appearances of "live" performances yet they are not physically "here and now", they exist in time and place differently than ordinary wayang performance—moving through walls, appearing at more than one place, coming from other times. They are bodiless appearances of life that exist beyond the present time of any live performance, and they come to haunt the "living present", they exert their power over the production and perception of performances. A televised wayang performance taking place in front of the television cameras has its spectral afterlife as a television show already within it: the performance—normally a transient, unrepeatable event—is now performed and watched with the awareness that it will appear as its double, an image of itself, at a later time and in a different place. Here we are somewhere beyond the distinction between "actual" performance and televised performance, and even performances that take place without television cameras are haunted by the spectral performances, by visions of the afterlife. The performers', spectators', and sponsors' perceptions of the performance are haunted by televised performances. The relationship between a physical performance and a television programme cannot be fully thought in terms of actuality and virtuality, absence and presence, sameness and otherness. Thinking in terms of spectres and haunting helps us to see how what happens constantly challenges these distinctions. Visibility is a key theme in this chapter, perhaps because it is the mode of the spectre's existence: it is through an unusual kind of visibility, of appearing, that the spectral puts to doubt notions of place, time, and reality.

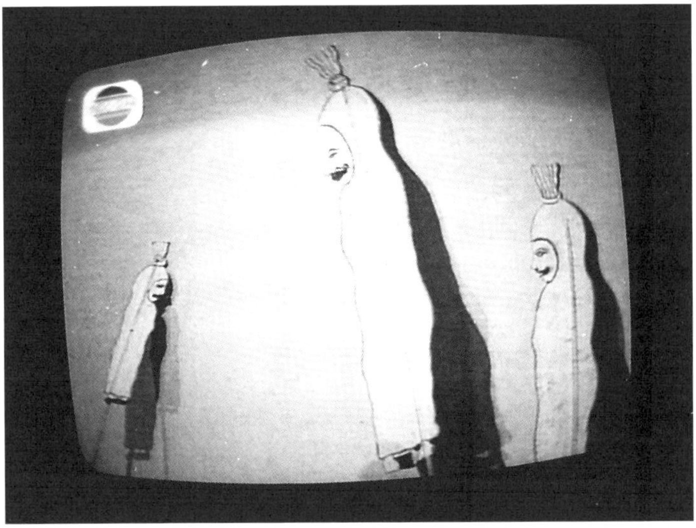

1.1 A family of wayang spectres on television (Indosiar broadcast).

At the same time, this does not happen without a struggle, without human attachments to certain realities, liveness, appearances, distinctions, ways of seeing, and perhaps above all, the resistance to certain—television-generated—spectrality. Certain spectrality: for wayang, too, is a medium, a medium that is not and never was simply present, and that makes visible beings that are and are not physically present—and with them stories, ways of being, acting, and thinking—in whose company people live, whom they admire or not, and from whom they learn. The saying goes that wayang is *tontonan* ("show") and *tuntunan* ("guidance"). It is as if living beings were accompanied and guided, and presented with edifying examples by spirits, teachers and ancestors. Ritual performances make communication with local spirits and demons possible by making them visible on the screen, and the spirits are part of the audience of these performances. Even ordinary performances, especially those less affected by television and entertainment business, are felt by many people to be involved with spirits, invisible powers, and ancestors. On another level, wayang brings wisdom, words, and images from the past into the present, it enables people to communicate, to be in communion, with the spirits of the past.[11] It reanimates particular ways of being—feeling, thinking, acting—and a particular world. Perhaps one difference from television is that wayang's spirits—even as they are always new and alive—are old, ancestral, familial; they come from the Javanese past, as part of an inheritance from "our" ancestors. Thus people are with them somewhat differently than with television's spectres, and the spirits make themselves visible, communicate with people, somehow differently. The resistance to television's spectrality, may be in part a matter of resistance to disrespecting the spirits of wayang, to giving up being with them, and giving up learning from the older wisdom of wayang. It seems to be precisely in performances that are most like television entertainment that the aura of the spirits' presence disappears.

If television haunts wayang, wayang's spirit, too, haunts television. A disembodied appearance of wayang, wayang in its afterlife, appears on television screens, and affects the time and workings of television. Just like a live wayang performance may become more like a television programme, so too wayang infiltrates television, and the latter becomes a strange, different kind of television, like a person possessed by a spirit.

One of the aims of this chapter is to show that the more direct moments of the encounter which we will discuss in later chapters—television production of wayang, watching wayang on television—need to be seen with a sense of the less direct interaction between, and co-existence of, wayang and television, their cultures, their pasts, their spirits; and with a sense of the complex, disjointed present of which the encounter is a part.

As explained in the Introduction, rather than presenting a historical narrative, the first three chapters focus primarily on the "Indosiar era" (roughly 1995–2005), when wayang on television was a much talked-about phenomenon. In the last part of this chapter, I reflect on how various phenomena and issues of this time were foreshadowed in the "prehistory" of the encounter between wayang and television.

Mass Wayang

I ask Handoko, Indosiar's president, if the network is interested in supporting and caring about the condition and quality of wayang, as some people say it should be, and as it publicly often claims to be. "*What we need is ratings*," he says in English, with emphasis and respect as if he were uttering a phrase from a holy book. "When we have {ratings}, when there are people who are interested, we get sponsors for advertisements. So we tend to be more {business minded}, we tend more toward a {business point of view}, rather than any other view." We need to take him seriously—from his powerful point of view at least, this marriage is not about supporting and caring. We need to learn to see the encounter between wayang and television from a "business point of view": in terms of ratings, advertisers, advertisements.

The president's statement puts the audience—which wayang and television potentially share—at the centre. It is impossible to think an entity so heterogeneous, evasive, and alive, as the millions of human beings watching wayang and television. However, the quote above suggests that we don't need to worry about nuances if we want to see in the way television business does. "What we need is ratings." Ratings represent satisfactorily what we erroneously thought were human beings. The audience is a homogeneous, measurable mass. Audience= ratings=sponsors=advertisements=money; thus: audience=money. In a variation of the equation, wayang broadcasts function as a form of "image-building", a self-advertisement for the television station, the ultimate goal of which is again attracting audiences and thus profit. In either case, the television's ambition is to be as popular as possible, and when it looks at wayang as a potential television programme, it is concerned about whether it will attract an audience.

This representation of audience ignores what wayang is (an event, an experience, an imagined world) and how diverse the people who watch wayang and television are—their lives, thoughts and feelings. But its power derives precisely from framing and zooming that leaves certain things invisible, and from quantifying everything (people, events) in terms of money—incidentally, a simulacrum in some ways comparable to television images. It is a clean, neat, luminous representation of reality.

Like television images, the representation invades reality and the two dissolve into each other.

The urge to make money by attracting masses of spectators is entangled in various ways with politics. Wayang has a long history of involvement with the political culture of royal courts and colonial and post-colonial states, and particular notions of power and power relationships are central to the values of wayang mythology, which are sometimes criticized (somewhat correctly, somewhat simplistically) as "feudal". The ability to attract large audiences is seen traditionally as a manifestation and enhancement of the sponsor's influence and status. Some large-scale performances are sponsored by political parties, government bodies, politicians, or army officers. Some events become in effect political rallies.[12] For puppeteers to be successful, they have to be on good terms with rich and powerful people—politics is inseparable from business. Commercial television stations, including Indosiar, are owned by people powerful both politically and economically—during the New Order and well past its end, Soeharto's family and close associates. But perhaps this entanglement can be discerned also on a more general level: it is not only in the case of commercial television that people are controlled through a transformation—by means of representations and images—into a quantifiable mass, and that success is measured easily in terms of numbers (consumers, voters, rupiah). The same is true about a "free market" economy generally, and about democracy, a powerful tool to control people with bright, neat images and staged events, which in Indonesia include both wayang and elections.

A common theme in the discussions surrounding new developments in wayang are the *penonton*, or spectators, as a new and powerful reality and as something that is felt to be modern. In a typical statement, the various new developments in wayang are said to be responses to "the demand of the times, or more specifically, the demand of the audience in these times".[13] This new audience is imagined quite differently than the members of the extended family, neighbours, invited guests, and onlookers from local community that are part of traditional performances. Personal, familial, and social relations figure strongly in smaller-scale, less televise-able wayang events. Even though it is a matter of prestige and satisfaction to attract people, traditional wayang is to a large extent a celebration through which the community spirit and personal relations are reaffirmed.

Amien Nugroho wrote in a 1991 newspaper article titled "Does Wayang Kulit Performance Need Renewal?" in the subsection "Modern Spectacle" (*Tontonan Moderen*; the connection between spectacle and spectator in the translation reproduces the shared root of the Indonesian words *tontonan* and *penonton*):

> [W]ayang kulit has to clean itself up [*berbenah diri*; to make itself neat and correct] so that it becomes a modern spectacle which is ready to be on the same level with other modern spectacles. [...] In a traditional society, the sponsor is a powerful person in the area or someone who has a celebration, and the spectator is whoever is directly involved with the artistic production. In the modern world, the organizers are the impresarios, and spectators are those who are willing to buy entrance tickets. Thus, in the modern world, an artistic performance will not take place without the presence of spectators. Spectators will come if the artistic performance is attractive. Because modern spectators' basic need is to look for "fresh air", for releasing the tension of everyday life. [...] In this situation there is no other choice except for wayang kulit to "go public" [*sic*], or in other words, it has to be able to sell (commercialized) to spectators.[14]

Here spectators are conceptualized as increasingly important in wayang as a "modern spectacle" and attracting audience and "selling" wayang is part of wayang "modernizing itself", which involves "cleaning itself up" so that it is "on the same level with other modern spectacles". This and many similar texts were written several years before wayang appeared on commercial television, yet at a time of some very modern wayang spectacles. By the way, as is common in these debates, there is an element of fantasy about the future: more than a quarter of a century after this newspaper article was written, the traditional model of sponsorship persists, and there are almost never "entrance tickets" for wayang.

The new wayang audience, in these discussions, is more like the imagined television audience—more like a homogeneous mass, characterized primarily by size, of anonymous individuals, always demanding to be entertained. These are conceptualizations—but again images and reality mirror and invade each other. When one attends a large-scale wayang performance by a famous puppeteer and stands in a crowd of many thousands of spectators, one feels, relates to others, and enjoys wayang differently, than when one is warmly welcomed by the sponsors to a small-scale village performance, and participates in what is a cosy community celebration.

To attract spectators, popular puppeteers adopt strategies of the modern entertainment industry, and become to some extent "business-minded", and are happy to profit from this. At the same time, the responsiveness to the audience's desires and the attempts to attract as many spectators as possible, create a conflict. For instance, one aspect of the unity of wayang performances derives from the sovereignty of the puppeteer. The puppeteer's catering to the wishes of the mass audience is perceived as a sign of the *dhalang*'s lack of authority. Even Ki Manteb Soedharsono, a top dhalang who has introduced and popularized many innovations, and is in many ways frankly "business minded", says:

> It is a great mistake if young dhalang say as an excuse that they follow the audience. Because it is precisely the audience that can be controlled, and they [the audience] would also have the same perception of the performance [as the dhalang] if they were presented with a performance that has its foundations.[15]

Dhalang are criticized for jeopardizing the integrity of wayang:

> Ki Manteb understands what the intention of young dhalang is, they want to do anything as long as it is new and crazy, as long as the spectators clap hands. Thus, the wayang performance will collapse, break down.[16]

Even as wayang approaches television, and even as a small minority of puppeteers get popular and rich, there is a pervasive feeling that something is deeply wrong, that the desire to prioritize mass popularity is foreign to wayang culture, and that it may be leading to wayang's collapse. Wayang is torn and energized by the opposing forces, and it is neither comfortably at home in the realm of commercial entertainment (in the way that television is), nor is it able to free itself from the "business point of view".

The development of the mass audience is indivisible from the changing character of the performance. Especially in the 1990s, there was a strong trend toward performances that were larger in scale, catered to large crowds (strong electric lights, amplification system, simulcast on television monitors, larger gamelan, and large stage are all part of this), emphasized light entertainment, humour, and variety, and presented new things (music, puppets, jokes) to keep people interested. These developments would leave a lasting mark on the character of wayang performances, even as later, different and even opposing trends, would complicate the situation.

A key concept in discussions of these developments is *hiburan*, Indonesian for "entertainment". Sometimes the English word is used, but never Javanese, wayang's own language. Here "entertainment" tends to mean "just entertainment"—light, popular entertainment. The talk of entertainment, such as that wayang is becoming "entertainment pure" (as the puppeteer Slamet Gundono put it, again using English) is often connected to the "collapse" of wayang. It is associated with (commercial) television and modern "showbiz". Slamet used "the world of entertainment" interchangeably with "the world of television", the meaning of one slipping into the other. Ishadi, a senior and influential executive in the television industry and author of publications on television, told me when we were talking specifically about wayang on television and how television encourages entertainment in wayang: "In the heads of television people there is {entertainment}. If they entertain, they get money—rarely are there idealists. Basically, the TV industry is business, West, Jakarta." In both wayang and television, entertainment is a means to attract audiences and thus to set the money-making system to work.

Mass popularity is a goal that modernized wayang shares with television, and it is something that—as puppeteers know—television people look for in wayang when they think about covering wayang on television. Although Indosiar to some extent tried to push wayang in the direction of a mass entertainment in order to attract an audience to wayang on television, wayang had already been moving in that direction even before wayang on commercial television became important. The new image of the audience, and the growing emphasis on easy entertainment in wayang, cannot be fully attributed to the influence of television, yet it is a movement toward television. It gives us a glimpse of the elusive love-hate relationship through which wayang becomes more like television.

A Struggle for Visibility: Seeing-at-a-Distance and Self-Advertising

The developments discussed in the preceding section are indivisible from the phenomenon of competition and a struggle for visibility. The puppeteer Enthus Susmono told me:

> I am very much indebted to Indosiar, to TVRI [the state television network], because I became well-known—"dhalang Enthus", "dhalang Enthus is like that." [...] Indosiar and TVRI have helped me very much in the matter of publicity. [... Before], frankly, I wasn't that well known, so the role of television is very, very great.

Sutami, then a singer (*pesindhen*) in the troupe of the celebrity puppeteer Warsena Slenk, talked about the effect of the puppeteer performing on television:

> The influence of course has been great. People from villages who don't know how handsome Mas Slenk is then [after seeing him on television] want to invite him. [...] When he was performing in Tritis, Boyolali, for instance, there was a group

> of people, who, when they were watching wayang, didn't want to see wayang, they only wished to see the puppeteer! Hahahaha! Isn't that funny? Because they had seen him on television, they wanted to see what the reality was really like. "On television and reality—are those different or not?"

Television seduces people to look at reality, guiding their vision to see in reality what they saw on television.

While the dhalang are the main "stars" in wayang—and the success of the group depends primarily on their popularity—other performers, too, may profit from appearing on television. Sutami told me about a man who saw her perform as a pesindhen on television:

> It was somebody from Sragen [a town some 40 kilometres away from Sutami's home]—he came here, I did not know him at all, he didn't know me either. He came with *informasi* [information, which he acquired thus:] when on Saturday night he turned on a *gara-gara* [a long interlude emphasizing entertainment, popular songs, and comedy] of Mas ["Brother", a term of address] Warsena on Indosiar, [when the puppeteer introduced the singers] he noted down where I am from, and came here. He asked the pedicab drivers at the crossroads. I was amazed, "Where are you from?" "I am from Sragen." "How come you know me? I don't know you yet!"—Because when he came he said 'Hello Bu ['Mother', a term of address] Tami!" Well of course I was shocked!

She mentioned other similar experiences. She said that there is a kind of pride, because "everybody knows me but I don't know them—a person like me is known to people far away!" Her pride in appearing on television is a matter of being visible in a way and at a distance—regardless of distance—that other people are not visible. The "positive aspect" of this is not only that more people invite her to perform, but also that, as she said with some amusement, "I am thought to be an expensive pesindhen", and people pay her more. Television creates an aura for performers from which they can profit in everyday life; television makes them special. At the same time, this is felt to be something new and strange: she is amazed and "shocked" (*kaget*) because the stranger knows her name and address, even though she does not know him. Television annihilates distance, both the social distance that people have to travel through when they begin to know each other, and geographical distance.

Indeed, one of the most important magic powers of television is the way it affects place and distance. In the past, older dhalang tell, each dhalang had his own area where he performed. Today, people are less bound to places than in the past. Famous dhalang are frequently invited to perform throughout Java. Television's powers amplify existing developments: a wayang performed at one place is seen on television "everywhere". Local dhalang now have to compete with these television performances. Because of the larger, delocalized field of activity and visibility, there is a growing desire for self-promotion: desire for one's visibility in a world where people can see more than before, and where people fantasize about visibility and fear invisibility. Performances on television are typically large, rich performances making it difficult for local dhalang to compete with them. Moreover, television "lifts" (*ngangkat*) shows and performers into a sphere of being everywhere at once, and gives them a special aura, a recognition, and a particular kind of visibility. Back in their world, they retain this aura: they have been in the luminous television world, they come from beyond-this-place where one is visible in a way that exceeds normal visibility. Competing with them means also competing with television and its powers, with the recognition it bestows.

A small number of dhalang become famous and in demand—on television and generally—while others are excluded, their performance opportunities are reduced, and they cannot compete with the recognized dhalang-superstars seen on television and sponsored by powerful patrons. The successful dhalang charge exorbitant fees, become rich and interesting to people—even those who never watch wayang—as celebrities. The top dhalang actively promote this image. Traditionally, dhalang are charismatic local figures, respected wise men in a community, but the superstardom of some of the dhalang today is new to wayang. Less well-known puppeteers imitate the performances of the superstar puppeteers, and the latter's individual styles become dominant. Thus, the "lifting" of wayang into a distanceless visibility, tele-visibility, and the struggle to be included in the sphere of light—processes in which television is a major force—affect wayang performers and performances in profound ways.

The Story of an Advertisement

A number of celebrity dhalang have acted in television commercials. The best known case is that of Manteb who acted in an advertisement for the painkiller Oskadon. This ad was first shown before Indosiar began to broadcast wayang in 1995, that is, before wayang became a regular programme on nationwide commercial television. It has had several sequels, seen on television over at least a decade.

The popular ad introduces images of wayang and a dhalang onto commercial television in a way that it is watched countless times by millions of people, including those not familiar with wayang. The commercial had a major effect on the (tele)visibility of wayang. When Panca, the Indosiar producer who introduced wayang on the channel, was about to look for dhalang who would first appear on Indosiar in 1995, Manteb was one of them, and Panca told me that he chose Manteb because he knew him from the Oskadon commercial. In the following years, Manteb was the dhalang to appear by far most frequently on Indosiar.

Panca was not the only one to learn about Manteb from the advertisement. In many articles about Manteb in the press he is referred to as "the advertisement star". He is known as such by many people, who see him first in the advertisement, close up, many times more often than in live performance. He was "lifted" into the tele-visibility of a popular television commercial, the heart and the purse of commercial television.

The advertisement became the object of passionate discussions. According to a Javanese article, one interviewed person likes very much the "wayang ad" (*iklan wayang*), "Because after they had watched the Oskadon Oye ad, my children changed and got to know about and became attracted to watching wayang. The ad is positive, why should it be problematized?"[17] Other people, the article reports, gave "the same reason". Manteb himself commented:

> My intention was to lift [*ngangkat*] wayang kulit by means of that ad. I envied other ads. Don't tell me wayang can't be like that. If someone disagrees, does he perhaps want television ads to be full of naked people? There was no thought of prostituting wayang. Stupid. I live for wayang![18]

Along with Manteb, wayang itself was "lifted" by appearing on television: it became visible in a new way. The medicine advertisement becomes wayang advertisement, *iklan wayang*. Yet, Manteb's motivation for "lifting" wayang and himself is primarily commercial in a specifically television-like way, as he himself emphasizes. He tries to attract television audience by making wayang into a television advertisement.

Manteb "lifts" wayang onto television. When "my children", as one of the authors puts it, watch the ad, they see a wayang performance, and are interested in seeing more of it. The introduction to the interview with Manteb about the ad begins by describing various controversial innovations in his performances, and talks about the ad as yet another wayang controversy. Detractors of the ad criticize it not as an ad, but as if it were a (strange) wayang performance: "there is no *lakon* Oskadon [Oskadon play]" is one critique; or: "What makes one concerned, according to Daniwara, is that the advertisement appears in the midst of a serious scene. In the midst of a battle—how come they interrupt it with a dialogue with the pesindhen which (strangely) advertises a medicine?" Another critic suggests that this should at least happen in the middle of a comic intermezzo. For many people, including the puppeteer, the ad is a case of wayang on television, and it is both "positive" and controversial because it is seen as wayang.

This case of wayang on television puts into relief what is also true about other cases: they, too, are permeated by the spirit of (television) advertising and multiple desires for (tele)visibility. If the Oskadon ad promotes headache medicine, a puppeteer, and wayang in general, other televised performances promote wayang, particular puppeteers and their styles, and also, as we will discuss further in Chapter Two, the television station and the performance sponsors.

How to Look Good on Television

The primary field of activity for all puppeteers consists of performances that are not televised. Performers are aware that a televised performance is lifted from the particular place and made tele-visible throughout Indonesia. The rare occasions when a puppeteer performs on television are important opportunities for publicity. Puppeteers try to make these performances into television advertisements for live performances. This is why they try hard to make wayang and themselves look good on television.

How do they do it? They try (1) *to perform extraordinarily well* when they perform on television, and (2) *to perform so that they look good specifically on television.* In part because television "just moves into people's homes" apparently "authentic" performances, here is no clear boundary between these two, or between innovations in ordinary performances and those that are made with television in mind.

The standards for looking good on television become part of live performances (and televised performances *are* live performances), spread uncontrollably like new fashions, and become the standards for looking good in the modern world. A major motivation for puppeteers to adjust performances to television is to become popular as performers of live performances: television and actuality dissolve into each other. The efforts are part of the complex growth of wayang toward television that is not simply an effect of television and, to the extent that one can speak of agency, it is not done while thinking simply about television.

Packaging and Innovations

Many puppeteers say that a performance on television should be better prepared and planned. Sutami, the pesindhen in Slenk's group, told me that before a televised performance, there would be rehearsals every day for a whole week, something not done normally. A particular story would be prepared (traditionally, the puppeteer often learns what story he will perform only just before the performance), and even in what are the freest parts, the comic interludes, "the songs would be packaged [*dipaket*] beforehand". It would be decided ahead of time what songs would be featured during the clown scenes and in which order, and who would sing each song—"so that there would be no confusion during the shooting [about which singer should sing], 'You!' 'You!' 'You!' 'You!'" On television, she said, "one can't be relaxed".

Performances become more pre-composed and less spontaneous. Traditionally, rehearsals are not essential, because all performances are built according to certain principles that are familiar to all performers and subtle cues are used to communicate, in ways that make wayang and gamelan into a performance of ideal social interaction, cultural values and notions of power, humility, and (self-)control. There is a standard structure and a repertory of performance elements and techniques, even as these conventions allow for much creativity and spontaneity. New performances—televised or not—both adhere to and diverge from these principles. If a particular section of the performance is pre-composed and rehearsed, new performance elements—often unique to a particular puppeteer—can replace those from the standard repertory. Written texts for new verbal passages and notation for new compositions become more common. People come to value the different character of discourse—more concise, less repetitive, less standardized, with more unconventional, flashy novelty.

One reason given by puppeteers why novelty is important on television is connected to the way television affects the performance's being in place and time and annihilates distances. When a puppeteer performs every night at a different village for a local audience, he can repeat some of the same jokes and tricks. When he does the same thing on television, however, the same audience will see the different performances and soon be bored because of the repetition. This especially applies to the many broadcasts featuring a small number of top popular puppeteers, and in the cases of some televisions stations that feature one dhalang for a series of performances.[19]

Puppeteers also mention that people watching wayang on television get bored or sleepy more easily than when they watch the same performance directly, in part because in the latter case, people enjoy the event as a whole, they socialize, and so on. The performance can be more repetitious and relaxed in tempo. But when a television spectator is bored, he is likely to either switch the channel or turn off the television.

Puppeteers try to keep people's attention by making their performances new and different every time.

But perhaps the most important reason is something else, something "in the air". It has to do with the aesthetics of television and commercial entertainment, and the general attitude to new things in modern society. People are interested in newness for newness's sake. And new sells.

Enthus Susmono told me: "If in the past [I did] this already, now it is replaced—that's why I am liked on television, because it is always different/other (*lain*). I am like Suzuki—constantly innovating [*inovasi terus*]." The new is appealing because it is "other" (lain). This otherness is essential. After describing the success of (the puppet of) the ghost of Lady Diana at the time just after her death when the media were full of news about the royal celebrity, he said:

> But if Lady Diana were to appear today, it would not be interesting anymore, because the affair is already rather old. One has to replace continually [*ganti terus*]. That's why I always have to watch shows other than wayang [such as television news, he clarified].

What he says about Lady Diana is true about many of his other puppets, such as George Bush boxing with Saddam Hussein, in a show just after the Gulf War. These puppets, like much else in the new performances, take inspiration from the "shows" that are television news, but wayang is also like the news in its dependence on presenting whatever is new, and on "replacing continually" (ganti terus). This is not growth. In growth, the new sprouts from the old. In this continual replacing, the new comes from outside, appears briefly, and soon disappears, replaced by something else. It is appealing because it is other than whatever came before it. Wayang is developing toward a medium which, at certain moments, becomes more like the television news, or television generally, and which depends on innovations that, in their newness and otherness, are nonetheless like each other—the replacement (*ganti*), the production of newness, is continuous (*terus*).

Sutami told me that for performances on television, Slenk

> has this politics: when there is a new singer, he always shows her off even though she might not be able to do things right, so as to make things new so that this recording and the previous one differ. For example, suppose this is the first time that Mbak Tami is performing, and if on the previous recording Mbak Jlitheng [was singing the most], to make things new, it is Mbak Tami that is focused on now, so that it is not same as the previous recording—even though Mbak Jlitheng is clearly better. The one who is focused on is continually replaced (*diganti-ganti*).

The new replaces the old even when the old is obviously better; what counts is continual novelty and change. The dhalang, Slenk, is famous for presenting the newest hits in his performances, and new songs continually replace those that are out of fashion. The Indonesian scholar Suratno writes about Slenk:

> He learns musical pieces—dramatic music and pop songs—from cassette recordings, the radio, and television. He buys tapes with gamelan pieces and new songs, and listens to them over and over again so that he masters the pieces or songs. Similarly, he often watches advertisements and pop songs on television, which he can use as spice in making jokes and as additional material for his performances.[20]

Part of the performers' work consists in collecting "news"—whatever is new and trendy at the moment—and presenting it in the performance.

The executives at Indosiar think about the wayang programme itself as an innovation. Handoko told me that "at that time, because we were still new, we had to offer a feature that was new on television". A high-level Indosiar executive told me, specifically with reference to the wayang programme, that "we have indeed looked for a {first idea}, new innovations [*inovasi-inovasi baru*]". In wayang, it is the newness and constant otherness of materials from television that attract audiences; on television, it is the newness and otherness of wayang. The mutual otherness of wayang and television has a certain appeal as the two media come together.

Television programmes such as foreign films, cartoons, and sports, are among the most important sources of innovations in wayang. Television not only broadcasts "authentic" wayang, but it is also "behind" what it records as a model to be imitated. Television is a source of the new and the Other, and by broadcasting wayang, especially in the beginning, television leant its sense of innovation to wayang by exploiting its newness and novelty. Even as it looks for something other than itself in wayang, it finds (traces of) itself most appealing. I asked how dhalang make wayang look good especially on television; it turns out that answering this means also looking at how wayang learns from a powerful representative of modernity—television—to make itself look good both on television and in the modern world. This is best seen on a further examination of the changes.

From Drama to Talk Show: Breaking Down the Structure of Wayang

When people watch wayang or television, they come and go, talk, eat and drink while watching. Both the wayang event and television programming last longer than most people care to watch. Yet, despite these similarities, wayang and television are structured quite differently.

In the "flow" of television programming, as described by Williams, "the elements of speed, variety and miscellaneity can be seen as organising".[21] One item is juxtaposed with the next, and advertisements, previews, and other announcements further fragment the flow. They keep viewers watching, not by creating a sense of continuity or gradual development, but by reasserting variety even within each programme, and by creating the sense that soon there will be something different. This fragmentation and variety give the flow a certain constant character.

A traditional wayang performance holds together differently. There is a variety in the alternation of dialogues, narration and visual action, in the alternation between philosophical discussions, battle scenes, humour, and so on. There is a variety of music, images, and moods. Yet, these elements are closely connected to one another and form a carefully built, architecture-like whole. Within each part of the performance and within each scene, there is a sense of unifying development, usually from slow and calm to faster and tenser moods. Each moment, like each scene and each larger part, is carefully joined to the next.[22]

However, wayang has been becoming more like television. One of the most striking developments has been the expansion of the comic interludes.[23] While traditionally the gara-gara, which features the male clown servants, consisted of only a few light gamelan songs with some comedy in between, in the 1990s it was expanded so that it commonly lasts around two hours, and it has become radically more open and freer. In addition, the *limbukan* which features the female servants Limbuk and Cangik, has become similarly important.[24] Even traditionally, the comic interludes are a break in the performance structure, or, in Rene Lysloff's words, "a rupture in the flow of time".[25] A.L. Becker writes that the "clowns, using modern language, modern ideas, and modern behaviour, step among the heroes and demons and gods like wide-awake men in a dream world".[26] During a comic interlude as performed today, only the clowns are on the screen, and they bring in the waking world, a world dominated by television and other modern phenomena. While at other moments the way the puppets are positioned and moved on the screen manifest the characters' relationships (status, family, etc.), during the comic interludes these relationships disappear. The clowns speak to each other in contemporary Low Javanese (the language used when one does not need to heed the other person's status) and occasionally some words or phrases from Indonesian, the language of the modern nation. What happens in the comic interludes is unrelated to the story or the musico-dramatic development of the performance. New and foreign elements and practices, including those associated with television, penetrate most easily here, and the emphasis on and expansion of the interludes has made wayang increasingly like television entertainment, with emphasis on novelty and variety. One attraction is juxtaposed with the next: for instance, today there are songs and dances in different styles and from various regions, "guest stars" from different forms of theatre and television shows, and so on.

The presence of guest stars changes essentially what happens on the stage. They are introduced as *bintang tamu* (guest stars)—an Indonesian, not Javanese, phrase, associated with Indonesian popular culture, such as pop music concerts, variety shows, and other television programmes. The guest stars bring with them into wayang "many attractions" (*atraksi banyak*), as people say, including other entertainments: dramatic forms such as *kethoprak* (a Javanese dramatic form, less ancient than wayang, accompanied by gamelan and featuring stories from Javanese history and literature),[27] *wayang orang* (a type of wayang theatre with human actors in place of puppets), and a variety of popular music. The inclusion of diverse attractions makes wayang more like the fragmented flow of television. Like on television, the other media and entertainments do not disappear into wayang, but continue to be (simulacra of) themselves, only partly transformed to fit the wayang frame, which is itself transformed into something more like a television screen. Pop singers, comedians, and actors from other dramatic genres do not become dhalang or puppets. They have substantial autonomy. While traditionally the dhalang is the single most important performer ordering all aspects of performance, today he is at certain moments only one among many stars.

Part of the new variety in wayang is the incorporation of entertainments from other regions. In the case of the dominant Solonese style, this means music and dances from other parts of Java and

1.2 Guest stars, including well-known comedians, a celebrity musician, and a clown servant (Gareng) represented by an actor of *wayang wong* (wayang theatre with actors), at a performance with two screens, covered by television (a camera is visible in the lower right corner).

Indonesia, as well as from outside Indonesia. This is an example of the general interest in anything foreign (for instance, non-Solonese, non-Indonesian, but also non-wayang). The foreign is in many cases also the sign of modernity (such as pop music, guest stars, etc.), but foreignness itself—as a relation between wayang and the other elements, a relation in which things are juxtaposed in a fragmented, decentred un-whole—is a modern, television-like phenomenon.

The incorporation of foreign elements relates to distance, and specifically tele-vision, remote seeing. Like television, wayang juxtaposes attractions from different places and while the attractions still refer to those places, distances are annihilated and places dematerialized and reduced to signs of otherness. What counts is the appearance of foreignness. A gamelan composition presented by a dhalang as "Balinese" is so only in certain superficial signs (the use of harder mallets and fast melodic figuration), and the performers do not actually perform Balinese music. One guest star, the *londo*, or "Westerner", is actually a woman who has never left Indonesia, dressed as (a caricature of) a foreigner. One can hear "Balinese music" without having to go to Bali. Like television, wayang presents appearances of the distant, the appeal of which is the annihilation of distance. Rather like—but not quite: wayang is never able to present appearances as pure as television, to separate appearances from places and annihilate distance as well. Wayang remains irreparably Javanese, and this is in some ways a limitation—especially on television—when for example, it cannot attract non-Javanese Indonesian viewers.

This bringing together of representative replicas of arts from different regions into wayang in some ways resembles a major cultural project of the New Order, the cultural theme park "Beautiful Indonesia" Miniature Park (Taman Mini "Indonesia Indah"), where different regions are represented through replicas of traditional houses, cultural displays, museums, and so on. Taman Mini was envisioned by Soeharto and his wife to create a model image of an orderly "Beautiful Indonesia" under the New Order, while the development of modern wayang was more organic and contradictory, but both are products of a particular cultural and political climate, and manifest certain attitudes to working with traditional culture in New Order Indonesia, traditional culture in the form of replica images. At the same time—seen in a larger picture, beyond the New Order—they annihilate geographical and cultural distance in two overlapping modern ways—in the tradition of modern popular culture (and media), and in the tradition of colonial exhibitions, ethnographic museums, and theme parks presenting national culture.

While developments are most intense in the clown scenes, the whole wayang performance has changed in character in such a way that it is more like the interludes. It is made more entertaining by incorporating more humour, a variety of musical styles, puppet dances, and new funny puppets. As one puppeteer put it, all the characters become clowns. There is an emphasis on separate attractions—puppet dances, fights, new musical compositions—and general variety, and less on the dramatic wholeness of the performance.

Indosiar, apart from encouraging entertainment and guest stars in its regular wayang performances, has broadcast a number of programmes that consist of comic interludes only. When Panca, the producer, was talking about his initiatives that foreground the interludes, he said about wayang:

> What do people actually watch? I am not so sure that they like the story, {the whole story}. What they need is to laugh, sexuality/sexiness [*keseksian*], sensuality [*sensualitasnya*] from a story, only that—[correcting himself:] not from a story, but precisely from an appearance/show, not its *whole*, but like one *part*.

The producer regards any kind of wholeness as undesirable on television, and emphasizes the "sexiness" of parts. Other Indosiar producers and executives also talk about the special value of the interludes because easy entertainment fits television well (as we will discuss further in Chapter Two). This process involves some serious violence to wayang, but the cut limbs are not visible on television and no pain is felt by television producers.

The views and initiatives of television producers demonstrate television's interest in the comic interludes as something that fits television, and they illustrate how television encourages wayang to turn into a comic intermezzo, or something that might make a good television programme. The emphasis on light entertainment, and the fragmented character of the comic interludes and increasingly the whole all-night performance, resembles the "flow" of images and shows on television "in which the elements of speed, variety and miscellaneity can be seen as organising".

Time, Speed, Rhythm

When puppeteers and television producers are asked about the challenges of showing wayang on television, they almost always mention time, speed, and rhythm. When performing in a traditional setting, "the time is long, we can be relaxed", as the dhalang Mansyur said; one is "free in time" as the singer Sutami said. On television, as another dhalang put it, "time is limited (*terbatas*), the puppeteer is not free, it is like being chased by time (*kadosipun dioyak wektu*)". When performing on television, as the puppeteer Sujiwo Tejo put it, "time has to be short, the rhythm has to be fast". When Yanusa Nugroho produced wayang for television, he called it Kalasinema, "Cinema Time", abbreviating wayang performance to a mere hour. He wrote that long performance time is one of the reasons why "traditional art is marginalized", and that he shortened the performance "because [he was] trying to avoid boredom. Because the effect is different when one watches wayang directly in a 'live' atmosphere, compared to presenting it on television at home." Boredom—the greatest fear in the age of entertainment—is one of the reasons, commonly pointed out by puppeteers, for the need for short time and fast rhythm. Another reason, mentioned both by television executives and puppeteers, has to do with the business mind of television. The president of Indosiar said that when Indosiar was thinking about broadcasting wayang, "the only problem was the expensive cost, not just the recording cost but the airing cost, because it uses up so much airtime". Ishadi, a senior television executive, also emphasized that television makes people "business oriented" and thus "television has to be very efficient about time—a seven hour wayang performance cannot be [efficient]—because it is business, a straightforward Western culture, straight to the point, while wayang kulit has to be enjoyed slowly". Here we are talking about commercial television, but it should be added that earlier, in the 1970s, televised wayang was even more constrained by time limits. Wayang broadcasts then lasted only an hour or less, and airing an all-night performance was unimaginable.

A different kind of time—short, calculated, limited as opposed to long, free, relaxed, slow—and fast rhythm is seen as one of the changes in wayang effected by television. But concerns with time in wayang—as in the case of other developments—cannot be understood simply in terms of television, but also in terms of wayang adapting to changing perceptions and experience of lived time. Calls for and experiments with the abbreviation of wayang performances, usually in the context of modernizing wayang, have been around for a number of decades.[28] Common explanations for the need to abbreviate the performance and to speed up its rhythm refer to the time and rhythm of modern life, such as people having to get up early in the morning to go to work, people being used to modern entertainments that are shorter in time and faster in rhythm, and so on. Performances have been getting shorter. My old dhalang teacher, Ki Naryocarito, was convinced that nights were longer in the past: when he performed in his old age, his performances went several hours past sunrise, which affirmed his belief. He said that in the past one could just follow the changing feeling of the night, while today puppeteers follow a watch. The present time was for him out of joint with his feeling of time. He felt that time used to be slower and freer, not measured by a machine but rather something felt, something in which one was immersed. The shorter, limited time and faster rhythm of television are part of larger changes in the modern world and in wayang performances.

The rhythm and speed of performances have been changing in a number of ways. Williams mentions speed as one of the basic elements of television flow. The new, fragmented structure of performances, the need to constantly change and replace, the speed at which the new replaces the old, are all part of the changing rhythm of the performance. The new tendency to plan and pre-compose performances also makes them faster and more "efficient", as in the case of the singers avoiding the situation in which they have to decide who is to sing a particular song. The puppet movement has been getting faster, many new musical compositions have prominent fast melodies, long classical compositions tend to be avoided as are long philosophical discussions, and many innovations aim at making the use of time more "efficient" and less relaxed.

We have spoken of many changes in terms of overcoming distance and increased visibility. They can also be understood in terms of time and speed. Distance is overcome by a new speed—the speed of electrons, speed that is experienced as instantaneity, as tele-technological "real time"—in which visibility is transmitted, or as Paul Virilio writes, "now it is speed which discloses and makes things visible";[29] "real time of the image prevails over the real space of vision, and instantly transmitted appearances supersede the usual illumination of places",[30] as "cameras and their monitors become so many precision watches or model 'light-clocks'" in a "chronoscopic system of under-exposed, exposed, and overexposed".[31] The power to make visible regardless of distance, the power to promote (expose) particular puppeteers and performances—speedy performances—can be thus understood as a new way of working with time and increasing speed, and the way in which cameras selectively overexpose and underexpose the world.

Infiltration: Film, Visualization, and Realism

Since about the 1980s, a new style of manipulating puppets (*sabetan*) has gradually become popular, and there is more visual action, with other components (narration, dialogues) given less time. Ki Manteb Soedharsono is widely recognized as the pioneer of the new style of sabetan, and he has been widely imitated. He emphasized that he was inspired by Chinese martial arts (kung fu) movies, popular in Indonesia, both in movie theatres and on television. "The process which led to my inventing the sabet[an] used today began from kung fu films," Manteb claims.

> [A]s he was watching kung fu films, ideas for sabetan were flowing to him, in addition to learning better to understand the bodily movements that captivate and the gestures that interest the audience. "I have translated [*terjemahkan*] all that into my wayang kulit performances", he said. "If there's a person crazy about kung fu movies, well, that would be me," he added, laughing in his characteristic way. According to

> him, every time there is an opportunity, even now, he finds the time to watch a kung fu movie on TV or on video.[32]

Manteb is not the only one who associates his sabetan with martial art films. One writer mentions that Manteb's "[f]ighting scenes appear like a scene of a Chinese martial art film full of action".[33] Another writes that new sabetan "resembles [*mirip*] a fighting scene in a film".[34]

The new, fast, virtuoso sabetan is characterized by what people describe as "acrobatic tricks": puppets are thrown into the air, "making" somersaults; weapons suddenly, as if by magic, appear in their hands, and so on. The movements, according to some critics, do not "feel" (*krasa*) and the puppets do not live (*urip*). There is a certain lightness resulting from the agility of the puppets as they fly in all directions; the movements are less physical. Yet, people say, such sabetan makes the performance more alive. There is a change of focus from making the puppet appear alive to another kind of liveliness: a new kind of excitement as the show gets louder, faster, more spectacular, and more visually sexy, rather like special effects action films. This is clear from a description of innovative techniques in the West Javanese "three dimensional" rod-puppet theatre (*wayang golek*), in some ways very much like those that I am discussing:

> From its [a puppet in a fighting scene] mouth spurts fresh blood. The spectators shout wildly. There are those who laugh uncontrollably, and there are those who keep screaming ... New things, or new techniques, make the performance more alive ... The head of an ogre can be severed and ... out streams blood![35]

Apart from horror movies and other films—dhalang speak about film-like "realism"—another kind of popular TV programming comes to mind: sport. Battle scenes in wayang are visually the most thrilling parts of the performance, and their excitement is not unlike that of watching football or a boxing championship. Again, here Sundanese wayang golek shares much with the new Javanese wayang kulit: "The battle scenes displayed seem to heat the atmosphere even more. [...] 'Come on, Gatotkaca! Hit his head, pull his hair!' shout the spectators."[36] Dhalang occasionally use references to sport, as well as puppets representing sporting celebrities. In a 1996 performance at the radio station in Surakarta, a young dhalang, Edy Sulistyana, half-joked: "Wayang is mixed [by other dhalang] with comedy, with dangdut, with [modern] theatre; I am also going to make an innovation: I will mix wayang with football!" But it is not simply sport that wayang looks to, but sport as spectacle, and primarily televised sport. Both football and boxing are popular and regularly broadcast on television in Indonesia, and Indosiar is especially known for sport. Crazy Djoko told me that while Manteb learns from kung fu movies, he looks for inspiration in TV cartoons and boxing. An ex-boxer himself, Djoko said that he is a "maniac" (*maniak*) when it comes to foreign boxing. As an example of how sports inspire his performances, he mentioned "slow-motion replay" which he incorporates into battle scenes. "Slow-motion replay" is thought of as part of sport: the "reality" that infiltrates wayang is already mediatized by television. Indivisible from particular filmic and televisual techniques that enter wayang is a new relation between images and reality.

Traditionally, a wayang performance, especially in the early hours, progresses through a number of standard scenes.[37] A striking change to this structure is the inclusion of a prologue (*proloog*) at the beginning, before the first audience scene. It may last for a few minutes to half an hour or more, and tends to emphasize spectacular puppet movement and often other effects such as coloured lights and sound effects. A wayang performance, typically preceded by formal speeches at the celebration, traditionally begins from the slowest, stateliest grand audience scene, dominated by long verbal descriptions, narration, and dialogues. As the night progresses, as the air gets cooler and the gathering more relaxed, the performance, through a series of gradually faster waves, increases in tempo, and there is less talking and more emphasis on fast visual action and battle scenes. Adding a spectacular, fast-moving prologue full of visual action where one expects the stateliest scene with long-winded narrations and dialogues is a radical change to the structure of wayang and to the way a performance is organically part of the celebration and the changing atmosphere of the night. It is also a move from words to a predominantly visual spectacle; and from the performance following and bringing out the lived time-structure of the night and the gathering, to television temporality. The prologue in wayang is generally associated with film and/or television. Hardja Susilo connects this practice specifically to television: "This recent use of 'pandemonium' to begin a drama can be traced to the television dramatic device known as the 'hook' or the 'teaser' which is designed to capture the audience's attention lest they switch channels."[38] Comparable to the prologue is the use of "flashback", typically a visual representation of events that might, in a traditional version, be only narrated by the dhalang or told by a character. Flashback—the English term is commonly used—is also readily identified as a film technique.[39] An old dhalang, for instance, said that "flashback imitates film".

The use of prologue and flashback exemplify a general trend: the tendency to substitute visual representation for verbal narration or description. As in the cases of other developments, there is no clear boundary between wayang learning from film and/or television, and wayang trying to look good on television. Manteb's emphasis on sabetan was inspired by kung fu films, and he was one of the first popular dhalang to use the prologue and flashback extensively, but he also talks about how when he performs on television specifically he tends to cut narrations and present visually what would traditionally be only narrated. He gave me this example: "'*Baladewa duka yayah sinipi* ...' ['Baladewa was extraordinarily angry ...']—it is already not relevant [to say this] on television; it is better to move the puppet [and thus show the anger through movement]." The most famous wayang golek puppeteer, Asep Sunandar, told me:

> I visualize utterances [*memvisualkan perkataan-perkataan*] from old wayang. In the past, dhalang were not creative in manipulating wayang puppets, and they were not creative in visualizing what was said [*memvisualkan apa yang dibicarakan*], such as when a minister reports to the king, "*Aduh*, O King, what shall we do, many have died on the battlefield, some have their necks broken, some vomit, some have their heads crashed, some have their arms cut off ...". Well, I tried to experiment and visualize these utterances in wayang, and it was accepted. But many older dhalang say that I don't follow the rules.

While Manteb is explicit both about television and film being his inspiration, and about the appropriateness of an emphasis on the visual for television, Asep talks about the "visualization" more generally as part of modern innovations in wayang: the two projects dissolve into each other.

The new emphasis on visual representation is connected to another tendency, a move toward what people call the *realis* (realistic). The dhalang Sri Sadono, the scriptwriter for one of the superstar dhalang, told me that wayang on television has to be realis because it has to compete "with Chinese films, with Indian films", and other programmes. What does "realis" mean? Sri Sadono's examples suggest that it is something like what other dhalang call "visualization". He said that one does not need to describe at length the king's chariot, but one should focus on visual representation, specifically one "complete with everything". He contrasted this against traditional wayang representation, in which objects, setting, and other aspects of the represented world are often merely described verbally, and many things may be implied visually (for example, through movement) but not actually shown. Note, first, that time and speed are at stake: for Sadono the main reason that visual realism is appropriate on television is that "TV has limited time" and because "television must save time, everything must be done in the shortest possible time"; thus the dhalang cannot tell stories in a long-winded manner (*bertele-tele*). Second, the effect of this "visualization" is that the character of representation is changed: it is now "complete with everything", rather than alluding to things. Asep used another illustration: When a character in wayang shoots an arrow, the bow is usually not represented, but, suggested by the movements of the puppet and the arrow, the bow is understood to be there. One of Asep's "visualizations" was to show a bow where it was previously imagined.

What is meant by "realism" here is quite specific: it is like a camera's "realism", like what people see in films on television. The realis contrasts with wayang's own manner of representation, which the dhalang Slamet Gundono calls "*imajinatif*". The new realism, his term suggests, requires less imagination from the audience, because they are presented with something that is closer to everyday reality in the way it is seen on television or in films. It is closer to television, which pretends to let one *see* the world, and thus satisfies the need for imagination with something that appears to be more real, namely (tele)vision. When I asked about Manteb's sabetan, Slamet Gundono commented:

> The tendency of puppeteers from Sragen—their strength is really in the puppet movement, such as the late Pak Gondodarman, his sabetan was extraordinary. [In Sragen] there is a tendency to try to adopt [*mengadopsi*] forms of everyday movements, and that is translated into wayang. ... Watching [that kind of] wayang is like [watching] everyday people, *very realis*. ... Wayang is imajinatif, and when it enters the world of *entertainment* [in English], whether television or the big stage [meaning the large-scale, spectacular, *moderen* wayang performances], that ["realism"] is what is most appropriate in the realis world. People have also already grown, and when they watch films, when they watch Donald Duck, when they watch whatever, killings—then the imajinatif world becomes something that is very foreign to them. Even looking at a statue—it is foreign. But when there is a naked person on the internet, *wah!* So perhaps that's why the Sragen puppet movements have been so successful. Pak [Gondo] Darman was realis, Pak Manteb is realis, and now it is *very realis* beginning recently, when Pak Sudjadi [a politician involved with wayang in the 1990s and working closely with the Semarang TVRI station] made wayang that was called *pantap*—that was an attempt to realis-ise [*merealisasikan*] wayang, with [puppets of] a bus, a train, and there were movements that were *very* natural(istic) [*alamiah*].

Wayang is made more realis to fit the realis world of television, and to appeal to people who have been educated by television so that they are now more familiar with the realis. Note also the example of pornography: we will continue to see that this kind of realism is often associated with sexual images, with exposure. What Slamet says concerns live performances no less than those on television, for both are part of the world that television affects. And as in the cases of many other innovations that bring wayang closer to television, the "realism" does not begin on television, but develops from something before it that happens to fit the moderen "world of entertainment", and that is thereby given recognition and becomes more widely popular, from a local style to a standard manner of moving the puppets in a world de-localized by television.

Slamet, in the quotation above, points to bus and train puppets as examples of the realis-ation of wayang. There are puppets representing motorcycles, cars, buses, trains, helicopters, fighter planes, guns, and new characters. They stand out because they are not from the mythological world of wayang, and because they are depicted in a different style.

Visually, the new puppets resemble television cartoons. When I asked Enthus, who uses many television and film characters, whether he gets inspiration from television, cartoons were the first example he mentioned, followed, in uncanny proximity, by the dinosaur movie *Jurassic Park* and the news of Lady Diana's death:

> Yes, very much! I am indeed a lover [*pecinta*] of cartoon films. Also a lover of films that are like *Jurassic* [*Park*]. After I watched that one, uuaaaaaa, I bought a biiiiig piece of hide [and made dinosaur puppets]; the first time they appeared on the screen—TUMULT! When Lady Diana died, it became interesting—I made a picture of Lady Diana's head and put white cloth on it ... A GHOST! Hahahahaha!

Mike Tyson, (the ghost of) Lady Diana, George Bush, and dinosaurs—these television and movie figures, as well as the modern means of transport, all look as though they come from television cartoons. The visual style is one indication of what realis is in wayang: it does not refer directly to reality, but to that which one sees on television and in films, the realis media par excellence. Cartoons and cartoon style of representation are said to be realis—Slamet cites Donald Duck as an example of the realis. Wayang learns to see and to show reality after television's image.

Even traditional characters behave "like a cartoon", as Crazy Djoko, who also cites cartoons as an inspiration, told me:

> Yes, like a cartoon! There would be a chase. Bagong [a small, fat clown-servant] is chased by Wrekudara [a powerful warrior prince], then they enter a rice field, now [Bagong] is cornered, he hides himself and only his behind is visible, Wrekudara gets close, this one [Bagong] farts, [Wrekudara] runs away! Hahaha! Scared! A general is scared by a fart! Hahahaha!

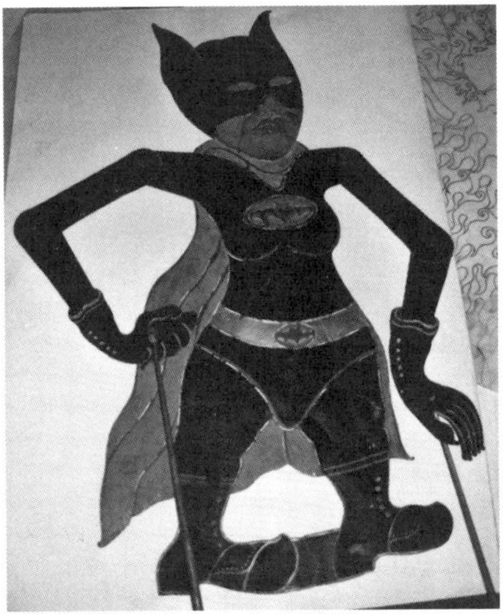

1.3 The puppet of the American superhero Batwoman: an example of puppets inspired by television and movies. (Collection of Ki Enthus Susmono, photo by author.)

1.4 The erectable Penis Ogre: an example of comic pornography in wayang. (Collection of Ki Enthus Susmono, photo by author.)

There are also puppets that are in some ways traditional, but their appearance has been changed as a result of the influence of film or television. Enthus says that his new superduperlarge puppet of an ogre was inspired by King Kong and (again) *Jurassic Park.*

There are many new versions of pornographic "devil" characters—females with huge swinging breasts, males with oversize moving penises or some that look like a walking penis (which can be made erect by pulling a string). These have many precedents, but they are now also readily recognized as *porno*. In the explicitness rather than the mere presence of sexual allusions, and in their dissociation from demonic or ritual function (they are first of all funny, pornographic "just entertainment"), they are seen as a part of the "modernization" of wayang. The connection of this realism to pornography or explicit sexual images is not accidental: the appeal of realism is in making everything visible, especially things that previously were just alluded to but not exposed to sight.

Asep, the wayang golek dhalang whom we have heard talking about the "visualization of utterances", says that, in addition to taking from kung fu movies,

> I have also learned from Western culture. For instance, the Westerners made the Mickey Mouse film(s). Kids in Indonesia who do not know English, do understand their movement language [*bahasa geraknya*]. Well, that too [is one of my sources]—[I perform] wayang golek like that. For example, the way a wayang golek puppet moves and whispers something into his friend's ears [he demonstrates with his hands]—the spectators already understand that.

While Manteb says that he "translates" kung fu movements into wayang, Asep speaks about using the "movement language" of cartoons in wayang. In both cases, either translation or using a foreign language is involved. Asep incorporates a foreign language that is now familiar to his audiences. In Slamet Gundono's terms, wayang's own visual language becomes foreign to people. At the same time, for Asep and Slamet Gundono, Mickey Mouse and pornography on the internet, respectively, are still identified as "Western culture", something foreign. The foreign is going wild.

Traditional sound effects which support visual representation[40] continue to be used, but new sounds are sometimes added. In the 1970s, Manteb popularized the use of Western-style cymbal and large drums. The kung fu movies, which inspired his puppet movements, feature highly stylized sound effects not unlike the sound of cymbal in Manteb's performances. In the early 1980s, Manteb introduced "realistic" sound effects, such as the sound of a flying arrow, fire, water, and so on. Manteb told me that his innovations were criticized because, for instance, the sound effect that he uses for a flying arrow is not really like the sound of a flying arrow in real life—it is only in films that an arrow makes such a sound, his critics said. Recounting the conversation to me, Manteb countered: "Is the sound of *dhodhogan* [the rapping traditionally accompanying the flying arrow in wayang] like the sound of the arrow?" The sound effects are called realis, not because they would be the sounds of real life, but because, like dinosaurs, they are from, and of, film and television.

While the older Manteb uses the sound of a triangle when two metal weapons clash, Enthus employs the same sound, but electronically reproduced on a keyboard. However, for comic and TV cartoon-like effect, the pitch changes as different parts of the metal weapon are hit, so that in the end the characters on the screen "play" on their weapons like on musical instruments. The conventionality of the "realis" (i.e., non-wayang) sound effects is brought out and played with. The "realis" is close to the world of cartoons: they both concern film and television.

More striking is the incorporation of filmic and televisual "realism" into wayang through the use of colour slides and videos projected onto the wayang screen. It is seen occasionally in mainstream performances, and is quite common in experimental forms of wayang. The wayang screen in effect turns into a movie screen, specifically one with the television-like quality of video. Wayang puppets may be moved against the background of the slide or video, "in" the picture, and realis sound effects are often featured. But the puppets never really merge into the picture, and there is an obvious discrepancy between the different manners of representations. As wayang and videotic media come closer together, the gap between them becomes all the more obvious.

Sri Hastanto, a former head of the Arts Institute in Solo, criticized the use of slides in wayang (mentioned in the following quotation, the *kayon*, also known as *gunungan*, is the sacred tree/mountain puppet, symbolizing life, life-energy, and the cosmos; it is also used to represent various things, such as fire, ocean, forest, power/energy, etc.; and it marks time of the performance, appearing at the transitions between major scenes and parts of the performance):

> A subtler act of damaging [wayang] is the shallowing of human feeling. Formerly, we could feel the circumstance

> of an ocean by looking at the skills of a dhalang moving the kayon accompanied by narration and the mellow tones of the *gender* [a musical instrument] that stimulate imagination [*imajinasi*]; this has been replaced by a slide of the ocean. Inner imagination has been replaced by a sight for the physical eye. Spiritual work has been replaced by the sound of a click of the tongue expressing astonishment at technology [*decak kagum teknologi*].[41]

Slamet says the realis is replacing the imajinatif as people become used to the realis from television and generally "the world of *entertainment*"; Sri Hastanto says that the practice of projecting a slide on the screen replaces the "spiritual work" of "inner imagination [*imajinasi batin*]". The slide or video projected on the screen is the next step from what Asep calls *visualisasi*, "visualization", or from what Sri Sadono talks as a representation "(more) complete with everything". We have seen how "the more complete", television-like realis representation leaves less space for, or does not stimulate, wayang-ly imagination. Projecting a slide or video makes the representation "even more complete" and, as Slamet and Sri Hastanto point out, replaces the work of imagination required by a wayang-ly manner of representation. And it does so instantaneously, saving time.

Wayang is in love with realism and is transformed by it, but its realism also betrays difficulties and resistances to this process, as when one tries to do something or be someone against one's nature—the result is sometimes more like a parody of television's realism.

Visibility, Electric Light, Spectacle, and the Clean and Tidy Stage

Television makes things visible in a new way. The developments in wayang's mode of representation discussed above—visualization, realism—are in part inspired by television, and are often believed to make wayang look better on television. Another major transformation, which also concerns new visibility, is the change in appearance of the stage at spectacular large-scale performances, which are widely imitated. There is now more light and less darkness. The connection between lighting and television is brought out by Paul Virilio's use of the phrase "indirect light" to describe the effect of "various electro-optical [...] prostheses".[42] Television generates a new, radically different form of "light" which allows people—as they see the world through television—to see what they could not see in ordinary, direct light. The increase in direct light at the wayang performance and the "indirect lighting" of television jointly increase wayang's visibility.

As everything becomes more visible, there is more attention to appearances. There is a tendency to make everything clean and tidy (*rapi bersih*). The stage where the musicians sit tends to be larger and often includes a space where people can stand and dance. The gamelan has grown larger. The female singers have been repositioned so that they are clearly visible. The screen has grown much wider, and its central part is flanked by ever longer rows of spectacularly expensive, gilded puppets. The musicians are more likely to wear clean and neat uniforms. Lights and spotlights illuminating the stage are now often part of the dhalang's hardware. Wayang has become, to use terms commonly employed in Indonesia to describe this development, *kolosal* and *spektakuler*. There are many forces that have moved wayang in this direction—economic/political/cultural—but here we will look specifically at how this is a part of wayang moving closer to television.

Depending on the occasion, television staff have a varied amount of authority to directly influence the performance. In the case of Indosiar, strong television lights illuminate the stage and change the atmosphere of the event and alter the space: traditionally, the light of the single oil lamp (*blencong*) defines the space where another world is represented, and the surrounding darkness supports this feeling. The strong modern lighting separates the stage from the surrounding areas, and the show from the spectators, creating an experience closer to that of watching Western theatre or television. Television producers try to make the stage clean and tidy, and avoid anything that might obstruct visibility, such as the poles supporting the temporary tent structure. When Indosiar has more leeway, the producer may arrange the stage in such a way that everything is "better" visible. For instance, the singers are located on a higher platform, and flower decorations may be placed in front of them.

(These initiatives of television producers will be discussed in more detail in Chapter Two.)

Ki Haji Mansyur, a Cirebonese dhalang who has never performed on Indosiar but watches wayang on the television station whenever he can, talked to me about the Indosiar wayang's "tidiness" (*rapinya*) and the appearance of the stage as the most impressive thing and something that he tries to imitate in his performances. He talked about the impressive size of the gamelan ensemble, the beautiful appearance of the instruments and the puppets, as well as the musicians' tidy uniforms. On Indosiar, he said, everything is "*Wah!*" ("Wow!"), and he contrasted it with the "dark, black, unexciting" appearance of the instruments that dhalang in his area use, and everybody is dressed "any old way" (*asal-asalan*). He performed at TVRI Bandung and was criticized by the television crew for precisely those reasons, and because of "the appearance of the dhalang and the musicians". They suggested that the performers "clean and polish the gamelan instruments and pay attention to their costumes [*kostumnya*]". He said that people in his area were asking him, "why can't Cirebonese wayang be like that?"—like the wayang they see on Indosiar. He is in effect saying: If only we could become more like what we see on television!

The development of the spectacular performances that Mansyur admires is not simply a product of television—the trend began well before Indosiar's first wayang broadcasts in 1995 (some colossal performances took place already around 1991, and even they have developed gradually from earlier tendencies). Yet, for Mansyur and his audiences—like for people in other areas—spectacular wayang is introduced primarily through television and for them it exists, or is visible, only thanks to television. It is this wayang made visible by television that Mansyur, as he says, imitates and with which he has to try to compete. He emphasized that people in the area generally don't get the chance to see the top dhalang live, so the influence is "really from Indosiar—indeed, what is called the "global era" leads in that direction—people switch to Indosiar and see wayang of [puppeteer-superstars] Pak Manteb, Pak Anom, or Pak Warsena, which is so pretty". So he "practices to be tidier".

As Indosiar makes visible certain performances and not others, it transforms wayang by promoting the kind of shows that are most like television. The tele-visibility that we have talked about earlier—making wayang visible regardless of place and distance—goes hand in hand with the visibility that is part of the spectacular performances full of light, because it is this spectacle that fits television, that is most appealing when it is made tele-visible. What is at stake *both* in making wayang visible across distances, *and* in making the performance spectacular (more light, attention to dress, polished instruments, arousing appearances), is an effort to increase wayang's visibility. The visibility/visuality itself is "arousing" (*merangsang*)—Mansyur used this word, which has a sexual connotation. Indosiar producer Panca suggested that people are not interested in the story, but in the "sexiness and sensuality" of the "presentation/appearance" (*penampilan*). What is arousing or sexy is not simply what one sees, but that one sees and how clearly one sees it. The gamelan was there before, but the trend is toward more light, and toward spectacle for the sake of spectacle—more instruments, better polished, neater dress, prettier singers. This increased visibility in/of wayang performances is a manifestation of television: it is the workings of television itself—as a new kind of vision characterized by unprecedented visibility—that is "arousing".

The choice of words such as "arousing", "sexy", and "sensual" by Indonesian commentators is not accidental. In addition to the more general connections between the new visibility of camera's realism and pornography, one can think more specifically about sexuality in wayang in a narrow sense. The increased visibility of the female singer—traditionally sensual and sexual—is a major development in wayang over the last few decades. Watching the female singer is frequently cited as one of the pleasures of watching wayang, live or on television. There are more singers, they have been repositioned to make them more easily visible, they play a more important role in the performance (not only singing but also speaking into the microphone, and increasingly often standing up), and their appearance is as important as their voice. Panca said that in the early Indosiar broadcasts, he looked for young and sexy singers, he would occasionally ask one to lower the front of her blouse covering her breasts, and ask the cameramen to take a high angle shot so as to make her breasts more visible. The singer and what is visible of her breasts has always been the object of eager eyes in live performances. But the television spectator can "get"—televisually—to the pesindhen much closer than usual, and the frequent close-ups of the singers that guide the spectator's gaze, the producer's awareness of the sexiness and sensuality of appearances, and his initiatives to make the appearances even more sexy and sensual, combine to make the erotic sensuality an important feature of wayang on television.

One should not be surprised to hear the president of Indosiar say in effect that before Indosiar, for most people wayang was invisible:

> When there is a celebration such as a wedding, only the VIP invited guests who sit in front are able to watch, but others are at the edges, happy to follow just the sounds, hahaha. They can't physically watch, only listen. Well, thanks to television, they can see what is in front of the dhalang, so automatically it is more interesting—usually they just hear the sounds, now they see it for themselves. [...] That has its own appeal [*daya tarik*: power to attract]. Not all people who have watched wayang necessarily know how the dhalang moves his left and right legs. On television, everything is visible [*kelihatan semua*]!

If television makes a performance visible across Indonesia, the use of close-ups annihilates distance on a different scale: one can see the performance from different angles and distances, and one can see the hands of a musician or the female singer as if from several inches away. And this is a motivation to keep everything clean and tidy.

Older people remember wayang without electricity. Interestingly, both puppeteers and audiences talk with nostalgia about the oil lamp that was used in the past—the flickering flame made the puppets' shadows appear to live and breathe. The puppeteer would adjust the wick to enhance the mood of a particular scene (for instance, the flame was made larger for a battle scene). In contrast, people say, electric light is steady and "dead" (*mati*). So why do people use it? The usual reasoning is that it is stronger and people can see the puppets more clearly and from a greater distance (think: tele-vision). Today, many puppeteers use halogen light because it makes the picture sharper (think: HDTV).

Strong electric lights are essential to the functioning of television, but even when a show is not televised, and regardless of whether the use of a particular light was inspired by television or not, electric light makes wayang more like television in that it increases visibility. The lights illuminating the stage and surrounding areas "compete" with the blencong, puppeteers say. While the old blencong, in the middle of a night, played with light and darkness, now darkness is annihilated and clear, steady light dominates.

Wayang performances today are strongly amplified. Electricity has made wayang more audible—more clearly and at a greater distance. The character of the sound, like that of the appearances, has been radically altered. The amplification is always extremely strong. The sound coming from the blasting loudspeakers is distinctly different from the sound of gamelan or unamplified voice, the loudness of this sound is appreciated by the wayang audience, though it often distorts the natural sound. Because of this, the amplification (the loudness) itself is celebrated, and no attempt is made to conceal the amplification or make it sound more "natural". Just as it is the new visibility that is "arousing", so electric amplification of wayang changes first of all, not what one hears, but how audible it is.

In the famous essay "The Medium is the Message", Marshall McLuhan uses electricity as his first example of a "medium without a message". He writes that in all media, "the 'content' of any medium is always another medium" and "the 'message' of any medium or technology is the change of scale or pace or pattern that it introduces into human affairs".[43] In our case, wayang is getting bigger, louder, brighter, and faster.

The new audiovisibility or audiovisuality, the cleanliness and tidiness, and a tendency toward the spectacular that come with it, permeate the whole performance, and are all aspects of a changing character of the performance. I have discussed the "visualization of utterances", the emphasis on puppet movements and the visual in general, and the changing appearance of the stage and the performers. I have talked about how many puppeteers tend to prepare "better" for televised performances, how these performances are more pre-composed so that momentary confusions are avoided, and this too makes performances generally more "tidy", like the illuminated stage. The kung fu-inspired sabetan is part of the same trend—it is, first of all, spectacular—as is the extension of clown scenes, which have become not only longer in time but also more spectacular. During the clown scenes strong lights are turned on to illuminate the stage, a stage that previously did not exist as a place for spectacle and for the "many attractions" and that is created and defined in part by the electric light itself.

Other/New Technologies and Modernity

Part of the incorporation of "other entertainments" and "many attractions" into the new spectacular wayang is the use of various new technologies. The new television-like visibility and audibility are attractions in themselves. The same applies to other new technologies, such as electronic keyboards, wireless microphones, disco lights, dry ice, amplification systems, and simultaneous television screening. As we have seen in the case of electric light, the incorporation of new technologies is often felt to make wayang less dramatically effective, but it makes it more spectacular. Part of this is that modern technology, like television, is itself an attraction as a sign of cultural, social, and economic modernity. We have heard Sri Hastanto talk about *decak kagum teknologi*, "the sound of a click of the tongue expressing astonishment at technology".

The presence of the television crew, with their camera and special lighting, helps to make live performances more spectacular. Typically, it is not Indosiar but the sponsor of the celebration who pays the performers, and the sponsor even pays Indosiar—often more than the performers to come, because, as a producer put it, Indosiar's presence is a sign of prestige. The large television cameras (located in conspicuous places above people's heads, often on the same level as the raised stage), powerful lighting, generators, the studio-bus, and trucks are part of the show and add glamour to it. At most performances recorded by Indosiar, the performance is simulcast on television sets placed around the performance area or video-projected on large movie screens. These visible signs of television's presence, spectacular though they are, refer to something even larger, something beyond the place. They are merely the visible parts of television, as a technology and institution, that makes the performance visible "everywhere" across Indonesia, as if throwing magical light on the event, magical light that makes it visible to everyone, regardless of where or how far they are ("Mirror, mirror on

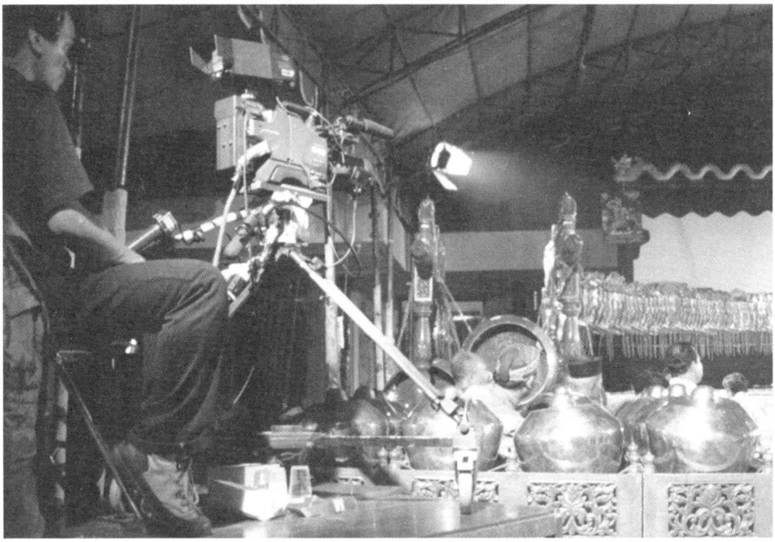

1.5 Television camera set up on a desk, and television light above, at the same wayang performance described at the beginning of the Introduction.

1.6 Behind the wayang screen (on its shadow side), people watching a "simulcast" of the same performance on a television monitor. The signal comes directly from the mobile studio of Indosiar, which was covering the performance. Other people watched the TV coverage on a projection screen attached to vans (see illustrations in the Introduction).

1.7 The Indosiar mobile studio and television crew have arrived at a wayang performance.

the wall, who is the fairest of us all?"). This makes the performance even more *spektakuler*.

These traces of television in wayang are signs of something else which, like television, is both here and beyond this and any particular place: modernity. Making wayang more modern and more television-like—these two are scarcely distinct—is in part motivated by the association of television with modernity: one attraction of wayang affected by television is that it approaches television, that it becomes modern technology. As Dr. Rahayu Supanggah, then the director of the Arts Institute in Solo told me, "what is positive" (*positifnya*) about "wayang entering television" is that "wayang can become a modern art".

Otherness and Comedy

Since the 1990s, a frequent comment by Javanese observers has been that the whole wayang performance is becoming comedy. According to one Javanese, "from the first audience scene to the end, there is only comedy [*anane mung dhagelan*]".[44] Pak Naryo said about Ganda Darsana, the precursor of many of the current trends, that "what is strange, the puppets/characters are all clowning [*anehe, wayange ndhagel kabeh*]". Not only critics, but the popular younger dhalang themselves and their fans agree that wayang is, at certain moments, becoming "crazy". It is intentionally made so, and the craziness contributes to wayang's appeal. Crazy Djoko (Djoko Edan) was one of the most popular dhalang of the nineties, the model followed by many minor dhalang. "Strangely, he accepts the title 'crazy dhalang' [*dhalang edan*] with pride. For he sought and fought for that adjective for many years."[45] He often advertises his clown scenes as *full edan,* "fully crazy".

How is comedy and insanity in wayang relevant to understanding wayang's relationship with television? When a clown in wayang makes a joke, sometimes his master calls him crazy (*wong edan*). That the whole performance—including the dhalang—is ostentatiously crazy can be seen as an aspect of the whole performance becoming more like a clown scene and the dhalang more like a crazy clown. The clowns (as A.L. Becker puts it) use "modern language, modern ideas, and modern behavior". Wayang's new craziness is related to the increasing opening of wayang to the present, "modern" world, because in wayang the modern—as introduced by the clowns—is, traditionally, crazy. An appeal of innovations, including the new technologies, is that, when they appear in wayang, they are crazy.

The clowns are themselves as if from the outside of the represented, mythical world. Their foreignness to the heroes' way of being is essentially comical—it is a joke that precedes any other jokes that the clowns may make. As the famous comedian Teguh points out, even their shape is "strange".[46] Today, all the characters are becoming to some extent clowns, that is, they are increasingly strange to themselves in the way that clowns are traditionally strange to them. This, in the context of wayang, means, as a spectator shouted out at a performance: "All the characters are crazy!" In many jokes, this foreignness-to-themselves is manifested as being modern in a mythical world. This happens when a prince rides a motorcycle or a police car; when another bribes the enemy so that he can avoid fighting; or when a military plane flies across the screen.

Having seen that global modernity is identified with the funny and the crazy in wayang, and that it is brought in by the clowns, we learn what wayang says about the modernity with which television is associated. It is *both* foreign, crazy, and funny, *and* it is one of the most fascinating and appealing things for the Javanese. This crazy and funny modernity is something that is now at the centre of wayang, of what many Javanese say is the most Javanese picture of their world.

Wayang approaches television. But if a part of the appeal of television in wayang is its foreignness and craziness, one wonders if the gap between the two media and their cultures, their otherness, is really closing. If television is to be "Other" in wayang and thus, appealing in the way it is now, there needs to be a limit to how close wayang can get to television before it loses its otherness and with it a certain appeal. But the fact that wayang's approach to television is often ironic or parodic reveals the complexity of their interaction. If wayang is able to see and show its televisation and modernization as a comedy, as a masquerade, it means that we have to be careful how to interpret any move towards television. If the move is in the spirit of comedy or parody, it may be a sign that wayang, at the same time that it is seriously becoming like television, maintains a certain distance, the clown's detachment, from the process, and sees it as something ridiculous or crazy. Perhaps like in any seriously humorous attitude to the world, one cannot draw a line between what is serious and what is a joke.

These are thoughts from the "age of Indosiar". In Chapter Five, we will see how the situation developed in the following years; we will see changes and a different atmosphere, we will see novelty and tensions wearing off, but the complexity, mutual infiltration, and the sense of a masquerade played with modern technology remain, when, for example, people around the world watch wayang on YouTube and, in the simultaneous chat, playfully pretend they are sitting, chatting and ordering food and drinks in a stall near the performance.

Roots and Spectres: The Net of Media, the Net of History

The foregoing discussion has focused on wayang and television and their interaction, as a storyteller might focus on two people and their relationship. But this interaction is part of a play with many actors.

Moreover, I have focused mostly on a time when wayang and television encountered each other most directly. But the (hi)story we are trying to understand extends into, and from, the past.

Javanese people often talk about the value of wayang as *pusaka*, "sacred heirloom", and its values and wisdom as that of the ancestors. According to a Javanese explanation, wayang originated when the king Jayabaya drew images of his ancestors, starting from Hyang Jagadnata (God-Ancestor King-of-the-World). Other accounts of the origins of wayang also connect it to ancestor worship. Its languages and images come from the past, and as A.L. Becker describes it, the puppeteer makes the past relevant in the present, through translation and interpretation, without replacing the past with its translation. Many passages in wayang are structured as quotes of archaic language followed by or interspersed with translation.[47] Both wayang and television bring their pasts with(in) them into the present through this interaction, which is never separate from the encounters between the living and the dead.

To think in another way about how questions about the past are part of the larger questions of this chapter, we can invoke again Derrida's spectre, as we did in the beginning of this chapter. Earlier, we were concerned primarily with how something of television infiltrates live performances; with the spectral appearances generated by television that haunt and seduce the living presence of wayang. Derrida's notion of the spectre intersects questions of tele-technologies, as well as the relation between the past and the present.

> If there is something like spectrality, there are reasons to doubt this reassuring order of presents and especially, the border between the present, the actual and present reality of the present, and everything that can be opposed to it: absence, non-presence, non-effectivity, inactuality, virtuality, or even the simulacrum in general, and so forth.[48]

We have seen how "live" wayang, even before it is put on television, is already affected by television, how virtuality invades actuality. To continue to think how wayang and actuality are never unmediated, we need to focus on the "non-contemporaneity with itself of the living present",[49] or the way things from and of the past—languages, media, cultures, technologies, works, including wayang and television—are alive in, *are* the living present, together with and not entirely separate from the spectrality generated by television and wayang. We need to pay attention to how the past foreshadows the present (foreshadows: the shadow before the body? The shadow generating the body?); we need to listen to resonances across time. What follows is not a history, but more like the invocation of ancestor spirits, particularly the ancestors of the spectral phenomena discussed in this chapter. This evocation of the past foreshadows my discussion of the latest developments in the last chapter, where I will continue to explore the "non-contemporaneity with itself of the living present" and the extended net of relationships among various media at the age of the internet and IT. Already in the following paragraphs, we will be caught in nets that in some ways foreshadow (and in other ways don't foreshadow) the Net.

Wayang, first heard on radio in 1934, has been broadcast regularly and increasingly more often since the 1930s.[50] In Central Java today, one can listen to wayang on radio practically every night (and this is true even in the age of the internet). According to Philip Yampolsky, a wayang kulit performance was first recorded on eight cassettes in 1973 (Lokananta Recording ACD-022); earlier, in 1968, there was one LP recording of the gara-gara, foreshadowing the popularity of the comic interludes on television.[51] Both the 1968 and 1973 recordings featured the popular "radio" dhalang Ki Nartosabdo, who would dominate the cassette market in later years, to be challenged only by the younger Ki Anom Soeroto, who became popular on cassettes, radio and, later, television.

At some moments, the radio and cassettes function as two elements of one medium. Live radio broadcasts of wayang are common, but many performances heard on radio are from private and commercial recordings of wayang. On these two media, unlike on television, wayang can only be heard and not seen—Ben Arps uses the term "audio wayang".[52] Dhalang who focus on spectacular puppet movement, such as Manteb and many younger dhalang, do not fit audio media as smoothly as dhalang famous for their beautiful voice, musical innovation, and skill with words. However, some puppeteers have been popular on both radio and television, and television is both a visual counterpart to the audio media and their extension.

Radio and cassettes, like television, lift wayang beyond a particular place (and often time), make it virtually perceptible "everywhere", endow chosen performers with an aura of recognition, and can help to make them famous and popular. Younger dhalang who appear on television continue to exploit the powers of radio and audio recording. Warsena Slenk, for instance, gives audio recordings of his performances to local radio stations, appears in interviews and phone-in programmes, allows his performances to be recorded by radio stations and even gives souvenirs to radio technicians to establish good relationships.[53] Ki Mansyur told me: "I recorded audio first, and only after the cassettes had been published and had promoted [me], did TVRI people from Bandung come." In his case, the "lifting" power of cassettes helped the puppeteer to get to the next level: television.

Even before television, radio and cassettes had begun to encourage wayang to become a mass, popular entertainment. Since the 1960s, Nartosabdo made singers more "visible" by joking with them during the comic interludes and by making light songs more central in his performances. Several older dhalang told me that the practice of requesting a song by a letter was first introduced in Nartosabdo's performances broadcast on radio, as an imitation of various radio programmes in which the studio audience or the radio listeners could request a song or a gamelan composition. The development of this practice—the beginnings of a dialogue between the dhalang and the singers—which relates to the increasing prominence of the singers (and by extension the "guest stars") and the increasing emphasis on entertainment, was the basis for further developments that define wayang in the era of television.[54]

Before wayang became a part of the television "flow", it had been part of the flow of radio programming. The fragmentary character of the performance—a flow of a variety of entertainments—can be thus seen as having (some of) its roots in wayang's encounter with radio. A characteristic of the music that Nartosabdo introduced into his performances is that it comes from a variety of "other regions", and this has been a trend ever since. This practice must be seen in relation to the being-beyond-place of the mass media, as well as to other realities of modern life, such as the fact that Nartosabdo and other famous puppeteers frequently travelled and performed in a variety of places. By incorporating songs from other regions, wayang has become more like the radio.

Radio and cassettes are obviously related to television. But the history we are tracing did not begin with them, and we need to go further back in time and look more broadly at the present. We have seen how electric lighting and amplification have brought wayang closer to television, but the process began before television became important: wayang was already becoming a modern, electric, mass medium. This means that recording wayang is not simply a matter of a modern electric medium recording a live performance. Since a wayang performance incorporates the mechanics of radio and television—electricity, electric light, sound amplification/reproduction, etc.—recording or shooting wayang is like "wiring" it to television, or like plugging television into an existing electronic apparatus, the already-electrified wayang. To an extent this is literally true. Microphones were used in wayang before television, and now the wayang's "audio out" is simply enhanced and connected to television rather than only to an amplification system. In terms of light, Indosiar "improves" on wayang's existing electric lighting by adding power to it, and by adding the "indirect light" that makes the performance visible everywhere. Radio's and television's relation to wayang can be seen, both historically and in terms of electrical wiring, as an extension of wayang's own amplification and lighting. The interaction between electricity and wayang, as two media and its new audibility/visibility, had prepared it for its integration into radio and television.

According to my teacher, the late Ki Naryocarito, microphones and the electric blencong were first used in wayang performances at the radio station and later in imitation of these prestigious performances. Radio and microphones were introduced simultaneously into wayang, and amplification became common in "live" performances as a kind of imitation of radio: the image infiltrating actuality. Another inspiration for the use of a microphone, according to Ki Naryocarito, was the charismatic figure of Soekarno, who used a microphone to amplify his electrifying speeches.[55] The microphone's associations with power and leadership are relevant here: like the mass media, it empowers the person who has access to it, it "lifts" him or her above the normal volume of other voices and other people. In this, too, amplification anticipated television.

An important aspect of the appeal of a wayang performance is the charismatic person of the dhalang.[56] If the use of the microphone in wayang was indeed partly inspired by President Soekarno's use of the device, the amplification of the puppeteer's voice can be seen as an effort to amplify his power. Later the female singers began to use the microphone, which elevated their importance. Technologically, they have become the dhalang's equals, and the dhalang has become only one of the people who can speak into the microphone. Gradually, more people were to have access to the microphone, such as the comedians and other guest stars, as well as members of the audience who today commonly come up on stage and speak and sing into the microphone.

In pointing out wayang's interaction with other media, my aim is, first, to show that wayang did not meet television in its virgin state; and second, it is to point to this *web of media*, to show the interconnectedness of events and technologies at a particular time as well as through time, to show that the early interaction between wayang and audio media, electricity, and so on, were not just "other cases" of interaction, but that they foreshadowed the future, they are part of the same flow of life, web of life, as the interaction between television and wayang, which in turn foreshadows future media liaisons. The net of language helps to capture the feeling of entanglement: when I say "flow of life", I have to think of the flow of television; when I speak of "the web of media", I evoke the Web and the Net, as the future of the past, as a medium which is part of the net-like history of media, and as a medium in which the web-like connectedness of the older media is further brought out.

Radio, for example, is not just another medium, because it shares with television many features—its relation to distance and place, something of the televisual flow characterized by variety and fragmentation, its "liveness" or "presentness"—it too runs on electricity, and it too is a manifestation of modern technology. When we talk about interaction of the media "preceding" television, something of television is already involved. McLuhan writes about electric light and power and how "they eliminate time and space factors in human association exactly as do radio, telegraph, telephone, and TV".[57] The interaction between wayang and "something of television" has started well before the first television broadcast in Indonesia. In fact, it is impossible to say when it began. Each medium is rooted in its complex past, and the interaction between them is both new and it is a moment in a multi-channel flow, a knot in a net.

A vast, entangled net that (dis)connects people, media, and other phenomena through "family relationships" (in an extended sense), through all kinds of links, friendships, enmities, echoes, also across generations; a net in which the knots are neither regular nor fixed, and connections are fluid: one is almost tempted to capitalize this Net (so as to amplify echoes across times and apparently distinct realms). To represent and make sense of this Net is in some ways counterproductive, in that it may lead us away from the field's vastness, and from the sense that there is no centre, no origin. But we can at least gesture toward that vastness, to begin to feel how the past foreshadows the present, how spectres haunt the present—the pasts living with us in the present—are impossible to limit, count, categorize, capture.

We have seen that the interaction between wayang and television is commonly conceptualized as a "marriage full of conflicts" between Javanese, local, traditional culture and global modernity associated with the West. As one reads about early modernity in the Dutch East Indies and Indonesia, one finds foreshadowing (or fore-lighting) of the sensations, physical traits, and workings of modernity in televised wayang that we have discussed in this chapter. In his book on early nationalism and modernity in the Indies, *Fetish, Recognition, Revolution,* James Siegel emphasizes the importance of communication technology; of the Malay language (from which later modern Indonesian developed) as a lingua franca; and the close connection (or functional equivalence) between the lingua franca and technology:

> A lingua franca by definition operates between peoples of different languages and cultures without belonging to any of them. And technology, too, is available to anyone who can use it or, more importantly for us, fantasize about it. It too, is a means, an in-between point. [...] [A]n understanding of the particularity of Indonesian history depends on understanding a middle point that produces cultural effects.[58]

One such cultural effect is "international overhearing"[59] across ethnic and cultural boundaries, and "the possibility of speaking to a broad range of peoples in a lingua franca and the interest in hearing of a wider variety of events and listening to a broader range of narratives than was previously the case".[60] We see some features (think family resemblances across generations) of television: television's way of being above and beyond place and distance. The lingua franca and communication technology were detached from any particular culture, ethnicity, place and tradition,[61] not weighted down by tradition,[62] and thus enabled (or stimulated fantasizing about) communication across cultures. Siegel writes about "translation to modernity" and modernity as transmission.[63] A special power of this kind of communication was a kind of (claimed, fantasized) universality, rather like that of television or the Net: it connected everyone and everywhere together, and anyone could participate in this communication across borders.

Together with these powers came a particular mode of representation in the literature in Melayu of that time, "reportive", "objective", "non-fictional"; in which the writer is less an author and more a reporter, publisher, or translator.[64] The same powers and modes of representation were admired about the camera. Siegel refers to the movies as "visualized lingua franca".[65] What attracted audiences were "technical effects", in particular the realism and clarity of the images (*terang*: clear, bright, well lit).[66] The reportive objectivity, realism, and clarity work across linguistic, ethnic and cultural borders: "works designed for one group—Chinese, 'native', European, Arab—were read by all".[67] The camera, "a version of the lingua franca", transmits "to everyone, thus across any borders, whether ethnic or political".[68] "Such clarity is the work of an instrument that performs as well in the hands of technicians in one part of the world as the next. It has the power to attract no matter what it shows, no matter what narrative it finds itself recording."[69] Can we see here a foreshadowing of the powers of television, infiltrating wayang, to be beyond any particular place and culture; tendencies toward realism, towards making visible rather than stimulating imagination; and generally a new visibility and audibility?

The texts in lingua franca and the camera's images in the Indies, were often translated from various local languages and cultures, and were read and seen by people from multiple ethnic groups and cultures: "It did not seem to matter who the readers were."[70] Siegel traces the development of new, mass, and increasingly anonymous audiences who have "the new identity of the audience of mass media";[71] of events on a massive scale (political rallies, cinema screenings) which brought together masses of people, regardless of their culture or ethnic background. Do not these developments foreshadow the development of new mass wayang audiences, and the associated transformation of wayang?

There was a "staggering polyphony and heterogeneity of printed materials".[72] In the case of visual representation, the "camera has the power to recontextualize [...] images that, no longer governed by their originals, mix with any other figures on the same page. The newspaper becomes a movie theatre, its commercial images responding to scenarios found nowhere in the actual world."[73] Should one think here of the fragmentary nature of new wayang performances and especially the comic intermezzi, in which various attractions, entertainments, languages, and musical styles, often from "other regions", are freely juxtaposed in a television-like flow?

In early popular fiction, various new technologies of visibility (and sometimes audibility) often have an effect of erotically seducing the viewer. This makes one think of a particular kind of eroticism in wayang, related to the new realism and increased visibility, that we discussed earlier as something encouraged by television. Then and now, the eroticism and seductiveness of technology are both an appeal and a threat. One may ask whether this erotic sensuality is inherent to images whose appeal is their clarity and technical realism; how technical realism and scientific objectivity always carry within themselves the appeal of pornography, through the possibility of annihilating physical, social, and cultural distance and thus enabling people to see what they desire from close up, without being seen.

The ability to communicate across boundaries with anonymous masses of people, and to employ the new verbal and visual languages in which images became reality, were new powers that various parties attempted to consolidate in order to gain authority over communication, representation, and what Siegel terms recognition, in a new environment which unsettled traditional and colonial structures of power. This story of early Indonesian nationalism could serve as a backdrop against which we can think about the present: to think about how puppeteers try to exploit television to "lift" them—and their culture—beyond a particular place, make them visible everywhere, and make them "recognized";

how there is a desire and competition among puppeteers to participate in modernity and in communication beyond their locality; how technological images of actuality—televised wayang performances—are strangely "in power", more so than performances taking place "merely" in actuality; how this is a struggle for power not only among puppeteers, but among different cultures; how this power consists in communication and visibility.

In Siegel's account of the late colonial era, the modern powers of communication create desires and possibilities to break away from local tradition and order, and at the same time an anxiety about threats to tradition. The persistence of tradition and the local appears at some moments as backwardness and an obstacle to modernity. Translation into modernity, as it annihilates distances and places, involves the annihilation of any conflicts between tradition and modernity "caused" by tradition, in particular any resistance to transmission. We may think about wayang on television as a case of the translation of tradition into modernity, of modernity encompassing tradition and trying to erase any conflict in the process. Wayang is torn between supporting television in this by becoming more like television—less bound to a place and a culture, more easily transmittable—and resisting modernization by persisting in making troubles for modernity, for perfect transmission, for technical realism, by asserting place and tradition.

Siegel writes about "the control of communication on the one hand and the breaking of that control on the other". He illustrates this with an example of New Order cultural theme park, Taman Mini, whose images, "close to the virtual reality produced electronically", he compares to television. However, an old Acehnese warplane disrupts the ways in which authority controls reality through images, because it "seems to provoke a flood of referents".[74] The warplane evokes conflicting, uncontrolled memories and feelings and thus–like a moment of darkness—disturbs the clear, clean and neat representation of Indonesian culture. Perhaps wayang on television–in the way it fails to translate smoothly into modernity—is another example of the disruption of the power of technological representation and a break of the control of the effects of technology. Siegel writes about a 1948 story by Pramoedya Ananta Toer which he presents as a break in language controlled by the "fetish of modernity": "It is, in fact, the failure of translation [think: televisation of wayang] that is really important. No true equivalents present themselves."[75] Whereas: "The fetish of modernity [think: television] claims that substitution always works."[76] Here we should remember the opinions discussed earlier in the chapter, according to which a form of theatre that used to stimulate and require imagination and "spiritual work", images that "provoke a flood of referents", has been "replaced" by realistic representation and astonishment at technology.

Siegel's initial and concluding case studies—Taman Mini and Pramoedya's short story respectively—demonstrate a certain historical continuity and the relevance of the study of the colonial period to understanding postcolonial Indonesia, including the age of television. Siegel goes beyond a narrow focus on the New Order period and situates Taman Mini—"a contemporary version of the colonial museum of ethnography", as he describes it[77]—and by extension New Order politics of culture, in a broader history of modern technology, communication, representation, distancelessness, and demonstrates the fruitfulness of such a perspective for understanding postcolonial cultural phenomena.

Rudolf Mrázek's *Engineers of Happy Land*, another book on the late-colonial Indies into which we can read family resemblances across generations, is about technologies, dreams, and anxieties of modernity and their localization: "while the people handled, and were handled by, technologies, their time, space, culture, identity, and nation came to feel awry".[78] He, too, suggests that there is a continuity, "the insistent sense of late colonial culture overgrowing into the post-colonial period and the present".[79] Specific images from the colonial period resonate with what has been happening with wayang and television recently: images of a technological struggle for cleanliness and against dirt, for light and visibility and against darkness, for high speed and against anything that makes one slow down; as well as the penetration of dirt and darkness into what has been lighted and cleaned.

Take, for example, roads: "The newness, the hardness and cleanliness —it was the roads' modernity."[80] Smoothness and general orderliness were admired, both contributing to increasing the speed and comfort of those passing on the roads. Public lighting systems were important, and in the journal of the Union of Motorcycle Riders, motorcycle headlights "were the most frequent and prominent presence.[81] In the "struggle for the roads",[82] this modernity had to be protected from mud and dirt which "came from outside, from the beyond of the modern road",[83] and from the crowds of "natives" who would slow down the motorcyclists. The fear of dirt, disorder, and darkness was a fear of something that would undermine modernity, "an alarming vision of breaking down of the ideal plan of empire through an invasion of physicality, crowding, and, most gravely, touching".[84] Siegel sees the "fetish of modernity" as suppressing "the ability to awaken references that were not intended, that seem to come from somewhere else".[85] Similarly, Mrázek speaks of the Dutch language in the Indies as "asphalt language"; language that is clean, hard and smooth, and works like a well-oiled machine; language that is "cultureless",[86] like modern technology, and in which—think wayang on television—"one could say anything about Java and Javanese culture no matter how sacred the subject".[87] Modernizing the lingua franca, "a language of the road",[88] meant cleaning it up, standardizing it, making it "correct", rather like cleaning, tidying and lighting the roads or the wayang stage. In all these cases, there was a sense that something was being destroyed: a Javanese writer's warning, in the 1930s, that "a language must not become a machine",[89] sounds like the voices saying, in effect, that wayang must not become television, or that the new, television-like realism in wayang kills imagination.

Roads, like television, are a means of communication, connecting places across distance. The transformation of the lived and travelled landscape by the development of a net(work) of hard and clean roads that make possible high-speed communication, foreshadows the televisation of wayang—making wayang clean, neat, well-lit, fast, overcoming distance and place, and otherwise modern—and the high-speed interconnectivity of the Net. What appears as dirt, darkness and disorder from the point of view of modern roads and television, as threats to modernity, as (in the language of the Net) broken links and slow connection, may be perceived differently from a different, non-modern point of view. What one calls dirt, another may call the soil. A Javanese scholar of wayang emphasized to me how walking to a village performance on muddy roads is part of the enjoyment of wayang. When television producers ask musicians at a wayang performance not to smoke and to remove or hide food and ashtrays because they spoil—soil, one could say—the televisually ideal clean and neat image, for the musicians this means spoiling some of the sensual and social pleasures of wayang and its atmosphere. Watching people as they eat, smoke and socialize is part of the enjoyment of wayang. The struggle over the modern roads is part of the same struggle. We find the same modern ambitions—to control the world by cleaning and tidying it, and making everything visible—and the same fear that the modern world will be subverted by dirt, darkness, culture, imagination, by "a sense of culture [...] as roots of grass breaking through armed or reinforced and culture-less modernity".[90]

To modernize the Indies meant to "put on the light in that poor dark world".[91] For the Dutch, lighting was part of defining their modern space—roads, houses—and separating themselves from darkness. There was also something like the "indirect light" of television: the modern optics which enabled people to see, and to shield and shelter them from what they saw. The optics discussed by Mrázek include the camera and the telescope, but also trains and airplanes—like television, technologies of modern seeing *and* of overcoming place and distance. Forms of tele-vision. From behind the television-like glass of the train window, one watched "a most easily and most comfortingly watchable modernity",[92] and travellers described the pleasing prettiness and peace of the colonial landscape seen from the train, like "beautiful Indies" paintings, "a late colonial image of the colony known and often more significant than the colony itself".[93] From behind the "unbreakable windows of the planes", the colony was "made more safely visible".[94] These technologies provided a way of seeing that is rather like the view of wayang through television (as we will see in Chapter Three): a comfortable way of watching without being in the midst of what is happening, without coming into physical contact with people, with one's view defined by the frame, yet also seeing in a stronger light, often in close up, enlarged yet in miniature, and under control. Yet this Java, brightly lit and seen through glass screens, grew from and was haunted by a fear of the other of modernity: darkness or bad visibility.

Wayang on television is like the native vehicles and life on the smooth and clean roads that threaten the safety of the racing Dutch motorcyclist with his powerful headlights, like the roots of grass breaking through concrete, like the darkness that is always possibly out of control; and the techniques, technologies, and ideals of television that wayang adopts are like the modernity first fantasized by the Dutch and later, almost in the same way but also differently, by Indonesians.

There can be no closure to understanding the extended family of wayang and television. To point to this lack of closure—like when a person on a ship makes a gesture trying to indicate the vastness of the ocean—one can look in any direction. In the past, wayang was always shaped by interaction, inter-netting, with different media, narratives, cultures. The Hindu epics—their truths, metaphors, ways of seeing, web of myths—have penetrated wayang, as did Islam and Dutch ideas.[95] Something like (and unlike) a marriage between wayang and television had happened in Java before Indonesian modernity. It is through these interpenetrations that wayang has become what it is, and past marriages remain a living past within wayang itself, foreshadowing, setting the stage and rehearsing for, later entanglements.

Or, one could look at how the encounter between wayang and television was prefigured in the history of television and Western culture. A part of European modernity is the return to modernity's other: from civilization to nature, from the city to the countryside, from mechanical production to crafts, from science and technology to art. These are returns which may be romantic, utopian, and escapist, but nonetheless they are sometimes felt to be a matter of survival: how not to become a machine, how not to be controlled by a single vision. This modernity's other is constantly appropriated by modernity (tourism industry capitalizing on masses in search of solitude, nature, culture, or unproductive time; book, art, spirituality industries), but at the same time it continues—perhaps in the form of a memory or a hope—to resist a total takeover, like grass ever breaking through the concrete, like wayang. The story of wayang and television—the rush to modernity, the returns to wayang—feels like a replay, a double, of what happened before, at a different place and age.

Let us think specifically about television. There is a social history of television and other communication and transportation technologies and institutions, which relates it to the social conditions in 19th and 20th centuries—increased movement of people across long distances, capitalism and industrialization, commoditization of pleasure and entertainment, creation of bourgeois homes, and so on. Here we can find obvious prefiguring of the specific themes we encountered in our case (overcoming of distance, lighting up the world, mass audiences, etc.). Most television genres—the news, soap opera, talk show, television drama—are like wayang in that originally they came from outside television. But since we are trying to gesture beyond the clearly visible, let us look into the uncertainty of misty distance, in search of the most shadowy foreshadowing of televised wayang in European thought.

The history of "the mother of the sciences", philosophy, is a history of recycling and reanimating particular images, gestures, and fantasies, as well as ways of thinking about and working with images, many of which happen to share much with television. Many prominent philosophers share a desire for all-encompassing, systematic visions, general and universally applicable ways of seeing and knowing the world, and philosophy is dominated by images and terms of light, vision, and image-production. In the spirit of making a point through caricature, as we sit and joke in the coffee shop, let us think how Western philosophy shares something with tele-vision.

In a 1935 lecture, Edmund Husserl describes the historical "outbreak" of European philosophy as the origin of all sciences. It is "*a new sort of attitude* [italics from the original] of individuals towards their surrounding world"—*television viewers?*—which grows into "a systematically self-enclosed cultural form"[96]—*television?* Husserl contrasts it to Chinese, Indian, and Babylonian philosophies, arguing that none of these is universal but rather they are oriented toward "the world which is concretely, traditionally valid for the civilization in question".[97] "Sharply distinguished" from this is the European philosophical, scientific, "theoretical" attitude, in which—*and does not the following quote evoke the television spectator, sitting on the couch, eating potato chips or fried tofu, and seeing the world through television with infotainment curiosity?*—

> Man becomes gripped by the passion of a worldview and world-knowledge that turns away from all practical interests [...] man becomes a nonparticipating spectator, surveyor of the world [...] the fully disinterested seeing of the world [...] obviously a variant of curiosity, which has its original place in natural life as an intrusion into the course of "serious living," either as a result of originally developed life-interests

> or as a playful looking-about when one's quite immediate needs are satisfied or when working hours are over.[98]

This theoretical attitude—*like technology, lingua franca, television*—lets the "nonparticipating spectator" be beyond and above place, tradition, distance: "Man views first of all the multiplicity of nations, his own and others."[99] The new attitude aspires to guarantee a universally true way of seeing, able to "cover" everything—*think television's realism, television's claim that it can cover everything*: "Through this astonishing contrast [of multiplicity of nations] there appears the distinction between world-representation and actual world, and the new question of truth arises: not tradition-bound, everyday truth, but an identical truth which is valid for all who are no longer blinded by traditions."[100] Seeing from a particular tradition—*such as wayang culture?*—becomes blindness, and something that this new attitude—*television*—supersedes. The "peculiar universality"– *think technology, lingua franca*—is "most essential to the theoretical attitude".[101] In a slightly later text, Husserl discusses the development of the theoretical attitude and of European sciences:

> The great ideal is soon anticipated of a science which, in this new sense, is rational and all-inclusive, or rather the idea that the infinite totality of what is in general is intrinsically a rational all-encompassing unity that can be mastered, without anything left over, by a corresponding universal science.[102]

Does not this "all-inclusiveness" of the new science, its ambition to "master" everything, resonate with attitudes we have encountered above in the discussion of modernity and colonialism in Indonesia—cameras, lingua franca, lighting up everything—and television's own self-propelling urge to cover and include everything? Husserl writes how there occurs "the surreptitious substitution of the mathematically substructed world of idealities for the only real world, the one that is usually given through perception, that is ever experienced and experienceable—our everyday life-world".[103] Thus the life-world is "forgotten"[104] in science, hidden behind the illusive "obviousness" of its representations of the world.[105] Again, we find a particular universalism coming hand in hand with a particular realism and illusive transparency, of science, of the camera, of television; realism that leads to the forgetting of the pre-scientific, pre-television life-world (*tradition, culture, wayang)*—or, as in the case of Husserl to some extent, and even more later phenomenologist, sometimes-nostalgic attention to the pre-X life-world, the fantasized time before the life-world became "live" world.

Husserl's own "transcendental phenomenology" is torn between a desire for a truly disinterested, objective, Cartesian, scientific point of view, on the one hand, and attention to the "pre-scientific life-world" and being in the world, which is hidden or "substituted" for by scientific representations, on the other—*between television and wayang?*

Two years after these lectures, Martin Heidegger presented a lecture on "The Age of the World Picture". Reading Heidegger's account of modern thought or "modern kind of representing", one might at times think that he is describing television. As always in later Heidegger, an essay on technology, science, or modernity concludes with a return to their others, to something like wayang: art, poetry, or the pre-modern world.

In science, "what is to be is defined as objectiveness of representing, and truth is first defined as the certainty of representing, in the metaphysics of Descartes".[106] The essence of the modern age is that

> the world [becomes] conceived and grasped as a picture. What is, in its entirety, is now taken in such a way that it first is in being and only in being to the extent that it is set up by man, who represents and sets forth. [ ] The Being of whatever is, is sought and found in the representedness of the latter.[107]

Today Heidegger could use the analogy of television: people live in a world of television and other tele-technological images, and they relate to and see the world more through watching these images than by being included in whatever is. The man-made, objective—"realistic"—television images substitute for the world, rather like when local storytelling is heard in translation into a lingua franca. In objective representation, the viewer is detached as a subject from the objectified world, as if sitting on a sofa and watching the world on television, surveying it, with a remote control in his hand, with an apparent power over the machine and the picture. Like modern roads, the objective representations (of science, of television) are man-made, structured, under control, engineered, neat and clean, a Cartesian fantasy of certainty:

> The fundamental experience of the modern age is the conquest of the world picture. The world picture now means the structured image that is the creature of man's producing which represents and sets before.[108]

In surveying and mastering the (represented) world, man is not master of this urge to master and "the modern age rages toward fulfilment of its essence, with a velocity unknown to the participants".[109] The struggle plays itself out in the realm of what is represented—something like a struggle over what happens on television. It is a "struggle of worldviews".[110] At the same time, "the world becomes a picture". Images surreptitiously substitute for the original, and representations and actuality dissolve into each other.

> The gigantic presses forward in a form that actually seems to make it disappear—in the annihilation of great distances by the airplane, in the setting before us foreign and remote worlds in their everydayness, which is produced at random through radio by a flick of the hand.[111]

These are images that we have encountered before—annihilation of distance through technology (including electronic media), the power to see or hear regardless of distances, a radically new visibility and audibility. But, just like in our previous examples, there is also something other than the modern lights, clear images, and clean and neat surveyability and calculability of the objectively represented. This happens when "the gigantic, and what can seemingly always be calculated completely, becomes [...] incalculable [...] This becoming incalculable remains the invisible shadow that is cast around all things everywhere when man has been transformed into subiectum and the world into picture."[112] What is this shadow? It "extends itself out into a space withdrawn from representation".[113] It is the incalculable that is "pointing to Being, which remains concealed".[114] The essay concludes with a gesture toward poetry and art as the truth beyond technology and science.

Resonances: Husserl's life-world forgotten by scientific representation, the grass under the concrete, the camera's images substituting of actuality, the darkness of the shadow puppet theatre hidden, but not captured, by television, objective realism replacing a less explicit, shadowy, imaginative performance, the "incalculability" of live performance that is problematic for television, watching wayang as a moving picture instead of being immersed in the performance event, and so on. And, thinking more generally about Heidegger's attitude to technology and art: isn't there, within his thought, an emotion not unlike the one we find behind Javanese discussion of wayang and television, an attachment to something older than new technology or modernity, to earlier art, poetry, media?

Such listening for resonances could be endless, and there are many perhaps more obvious examples, from Descartes's philosophical-scientific model of the mind as a camera obscura (an early form of television?) and his notion that the world is knowable only through objective images and representation produced by this camera-like mind and edited by reason and his mistrust of physical sense perception (like if one believed television more than one's eyes), to, in the realm of visual art, for example, the development of perspective ("seeing through") which transforms painting into a television-like "window" through which we see a virtual world, as "fully rational—that is, infinite, unchanging and homogeneous—space"[115] which, as Panofsky shows in detail, is "specifically modern"[116] and embodies current philosophical notions of the world—and indeed, the position of the television spectator as someone watching the world from outside, from behind a framed screen, is prefigured in Western painting. One could also think nostalgically back to the early unity of art and technology (Greek wayang and television) as *techne* and their later—modern—split into what have become opposing attitudes to the world, art and science—is this the original sin from which our conflict developed? But the caricatures above would be misunderstood if they were read as an attempt at an argument. Such argument might show wayang through theoretical distinctions (such as Husserl's and Heidegger's clear, purified and originary visions), and lead us away from the dusty and sweaty desires, struggles and confusions of life. The aim of my caricatures is, rather, to loosen the thinking of this chapter so as to let its images resonate more freely and broadly, across times and spaces, like when wine or love helps people to think and feel. I have tried to give an impression of how the marriage of wayang and television is involved in an endlessly extended family, living and dead, and how this particular marriage—the encounter, the fantasies, the interpenetration—is in some ways a repetition, reverberation, of its past. Wayang, television, their marriage, the world in which the marriage happens—none of these ever was a blank slate but each is saturated with, constituted by, media and media interactions, technologies, representations.

The Failure of the Marriage

Ishadi, at the time of writing the director of the TransTV television company, and formerly serving in the highest positions at TVRI, said that "we haven't yet found the right way to broadcast wayang". Ki Anom Soeroto, the most famous dhalang heard and seen more often than any other dhalang on radio, cassettes, and television, says that "we haven't found the right way to perform on television", a sentiment shared by many other puppeteers. Despite the continuous intercourse between wayang and television and their worlds, despite the many ways in which wayang has become more like television, and despite fantasies about their union, theirs has not been an easy marriage. Often, as wayang approaches television, the feeling that they are incompatible only increases. Elements of television and the modern world enter wayang but often they are appreciated either as humorous/parodic, and/or because of the anarchy they stimulate in the realm of wayang; that is, they retain much of their foreignness to wayang, which makes them appealing. The next chapter will explore the continuing presence of this split between wayang and television, and various forces pulling and pushing in different directions, by focusing on the work of production of television programmes, and the interaction between people involved with wayang and people involved with television.

2

A Marriage Full of Conflicts: Television's Production of Authentic-but-Entertaining *Wayang*

The production of *wayang* on television is characterized by a multiplicity of often conflicting visions, interests and values. People with different backgrounds discuss it, argue about it, try to co-operate, or fail to communicate and give up on co-operation but are drawn into the process because they have a stake in it. A creativity-killing frustration is common. These feelings and problems surface in the ways that people talk, but they are also apparent in the process itself as well as in the resulting television programme, which bears the marks of unresolved conflicts about what the programme should be, misunderstanding among the different agents, concessions made in compromises, and generally divisions of people, institutions, and cultures behind the programme. Considering these problems, the persistence with which wayang is televised is impressive.

There are many players in the game: performers, people associated with television, sponsors of performances (individuals and institutions), governmental and other organizations, art academies where puppetry is cultivated, and so on. Each has a particular vision, authority and culture; there are different fields of expertise and ignorance; and even divergent ways of communicating cause misunderstanding or discomfort. There are no absolute divisions. A television producer may come from the same village and a similar background as a puppeteer. Nonetheless, the difference in personal and professional culture among the puppeteers and the television people—especially in the case of Jakarta-centred television stations such as Indosiar—is often almost palpable, even in the ways they talk, move and dress.

Indonesian commentators speak about the different cultures and "principles" of wayang and television. This chapter explores how people, often from different social environments who would have no other reason to meet, were it not for the televisation of wayang, come together around and in the production process; how they bring their cultures, their "imaginative frames" (I think of O'Connor's seminal essay on local Southeast Asian and global "modern" connoisseurships[1]), or their "equipment for living" (a phrase A.L. Becker liked to use) into it; how the televisation of wayang is at the intersection of their desires, schemes and frustrations; and how the programme reflects the conditions of its production and the colliding imaginative frames. We are talking here about the interaction among people, but also between the media and their cultures, which compel particular ways of thinking and acting.

This chapter, too, focuses on mainstream wayang broadcasts dominant from 1995 for a short decade, with special focus on Indosiar wayang, supplemented by references to other cases, mostly around that time. This close-up, and the various issues encountered in this chapter, will be situated in a broader perspective in Chapters Four and Five, where we will look at a greater variety of cases, from local television stations to wayang on the internet.

Television's Production of Authenticity and Nostalgia

Even though Indosiar claims that "we just move what is there to people's homes", and it is stressed that wayang on Indosiar is *asli* (authentic, original), the previous chapter showed that this "what is there" had already been deeply affected by its interaction with the world of television, even before or without being made into an actual television programme. This chapter shows how television producers consciously shape the wayang performance in front of the cameras and, through editing, the programme seen on television screens. And yet, the "authenticity" of wayang on television is a key feature of both the discourse about wayang on television, and the audiovisual rhetoric of the programmes themselves.

This authenticity, as understood by Indosiar men and as apparent in the programme, is not a claim of absolute purity. A wayang performance that involves keyboards, pop music, and a George Bush puppet, is seen as authentic. Indosiar wayang's authenticity concerns the programme's relation to contemporary mainstream wayang performances. First, the wayang performance in front of the cameras is fundamentally the same as other performances (which are also affected by the world of entertainment and television)—after all, most performances on Indosiar are mainstream performances. Second, the programme is coverage of an event taking place in actuality, rather like the coverage of a football match or a concert.

Even as television penetrates wayang, it keeps its distance from it. The screen and frame of television do not pretend to become the wayang screen and frame; the world that one sees on television is not the world that one sees on the wayang screen. Television (re)presents the whole performance event. One sees a long shot of the performance area at one moment and close up of a puppet or a musician at another. Rather than becoming one with wayang, television looks at wayang from outside, with its own way of seeing and (re)presenting what is "out there".

Television controls what is seen of wayang, its image, its double, whereas wayang cannot control how television shows it. By keeping wayang authentic, by keeping it separate from itself as an object, television prevents wayang from active participation in the production process. The agency of wayang is kept *within* the frame of television. Whatever the puppeteer may do and say, he cannot control what is seen and heard.

It is as if television were telling us about wayang, without allowing it to speak directly for itself. Yet television does not speak *about* it, but claims to enable us actually *to see and hear* it, as if in an objective, unmediated way: images substitute for life-world, "the world becomes a picture" (Heidegger). In television studies, it is commonly emphasized that what one sees on television is manipulated, but the critique of the "transparency fallacy" sometimes misses the point that the transparency, qua illusion, is basic to television.

The illusion that television allows us to perceive reality, gives authority to television, similar to a scientist's claims that his methods are objective and his view disinterested (here we may recall that in many European languages, variations of the word "objective" mean "camera lens"). The authority gives credence to the claim that "we are just bringing wayang to people's homes"; it hides television's agency in changing or creating what it "brings". Television claims that what viewers see on television is wayang, even though what they see is wayang's double, a spectre pretending to be wayang, produced and controlled by television. The world becomes picture; wayang becomes television. Wayang disappears behind a television-generated vision of wayang. This substitution never works neatly, and we will see that puppeteers try to show, and audiences are mindful, that the "authentic" wayang on the screen is not quite, not simply, the wayang performed by puppeteers. Nonetheless, the illusion of reality and the authenticity claimed by television are essential to the relation between wayang and television.

In its discourse and categorization, Indosiar frames wayang as *seni tradisional* (traditional art). Like in some ethnographic museums, framing phenomena as authentic traditional art separates the perceiving subject and what is perceived, and presents what is seen as being from somewhere else. It allows the subject to define the terms of encounter. Even as it presents modernized performances, Indosiar uses the ethnographic category "tradisional" to frame wayang as something outside of the modern, outside television. Television paradoxically incorporates wayang *and* keeps it separate from itself. The traditional is a realm that is, in this particular manifestation, created by television. What one sees on television, claims: "I am not television, I am actuality."

The authentic "traditional art" on Indosiar is comparable to tradition as represented in New Order projects such as Taman Mini "Indonesia Indah" ("Beautiful Indonesia" Miniature Park), a favourite example in scholarship on the New Order. Taman Mini, too, emphasizes authenticity and conceals reality with its images in order to silence and disempower it. James Siegel, in the book that I have extensively referenced in the previous chapter, briefly evokes television in his discussion of Taman Mini (and we may think of Rudolf Mrázek likening the views from the train window in the colonial period to the Beautiful Indies paintings):

> The overhead train turnishes the perspective of Taman Mini. It reverses the situation of the viewer of television

> who sits nearly immobile in front of moving images. Here, the viewer moves and the stationary objects, by virtue of the fact that they are seen rather than experienced, turn into images. [...] That these objects are taken as authentic, that no difference is made between originals and copies, makes them close to the virtual reality produced electronically; but they are even more compelling.[2]

However, speaking more broadly about the effects of Taman Mini and its technology (including especially an Achehnese airplane from the revolution, with "a power of reference much less limited than the other objects in Taman Mini"),[3] Siegel also emphasizes that "it would be a mistake to think that these effects are necessarily domesticating and completely controllable by authority", and he uses the story of Taman Mini as an example of the "control of communication on the one hand and the breaking of that control on the other".[4] I also agree with Edward Bruner's interpretation of Taman Mini, in which he emphasizes that "local people operating within an official state-sponsored site impose their own meanings and social practices, make the place their own, and undermine the official interpretation of the site".[5] Still, in comparison to Taman Mini, to me Indosiar images seem in some ways less obviously manipulated and the illusion that they let us see unmediated actuality appears more powerful, or at least different. Because of their close link to the apparently "authentic", unpredictable actuality of performances (from which their illusion draws authority), the images—and I am trying to share my impressions here, rather than stating an indisputable fact—seem somewhat less controlled than those of Taman Mini, in the sense that unwanted, uncensored elements of actuality often leak through into the images, while at the same time television images infiltrate reality and enter people's homes and personal life more easily and pervasively than the walled-off Taman Mini does. In this and other ways (such as the different though overlapping interests of a nation state and a commercial company), a view of wayang on television in the New Order period gives a comparable, but somewhat different picture of the cultural politics at that time, to interpretations of Taman Mini. Indosiar controls what is shown on the one hand, yet allows for—indeed highlights—(mediated-but-seemingly-not) liveliness in order to make its illusion of authenticity more believable. Incidentally, Taman Mini and Indosiar are, in more than one way, part of one family. Senawangi, a governmental organization that, especially during the New Order, oversaw wayang, including wayang on television, had its head office in the Taman Mini complex. One could also explore the resemblances and family ties with the representation of culture on the state controlled TVRI, especially before the era of commercial television. Supanggah, for example, said that on TVRI, especially in the past, traditional art was decontextualized and "always artificial, [for example] a dance from Irian would be danced by a person from Jakarta, the child of a government official"—which suggests that Taman Mini is even more like certain programmes on TVRI.

"Authenticity" and the appearance of transparency allow Indosiar to control and possess the images of wayang. This enables television to exploit wayang in a number of ways. Let us listen to the president of Indosiar, Handoko (note, by the way, how he skilfully employs culturalist rhetoric, often used in nationalist politics, for business ends):

> Traditional art represents the people's culture that is present in each ethnic group. [...] Whoever the people may be, they will surely like, or be familiar with, their culture. If I am a Balinese, for instance, and I stay for a long time in Russia among the Eskimos, and suddenly I hear Balinese gamelan in Russia, I will certainly be touched. That is the basic principle—that traditional culture or traditional art is a root, it is rooted in, it exists in the heart of every person. Now, the problem is, in these times of progress, many people move [from villages] to cities. Transportation is easy, and it is easy for them to go to work away from their homes, and they rarely can listen to, rarely watch, their own traditional art which they often used to hear when they were young [...]. This means that no matter how much a person may like his new place, at one moment, perhaps in the evening when there is nothing to do, or perhaps when he is sad, he will suddenly be happy, he will feel something is right for him, when he hears something familiar. It is just like when you are here and you hear a Czech song, you will certainly be easily reminded. That is the basis [*itu basic-nya*]. [...] So, to

> answer why we show [wayang], it's like this: first because people like it, second because there are many devotees.

Television exploits people's familiarity with wayang and the fact that wayang, as a part of a person's culture, is "rooted in people's hearts". Therefore, television presents authentic wayang, that is, wayang that evokes the kind of wayang that people know, rather than framing the programme as something newly created by television. Handoko connects the appeal of authentic wayang to the present situation in which many people live away from their homes. Authentic wayang on television is specifically appealing in the modern world, when people are on the move or are displaced: this appeal of authenticity is a modern phenomenon.

Television exploits a rupture in people's lives. The programme, itself full of conflicts between tradition and modernity, is hoped to attract people whose lives are characterized by a conflict between attachment to a place (with its culture, its traditions) and modern displacement or mobility.

Television executives and producers often say that wayang on television "cures nostalgia" (*mengobati nostalgia; obat* means "drug, medicine"). According to Panca Cahya Utama —the Indosiar producer responsible for wayang during the early years—when wayang was first shown, many letters from viewers requested that wayang be shown on a regular basis. Many of these letters were from Java, but the majority were from Javanese living away from home, such as villagers who transmigrated to other islands. The principal reason for their interest in wayang on television was that they *rindu*, which is a feeling of yearning or homesickness. These feelings often make it into performance. During a wayang programme on Indosiar, a *dhalang* mentioned, for example, that he hopes that the performance seen on television will "be a medicine for the feeling of homesickness for our brothers in *transmigrasi* [transmigration]".

To explain the appeal of wayang on television, Indosiar people talk about Javanese who have transmigrated and people working in cities. Their displacement and alienation is most apparent, but it is also characteristic of Javanese wayang fans in general. That is, even in Java and even for people who live in their villages or towns, there is a degree of alienation from people's own culture as well as nostalgia for things like wayang. It is as if Indosiar people were saying: if you want to understand why people watch wayang on television in Java, it is best to look at people who live away from home.

We are getting a picture of the Javanese condition, but our case is never entirely unique. I suggested in Chapter One that a desire for a return to something before or outside modernity has always been a part of modernity. Derrida said in an interview about television:

> [T]he global and dominant effects of television [...] is that the here and now becomes uncertain, without guarantee: anchoredness, rootedness, the at home [*le chez-soi*] are radically contested. It has always been this way. The at-home has always been tormented by the other, by the guest, by the threat of expropriation. It is constituted only in this threat. But today we are witnessing such radical expropriation, deterritorialization, delocalization, dissociation of the political and the local ... that the response, the reaction becomes: "I want to be at home, I want finally to be at home, with my own, close to my friends and family."[6]

The "at home" may be a place, but also a time: when people talk about wayang on television, they often speak of the past, and especially their childhoods. Wayang's authenticity appeals not only because it "reminds" people on the move of a special place in an age when places and distances are annihilated, but it may also be, as Germain Bazin wrote about the appeal of museums in modern Europe, related to "a need to escape from the vertigo caused by the acceleration of time, some secret nostalgia for the past ... a need to flee the present, to seek refuge in the warmth of an ancestral ambiance".[7]

Television plays on people's nostalgia and this is related to presenting authentic wayang and presenting it as a (social) event—as a slice of life at a virtually particular place, and a different, slower, more relaxed time (note the sleepiness and the laughter in the quotation below). But of course, television's primary motivation is not to cure nostalgia, but to profit from the existence of this "sickness" by presenting itself as medicine. The executive director of Indosiar, Soewastomo, says about wayang explicitly that "this is like drugs"—using English in the middle of an Indonesian conversation—and makes it clear that Indosiar presents wayang in such a way as to encourage and profit from its addictiveness (words in italics were spoken in English).

> It [wayang on Indosiar] is authentic [asli] just like whatever there is [in actuality]. We have been criticized once: Why don't we use *lighting*, *colouring*, and *sound* like in a studio? Because [the critics argue] this is television wayang [*wayang televisi*]. We don't want to do that, because we want to capture its character a hundred percent, so that people like me—I have been watching wayang since I was little, and I like very much to watch wayang, and when I was circumcised we sponsored a wayang—the story [in wayang] is always like that, Pak Jan, same, *everybody knows*—but why do we enjoy watching? *This is like drugs*, but this is positive. So, if we [Indosiar] can lift [i.e., show] it as far as possible precisely like that, and if the performance conventions are not changed, then we [the viewers]—*so many ringings in our mind*: Oh, it was like this in the past! It was like that! And we also show that on TV: there is someone sleepy, there is the person who plays the gong and is sleepy, there is the person who keeps laughing—the {whole} atmosphere, the whole culture.

It is the kind of medicine that not only relieves the symptoms of the disease, but also revives it and creates dependence on the drug. Didik Yulianto, the executive producer responsible for wayang programme after Panca left Indosiar, makes this clear when he uses the words *menghidupkan suatu nostalgia*, "bring a nostalgia to life":

> Actually, for people in large cities, like me, watching wayang—that is a way to bring a nostalgia to life. In the past, in the village, I used to wear sarung, was eating peanuts, while watching [wayang]—in fact, *that* is the pleasure, next to the sound of gamelan, *te te te*—the atmosphere, people

> laugh, people gather. We make the authentic atmosphere present on television [*menghadirkan suasana aslinya ke televisi*], that's why I say, wayang *on* television [*wayang* di *televisi,* in contrast to *wayang televisi,* "television wayang"].

Even as wayang on television cures nostalgia, it brings it to life, just as addictive drugs both satisfy and perpetuate a desire.

This cultivation/curing of nostalgia is related to the public rhetoric of Indosiar, especially the claim that the wayang programmes help the popularity of wayang and that Indosiar cultivates (*melestarikan*) the "traditional arts." Cultivating and promoting the traditional arts is—among other things—a way to create an audience for Indosiar's programmes, to promote *television* programmes. Indosiar is interested in wayang because it is addictive, and by encouraging this addiction, it also makes people addicted to (wayang on) television. Indosiar tends to encourage and popularize the kind of wayang that it deems appropriate for television (for itself), that is, wayang that features light entertainment and that attracts as many people as possible.

Wayang's authenticity is television's attraction. It has not been created by television out of nothing. It is rather like what Heidegger describes as technological "revealing", in which everything is made available for use and transformed through a particular conceptualization: "The earth now reveals itself as a coal mining district, the soil as a mineral deposit."[8] Wayang on Indosiar cultivates and exploits people's existing desires and attachments, many of which grow from the current cultural situation. Etymologically, nostalgia means homesickness, but it is more often used to refer to a desire for something that took place in the past and can be no more. In our case, the Java and wayang on television that appeal to people both does and does not exist, and people both can and cannot return to it. Home can be simultaneously a reality and a fantasy.

The quotations from interviews with Indosiar people show that even simple familiarity can be exploited by Indosiar. Familiarity, as is well known, is an important part of the appeal of various television programmes such as television series, and in the Indonesian context I think especially of soap operas. Wayang audiences are familiar with the wayang medium, with the characters, with the stories, rather like they may be familiar with the style, performers, and characters in a soap opera.

The star quality of the dhalang that Indosiar encourages can also be seen in this context: people become familiar with particular performers, as well as with particular performing styles. This is an aspect of the appeal of the authentic wayang on television.

The dilemma that characterizes wayang on Indosiar derives from the fact that television is self-asserting and self-effacing at the same time. On the one hand, as seen in Chapter One, the principles of wayang are said to conflict with the principles of television, and wayang is modernized, made more like television. On the other hand, Indosiar is interested in authentic wayang, something other than television. This, however, becomes on television, something other than television, television's major appeal. Television says, pointing at the invisible television screen: "Watch this, this is wayang!"—and thus makes people watch television.

The dilemma for performers and producers is this: how to perform/produce wayang that is as much as possible and at the same time as little as possible like television. If one looks at what happens in performances of mainstream wayang, the dilemma can be clearly felt: how far to move away from wayang and toward television? Dhalang and television producers are criticized for being too traditional, for not modernizing wayang enough, for not adapting it to television enough, and they are criticized for changing it too much; they argue and disagree about it among themselves. The production of wayang on television can be seen as a part of the process in which wayang approaches television, yet the appeal of authenticity, cultivated by television, is one of the forces that keeps wayang separate from television. Even as television attracts wayang towards itself, it tries to keep wayang in place and separate from itself so that it can control it as an object, and so that it can exploit people's familiarity with wayang.

Image-Building: Wayang Promoting Television

According to Soewastomo, the director of Indosiar, the company does not profit from wayang programmes. The expenses (especially airing cost)—high because of the length of the weekly programme—are hardly covered by the paid advertisements shown during the programme.

Many of the advertisements are shown for "free" as a "bonus" given to the advertisers for purchasing a package of advertising time. If this is true (or close enough to truth), why does Indosiar show wayang at all?

Indosiar profits from the wayang programme indirectly. Soewastomo gives some hints:

> Wayang does not make *profit for the TV industry*, but, *on the other way* [sic], there emerge certain *feelings*, including a feeling of possession, *sense of belonging*, from the *public* toward Indosiar. That is what emerges: a feeling of comradeship among them, it's watched by *so many people*, and that creates social harmony, a certain friendship which, you know, is very positive.

I asked Handoko why Indosiar shows wayang even though it is not profitable:

> Because [wayang] has already become a certain specialty [of Indosiar], it has become a certain—like if you had a hardware store, OK? You have {nails}, {screwdrivers}, building materials, {bricks}, all kinds of things, but if you don't sell cement, {it doesn't make sense}, right? Even though the profit from cement is very slight, but {you need to have that}, hahaha, right? In the programming of Indosiar, wayang is just like that. It has its own importance. [...] Or if you want to use more blunt language, just consider it {promotion cost}.

(Handoko was also the president of Indosemen, a company producing cement, part of the same conglomerate as Indosiar.) Terms such as "building channel loyalty" and "image-building" spring to mind—they remind us that we are speaking of television culture.

What kind of image is built for Indosiar? "Indosiar promotes wayang and traditional arts generally." This claim is made not simply by the existence of the programmes—although it is far from clear and simple how the programmes affect wayang—but also frequently in the wayang programmes. The Indosiar logo (a sticker, I am told) is visible on one of the *kayon* (tree of life) puppets used in many performances, and occasionally the camera zooms in on it. At one performance, to cite another example, the puppeteer lifts his mug with the Indosiar logo on it and uses it to give a drink to a puppet on the screen—again shown in close-up. The performance area is sometimes decorated with large banners with the Indosiar logo and its slogan, "Indosiar is indeed for you."

2.1 A close-up of the Indosiar logo on the sacred tree/mountain puppet, as seen on television. The same logo is visible in the upper left corner of the screen. This is one of the early performances covered by Indosiar, in Sukoharjo in 1995.

Indosiar is commonly mentioned by the dhalang in performances broadcast by the television station. The reason for the wayang broadcasts appears to be charity: Indosiar helps wayang and wayang performers to become better known and thus helps to cultivate traditional arts. In one performance, for example, the dhalang Warsena Slenk says:

> Indosiar performs an art mission through wayang broadcasts. How extremely lucky we are to be inside television! That's a great progress! Why? It raises the standing of artists. ... Thanks to Indosiar for its help!

Sometimes the dhalang adds a wish that other stations would be like Indosiar, or in other cases he may just shout well-known trademark slogans such as "Indosiar is indeed for you!" or "Indosiar, television of our choice!" A longer discussion of Indosiar in a wayang performance may go as follows. In the following example, the dhalang was Manteb.

> Great is the love of [people's] own culture and especially *wayang kulit*, particularly on Saturday evening when they wait for the Indosiar television programme "Wayang Kulit". Oh, God be thanked! I, too, am happy! I, too, like it! And I thank very much the Indosiar company for broadcasting not only the famous puppeteers but also those who are not yet famous, so that their well-being will be equal [this is an obvious reference to the frequent criticism that Indosiar features primarily superstar puppeteers]. Here is a famous dhalang, my younger brother [term of address] Ki Djoko Hadiwidjojo, famous as Crazy Djoko, from Pudak Payung. Good evening, brother Djoko Hadiwidjojo! [Djoko is shown holding a microphone and a paper with responses to be used in the dialogue that follows, clearly prepared beforehand.] Now, I will ask about your view of Indosiar wayang. What do you think about it?
> Djoko: Yes, agreeing with what you said before, it is very positive.
> Manteb: Yes!
> Djoko: For artists and in particular puppeteers
> Manteb: Yes!
> Djoko: Because Indonesia, excuse me, I mean Indosiar, is a television station which gives opportunities for puppeteer-artists to show their skills and at the same time for marketing them.
> Manteb: Yes! Yes! Yes! Beautiful! Beautiful! Beautiful! [Djoko smiles, embarrassed, and there seems to be a touch of irony in Manteb's entusiasm. The fun of this moment, and people's obvious enjoyment, derives from the fact that obviously this exchange is not spontaneous.]
> Manteb: Now, brother Djoko, I am going to ask you: do you know the hidden meaning of Indosiar?
> Djoko: Indosiar is P.T. Indosiar Visual Mandiri, but if we look

at the letters one by one, I can indeed interpret them.

Manteb: Let's see if you can do it. I.N.D.O.S.I.A.R. How about I?

Djoko: [Reading from his notes, in Indonesian.] This [*inilah*] is the latest hit of Indosiar television.

Manteb: Yes! N?

Djoko: Far [*nun jauh*] reached the dreams of the people—now they came true thanks to television broadcasting.

Manteb: Yes! D?

Djoko: The puppeteers [*dhalang-dhalang*] yearn to each get their turn [to appear on television]. [Laughter in the audience.

Manteb: Yes. O?

Djoko: The fee [*ongkos*] is not important; principles are. [Djoko and audience giggle.]

Djoko: Sorry, brother, I don't mean the puppeteer's principles, but Indosiar's. [The joke is that Djoko also hints at Manteb, who can be seen as prioritizing commercial gain over artistic principles.]

Manteb: Oh, okay.

Djoko: It turns out that this is not just mutual assistance.

Manteb: It can't be that!

Djoko: [Screaming, to the audience and pointing at Manteb] HE GETS 13 MILLION FOR THIS EVENING!!! [Wild laughter.]

Manteb: Now, S, what about S?

Djoko: First-rate artists [*seniman yang jempolan*] emphasize service and responsibility toward the perpetuation of culture.

Manteb: I?

Djoko: That [*itulah*] is what makes Indosiar broadcast wayang every Saturday night.

Manteb: Yes! A?

Djoko: The God be thanked [*Alhamdulillah*], Manteb the Devil is the dhalang this evening.

Manteb: R?

Djoko: Prosper [*rahayu*], be victorious and prosper, Indosiar!

Manteb: Yes! Applause for my brother Djoko!

A similar exchange may take place between two clowns, or the female singers and musicians can be involved. It is common in contemporary performances for the audience to request songs by means of a note sent to the puppeteer, and the Indosiar crew frequently makes its presence known in this way as well, as *kru Indosiar*, "Indosiar crew". In one case, when the Indosiar crew requested a large number of songs, the dhalang exclaimed into the microphone: "That's really a lot! Are they requesting songs or buying cassettes?" There are also specially composed songs promoting Indosiar incorporated into the clown scenes, such as *Indosiar televisi pilihan kita* ("Indosiar, television of our choice") and *Pangkur jenggleng Indosiar* (a new version of an older melody, with lyrics about Indosiar promoting traditional arts).

These references to Indosiar and its support of traditional arts tell the spectators what to think about wayang on television. But the Indosiar strategy plays on a discrepancy between what is claimed and the effects of claiming it; on the difference between the content and the effects of the utterances. The message of these references is that "Indosiar promotes traditional arts", but in effect this message promotes Indosiar. On the other hand, when the wayang scholar Bambang Murtiyoso says that Indosiar shows wayang "only for the purposes of its own promotion [*promosi*]," this is not the image that Indosiar wants to create, although, as we have seen, even Handoko privately says that wayang can be considered "promotion cost" for Indosiar. So, the real motivation of Indosiar, its self-promotion, has to be hidden behind the image of its charity towards the traditional arts.

It is difficult to overestimate the value that Indosiar places on this image and on its effects. Indosiar has indeed become known as the station that shows and promotes traditional arts. In November 1995, only a few months after the first broadcast of wayang on Indosiar, the magazine article "The Story of Petruk's Success on Indosiar" noted:

> It seems that Indosiar wants to build an image [*membangun citra*] in the hearts of the viewers as a television station which gives ample space to traditional arts. "Indosiar succeeded in building a self-image [membangun citra diri {image}] as a television caring about traditional arts," said the mischevious/trickster dalang [*dalang mbeling*] Ki H. Sujiwo Tedjo.[9]

As Handoko said, when Indosiar first began to broadcast wayang, it was "the talk of the town" (he used the English phrase), and it seems that any discussion of traditional art in the era of Indosiar and even in following years was incomplete without the mention of Indosiar. All this meant publicity for Indosiar. When Indosiar, as a new station, had to compete with established stations, this was a strategy to attract public attention. Handoko said that "at that time, because we were still new, we needed to provide the new television station with an identifying characteristic." This "new" thing, this latest hit, was the traditional arts.

A senior Indonesian television executive and writer on the media told me that this image was especially important "because the person who owns Indosiar is a Chinese—in order that it is not [i.e., make people think that it is not] just business". In his history of Indonesian television, Kitley reports on the Chinese workers affair and the bad image it created for Indosiar at the time the television station was about to begin broadcasting.[10] The presence of a large number of expatriate television staff, reportedly mostly Chinese from Hong Kong, and Indosiar's association with the Hong Kong television industry, sparked criticism and a debate in the press, which resonates with the controversies surrounding wayang on television: when "*local* programming material is *produced by foreigners*",[11] what is at stake is Indonesian "culture" and its "cultural infiltration" (*inflitrasi budaya*) or "attack" by foreign cultural values, the "process of cultural imperialism and colonization that would result in the domination of indigenous culture and the alienation of Indonesians from their own cultural values".[12] The Chinese workers affair, and the fact that Indosiar was owned by the most powerful Chinese-Indonesian conglomerate, created an undesirable image for the company, evoking ideas about foreign culture threatening indigenous culture, and of Chinese business managing Indonesian values. Krishna Sen and David Hill write that Indosiar Visual Mandiri [*mandiri* means "independent"] "was denigrated as Indosiar Visual Mandarin, in part because its owner is Indonesia's most powerful Chinese businessman" and because of the Chinese workers affair.[13] They write: "Remarkably, and perhaps a little ironically, given the anxiety about its Chinese connection, within a year of going on air Indosiar was presenting 45 percent domestic material."[14] Perhaps this was not so ironic, if the Chinese connection was a reason to emphasize local programming, and include even local performing arts. Indosiar's broadcasting of Javanese "traditional art", the emphasis on wayang's authenticity, its evocation of Javanese village home and childhood, is, as the statement of the television executive quoted in the beginning of the paragraph implies, a way to change its image as foreign, non-Javanese, and "big-business," and thus attract Javanese audiences.

Indosiar's reaction to its "Mandarin" associations betrays a more general quality of the images produced by Indosiar. In a quotation from a performance earlier in this chapter, we heard Crazy Djoko's slip of the tongue, when instead of "Indosiar" he said "Indonesia": "... Indonesia, excuse me, I mean Indosiar, is a television [station] which gives opportunities ...". When one listens to the dialogue, the slip of the tongue is not surprising: what is said about Indosiar there, and the tone, is much like the nationalistic discourse that paints a positive picture of Indonesia and its government, although Indosiar here functions more like the government than the country: it is presented as benefiting and caring for society in the way an ideal government does—"Far reached the dreams of the people—now they came true thanks to television broadcasting." Regardless whether one believes in the truth of Freudian slips, one finds the same rhetoric in the images Indosiar projects, as well as in the statements of Indosiar executives. For example, when Soewastomo talks about a "sense of belonging of the public to Indosiar", the imagined community here is that of Indosiar viewers, but there is again a slippage to an implied larger community, the nation, when in the next sentence he says that wayang on television "creates social harmony". In the case of the Chinese workers affair, the discussion of television programming slips into thinking about "cultural infiltration" and "alienation of Indonesians from their own culture"—that is, television programming becomes a matter of national culture and national security. Phrases like "dreams of the people", "social harmony" and "cultural infiltration" blur the distinction between the realm of commercial television and national culture as it is construed in political rhetoric, between channel loyalty and nationalism. Both the official Indosiar discourse and the New Order political discourse, or its cultural expressions like the Taman Mini, are non-confrontational and on the surface apolitical—exactly because the positive images of "social harmony" hide aggressive political and commercial interests.

The visible signs of Indosiar—the Indosiar kayon, the mug, the banners—as well as the more explicit mentions, slogans, discussions and songs, give an image of a harmonious, friendly co-operation of Indosiar and the performers as well as the sponsor. The performers and the Indosiar people seem to be good pals, joking with each other. Sometimes the jokes border on mutiny, such as when Djoko, in the excerpt above, hints at the financial gain of the puppeteer, contrasts the fee to the principles, and so criticizes the commercial nature of what is happening and the hypocrisy (this is one of the many examples in which uneasy reality leaks into television's pleasant, optimistic images), but in general Indosiar tends to keep the impression of a convivial spirit. This is the atmosphere created by Indosiar in which its charity can be displayed. It also masks a more complex and less harmonious reality.

Note that much of what is at issue in this interaction between wayang and television is visibility and appearances—self-promotion, image-building, looking good—as well as a struggle for perfect translatability, for eliminating any conflicts that may cause obstacles to smooth transmission, or that may make people think that there is more to (televised) wayang than they can see. In Chapter One we saw how puppeteers want to look good on television, and how their major motivation to get involved with television is their desire to become visible and to "build an image". Here we see that Indosiar is involved with wayang because it too wants to look good and be seen by as many people as possible.

Politics and Economics of Production: Performers, Television Producers, Television Stations, Sponsors, Art Academies, the National Wayang Secretariat, and Powerful People

When television producers and puppeteers collaborate or disagree, they care not only about producing wayang on television, but also about their image, career, wealth, personal authority, issues of justice or fairness, and so on. When a puppeteer says that a television producer is stupid because he does not know anything about wayang, such a statement may be more about the struggle over authority than the wayang programme itself. Even arguments about technical details have (inter)personal dimensions. There is a multiplicity of foci and interests with which people perceive what happens. Producing the programme is merely one knot in a net of desires. People are drawn together because of the wayang programme, but the production and the different actors are all caught in the thickness of the situation and in the plots of individual lives, with their many views, interests, passions, obsessions, ambitions, loves and hates. A novel might capture this better than scholarly analysis. A selection of particular cases—described by people in interviews, reported in newspapers—may be helpful. The specific must not be lost in generalizations.

From the first, there was enthusiasm, and there were frictions. A high-ranking government official is rumoured to have first suggested the idea of producing wayang to Indosiar's executives—we are reminded again of Soeharto and his family's involvement with commercial television and Javanese culture. An important stimulus came from audiences who requested that wayang be broadcast regularly. There were disagreements within Indosiar. Foreign consultants—"people from Hong Kong and England"—especially opposed the idea. From the beginning, there were tensions between some puppeteers and Indosiar producers trying to organize recording sessions. The producer Panca told me how, when he was first looking for puppeteers, neither he nor Handoko, the company's president, knew anything about wayang, except that Panca had seen Manteb in a television advertisement and had heard about the famous puppeteer Anom Suroto. He went to Anom's house in Solo, but was "flatly refused, [even though] I am from Solo, I am from the Palace". According to Panca, it was because Anom "didn't know what Indosiar is and what it is for". "Frustration happened" (*terjadi suatu kefrustrasian*), Panca said. In his hotel, there happened to be a celebration where he met the *bupati* (district head) of Sukoharjo who told him about wayang and dhalang. Only a few months later, the bupati and Indosiar organized jointly some 50 performances, which took place nightly in Sukoharjo. A dignitary like the bupati is traditionally a sponsor of wayang, and in this case the bupati helped Indosiar to enter the wayang world, setting a pattern of collaboration between the television company, local government and army officials that would be important for Indosiar in the following years. The recordings from Sukoharjo would be broadcast and rebroadcast for a number of years. And so, from the very beginning, there were not only decisions, much happened by accident; love of wayang, desire for money, and politics were all involved; there were frictions between wayang and television personnel, and there were influential third parties involved, such as the mysterious voice from the central government and the very generous and visible co-sponsorship by the head of the local government.

Many puppeteers and wayang viewers were excited by the possibility of regular wayang broadcasts on television, but even then performers felt uncomfortable with some of Indosiar's requirements, such as abbreviated performance time, strong lights, and the unusually orderly stage. There were practical problems: traditionally, puppeteers are paid at the performance, but, some performers reported, Indosiar was going to send them a cheque later—a practice unusual for village puppeteers, who were expected to pay their musicians immediately in cash. Performers tell how they were prohibited from eating and drinking during the performance because of television's desire for a clean and tidy picture, how the performance time was limited, and so on. In general, however, there was a degree of enthusiasm and willingness to overcome differences which was to decline as more problems arose.

Major problems concerned not the technical process, but the co-operation of the performers, Indosiar, and the sponsors. In March 1996, a Javanese magazine reported on one such case. Below the title of the article, "Wayang Indosiar: 'Stumbled over Ki Anom Suroto'," large letters asked "Will the famous puppeteer from Solo sue TV Indosiar because his name was stained?"[15] In a scenario that foreshadowed similar clashes in the future, the puppeteer was unwilling (*wegah*, a word that implies a degree of irritation) to be recorded by Indosiar. The problem was that Indosiar planned an "Anom Suroto Tour", a series of 19 performances in different parts in Java, apparently in co-operation with local bupati. During the initial planning, Anom wanted to change the date of one performance, but Indosiar "stubbornly insisted" (*ngotot*) that the performance take place on that date. Later, Indosiar suddenly cancelled the whole tour, "without a clear reason and by telephone", which upset Anom. But the main problem was that, according to Anom's version of the story, Indosiar failed to inform the 19 bupati about the cancellation. The climax came when in the Tegal district the stage with the gamelan and puppets was set up and VIP guests and large crowds were waiting for the performance of the superstar Solonese puppeteer but Anom Suroto didn't arrive and was in fact performing in his hometown. The crowds in Tegal protested and according to the spokesman of the bupati's office, the regional government headed by the bupati was accused of "being unable to pay the puppeteer". The angry bupati called Anom Suroto, believing that the cancellation of the performance was the puppeteer's fault. Anom—known for trying hard to have good relations with powerful people, and especially government officials—felt that his good reputation was stained.

Indosiar's version of the story was different:

> The Indosiar public relations manager, Andreas Ambesa, insisted that it was Anom who cancelled the whole contract, not Indosiar. For the event in Pasuruan and Tegal, the contract, he said, was not cancelled. "So it's not at all the fault of my TV!" he said. This made Ki Anom to go into rage [*sic*]. Because he felt put down and slandered. "The Indosiar side has to straighten this up. If they don't admit their fault, I will sue them!" he threatened.[16]

Anom was angry because his reputation had been stained or *dirusak jenenge*, "his name was broken". He asked Indosiar to admit their mistake, and he wanted to sue them, not because of any immediate economic loss, but because of slander. The local government official was angry because people thought that he could not afford to pay the dhalang. The story is not about any technical difficulty of showing wayang on television. It is about anger and multiple accusations. The damage done is to names, images, reputation, and people's dignity. Self-promotion and self-image is on everyone's mind. From the puppeteer's perspective, Indosiar also disturbed his relationship with traditional sponsors, and thus something of wayang culture.

Two producers used the same expression to describe Indosiar's main problem: the puppeteer considers himself "the little king in his domain".

Panca told me that when he asked puppeteers to do certain things, "many, many" disagreed.

> Pak Anom, for example, was fighting with Waldjinah [a famous singer and popular guest star at wayang performances], he didn't want [to perform with her], but I forced him. Well, one needs to be professional, right? [JM: "Was he paid by Indosiar?"] Yes, but even so, he is a Javanese—what's more, he is a puppeteer! He feels he is the king: "You are below me, I don't want to [follow], I have my way, you have to follow me!" *That* is what causes collisions. So I am often in the newspapers. [They claim] I haven't paid yet, I haven't done this or that yet. [...] [The puppeteers] don't want to listen. [...] They all feel they are better than us—*that's* it, *that's* what I don't like!

Each party feels that it has the right to be in control and the other party should follow, and because the other party does not, the first party feels that it does not get the respect it deserves.

Panca does not speak only about Anom, but puppeteers in general. They form a class, and Anom is merely an example. Still, he makes some distinctions: Enthus is an exception—he listens. Timbul Hadiprayitno, a famous senior puppeteer, "dislikes me the most", noted Panca.

A few months after Indosiar's "tripping over" Anom, Manteb was offered a contract for 30 performances on Indosiar. He refused. Among his reasons was that "in a performance on television, the television side makes all kinds of requests, which sometimes presents a difficulty for the puppeteer".[17]

Occasional crises characterized the relations between Indosiar and the puppeteers in the following years, and tensions and mutual criticisms perhaps grew even sharper. For instance, in 2001, five years after the incidents described above, the press—from *satunet.com* (then a major Indonesian online portal owned by a South African company) to *Suara Merdeka* (a newspaper published in Indonesian in the provincial capital Semarang), and the Javanese magazine *Jaya Baya*—reported on a conflict between Indosiar and Manteb and a number of Solonese puppeteers, including Anom. It started with a performance by Manteb on 3 March 2001, broadcast several weeks later. The main problem was the presence of the pretty *dangdut* singer Cucu Cahyati.

> It was not the way [Manteb] performed as a dhalang, but the *gara-gara* scene that made everything break down. That night, the performance of Ki Manteb was chaos/anarchy. The viewers climbed onto the stage and joined in dancing next to the guest star Cucu Cahyati, who sang the song "Pria Idaman" [Dream Man]. Strangely, the *campursari* music was played by the Sanggar Bima group lead by Danang, the puppeteer's own son. So it appeared that this was the plan. But actually it wasn't! Actually, according to Manteb, he was trapped—he didn't know that Cucu Cahyati was there. That evening, there were already the guest stars Bu Waldjinah and the comedian Mbah Ranto Edy Gudel sitting close to the puppeteer [on stage]. Suddenly, in the middle of the night, there was a note from the Indosiar side, pushed under the screen: "Pak Manteb, there is the guest star Cucu Cahyati here." Even though that wasn't agreed. That is what made the *oye* puppeteer angry.[18] He felt trapped. [Of] the five performances for which he was contracted by Indosiar, he performed only two. The rest [...] he refused.[19]

Anom was among those many puppeteers criticizing the performance and particularly Indosiar.

> Ki Anom criticized Indosiar even more hotly, more harshly. [...] "I know that Indosiar is going to destroy wayang. They claim to cultivate it, but in fact they poison it. If the reason is that the advertisers want it that way—I can't believe that wayang has been defeated by money. If so, is the weight of money going to outweigh the destruction of wayang?"[20]

Indosiar replied:

> It's strange that Pak Manteb says that he didn't know about the guest star Cucu Cahyati. Because, it is Indosiar's policy that before the puppeteer goes on stage to perform, he is told by the producers who the guest stars are. If he doesn't agree, it doesn't go through. It's inconceivable that Pak Manteb wasn't told.[21]

To which Manteb reacted: "If I lie, may this mouth of mine rot" (*Lha nek aku ngapusi, mbok cangkemku iki bosok*).[22]

Manteb was criticized by his colleagues. He blamed everything on Indosiar, said that he regrets what happened, and that it will be a lesson for him and others. He thus positioned himself on the side of the puppeteers, and the situation crystallized into a conflict between them and Indosiar, between wayang and television. Anom said that he, too, was criticized for his performances on Indosiar. In his case, this was because he used a kayon puppet with a large Indosiar logo which had been prepared by Indosiar. One newspaper article, entitled "Puppeteers are Sick of Indosiar Broadcasts", began:

> Ki Anom and Ki Manteb Soedharsono together with all professional puppeteers from Sala [Solo] and environs, announced that they are sick of broadcasts of performances of *wayang kulit spektakuler* that have recently taken place on Indosiar. [...] "Pak Manteb and I have agreed not to honour Indosiar's requests [to perform on television] as long as the performance material is like that. Now it is up to our colleagues, especially young puppeteers, if they accept these [Indosiar's] ways or refuse them," [said Ki Anom Suroto].[23]

The main problem is who is in control and who decides what the rules are. The puppeteers are not angered by just a single incident, they object to the whole system, and to the fact that it is Indosiar, rather than they, who sets the rules.

Not all puppeteers united against Indosiar. Enthus Susmono said in an interview published in a Javanese magazine:

> Pak Manteb himself is not consistent. Why couldn't he just openly admit it? The fact is that before shooting, they [Manteb and Cucu Cahyati] practiced together. But when people in the audience got up and began to sway their bodies and dance out of control, and when he was sharply criticized, Pak Manteb was confused and afraid, and he said that he was trapped.[24]

Indosiar said that it invited Cucu Cahyati to "make wayang look more interesting", and that Indosiar broadcasts wayang because "it wants to join in preserving traditional culture, even though the expenses are great". It denied Manteb's claim that he hadn't been told about the presence of the guest star.[25] An Indosiar producer involved in the situation kindly provided the following account in an e-mail.

> I have produced *wayang spektakuler*, perhaps if mas jan [you] saw it you would find it very interesting, because I made this wayang to deviate from the conventions of classical wayang, and in the performance I added several modern elements. for example ... I presented famous comedians, dangdut singers, pop singers, even rock singers. also, I organized the stage as in an Indosiar music show and I also used lighting that is usually used for rock concerts such as laser ... in short, interesting. I have already made 20 episodes, from solonese wayang kulit, yogyanese, banyumasan, alternatif, to wayang golek.
>
> there is a funny story ...
>
> for example ki manteb, participated in *wayang spektakuler* and he was happy about it, I have already confirmed ahead of time his willingness to participate in the format of *wayang septakuler* [*sic*] and he agreed to participate, and during the shooting he had no problem with it and everything went smoothly. but after it was broadcast ki manteb wrote to a newspaper about the wayang spektakuler that he felt trapped by the *wayang format spektakuler* and felt that Indosiar did him wrong, even though every time I choose a puppeteer to perform in a *wayang spektakuler* I always ask about his

> acceptance of the format, and I always say if you are not willing I will look for another puppeteer. so the wayang spektakuler event that I made turned into a controversy [*pro dan kontra*]. because puppeteer circles and old people who like classical wayang all say they don't like [*wayang spektakuler*] but young people/teenagers all like this kind of wayang very much, and maybe the adolescents who didn't used to like to watch wayang, do like it now. even though the fans of classical wayang refuse to accept it, still we continue to broadcast it because we want to find a solution to how can wayang be liked by adolescents today, because when the granddaddies all die, who is going to watch wayang then....:):):):)[26]

A few months later the producer emailed:

> We still produce wayang but we select that which can be made *spektakuler* and that which we will not make *spektakuler*. For example, classical puppeteers are produced in classical format, and those that can be made *spektakuler* we make more *spektakuler*. All this is so that we can normalize again [*menormalkan kembali*] classical puppeteers so that there is no more protest.[27]

In October of the same year—only about half a year after the beginning of the incident—a newspaper article, "Recording Again, Ki Manteb Agrees with Indosiar", recounted the history of the misunderstanding, the "boycott" of Indosiar by Solonese puppeteers, and criticism by national puppeteer organizations, and reported that Manteb had agreed to perform again, but now with a written agreement (*surat perjanjian*) specifying the "performance format". Manteb said: "There can be guest stars, but I have to be consulted first, and I shall evaluate if they are appropriate to perform as guest stars or not. If I refuse, Indosiar cannot force me." According to Manteb, Indosiar was compelled to approach him because "it appears that wayang lovers and advertisers protested, because Indosiar was re-broadcasting Manteb's older recordings and was not showing any new ones".[28] Manteb's account makes clear how he sees his interaction with Indosiar as a kind of power struggle, in which he asserts the control over wayang, and in which the audiences and advertisers are also involved.

The stories are full of accusations, but the greatest threat is nothing more than a conditional refusal to co-operate, or ignoring the other side. There seem to be no lawsuits, only threats of divorce in the heat of a crisis, after which the situation is "normalized". However, the reports give an impression of bad relations, culminating into disgust with the other side. Even when the two sides co-operate, they appear to try to avoid closer contact. One gets the impression that there is something generally wrong in their relationship. To articulate some of the general problems, let us review the business and political aspects of the relationship between puppeteers and television, keeping in mind that the particulars vary somewhat with every case.

Exceptionally, a performance is sponsored solely by Indosiar. In most cases, there is another sponsor. Sometimes, especially in earlier years, the sponsor and Indosiar shared the expenses. It has become increasingly common that the sponsor pays all expenses connected with the live performance, pays Indosiar a substantial amount, and provides food and lodging for the crew.

There are many variations to the set up. In some cases, Didik said, it was a condition of Indosiar's—a part of the contract (apparently always written by Indosiar, and more or less respectfully signed by other parties)—that the sponsor invites and pays for certain guest stars. Even when the condition is not incuded in the contract, Didik said that

> in some cases, people who invite us also include [the guest stars], as a package [*paket*]. They already know that this addition to wayang is nice. That is our good fortune/profit. They already get ready a wayang in our style [*sebuah wayang dengan style kita*], just like before when we added a thing here and there.

Indosiar has great control over the "style" of wayang without having to pay much or anything at all, or even while getting paid by the sponsor. Indosiar justifies this by saying that it has many expenses, the cost for the four or five hour airing time is high, and the wayang programme is not profitable. According to Indosiar, it is the puppeteers who profit from the system. As the president of Indosiar told me in his luxurious office in Jakarta ("he" in the following quotation refers to a generic puppeteer): "He also gets promoted! He should pay me!"

Certainly puppeteers hope to profit from appearing on television. Still, many do not consider this a proper argument, and think the whole system is flawed. The performers see that their performances are shown on commercial television, often repeatedly, with long commercial breaks, which the puppeteers perceive as a source of Indosiar's profit, while the puppeteers receive no money for this. They perceive Indosiar—a large company owned by one of the richest men in Indonesia—as making a profit on their performances, while they are not paid anything by Indosiar. They feel exploited.

Slamet Gundono, a puppeteer famous for his unconventional style and the inclusion of modern artistic elements in his performances, is an articulate critic of Indosiar and commercialism in wayang. He said that in an ideal world, it might be possible that television and traditional artists profit from their co-operation, but this would have to go beyond superficial promotion.

> Ideally, they could both benefit, in the sense that benefitting traditional arts would not consist only in publicity, or in making the puppeteer into a Michael Jackson—I mean very famous and rich—but the television world should have experts who completely understand wayang's growth and development and its true originality.

When I mentioned the common complaint that Indosiar does not understand wayang, Slamet retorted:

> Didik [the Indosiar producer in charge of wayang then] understands wayang *very* well! Precisely this Didik Yulianto, precisely because he understands wayang, because he understands the weaknesses of the puppeteers—he gives them a million [rupiah] and that makes it *healthy*? Just like *that*? Well, that is exploitation. I don't believe Indosiar doesn't understand; he/it understands very well the weaknesses of Javanese puppeteers. [...] And that is exploitation: so, not

> because people wouldn't know, but because people do not have a moral commitment and sense of care, and zest—at the same time that they may be selling wayang—to make a healthy contribution to the world of wayang. Precisely because Didik knows, he treats Anom Suroto in one way, Slenk in another, and poor puppeteers in yet another.

Indosiar understands wayang in such a way that it can profit from it. The fundamental point, Slamet emphasizes, is that, "television is a kind of 'company,' the tendencies of which will always start from profit making—how to make the broadcast have high rating and get big advertisements".

Fred Wibowo, the director of a media studio in Yogyakarta, expressed a similar sentiment when I asked him if in his view Indosiar exploits performers: "That is always so with every television station. They follow economic principles: to get the largest possible profit with the smallest possible sacrifice."

Slamet says that entertainment is not necessarily bad. But there is no serious effort to make wayang into entertainment in such a way that it retains its character, rather than becoming "entertainment pure". One reason, according to Slamet, is that "now we are still at a stage when [wayang] is only exploited," rather than Indosiar caring about "making a healthy contribution" to the quality of wayang. This would cost money which Indosiar is unwilling to spend—"Indosiar is actually poor," says Slamet, because it "has money but doesn't dare to experiment."

We have seen that Indosiar emphasizes that it leaves the performance unchanged for the sake of "authenticity". But, as Slamet describes it, Indosiar simply exploits what is there because that is the cheapest possibility. Moreover, "the puppeteers are defenceless", "tend to be very simple and just accept everything", and "this situation is exploited by television". The defencelessness that Slamet speaks about is best understood in economic terms, but money, together with other factors, gives Indosiar a kind of superiority which has wide-ranging effects, and allows Indosiar to manipulate wayang and the puppeteers, who indeed appear "very simple" in certain respects compared to the giant company—like a small village shop next to hypermarket chain.

Having mentioned the hypothetical ideal of a "healthy contribution" from Indosiar, Slamet began to feel uncomfortable in the realm of optimistic possibilities:

> I am afraid to talk about what is ideal. I know Indosiar is not ideal. I know Didik—Ah!—so I don't have any idealistic hopes. He is just [concerned about] competition and rating. [...] Perhaps we shouldn't talk about what would be best but about how now, in the present condition, without funds and with Indosiar only taking advantage of sponsors—how, with what we have, we can experiment or educate.

Slamet says that Indosiar takes advantage also of sponsors. The amount paid by them to Indosiar varies and is not readily disclosed, but many people say that often it is more than the performers' remunerations. Performers see this as additional profit for Indosiar. This amplifies the performers' feeling that they are exploited.

What is the sponsor's motivation for inviting Indosiar? It seems that he is sponsoring as much, or more, a television event as a wayang performance. As discussed in Chapter One, television's presence adds glamour to the live event, because of the spectacular technological hardware, because people are aware that this visible machinery is a part of a much larger system which allows the performance to appear on television screens across Indonesia, and because of the presence of Indosiar—a major and well-known Jakarta based company and a television station. All this impresses the people present at the event as a sign of the sponsor's power, status and connections. In this sense, the reason for sponsoring television is similar to sponsoring wayang: to gather as many people as possible at the event, entertain them, and impress them with the event and thus with the sponsor's power. One could also liken the motivation to sponsor an Indosiar broadcast to the reasons for inviting a very expensive guest star. However, it seems from talking to people that perhaps the major motivation is that the sponsor—his house, his celebration—appear on television. His name or his organization's name is mentioned by the puppeteer during the clown scenes, usually with a flattering introduction. The sponsor usually puts up a large sign near or even on the screen which is intermittently visible on television, from a distance in long shots and in occasional shots that zoom in on the sign. At a performance of Anom Suroto that I attended in Kediri, described in the Introduction, the sponsor, a local army commandant, went to great pains to create and put up a sign on the top of the screen with the name and number of his army unit, and as I was sitting with the producer in the mobile studio at the beginning of the performance, a messenger came from the sponsor asking if Indosiar would show the sign close up. The desire to appear on television can be seen as an extension of the sponsor's desire to show his power locally, but it is also a desire motivated by television itself—to be visible "everywhere".

Tensions and conflicts between the sponsor and Indosiar are common. This can be seen in some of the anecdotes recounted above. At the Kediri performance just mentioned, the tension was very clear. First, Indosiar wouldn't show the sign often enough. But the crises came when the sponsor asked that Indosiar broadcast not only the performance, but also the speech preceding it. Indosiar refused, but the broadcast was postponed because of the conflict. All parties collaborate but each has its own agenda, and tensions arise because each party seeks to control the process.

Everyone is primarily concerned about image-building or self-promotion. This is related to what has been said in Chapter One about television's power to make things visible in a new way, puppeteer's interest in this possibility of greater visibility, and Indosiar's emphasis on "image-building". Self-promotion, unlike money, is not directly quantifiable. This helps to explain the frequently conflicting views about who profits and who is exploited—it is difficult to prove anything. And, at certain moments at least, each party seems to echo Handoko's words: "*He* also gets promoted—*he* should pay *me*!"

Most wayang performances in Java are sponsored privately, often on the occasion of marriages and circumcisions. In the case of the large-scale, spectacular performances prevalent on Indosiar, the sponsor is typically an organization or its head, such as a bank, a university, a private company, or often a (local) governmental, political, and/or military organ. In the Soeharto era, many performances were sponsored by his ruling party. In these cases, powers such as the government, political parties, and military influence which puppeteers and what kind of performances appear on television, as well as the content of the programme (for example, the inclusion of propaganda, promotion of a politician, a political party, a particular agenda or "message", and so on).

Government and army officials and rich businessmen represent a major force in the puppeteers' professional lives. Those puppeteers who are in favour with people in power—"close to power", as Slamet put it—have a chance to appear on Indosiar, while for others it is almost impossible. This means that puppeteers are compelled to "continually beg " (*ngemis-ngemis*) the powerful institutions and people who can afford to sponsor the spectacular performances that Indosiar prefers. "We always have to face what's called power," said Slamet. "The problem is not only Indosiar, but also the patrons, the people who have money." Said Ki Haji Mansyur, a dhalang from Cirebon (and his perspective also reveals yet another inequality, that between different districts and parts of Java):

> For us in West Java, it's difficult to enter Indosiar, with the *live* system, Mas. They are only shooting live, on the stage, not in the studio. Indeed, it looks nice, but, hmm—when I propose [a performance to Indosiar], there is a condition: "You should propose it to the local government, the functionaries at the *kebupaten* [district government]." That's what's difficult. [...] [But] the local government helps the local artists and the local art only in slogans. It's not like what I see when Pak Manteb performs in Kabupaten Sukohardjo, there is the "Sukohardjo Makmur" sign [Prosperous Sukohardjo], and Pak Bupati even sings a verse—they are very close, Manteb and the functionaries. [...] After all, it is also a pride for a bupati to appear on Indosiar.

Some puppeteers that are by all standards bad, appear on television because of their connections. Others, sinking into televisual invisibility, try to "continually beg " or resign themselves to being "village puppeteers", which now feels inferior. Television's involvement in the system augments the power of powerful sponsors by further increasing their visibility. Indosiar becomes the instrument of power of the government, the military, and the very rich. Less powerful or less wealthy sponsors, and with them less widely known puppeteers and smaller performances, are excluded from the system. It is worth noting that the powerful sponsors, from the point of view of the wayang world, included, even in the New Order, not just Jakarta-based, but perhaps even more importantly, regional and local government and army officials—the bupati in the anecdotes above (from the initial recordings of wayang to the later conflicts) or the local army official in the performance described in the Introduction are just a few examples, but there are many others, including the notorious monthly performances sponsored in the 1990s by the Governor of Central Java in Semarang, which were also broadcast on TVRI Semarang. If scholars associate the New Order era with a strong central government (in contrast to the growing regional autonomy in the post-Soeharto new New Order), our case shows that even under the New Order, local government officials figured as a major force in the wayang world and found ways to express their political power and personal prestige—in sponsoring a wayang, the distinction between the two is usually blurred.

There are other actors in the play. Senawangi (National Wayang Secretariat), was powerful especially during the New Order era, even though its exact manner of influence is not easy to see. It is a government institution that officially cultivates wayang, but also serves to control it. Many of its members are rich businessmen and/or have close connection with the army and/or the government. Senawangi sponsors performances that are sometimes broadcast on Indosiar, but it also has less visible powers. For example, an Indosiar producer told me that when he began to broadcast a particular wayang programme focusing on entertainment (the *Lakon Goro-Goro* discussed below), the plan was aborted because Senawangi didn't like it. It is hard to say who and what exactly Senawangi is, and its exact manner of influence. It is said that a top Senawangi officer was also indirectly involved in the management of Indosiar, and even he, it was suggested, was only the communicator of the wishes of President Soeharto. Senawangi has also sponsored extensive research on how to best show wayang on television (discussed in Chapter Four). Senawangi forwarded its recommendations to Indosiar, but Indosiar seems to have largely ignored them. A Senawangi member who wrote some of the recommendations told me that he was not pleased about this. Indosiar producers didn't feel that they needed Senawangi's recommendations, and considered it an unwelcome intrusion.

Other parties involved include the art academies in Yogyakarta and especially Solo. They are the artistic and scholarly elite. Senawangi has connections with the academies, and certain individuals are involved in both organizations. The position of the academies resembles Senawangi in that they would like to advise Indosiar and they feel that their expertise would make the programme better, but Indosiar mostly ignores them. Said Rahayu Supanggah when he was the head of the Solonese academy:

> I am not that interested in watching wayang on television, except when there is a puppeteer whom I haven't seen yet. [...] It's ugly [*jelek*], there is no content, I don't get a new experience, and aesthetically, too, I am annoyed. [...] I often have a discussion with the television side, but they never listen. I mean: they don't want to hear about their weaknesses, they consider it good already. [We suggested:] "Invite us to work with you, you don't have to pay us." But perhaps they feel threatened. It would be better if we just did it ourselves.

The academies tend to be critical of Indosiar and there is little institutional co-operation. Their vision of wayang as serious "High Art" is very different from Indosiar. They tend to perceive "entertainment" as bad. However, some of the famous dhalang have connections with the academies and some academy instructors occasionally perform on Indosiar. Some innovative ideas that originate in the academies find their way into popular mainstream performances. Despite the general unwillingness to work together as institutions, there is a degree of traffic in people and ideas between Indosiar wayang programmes and the academies.

There are also other parties that try to influence the shape of the programme. For example, Studio Audio Visual Puskat (Audio Visual Studio, the Catholic Centre) in Yogyakarta, directed by Fred Wibowo, sponsored a number of seminars on the production of traditional arts on television at which Indosiar producers were present. While Fred Wibowo takes credit for the success of Indosiar wayang, his contribution is not acknowledged by Indosiar producers. They don't feel they need outside help, and at least some of them have little respect for Fred Wibowo and consider him only clever at writing grant proposals with which he is able to get big money from the Ford Foundation.

There are two other important forces: the advertisers and the audiences. The influence of one depends to some extent on the other. Advertisers are attracted to ratings, which means that in order to attract advertisers, Indosiar has to attract audience. But these audiences are to a great extent imagined—there is no audience research done specifically for wayang, and the ratings, as everybody seems to be aware, are especially misleading in the case of wayang. They are based on selected viewers in the largest cities of Sumatra and Java, so the system ignores people living in villages and towns, where certainly wayang is watched. All this does not mean that the audience does not influence the programme. I have noted before that the impetus to start the regular screening of wayang came in part from the audience, and the letters to Indosiar do to some extent affect the choices made by the producers. The producers often mention requests or protests that appear in audience letters, and they take them into consideration.

The interest of advertisers in the programme is cautious, and Indosiar is resigned to the fact that it will not make a (large) net profit on the advertisements shown during wayang programming. The "image-building", as we have seen, may be the more important consideration. Nonetheless, the importance of advertising does influence the wayang programme in various ways. The decision to schedule wayang late at night rather than during prime time, the desire to make wayang into commercial entertainment appealing to as many people as possible, and even the unwillingness to spend too much money on wayang—all these decisions can be understood in the context of the commercial character of private television.

Performers, television producers, rich sponsors, government officials, military commanders, government agencies cultivating and/or controlling wayang, art academies, audiences, advertisers—the production of wayang happens at the intersection of their desires and ambitions (for money, visibility, image), professional and personal, in the midst of their alliances and enmities; it is caught in the midst of multiple intentions and accidents.

Altering Wayang for Television: The Worksphere

Both dhalang and producers want to make wayang look good on television, but their views on how to achieve this differ. In Chapter One, I discussed performers' efforts to make wayang look good on television and, inseparably, in the contemporary world. In this section, I focus on the work of the television crew.

We can think about the work of the television crew as a "performance"[29] that interacts with the wayang performance. The television producers try to show what is significant or interesting at a particular moment: when a battle is going on, they focus on the screen and the puppeteer's action; when the *pesindhen* (female vocalist) is singing, they focus on her; when they feel that there is nothing visually interesting on the screen, they show the musicians or, less often, the audience. During dialogues, the editing may alternate between the puppet "speakers", focusing on the one who is speaking at the moment.

2.2 Simultaneous editing of a wayang performance inside the Indosiar mobile studio. The input from different cameras is visible on the monitors.

According to one Indosiar producer, the length of each shot and the resulting tempo of cutting from one shot to another follows the tempo or mood of the music—during calm musical compositions and periods of calm in the play, editing tends to be slower, while during faster-moving music and dramatic action, the tempo tends to be faster.

Performers generally agree that this is what the television crew should do, but they disagree about how it is executed, and this is a source of much bitterness. A common criticism is that the television producers do not understand wayang. Almost every dhalang who has performed on television seems to have an example of this. Typically, the puppeteer may complain about a moment when something very important is happening on the screen, but the television shows, for example, a musician or the female singer instead. Another common complaint concerns post-production editing, such as when a commercial break is inserted at a time that the puppeteers consider inappropriate, or when, in the process of abbreviating the performance, the producer deletes a segment that the puppeteer considers essential. Puppeteers find this frustrating.

But is it simply that—to use the language of a famous dhalang when he was complaining about one such case—the television cameramen are "stupid" (*goblog*)? From the puppeteers' perspective, the answer is yes. With some exceptions, the understanding of wayang among the television crew is limited. The cameramen mostly do not know the names of the musical instruments or even the most basic characters, which makes communication between the producer and the cameramen difficult. Even when the producer wishes to do something that the puppeteer might consider correct, it may not be realized. The producer might ask the cameramen to quickly focus on *gambang* or Kresna, but the cameramen has no idea what or who this is. More generally, puppeteers say that television people do not understand the aesthetics and meaning of wayang.

Yet, while one can understand that the puppeteer may see the crew as "stupid", this stupidity consists of not understanding wayang. It arises from the encounter itself, and from a lack of mutual understanding. The Indosiar crew do not feel that they have to understand wayang well. The television institution does not encourage them to. There is no team of cameramen permanently assigned to wayang, so they have no chance to learn about wayang by experience. A producer may become to some extent familiar with the shooting of wayang, but soon he is reassigned and replaced by a new producer who has to start learning from the beginning. It also happens that a producer not normally in charge of wayang substitutes for one who has some experience.

While puppeteers complain about the stupidity of the television crew, the television crew complains about the ignorance of the puppeteers. Puppeteers, it is said, are villagers who do not understand modern technology and modern business, or they are "idealistic artists" who do not grasp the practical requirements of television and the need for compromise.

To some extent, it is possible for each party to do its part of the job, without understanding well what the other party is doing. But some degree of interaction is necessary. As a result, there are conflicts in which both parties struggle to have a degree of control over the process, at least to the extent that they are able to work as they wish to, rather than being forced to follow the other party which, in the first party's view, does not understand the job.

In this atmosphere, which is itself a result of the workings of television, producers work in such a way that they don't need to understand wayang. This relates to what has been said in the discussion of authenticity. Television "moves whatever is there to people's homes". A deep understanding of wayang, it is felt, is not essential—television records and transmits it just like any other event, following its own universally applicable methods. Most Indosiar executives and producers (Panca, who is not working at Indosiar any more, is an exception) say that they don't want to interfere (*campur tangan*) in the performers' business—wayang remains authentic, with television in control of the images of wayang.

According to Kristiyadi, a dancer and a producer at the state TVRI Yogyakarta, the problem is that television uses "norms" (*norma-norma*) or "expertise" (*ilmu-ilmu*) that are used for the news and other programmes, but nobody yet knows what the "norms" or "expertise" for televising wayang are. He said that even if the television crew understood wayang—which, in his view, is not likely in practice because they have to produce many kinds of other programmes—he is not sure if that would be the solution, because they would still have to follow the standard "norms" of television (as an example, he mentioned that one shot should not be much longer than 30 seconds, because of the visual variety expected on television). A good dhalang, musician, or dancer does not necessarily make a good television producer, because that it not his "field" (*bidang*). This is an important point: it is not just television producers and cameramen who control or expose wayang. The technological system and the dehumanized *norma-norma televisi* (television norms), which no single person controls, are a powerful force in managing the process and controlling what people do.

Kristiyadi thus affirms the separation between the two fields, and the fact that television presently covers wayang using universal "norms", rather then changing its "norms" to fit wayang. If I have said that the television people can be considered as performing alongside the wayang performers, it is also important to see that part of the relation between these two "performances" is that television treats wayang as the raw material for its own performance and for their product, productively consumes it, treating it in fundamentally the same way as any other raw material.

Altering Wayang for Television: Manipulating Performance

In Chapter One, we discussed the tendency toward more visibility and more light in contemporary performances. By far the strongest lights illuminate televised performances. Indosiar uses powerful television lighting to illuminate the whole performance area, as well as mobile hand-held spotlights. This relates to other changes. Producers believe that, because of the increased visibility and the use of close-ups (close-ups, in turn, require more light), it is necessary to make wayang clean and tidy if it is to look good on television, and they strive for such a clean and tidy spectacle. Part of this is arranging the stage in such a way that it looks good specifically on television. Panca told me how, especially in the early years when he had more leeway, he asked wayang performers to arrange the instruments so that the stage looked tidy and that the cameras could easily focus on different musical instruments. Care was taken that the pesindhen were visible and that

2.3 Neatly seated female singers on a clean stage decorated with flowers, as seen in Indosiar television coverage of a 1995 performance in Sukoharjo.

there was nothing between them and the cameras that would spoil the picture. The performers were asked to keep the stage clean and not to put food or glasses in places where the camera might "look". Something that is so much part of the enjoyment of wayang—eating and drinking, and watching others eating and drinking—is considered ugly by television! (The writer is shaking his head in disbelief.) In the series of performances sponsored by Indosiar in Sukoharjo in 1995, there was no food served to the musicians during the performance—something unimaginable at a normal performance, as performers' indignant comments made clear. "At that time, I was keeping discipline," Panca told me. "No one was allowed to smoke, and that is very difficult for [the performers]. There were no bags allowed, no thermo bottles—that makes the picture ugly, when there is a thermo bottle, or a piece of bread." Performers were reprimanded when they talked during the performance. Garlands of flowers were arranged on the stage to beautify it, and singers were told to keep their notebooks low so that they would not disturb the picture. Panca complained that sometimes musicians do not keep their instruments clean and, he said, they write "I love you" or draw pictures on their instruments or mallets. He asked the performers to clean their instruments.

These alterations are disconcerting for wayang performers, who see them as arrogant interventions in their work and art by people who do not know what they are doing. Smoking, eating, drinking, and talking in a relaxed atmosphere *is* wayang. One senior, highly respected dhalang told me how Indosiar crew asked to put the *rebab* (musical instrument), which is normally fixed vertically in a stand, down on the floor, because it blocked the view of a camera. The old puppeteer was furious: "This is the way that rebab is always put!" Laying the rebab down would be disrespectful to the instrument. Moreover, when Indosiar rearranged the instruments to make gamelan look good on television, the musicians said they could not hear each other well.

Indosiar people say that the main change they try to effect in wayang is to "add entertainment", which, we have seen, is one of the main developments in mainstream wayang. Handoko told me about what he called "protest in quotation marks" that followed the first Indosiar wayang broadcasts.

> "What kind of wayang is this? *Wayang purwa* [the most common kind of wayang] is not like this!" Well, I told them, "This is Entertainment Wayang [*Wayang Entertainment*], and if you don't like that either, it's Indosiar Wayang [*Wayang Indosiar*]!" Hahahaha!

Other Indosiar executives and producers also emphasized the importance of entertainment in "Indosiar Wayang", and talked about the comic intermezzi as the most entertaining. Why, Handoko was asked by critics, were the comic intermezzi foregrounded in the early Indosiar performances?

> Because even people from Central Java or East Java, or even people from Sunda in the case of [Sundanese] *wayang golek*—not all of them will understand precisely the meaning of words [in wayang]. Perhaps he is already sleepy, and he can't stay up till 3 o'clock. Well the comic intermezzo is an interesting part [of the performance] because there is a great freedom and it is usually funny, and it is {entertaining}—there is the pesindhen singing and so on. Well, why did we move it to an earlier time? To *grip* them!

According to Panca, the producer who organized and shaped the first broadcasts of wayang understood that

> in Indonesia ... a person buys television not in order to watch the news ... [but] because of entertainment. Whatever is shown, all the programs, all entertainments, even the news, becomes entertainment. [Wayang on television] will *inevitably* move in that direction.

This may remind us of a puppeteer's statement quoted in Chapter One: "In the heads of television people there is *entertainment*. If they entertain, they get money—rarely are there idealists. Basically, TV industry is business, West, Jakarta."

There is, of course, a political dimension to this emphasis on business and entertainment. Entertainment can become a space for popular expression. At the same time, the apparent absence of politics conceals an Aldous Huxley-esque appeasement of people (even those in power, such as the television executives, who, too, are caught in the system), with happiness and well-being, and the suppression of "idealism" ("rarely are there idealists") with money and pleasure as the ideal, as the object of desire. One thinks of what the dhalang Slamet Gundono said, counterintuitively but profoundly: "Indosiar is actually poor."

The entertainment that Indosiar producers encourage encompasses many initiatives—adding guest stars, encouraging the inclusion of comedy and pop music, emphasizing the comic intermezzi. We have seen that the emphasis on entertainment is related to the increasing level of light and the increased visibility, and thus also to the ideal of everything being clean and tidy. These connections may seem tenuous or "theoretical", but when one sees television celebrities in strong light on a giant, spectacular, clean stage accompanied by the sounds of electronic keyboard, one feels that all these qualities combine to a particular effect, style, culture, and the creation of spectacles of which the main aim is to attract as many spectators as possible.

Manipulating and digesting the electronic images of wayang—recording, editing, broadcasting—may be television's most obvious practice, but because the distinction between reality and image is hidden by the claim that on television one sees authentic reality, it turns out that television manipulates what goes on in front of the cameras as a kind of extension of the manipulation of wayang's images. It manipulates reality so that reality can fit television's "norms".

The discussion above overlaps with the previous chapter not only because we are talking about the same performances, but because the initiatives of television producers are sometimes more and sometimes less direct, and they consist in, not only introducing or forcing changes, but also encouraging certain existing practices, some of which may have been initiated by puppeteers in their attempts to adapt television materials and aesthetics to wayang. The direct, conscious initiatives of Indosiar examined here are in practice indivisible from the complex and gradual movement of wayang toward television and the world of modern entertainment in which television is only one factor, as discussed in Chapter One. In this section, we will return to issues that we have encountered in the previous chapter, but now we consider them from the perspective of the television production process.

Puppeteers make wayang in many respects more like television, but a puppeteer's perception of an innovation depends on whether it is his own initiative, or something that is forced on him by the television crew. In the latter case, what might be under different circumstances done by the dhalang himself, or what may appear to be an extension of a puppeteer's initiative, is felt by the puppeteer to be television's unwelcome interference. Social relations and personal feelings are intertwined with the formal changes in wayang performances and programmes.

How far Indosiar is able to control what happens, depends on the particular sponsorship arrangement and the puppeteer's view of it. When a puppeteer sees Indosiar as the sponsor, the television company has greater authority. If the puppeteer considers Indosiar only a parasite at a live performance, he will be less accommodating. When, in the early days, Indosiar co-sponsored a large number of performances, it had substantial control. The producer requested that the performance would last only four hours, made decisions about guest stars, and was allowed to substantially rearrange and decorate the stage. In other cases, sometimes the dhalang follow Indosiar's wishes (and may even comment during the performance that, for instance, this performance will be kept short at the request of Indosiar), while at other times they ignore them. A producer complained to me that performers still prioritize the live-event aspect of wayang and thus the sponsor, rather than thinking about the performance as a television programme and adjusting it according to the wishes of the television producer. Several dhalang complained that the producers are so arrogant that they come, often without paying the performers and even getting money from the sponsor, and they think they can order the performers around and ask for things that would spoil the performance, such as shortening it—after all, as many puppeteers, sponsors, and viewers say, one is not "satisfied" (*marem, puas*) if wayang doesn't last whole night.

The introduction of guest stars exemplifies the power struggle that is part of the production process. Indosiar's agency here is an extension of an existing practice: there were similar guest stars several years before Indosiar began to broadcast wayang, and the growing importance of the pesindhen in the past few decades can be seen as a precedent of the guest star phenomenon. There is no doubt, however, that Indosiar stimulated this practice. When the guest stars are introduced into the performance by Indosiar, but also when they are paid by the sponsor because Indosiar requires it, or because the sponsor knows that this is normal in televised performances, the presence of guest stars is an example of the more or less direct intrusion of Indosiar into the work of the wayang performers; an example of Indosiar changing the performance before the television cameras. Dhalang are aware that the inclusion of guest stars is a powerful means to attract audiences, some have "guest stars" in their troupe, and yet this is one of their most common objections about Indosiar. They say that famous guest stars can be a nuisance. The puppeteer cannot control what they say and do, and he loses the centrality and supreme authority that he had in traditional performances. From his perspective, this means breaking down of the traditional order. When the guest stars are sponsored by Indosiar, the puppeteer feels like the intrusion of the guest stars is part of the Indosiar's intrusion—it is as if the guest stars were Indosiar employees, performing on stage and pushing the puppeteer and the puppets aside. After all, Indosiar itself "performs" like a super-guest-star in many ways, both from the perspective of the sponsor, when he pays Indosiar to come, and from the perspective of the puppeteer, who struggles with Indosiar for control over what is happening in the performance. Indosiar, the sponsor, the puppeteer, and the guest stars are involved in a complex struggle for authority, both on and off stage.

Altering Wayang for Television: Manipulating Electronic Images

Whatever may be the unique features of the manipulation of the images and sounds of wayang, the editing style remains close to other similar programmes in which television claims to present authentic reality. It is when the standard manner of editing reality does not work for wayang that television (sometimes) tries out something else.

Indosiar wants wayang to be both "authentic" and entertaining, but "authentic" wayang is not necessarily entertaining on television: this dilemma affects the manipulation of sounds and images on many levels, from basic editing to programming. Many wayang fans who usually enjoy wayang live say that they are often bored when they watch it on television (as we will discuss in the next chapter). Many television producers say that they feel that a straightforward coverage of wayang would bore viewers, and, some admit, they too are often bored during the production of the programme.

Producing an authentic wayang and entertaining television programme means aiming at an editing style that does not call attention to itself, yet simultaneously makes the programme more entertaining through editing, such as: presenting shots and sequences that are somehow striking, often precisely because they show wayang in ways in which it cannot be seen at a performance, and/or because they foreground televisual technique, such as extreme close-ups; extremely slow transitions between shots with a long moment (sometimes as much as a minute), during which two images are superimposed, so that, for example, both sides of the screen can be seen at the same time, or one can see a close up of the female singer's face mixed with a long shot of the screen; shots of musicians and instruments from unusual angles, such as from above, or with the camera deviating from the standard horizontal orientation; and so on. These kinds of playful foregrounding of the television technique would not be unusual in programmes such as pop music shows, but they stand out in the wayang programme. One

2.4 A photo of a television tuned to a wayang performance: a very slow transition from one shot to another, during which the puppeteer's face and the wayang screen blend into one image.

2.5 Simultaneous editing of a live wayang performance, inside the mobile studio of Jogja TV, 2007. The producer communicates with the cameramen using a walkie-talkie.

producer said that at one point he began to use more television tricks because he felt that wayang was boring without them and he wanted to make the wayang programme more like television pop music shows, but he received letters with complaints from viewers and he was reprimanded by his superior and asked not to go *too far* from the low-key style that presents wayang as "authentic".

The manipulation of images and sounds consists in selecting and showing certain limited, partial views of what is before the cameras, while leaving much invisible; recomposing them into larger wholes in which they are seen in new contexts; and integrating the results into the flow of television programming. These processes take place on several interconnected levels: from editing to programming. The desire for entertaining variety and selection of what looks interesting specifically on television is key. Standard television principles give rise to specific problems in the production of the wayang programme.

One persistent problem concerns—again—time. The wayang performance lasts the whole night, and from television's point of view, it progresses very slowly. In wayang, occasional moments when "nothing is happening"—as when the puppeteer looks for a puppet, drinks, or lights up—are common and are part of the atmosphere of wayang. There are long periods of time when puppets are still on the screen while music plays, and dialogues during which only the puppet's arms are moved slightly from time to time. Even during scenes that emphasize visual movement, there are moments when the screen is blank, such as when the puppeteer is looking for a particular puppet. This may become a minor cosmetic flaw even for people watching the live performance, but on television, a long moment when the screen is white and empty is unacceptable. More generally, the rhythm of the all-night performance is very different than the feeling of time on television, where something has to be happening every second.

Despite the "authenticity" claims, producers see the slow tempo of wayang and visually static or "empty" moments as problematic. The producer tries to compose an interesting sequence of shots from whatever he can find—close-ups of puppets, people's faces, musical instruments and musicians' hands, combined with an occasional longer shot, or shots with ostentatiously interesting camera movement. He tries to compensate for the lack of movement in the performance with motion produced by television, thus changing the feeling of the moment. During dialogues, the producer may use a standard television technique, common in television drama: the camera alternates between the close-up of "speakers", depending on who is speaking at the moment. Here the "speakers" are puppets, which, puppeteers say, look "dead" in close-ups.

Battle scenes and other visually spectacular moments are often felt to be more appropriate for television, but when a battle scene lasts too long, on television it, too, may become "boring", as both television producers and some puppeteers say. Puppeteers, with Indosiar's encouragement, introduce more variety, spectacle and humour into action scenes, but the producer may still feel that a scene is boring after a while and will zoom in on the female singer or the musicians while the battle is continuing on the wayang screen.

I have mentioned that performers often complain that at a particular moment, television "looks at" something other than it should. Moreover, performers say that they dislike certain kinds of shots that the producers are fond of, such as extreme close-ups of puppets. They also tend to dislike shots that distract from what they see as being important in a particular moment—such as close-ups of a singer's face during a battle scene. The performers do not have any say in the electronic manipulation of the images of the performance, which conditions their views and attitudes.

The next level of the manipulation of images takes place in the Indosiar buildings in Jakarta, where the producer works with the videotape of the performance (there is no post-production for live broadcasts, which are more common on TVRI). Post-production again involves choices about what is shown and what is not. Here, too, time and speed are important: the most radical part of post-production involves cutting the length of the programme, often by as much as one third and sometimes even more. The live performance usually takes about six to eight hours. The programme on Indosiar usually lasts between four and five hours. This editing process involves deleting small fragments of several seconds as well as long segments. On this level, the producer tries to solve some of the same problems that I have discussed in the previous paragraph: (tele)visually "boring" moments may be cut out, even though in live performance these moments may be aesthetically among the most memorable, such as parts of long musical compositions during which there is no action on the screen. Parts of long battle scenes are also often deleted. Those shorter, televisually awkward moments when a puppeteer looks for a puppet or takes a sip of tea and the screen is blank may be cut out. In the comic interludes, which may take up more than a third of the performance time, the producer sometimes cuts out a song and a portion of dialogue. This also enables him to censor the performance, such as cutting politically sensitive or risqué comments, as well as mistakes of the editor or other mishaps, such as a person walking in front of the camera. When he works with an older recording, the producer deletes whatever is "out of date." For example, after Soeharto's downfall, the producers re-editing older recordings deleted statements that celebrated Soeharto along with shots of Golkar banners.

The post-production editing is done by a producer in one session, which means that he cannot listen closely to every dialogue or attend to the nuances of the plot. Performers are aware that their performance has been cut when they watch it on television, and they express dissatisfaction both with the fact that the performance is radically abbreviated and with how this is done. As in the case of shot selection, they talk about the producer's ignorance of wayang, and the ways in which the producer, in the performers' eyes, makes the wrong choices and ruins the performance that is seen on television.

The need for radical abbreviation of the performance is related to what we said about television's desire for entertainment and the difference between television time and wayang time. On television, time is money, and it is counted in minutes and seconds, each of which costs something. In wayang, time is not divided into seconds and minutes, but the whole night is one unit of time, and the performance time follows the changing mood of the night rather than rushing to its end. Time as measured by clocks is only an aid to understand the progress of the night, and neither the performance nor the night follows the clock strictly. This is one of the many ways in which the images of wayang do not fit easily on commercial television and are therefore radically altered.

Not all Indosiar performances have to be radically cut in post-production. The above discussion applies to the most common scenario in which Indosiar covers a performance sponsored by a third party, and at which Indosiar can make suggestions but has to respect the sponsor's idea of the performance. However, in some cases such as at the event in Sukoharjo, performances are significantly shorter. The puppeteers and musicians remember the strange feeling when during the performances, every once in a while an Indosiar man would appear with a signboard announcing how much time remained. Even some of these already shortened performances were further cut in post-production. This is another example of the continuity between manipulating the images of the performance on the one hand, and the performance that takes place in front of the cameras on the other.

In some cases, the post-production involves more radical manipulation. Once a month in January, February and March of 1998, at the time of its regular wayang programme (on Saturday nights), Indosiar broadcast *Lakon Goro Goro*—rather paradoxically, since gara-gara (*goro-goro*) is not a *lakon* (story, play) but an interlude that provides a moment of rest from the lakon. The producer took the gara-gara part from a number of previously recorded performances and showed them one after the other in a four-hour programme. Each *Lakon Goro-Goro* consisted of clown scenes taken from wayang performances by a single puppeteer. According to Panca, the Indosiar producer of wayang at that time, the original plan was to schedule the *Lakon Goro-Goro* regularly once a month: "First week *serius* [serious], second week gara-gara, third week serius, fourth week wayang golek." After three months, this plan was abandoned, reportedly because of the protest of high government officials who preferred that wayang remain "authentic". Panca told me that he made these programmes as a kind of experiment:

> What do people actually watch [in wayang]? I am not so sure that they like the story, *the whole story* [in English]. What they need is to laugh, the sexiness [*keseksian*], sensuality [*sensualitasnya*] from a story, only that—no, not from a story, but precisely from an appearance/performance, not its *whole*, but like one *part*. So I cut it at the gara-gara. And the *rating* went up.

While at a regular shooting of wayang, the producer selects the shots and composes them into sequences, *Lakon Goro-Goro* is an extreme example of how the television producer cuts large pieces of performances and composes them into a television programme.

Again, there is a continuity between manipulating the electronic images and the performance in front of the cameras. In January 1999, on the occasion of its fourth anniversary, Indosiar produced two shows, called *Paket Wayang Spesial* (Special Wayang Package), which again replaced the regular wayang programme with its comic intermezzi. This time, however, the cutting was not done in the editing room, but on stage in Indosiar's studio, where the dhalang, Ki Enthus Susmono, began by performing the *limbukan*, the first comic intermezzo, and then the second one, the gara-gara. The limbukan was broadcast on one Saturday night, at the time of the regular Indosiar wayang, and the gara-gara was broadcast one week later.[30] This *paket* went a step further than usual, not only in throwing out all of wayang except the comic interludes, but it was made even more spectacular than usual, with the puppeteer acting, in the words of the executive producer Didik Yulianto, as an MC (master of ceremonies), introducing various guest stars and guest spectacles (dances, comedy), and the studio environment also enabled more showy camera and lighting techniques. The dhalang himself, even though he is known for his flexibility, experimentation, and disregard of conventions, told me that he felt "uncomfortable".

This show resembled another event organized by Indosiar several years earlier. On a Saturday night in August 1996, about a year after its first wayang broadcast, Indosiar, sponsored a large-scale show in Surabaya called *Pesta gado-gado Indosiar*. Pesta means "party, festivity, celebration". *Gado-gado* means "mixed salad, a mix of diverse elements". So: something like "Indosiar Mixed-Salad Party". The show featured famous pop and rock singers, set against the backdrop of a gigantic wayang screen. Spectacular moving coloured lights were "played" on the screen and the space around it as tens of thousands of spectators watched. Soon after midnight, an abbreviated (about three-hour) wayang performance took place, which itself emphasized a comic intermezzo during which a celebrity comedian took the place of the dhalang. Instead of just television-like entertainment being a part of wayang, here we have wayang becoming, in a live show, one of the attractions in a television-like entertainment which is not contained within wayang but which contains wayang—which is what happens whenever wayang becomes one element of the television programming. The first part of the show, with the giant wayang screen visible in the background, was broadcast live on television, but after midnight, a recording of another wayang performance (by Manteb) was broadcast instead of showing the Surabaya wayang. On television, the night's programme combined two performances. Distinctions between a television programme and a live event, between wayang and a television variety show, and between manipulating electronic images and manipulating material reality, become blurred.

Indosiar is not the only station that experiments with the comic intermezzi, cutting the performance through methods other than editing. For instance, several times TVRI Semarang broadcast not a complete wayang, but only the gara-gara. The comic intermezzo was not an excerpt from a performance, but the puppeteer (a number of times it was Warsena Slenk) was invited to the studio to perform specifically a single intermezzo.

Programming choices made by Indosiar are another aspect of the manipulation of wayang's images. Again time is at stake. While a wayang performance usually begins at about 9 o'clock (sometimes somewhat later if it is preceded by speeches), on Indosiar the programme starts close to midnight. This allows Indosiar to show other programmes that have higher ratings during prime time, while wayang is allocated a time when it is likely to be watched by fewer viewers, most likely those with special interest in the programme. This is a vicious cycle: while the reason given for showing wayang later at night is that it has relatively smaller television audience than prime time television programmes, showing wayang late at night in turn ensures that it cannot compete with other programmes in attracting larger audiences. This policy follows from Indosiar's commitment to "authenticity": while Indosiar tries to make wayang more interesting, it is resigned to the fact that this programme is primarily for wayang fans or for the relatively few people who stay up after midnight. Indosiar does not try to make wayang into a television show that could compete with soap operas and other popular programmes for the prime time spot. Instead, the wayang programme competes with live wayang performances. Saturday night is "prime time" for live wayang performances, because the next day people don't have to get up early to go to work, and celebrations of which wayang may be a part are often held on the weekend. Some observers criticize Indosiar for selecting this time and accuse it of diminishing the audiences of live wayang.

The regularity with which wayang can be seen on television every Saturday is often pointed out as one reason for the relative success of Indosiar wayang. While wayang performances are generally organized on special occasions and people learn about them mostly from hearsay, it is important that people always already know that on Saturday night they can be sure of a wayang on Indosiar. From soap operas to news, this temporal regularity is one of television's basic structural principles, and making wayang a regular occurrence is a part of adapting it to television's being in time. Regularity establishes expectations and works to attract audiences for "the next time". Each "episode" (as the executive director called it) is an advertisement for the next. Each wayang programme becomes one link in an endless chain, one "episode" of Indosiar wayang. Wayang becomes a sort of television series. Regularity leads to familiarity, and, the hope is, the programme becomes a part of people's routine. Wayang on Indosiar comes to mean not only watching wayang on television, but it is associated with one of the more pleasant times of the week and its specific pleasures—staying up late with friends. It is incorporated into the structure of television time and through it—thus differently than before—it becomes part of people's lives.

The familiarity of Javanese people with wayang was an important consideration when the Indosiar executives first decided to begin the broadcasts. Looking at wayang with the eyes of a television producer, one can see many features that resemble a television series, such as the standard set of central characters in the stories used for all "episodes", the multiplicity of rather loosely related story lines, and the relatively open ending with which each episode concludes. One can discover soap opera in wayang. With its pretension of "authenticity", Indosiar has not tried to completely transform wayang into a soap opera; but, through the regular programming and in other ways, wayang on Indosiar has, as if by itself, "turned out" not so different from the television series: "the earth now reveals itself as a coal mining district". Soewastomo, as we have seen, described wayang's potential for its success on television by saying that for Javanese, wayang is "like drugs", and the familiarity-breeding regularity of Indosiar wayang cultivates the addictiveness of a television series.

There is a standard set of characters represented by the puppets, and there is a set of performers who appear repeatedly in wayang on

Indosiar. The programme is dominated by a small group of superstar puppeteers, with less well-known puppeteers appearing occasionally. Several notoriously famous guest stars—singers and comedians—appear again and again in Indosiar wayang performances, and television viewers are also familiar with them from other television programmes. The performers are familiar not only in that they are seen often, but the puppeteer talks with the guest stars in a sphere of relaxed, party-like familiarity, joking and gossiping. Commonly they talk about the performers' personal lives. The television viewers do not simply watch a singer singing: they spend the night with her—in the friendly atmosphere of the wayang performance. This is comparable to watching a talkshow or a soap opera regularly.

In the previous chapter, we saw how the practice of inviting guest stars and the inclusion of various kinds of entertainments and "attractions" in wayang brings wayang closer to television, turning wayang itself into a kind of "flow" of a variety of entertainments, often from different places and cultures. Indosiar invites "guest stars" or asks sponsors of performances to invite them if they want Indosiar to televise the performance. This is cited by television producers as an example of encouraging "entertainment" in wayang. In Indosiar's Paket Wayang Spesial, the brainchild of Didik Yulianto, there were dancers and dances from the 27 provinces (Taman Mini again comes to mind, as do school textbooks), in addition to many other entertainments and guest stars. In another Indosiar production, called *Wayang Koalisi* (Wayang Coalition) or *Wayang Kompilasi* (Wayang Compilation), Javanese wayang kulit appeared next to Sundanese wayang golek, and between the two groups of performers was a stage upon which dancers, comedians, and *kethoprak*-like actors performed. The incorporation and juxtaposition of entertainers and entertainments is television's way of being. By encouraging wayang to include guest stars and entertainments from a variety of places, television encourages wayang to be more like television itself.

On television, wayang is seen as a part of the television's flow. It appears next to sports (from which it borrows Mike Tyson and more), Chinese films (it resembles them in the kung-fu puppet movements), Indian films (the dangdut music, inspired by Indian film music, is featured in the clown scenes in wayang and in other TV programmes), video clips and music shows (and the most up-to-date hits heard on radio and television are also played in wayang, often with disco-lights and appropriate dancing), cartoons (from which wayang learns new jokes and styles of representation), films like *King Kong* and *Jurassic Park* (which have inspired the extra-large puppets of a Javanese demon and wayang-dinosaurs), television news (from which wayang takes the ghost of Lady Diana, George Bush, Saddam Hussein, Indonesian politicians, and more), other "traditional performing arts" shown regularly on television such as kethoprak (a form of traditional Javanese theatre; the conventions and humour of those genres are brought by their performers who are featured as guest stars in wayang), and more. It is not only the general character of the flow of television and wayang that come closer together, but the "many attractions" in wayang performances are also the attractions of television, or are at least inspired by them.

The wayang programme is also penetrated by advertisements, a television genre that is often the most intense and dramatically powerful (according to television standards). As I spoke to the executives at television stations, I realized that they think about all programmes as the setting or background for commercials. Ads themselves incorporate "many attractions", including wayang puppets and puppeteers, actors from both traditional theatre and soap opera, pop music singers, and so on. In addition to advertising commodities, there are also advertisements for other programmes, which are very common during wayang broadcasts. They typically include excerpts from the programmes they advertise. As one watches wayang on television, one finds oneself watching excerpts from—"the best of"—American action movies, Chinese martial arts movies, Sri Mulat (a popular modern comic theatre, first performed live on stage, starting in Solo the 1950s, later becoming very popular on national television, including TVRI in 1986–1987 and Indosiar in 1995–2003 and 2006), Ketoprak Jampi Stress (the name of a kethoprak group and, starting in 1999, an Indosiar television show; *jampi* is traditional herbal medicine or curing method; "jampi stress" means "cure for stress"), boxing matches (which are broadcast regularly on Indosiar), soap operas, music and variety shows—those programmes most often advertised during wayang on Indosiar.

Wayang also penetrates into other parts of the flow, into other programmes, both in the form of the different advertisements in which puppeteers become "advertisement stars" (*bintang iklan*) or in which other ad stars act as wayang puppeteers, and through advertisements for the wayang programme, which consists of images from wayang performances on television. In some cases, puppeteers become guest stars on other television shows—but in a sense they are always "guest stars" whenever they appear on television.

Wayang, which is already permeated by television, appears as one sub-stream in the flow of television programming. Each programme is a fluid entity, and they freely overflow into each other. Much of what one sees during the clown scenes has only an incidental connection to wayang, and can be seen and heard in other television programmes: pop stars and pop music, comedy, and so on. The two media and their attractions freely mix and often it becomes difficult and irrelevant to distinguish between wayang and television, or between their respective attractions. One could get the impression that wayang and television mix as two equals. But on television, all this happens *within* television, and wayang is merely one of the many attractions of television.

We also need to remember that images and actuality dissolve into each other: the mixing and interpenetration that is characteristic of television is also characteristic of contemporary live wayang performances, televised or not. Wayang is part of the "world of entertainment". Performers and audiences attend wayang performances as a part of a television-like flow of entertainments that mix and interpenetrate. The television stars from all kinds of entertainments are part of, not only performances on television, but also of live performances. As performers perform and audiences watch, they shape and enjoy the wayang performance with their familiarity of other entertainment and with the awareness that wayang is a part of a larger flow of entertainments.

We have been tracing how, on different levels, television selects cut-out images of the world and recombines them to form a television programme, from the simultaneous editing of shots to the post-production editing and finally to the incorporation of the wayang programme into the larger flow of television programming. There is one more level on which this selection and recombination takes place: the selection of performances. Only a tiny percentage of wayang performances are shown on television, and their selection is an important way in which Indosiar manipulates what is seen as wayang. In the same way that the editor looks for interesting shots and selects them, Indosiar looks for what might be interesting on television. The choice—spectacular performances with guest stars and abundant entertainment—in turn affects the wayang world by giving a special authority to these performances, performance styles, and performers, as we have seen in the previous chapter.

Performances are not only selected, but decisions are made about when a performance is actually going to be broadcast. In the decade after 1995, there were three performances of Javanese wayang kulit followed by one performance of Sundanese wayang golek. This cycle introduced regularity on this level and composed the four performances into a distinct "3 plus 1" unit, and this practice reveals for whom the wayang on Indosiar is intended: three quarters for Javanese and one quarter for Sundanese. This articulates the majority politics of television. There is no Balinese wayang, for example, and even wayang in other styles than the dominant Central Javanese styles are rare (East Javanese, Cirebonese, or Banyumas). Here again, Indosiar prefers to privilege a small number of dominant performers and performing styles, with which the television audience becomes familiar.

Indosiar also makes choices about how many times a particular performance is shown over the years. A performance by a familiar superstar puppeteer tends to be shown more often—two or three times—than a performance by less famous puppeteers. In some cases, a recorded performance is not shown at all. A striking example of this is a number of performances by woman puppeteers that were recorded but never actually broadcast. This is another way in which Indosiar further manipulates how wayang on television is represented—it selects and makes visible certain things while leaving others invisible.

The Capital: Video Recording

Recording technology plays an important part in how Indosiar controls and manipulates wayang. While a live broadcast of wayang frees a performance from a particular place and annihilates distance, recording also separates the performance from a particular time. A live performance is an ephemeral event in time. A recording is an object that can be owned, stored and reused. Elsewhere, I have described wayang performance as work without a material product, work for the sake of working, a journey for the sake of travelling.[31] Indosiar fixes the live performance into a product of work. Marx comes to mind, and to our coffee shop: "That which in the labourer appeared as movement, now appears in the product as a fixed quality without motion."[32] The work of the performers, in its original transiency, is difficult to control totally. As an object, the performance is owned and controlled by Indosiar in an unprecedented way. "[T]he product is the property of the capitalist and not that of the labourer, its immediate producer."[33] Recorded, the performance can be seen anywhere and anytime the owner of the recording choses. It can be manipulated and repeatedly altered in a way that a live performance or a live broadcast cannot. A recorded performance can be edited, cut so as to make it shorter or for other reasons, and scheduled at a particular time in programming. Recording also allows Indosiar to rebroadcast the performance, usually altered again and framed anew.

It is Indosiar, the owner of the recording, that controls all these processes, while the performers have no control at all. "We are always the object, never the subject," the puppeteer Slamet Gundono told me about the relation between performers and Indosiar. The change of being in time and the objectification of the performance that recording effects, is an aspect of Indosiar's capitalistic exploitation of the performers' work. In separating the performance's images from the moment of the performance—when the performers are to a certain degree in control—Indosiar frees the objectified performance from the performers' power. This allows Indosiar to use the recorded performance for profit again and again, with no rights reserved for the performers.

To record the performance means to store it for future use. Earlier I have suggested that when television takes advantage of and profits from existing situations, the "earth now reveals itself as a coal mining district, the soil as a mineral deposit", in Heidegger's words. Storing for future use, creating a stock, is, in Heidegger, another stage of technological revealing: "Everywhere everything is ordered to stand by, to be immediately at hand, indeed to stand there just so that it may be on call for further ordering."[34] The "regulating and securing" that happens to wayang is like what happens to the river Rhine when it is "dammed up into the power plant" and "appears as something at our command".[35]

Indosiar has a collection, or stock, of recorded wayang. To understand how Indosiar secures and manipulates the performances, we need to consider not only an individual performance as it is recorded, stored, and broadcast repeatedly, but rather the whole collection kept at Indosiar. Indosiar broadcasts not unique performances but replaceable specimens from a stock—wayang performances turn into something like money. Indosiar can choose from the collection, and through each choice Indosiar manipulates how wayang is seen on television, and reduces the performances and the performers to stock, ever on call for further manipulation. "Unlocking, transforming, storing, distributing, and switching about are ways of technological revealing."[36]

When Indosiar decided to broadcast wayang regularly, the first step was to sponsor a large number of performances, that is, to build the collection that would be stored and used in the future. This allows Indosiar to broadcast wayang every week even as it records wayang performances irregularly or perhaps, much more rarely, once a month. The collection, the capital, allows Indosiar to transform the irregularity of live performances into the regularity of television, and broadcast many more wayang programmes than the number of wayang performances it has recorded. The impermanence of individual performances is transformed into the permanence of the regularity of television broadcasts. We have seen that this regularity is a powerful way to attract and keep audiences, and to compete with live performances. Regularity: we may think back to the desires for neat, clean, orderly appearances on wayang stage, which we have found to be a feature of modernity beyond our case, as well as part of the desire to control the world. We may also think back to the securing, regulating and ordering of technological revealing directed "toward driving on to the maximum yield at the minimum expense".[37]

This regular continuity is also, in Marx's words, the "restless never-ending process of profit making".[38] Indosiar, treats the performances in a radically different way than does a traditional sponsor. The traditional sponsor can be said to "use" the performance the one time it is performed. Indosiar treats the performances rather like money: each performance, like a dollar bill, is one item in a collection of equivalent items, and each is reusable. Like Marx's capitalist, Indosiar achieves "the never-ending augmentation of exchange-value [...] by constantly throwing it afresh into circulation". Indosiar is able to transform the performances, by recording and collecting them, into a form of capital. "Use-value must therefore never be looked upon as the real aim of the capitalist; neither must the profit on any single transaction. The restless never-ending process of profit making is what he aims at."[39]

Comments by Manteb and Anom—the two dhalang shown most often on Indosiar—make it clear that they see the system, which is made possible by recording, as an exploitation of their work. They complain especially because they believe Indosiar profits from multiple rebroadcasts, while they get nothing. Manteb told me that not only does he get nothing from Indosiar the first time his performance is shown, but Indosiar then shows the performance "played over and over" (*disetel ping bolak-balik*). (Manteb uses the word (*di*)*setel*, which is normally used to refer to playing a cassette tape or turning on a machine: this suggests how he thinks about these rebroadcasts. *Setel* is related to Dutch *toestel*, "device, machine, etc."; and, how can we resist thinking of that more distant relation, among others, Heidegger's *Gestell*, translated as "enframing.") Manteb says he "suffers loss" (*rugi*) when his performances are rebroadcast. and, he continues: "The one whose cassettes [*kaset*] are the most numerous at Indosiar—that's me. In the past, I wasn't aware. It was just my ambition to perform on Indosiar, that was all. I wasn't thinking that I would in fact suffer a loss."

Manteb here brings up the image of the collection of "his" cassettes at Indosiar, and other people making money on "his" cassettes. Indosiar, no doubt, would claim that these are not Manteb's cassettes at all, but are Indosiar's. For the performer, the cassette recording is indivisible from his performance and therefore it is "his"; the product being indivisible from work. For Indosiar, the cassette is an asset, and the performer's work is something separate and a matter of the past, something for which he has been paid already, by someone else.

Anom's views are similar and he, too, finds that he "suffers a loss":

> So, frankly, many puppeteers find it rather disturbing, especially in the case of Indosiar—why do they record once, but it is broadcast repeatedly? And the dhalang doesn't get

> anything. Many [dhalang] complain about this. It's not like abroad. For example, I still get royalty every year for my *Dewa Ruci* performance which was recorded during a dhalang festival in the Netherlands in 1991. When they want to broadcast that recording on the radio, I get *teleks* from there: "May we broadcast your wayang on our radio? If yes, you will get royalty, this much." That's how it is there—but that's not how it works here, Mas Jan. Yes, yes. On Indosiar, the old recordings, mine, Pak Manteb's, they are repeated all the time.

Like Anom, Manteb referred to his experiences abroad:

> Once I got money sent to me from America, University ... eh, U ... what was it? [me: UCLA?] Yes, yes. I performed there once and, hey! I got paid twice! I got money from the television station, I got $500 from that TV, and from the students I got $2,000. And until today it is broadcast and I get $250 in the mail! Pretty good, right?

Another puppeteer present at the conversation commented, "We should have rules like that here too; here it should be that way too."

These foreign examples suggest that royalties and a sense that artists' performances are their property are foreign to puppeteers, who indeed "steal" ideas from each other all the time, a practice that is considered normal, but it is precisely this practice that Indosiar exploits.

Wayang is not recorded only by Indosiar or other television stations. An interesting phenomenon is the renting of video equipment and cassettes that contain wayang previously recorded from television, especially Indosiar. A sponsor of a celebration rents the tapes and the equipment instead of sponsoring live wayang. Indosiar's president is aware of this practice:

> I was back in the place where I grew up, in Central Java. There was a wedding, and on the invitation it was stated that there is going to be wayang kulit, who is the dhalang and what is the lakon. Even though it was only a common person, a

> farmer. Well, what happened was that he rented speakers, a television, and video [player]. That is, our programme [*kita punya program*] was taped by him, and he had a collection [*koleksi*]. When there was a ceremony, he installed the television [and played the recording for a fee]. So, there are people who take advantage of it again [*memanfaatkan lagi*].

This *memanfaatkan lagi* betrays that Handoko recognizes that when the person builds up a collection of cassettes which he has recorded without paying anybody for it, and then shows the Indosiar programmes for profit at celebrations, he is doing, on a small scale, something like what Indosiar does, "again". In both cases, a person captures wayang on a cassette and thus takes control over it, and, with a collection of tapes as an asset, he is able to play it repeatedly and thus achieve "the never-ending augmentation of exchange-value [...] by constantly throwing it afresh into circulation". Just like the puppeteer doesn't share in Indosiar's profits, so Indosiar doesn't share in the profits of the person who rents out the recordings. The additional irony of this is that the villager plays a comparable role to that of the puppeteer—he, too, offers wayang to enhance festive occasions—and the two compete with each other, as well as with other possible entertainments that can be sponsored for such occasions. While recording allows Indosiar to tear wayang away from its original context and integrate it into television programming, it is also recording that allows the village renter to lift the performance from its television context and reintegrate it into village life, not as a television programme seen regularly on Saturday night, but as entertainment at a celebration where wayang would be traditionally performed live. This return of (recorded) wayang, and the participation of people beyond the television company in using and manipulating the wayang videos, in some ways foreshadows what happened in later years, in the age of YouTube, as we will discuss in the final chapter.

While many wayang performances have been commercially produced on audio cassettes, wayang has not, to my knowledge, been commercially issued on video cassettes. However, it has been issued commercially on VCD, a later technology. For example, in 2000, a private company released a VCD with a one-hour performance by

Manteb. According to a newspaper article from April 2001, four other similar performances featuring the same puppeteer were produced but not distributed because it turned out that the first recording quickly multiplied into many "pirate" versions that flooded the market. The fear was that the same would happen to subsequent recordings.[40] In August 2001, another article announced that ten special, short wayang kulit performances were planned at the house of Anom Suroto in Solo that would be published on VCD. Two other wayang performances would take place in Jakarta for the same purpose.[41] When I spoke to him in summer 2000, the top Sundanese dalang Asep Sunandar told me that a VCD with wayang golek should appear soon. I will discuss these cases in detail in Chapter Four.

Let us look at the appearance of wayang VCDs through the eyes of wayang fans, by examining a discussion on the Javanese-language internet mailing list "Jawa" in late March and April 2001. The discussion began when one subscriber wrote: "I cannot afford to sponsor a wayang performance yet, so I need one that can be played using video, cassette, or CD + PC + amplifier." Others wrote that they would be interested too. One person recommended the *Dewa Ruci* VCD mentioned above, and said that it can be ordered from the publisher, giving the address. Another wrote: "Once, I saw a VCD seller with a VCD with a two-and-half hour wayang by Uncle Manteb Sudharsono. (This was back in my village, near Nganjuk.) I think that in other towns there should be that VCD as well."

It is likely that this was a pirated version of either *Dewa Ruci* produced on VCD, or perhaps part of another performance by Manteb copied from television. Another person wrote:

> Yesterday I was walking around the market, and there was a wayang kulit VCD. I bought vol. 1 to vol. 4 (4 VCDs but [the performance] is not complete). The dhalang was Warseno Slenk (the story, Romo Nitis Makuthoromo). Then I tried it at home and it turned out to be a [pirated] recording from a private TV station.

Another person commented:

> [I]t may be true that the Rama Nitis VCD was made while "breaking the law". I have also seen those VCDs at the sidewalk vendors in Batavia (specifically in Jatinegara or Glodok), and they cost only Rp6.000 per CD. There were other wayang VCDs, namely *wayang orang humor* ([a television programme] with actors Topan and Lesus) and Ki Manteb's Dewaruci (pirate version [*versi bajakan*]). Of course, it's pirated goods, the quality is not guaranteed ... he,he,he.

Yet another joined in:

> While I was walking around in Solo, I stopped by a store with various recordings of Javanese traditional music, wayang, and Javanese arts. [...] In front of the store there was a cigarette vendor who also had recordings of wayang on [V]CDs.[42] A bit to the north, in the store facing west, they also had them. The stories that were in store included: (1) Bima Bungkus, Ki Anom Suroto, 4 *kasets* [meaning VCDs], cost 25 thousand rupiah; (2) Rama Nitis, Ki Warsena Slenk, 5 *kasets*, cost 30 thousand rupiah; and (3) Goro-goro, Ki Jaka Edan, 2 *kasets*, cost 12 thousand rupiah (there are many sorts of goro-goro). About "quality" and about whether the recording is original or pirated I don't know. But in the least, it can serve as "*tamba kecelik*" ["medicine for disappointment" i.e., better than nothing].

One of the sets of VCDs mentioned above, for example, with the play *Bima Bungkus* performed by Anom Suroto, is clearly a performance recorded by Indosiar—the dhalang thanks Indosiar during the clown scenes—and it is probably one of the wayang spektakuler performances described by Yayang. In the left corner of the screen, where one usually sees the round logo of Indosiar, is a logo-like image in the shape of the *gunungan*/kayon puppet, which serves to (imperfectly) cover the Indosiar logo. The labels on the VCD and the VCD cover—the set was sold in plastic foil—look just like labels of other pirated Indonesian VCDs, and the hazy images are clearly screenshots taken from the recording itself. Ki Warsena Slenk, whose *Rama Nitis* performance also appeared on VCD and is mentioned above as being sold in Solo, observed:

> The performance was recorded almost whole, except that information [titles] at the beginning and at the end had been deleted. One can see that the logo of the private television station which usually appears on the upper left of the television screen has been covered by a logo with the gunungan image and the letters "Slenk" in orange colour—even though my own logo has the letters "Slenk" in blood-red letters.[43]

At about the same time that this discussion was going on, there appeared a number of reports in newspapers discussing wayang on VCD. The article "Pirated CDs of wayang performance sell well in the market" from which I have just quoted, provides a dhalang's perspective. While wayang fans seem to be eagerly buying up VCDs of wayang, pirated or not, the dhalang has other concerns. Interestingly—considering the strained relations between puppeteers and Indosiar—the puppeteer believes that it is Indosiar who is behind the VCDs:

> Feeling that he never made an agreement for the production of recording from his performance in a private television station [Indosiar], Ki Ir Warsena Slenk Msi, too, was affected by the distribution of VCDs of the wayang kulit play *Rama Nitis Makutarama*. One set consists of five VCDs and it is believed to have spread in markets—among others, in the Surakarta area—with prices from Rp 35,000 to Rp 60,000 per set. "I don't know exactly if this can be called pirating. But I feel that there are people who have breached and stepped on my rights, because the agreement that we made with the private television was only for broadcasting, and not for reproduction/multiplication and sale,' said [Slenk]. [...] [T]he brother of the famous puppeteer Anom Suroto [i.e., Slenk] cannot ascertain the source and who plays the main role. But he guesses that there is a co-operation between the production team and

> a marketing syndicate, or perhaps it is handled directly by the production team of the private television station.[44]

I asked Yayang at Indosiar about what he knows:

> There are people who take advantage [*memanfaatkan*] of Indosiar broadcasts, because at Indosiar we do not make VCDs for distribution for the public at all. As far as I know, the VCD was made [by a third party] when wayang was broadcast on Indosiar. If Indosiar made a VCD, I would certainly give one to Mas Jan.

The puppeteer "feels" that the VCDs are just another means of exploitation controlled by Indosiar. His suspicions show the mistrust that puppeteers feel toward Indosiar.

It is interesting why exactly the dhalang is upset. The article described this in a section entitled "Image-building" (*bangun citra*): "[H]e asserted that he has suffered great loss, because so far he has been building an image of himself [*membangun citra diri*] through direct live performances or television broadcasts. Because of that, so far he has not produced [wayang] in the form of CDs."[45]

The damage done, in the puppeteer's perception, is not financial, but it concerns his image. We have seen that image-building is a major aim of all the parties involved, and a major problem in the skirmishes between the different parties are "broken names".

Let us assume that the VCDs were made by a third party and not by Indosiar. This is a real possibility, considering the technology is easily available. The *Dewa Ruci* VCDs, which were not produced by Indosiar, were also extensively pirated. This would mean that, rather like in the case of the village renter of wayang video cassettes, recording enabled more people to make profit on the performances. It is not only Indosiar controlling the recorded performances and taking advantage of the puppeteers, but with the recording technology being mastered by multiple parties, there are now many parties profiting from the performer's work, "productively consuming" it, with the help of recording technology. The process is not entirely under control any more. Even broadcasting technologically multiplies the performance—it is seen on many televisions in many places. But the commercial reproduction and distribution of wayang on VCDs results in a new form of multiplication. The performances can now be stored and controlled by a multitude of VCD owners. On multiple copies of widely distributed recordings, the performances and the Indosiar programmes begin to live a new kind of life and fit into people's lives differently. What remains the same is that the puppeteers have no control over the process in which other people make profit. Speaking of the possibility of people recording and distributing copies of performances for profit, Slenk is quoted saying: "I really don't know about any way how to overcome/master it [*mengatasinya*]." Manteb is said to be *apatis* (apathetic).[46]

There is of course the possibility that the puppeteer himself may try to control the recording technology and profit from it, just like modern performing artists are able to do. The case of Manteb's *Dewa Ruci* is an example of wayang VCDs produced "legally". The recordings were made with Manteb's permission, he shared in the profit, and he was also marketing the VCDs at his performances. In this way, the video recording industry becomes part of the puppeteer's business. However, the first thing that happened was that the VCDs began to be (re)produced/copied by other parties.

There is no enforcement of copyright, and there is a long-standing tradition of what modern business calls "pirating". And while some dhalang—especially those who have been abroad and who are generally closer to modern commercialism—may dream about a modern system which would protect their individual rights, it is difficult to imagine how intellectual property law would fit with the conventions of the wayang world, in which individual creativity and borrowing from others are viewed very differently than in modern Western arts. During the New Order, Anom, Manteb, and Slenk all used scripts written by a puppeteer who was not allowed to perform, and even though they paid him, they never mentioned his name and he did not get paid for subsequent uses. Some of these scripts are copied from older sources, such as periodicals focusing on wayang.[47] Heard on radio and television, they are noted down and used in performances by other puppeteers. The same happens with published texts of wayang plays, new musical compositions, puppet movement, and other innovations.

Here we see again conflicts arising from the difference between the cultures of wayang and television. The puppeteers, as they perform for weddings and circumcisions in villages, but also on television and VCDs, are caught between two different attitudes to copying or learning from others, however one chooses to call it. Indosiar is able to exploit the situation by selectively combining practices and ethics of the two cultures, often justifying its exploitation by referring to traditional practices of copying, as if saying, "look at the puppeteers, they traditionally steal from each other, so it is OK for us to steal for them"—even as the puppeteers look to modern/commercial ideas of copyright when they criticize television.

Sneak preview: We will return to many of these issues—such as the various ways in which video recordings, made by television companies and otherwise, are controlled, manipulated, used, recontextualised and/or enjoyed in a variety of ways by multiple parties, people's views of "piracy", and so on—in the last chapter, in the discussion of wayang videos on the internet, particularly YouTube, where even many years after they were recorded, Indosiar wayang videos (among others) are watched and used. The spectres of wayang produced by Indosiar continue to live a lively afterlife. Some of the illustrations in this chapter [2.1 and 2.3], showing the earliest Indosiar-sponsored performances from 1995, were captured in 2018 from Indosiar videos available on YouTube.

Whereas in Chapter One there was more emphasis on how wayang is haunted and seduced by television and modernity in general, this chapter has focused on how television—the people, the system, the "norms"—tries to objectify, control, manage, and make profit on wayang. In both chapters, there are recurring moments of failure and disappointment. In many cases one feels the resistance to television. So far, the spectators and their images were considered mostly as a force affecting the making of wayang performances and television programmes. The next chapter focuses on the experience of watching wayang on television and on the perspectives of wayang/television viewers.

3

To Be or Not to Be There: Watching *Wayang* on Television[1]

It is late in the afternoon. The hot air makes everything still. I sit on the veranda quietly, only now and then clapping my hands as I try in vain to assassinate a mosquito, and I look forward to going out to watch *wayang* in the evening. I feel refreshed even as I imagine the coolness of the night, the buzz of the many voices and people moving around, the mixture of smells from the food stalls.

I can be sure that there will be several performances in the area on a Saturday night. Which one I decide to go to depends not only on who the puppeteer is, but also on how far away it is, the weather, if I must get up early the following morning, and so on. Usually I prefer watching a performance directly, which means also enjoying the atmosphere, talking to people, eating and drinking at the food stalls, and so on. But there are times when I prefer to stay home and watch a wayang performance on television. You can say I am lazy—but when I am tired I just don't feel like socializing, and, especially if it's raining, the idea of having to go out, getting to the performance, and having to stand for hours in a crowd and to smell other people's sweat and worse, just doesn't appeal to me. Yes, there are times when I prefer to sit on the sofa, sip sweet, hot tea, and watch wayang on television—and if the *dhalang* is no good, I can easily switch to another channel and find either another, hopefully more entertaining wayang performance, or another exciting late-night programme.

One day one watches wayang directly, another day on television. Sometimes one must choose. For Javanese who like wayang, this is a practical question: to watch wayang directly or on television? People answer not theoretically, but by physically moving in the world: staying at home or going out. They answer on the basis of their perception of the differences between the experience of watching wayang directly and watching it on television. This chapter is about this question posed by the present world, and about the basis on which it is answered by people who watch wayang. (In this context, I have hesitantly chosen to use the word "directly" in part because it best approximates the word *langsung*, which is most commonly employed in this context by Indonesians—although some speakers, especially in Javanese conversations, use other phrases, such as *wonten njawi,* "outside". The oversimplification involved in using either "live" and "directly" reflects the intrinsically muddled relationship between the different ways of watching wayang.)

Some people tend to prefer watching wayang directly; others on television. In many cases, the choice depends on the particular moment, the particular circumstances, even the mood. However, as I was talking to people in Java, it became apparent that their comments had one particular attitude about the experience in common, and I was reminded of Maurice Merleau-Ponty's way of describing perception. Both Javanese wayang viewers and Merleau-Ponty talk about perception as inseparable from my body—not a body-object, but my body as I experience it, as it hurts me, as it feels good or cold or hot; as my means of being at a place and in the world. Not everything, but much that is said about watching wayang on television concerns *my body and where I am.*

Especially in this chapter, when I say "television" I mean specifically television in the case of televised wayang. I avoid hypothesizing how televised wayang "could be" watched, but limit myself to the mainstream televised wayang (such as Indosiar and TVRI) as discussed by the Javanese viewers, puppeteers and television producers to whom I have spoken. I focus on their experience, and I do not question to what extent their statements are universally true.

A Taste of Merleau-Ponty's Body

In Merleau-Ponty's descriptions of perception, I perceive with my body, always from somewhere. The perceiving body is not a collection of organs, or an object looked at with indifference, or a being constituted by thought, but my body as I experience it. My body is my means of being in the midst of things. I see through my lived body, and my eyes are organically, indivisibly part of it, because it is a (seeing-hearing-touching-etc.) whole through which I inhabit the (visible-audible-tangible-etc.) world and make it whole. This perceiving body is made of the same stuff as the world, and "[t]he look is itself incorporation of the seer into the visible".[2] Perception is never a "pure sensation", a mechanical, objective registering—as if I were external to the world—but between the visible and me there is "an intimacy as between the sea and the strand".[3]

> The sensor and the sensible do not stand in relation to each other as two external terms, and sensation is not an invasion of the sensor by the sensible. [...] My gaze pairs off with color and my hand with hardness and softness [of an object], and in this transaction between the subject of sensation and the sensible it cannot be held that one acts while the other suffers the action, or that one confers significance on the other. Apart from the probing of my eye or my hands, and before my body synchronizes with it, the sensible is nothing but a vague beckoning. [...] Thus a sensible datum which is on the point of being felt sets a kind of muddled problem for my body to solve [...] And yet I do so only when I am invited by it, my attitude is never sufficient to make me really see blue or really touch a hard surface. The sensible gives back to me what I lent to it, but this is only what I took from it in the first place.[4]

All sensation happens within a totality, "the thickness of some *primal acquisition*" that is beyond that individual sensation, and every sensation is illuminated by this totality, by "*sensibility* which has preceded it and which will outlive it".[5]

There is an intertwining of the seeing and the seen, the touching and the tangible, my body and the world, through which perception becomes possible. Perception is indivisible from being situated and moving in the visible, tangible world, in the midst of things and others; just as my body, if it is to perceive, is indivisible from the flesh of the world; and just as my eye, if I am to see with it, is indivisible from the flesh of my body. It is only by being bodily in the midst of things that I can perceive: "The thickness of the body" is "the sole means I have to go unto the heart of the things, by making myself a world and by making them flesh".[6] The spectator, together with others like him, is part of the spectacle: he "is one of the visibles".[7]

Every perception is organically part of bodily movement and position in the world. When I feel a surface with my hand, the movement, its direction, its speed, are directed by perception, by the thing itself; and perception is only possible because of the movement of my body. "[T]here is not a perception followed by a movement, for both form a system which varies as a whole."[8] It is not my consciousness that moves my eyes or turns my head to see; the eyes move themselves and thus perceive, in response to what they see and anticipate to see, or fixed for a moment by it, in response to the "vague beckoning" of things to my body—in an intimate, silent, sensuous dialogue between my body and the world.

A Difficult Choice: My Body or My Television

While Merleau-Ponty's phenomenology of perception resonates with how Javanese spectators talk about watching wayang, it does *not* apply to watching wayang on television.

As I watch television, I can see and hear things without being bodily present in their midst. Samuel Weber writes: "Ever since Plato, one of the most decisive purposes in the development of art, artifice and technology has been interpreted to be that of overcoming the shortcomings of nature, human or otherwise."[9] In the case of television,

> the limitation that is to be overcome is tied to the individual body. The body as such has always been defined by a certain spatial limitation. A body is understood as something that occupies a determinate extent of space and occupies it exclusively. [...] If television thus names seeing at a distance, what it appears to overcome thereby is the body, or more precisely, the spatial limitations placed by the body upon seeing and hearing.[10]

For Merleau-Ponty, the body is not simply a limitation, but *the* means to perceive and to communicate with the world, the medium of being in the world. Thus, perception for Merleau-Ponty is never absolutely direct or pure but—if we think about the body as something like a medium through which I perceive (even as this "I" cannot be separated from the body)—perception is always already "mediatized", that is, embodied. "Overcoming the body" means giving up this medium of communication with the world. To watch television or to watch wayang directly is a choice between experiencing wayang while being in the midst of the event with my body, and perception which frees me from my body and allows me to see and hear without being physically in the midst of what I see and hear. These are different modes of perception and of being in the world. However, it is not a question of which is better. To be in the midst of things, to have one's perception bound to one's situated body, has its advantages and its disadvantages. Javanese viewers are acutely aware that the experience of watching wayang directly is not limited to the visual and aural registering of what happens on the screen. The pleasure of watching wayang is precisely that of being there, in the midst of it all; being incorporated into the flesh of the world. But having to be there in order to perceive it also has its disadvantages. Similarly, the main disadvantage of watching wayang on television is that one is not physically present in the midst of what one sees and hears. The main advantages of watching wayang on television are connected to being able to stay home, and not having to go to and be present at the performance.

A Problem: Going There and Getting Back

One point that frequently came up in conversations about wayang and television was the problem of going to the performance and getting back. "Not having to go anywhere" is mostly, though not always, seen as an advantage of television, and it is mentioned frequently, even by people who for other reasons prefer watching wayang directly. This may seem banal and unrelated to wayang performance, but if the experience of wayang is seen as a part of life, as it is for Javanese viewers, rather than cut out of the flow of life as an object of study, getting there and back is part of the wayang experience, and it is one way that the experience connects into life. Judging from the frequency with which this motif appeared in the discussions, the fact that one does not have to go there is an important way in which direct experience of wayang differs from wayang on television.

Television enables the spectator to see wayang without him having to go there. What is at stake is distance, and moving from one place to another. Tele-vision overcomes distance. But it is not an "objective" distance measurable in kilometres that is at stake. When wayang spectators talk about getting there, they talk about distance in terms of travelling through it, as bodily effort and comfort or discomfort, as the fatigue and the sore legs, or as the pleasure of travelling, seeing things, and meeting people. This distance may also be expressed in terms of time, but not homogeneous time measurable in minutes and hours, but time as it is experienced, as it makes me tired or relaxed, or as time in which I could do something else. To what extent getting there is a problem is conceived in terms of how busy I am, whether tomorrow I have to get up early, and generally as an experience that is part of my life. Wayang spectators often talk about their mood and about the weather. Often the first response to the question "what is the advantage of watching wayang on TV" is "I don't have to go out into the rain". Getting there is never separate from these various aspects of experienced distance.

How does television cover this distance? Television does not travel through the same space, the same distance that I have to travel when I go to see wayang, a distance that is inseparable from the landscape, my means of travel, the weather, my mood, and my situation. We have seen in previous chapters how television annihilates distance, and the effects of this on puppeteers and wayang. In this chapter, we focus on the experience of the audience, and here again distance is at stake: television conceals—covers—this phenomenological, physically experienced distance, it makes distance disappear, as if by magic: I can stay home, and yet be there.

Thus, when I watch television, I do not move through the same kind of space, in the same world; I do not move in the way that bodily movement is described by Merleau-Ponty. Weber says that television "transports vision as such and sets it immediately before the viewer

[...] it involves a transmission or transposition of vision itself".[11] But what kind of vision is it? It is not (simply) human vision, a vision indivisible from a body. Television is the "most detached kind of vision and audition" and it is "first and foremost a method of *transmission*; and transmission, which is movement, involves separation".[12] This is in a way also true about other kinds of media, and even about listening to a story or imagining. However, there is a difference—and this difference is especially relevant to our case, "event television", or television that claims merely to let people see something taking place elsewhere—which is due to television's

> power to combine such separation with the presentness associated with sense-perception. What television transmits is not so much *images*, as is almost always argued. It does not transmit *representations* but rather the *semblance of presentation as such*, understood as the power not just to see and to hear but *to place before us*. Television thus serves as a surrogate for the body in that it allows certain sense-perception to take place; but it does this in a way that no body can, for its perception takes place in more than one place at a time. Television takes place in taking the place of the body and at the same time transforming both place and body.[...] [Television] overcomes spatial distance but only by *splitting the unity of place* and with it the unity of everything that defines its identity with respect to place: events, bodies, subjects [italics in the original].[13]

Television, as a "surrogate for the body", is present at the wayang performance. It substitutes for my body in the sense that normally I see by means of my body, but now I see by means of television. In the light of what Merleau-Ponty says about the body, we can understand that the effect of television is not only that it makes perception easier by eliminating the lived distance between my body and what I see. The manner of perceiving is essentially different; perception is no longer what Merleau-Ponty claims it to be. Between my body and the world there is television. My perception is no longer inseparable from physically being and moving in the midst of the visible and tangible, my body is no longer part of the world by moving in it and perceiving it, a world in which the visible is also tangible, and the seeing body is also a touching body. The unity of my body, and the unity of the world, is *split*, and my sight is detached from my body, from the place and the movements of my body.

To see how this difference is important specifically in the experience of wayang, we will have to look at more than going-there. At this point, however, note that by bringing up going-there as a major difference between watching wayang on television and experiencing it directly, Javanese viewers point to what is at the heart of the difference between experiencing wayang directly and watching it on television: the difference between distance—space, world—which I have to travel if I want to experience wayang directly and the (non)distance of television; the difference between moving with my body in the midst of things, and being beyond lived space and distance. We see here, now from the perspective of the audience, the annihilation of distance that we discussed in previous chapters. Javanese spectators talk about their experiences in a way that suggests that perceiving (wayang) directly is indivisible from physical movement (going-there, for instance), from *where* I am physically, from the situation; and that watching wayang on television alters perception by altering my relation to what I see—the relation between vision and the visible, me and the world—in terms of bodily position and movement.

I should note that while most people attend to the unpleasant aspects of *having* to travel to the performance, some also note that there is something pleasant about the "suffering".

> If you watch [wayang] in a village, you walk in the mud, the only light you have is a torch—it's between complaining and enjoying it [*antara mengeluh dan enjoy*], hahahaha! "*Wah*, it's so dark on the road!"—but you enjoy it too, hahahaha! That can't be replaced!

One may think again back to our discussion of light and darkness in Chapter One. Television annihilates darkness, not only by lighting up wayang and making it visible in new ways, but also by annihilating the experience of walking on a dark and muddy road.

To Be or Not to Be There in the Midst of It

Watching wayang on television is different from watching it directly not only because I do not *go* there, but also because I *am* not there. When contrasting watching wayang directly and on television, wayang spectators speak about watching wayang *langsung* ("directly"), but also about wayang *wonten njawi* ("outside"), *wonten tarub* ("in *tarub*"; *tarub* is the temporary open shelter in which wayang usually takes place), or *wonten ndhusun* ("in the village"). These terms suggest that the difference between watching wayang directly and on television relates to the *place* and *situation*; and that it is this watching-as-being-at-a-place, this situated watching, that is affected when wayang is watched on television. In the following sections I consider specific aspects of what being-there and not-being-there involves for Javanese wayang spectators.

To Be or Not to Be Among Other People

One aspect of being there in the midst of it is being in the midst of other people. This, it appears from various comments, is an essential part of the experience of watching wayang and one motivation to watch wayang directly rather than on television. It is often pointed out that—in contrast to watching wayang on television—when watching wayang outside, the atmosphere is important. When watching wayang directly, people say, one usually watches with friends, with many other people (*kancane akeh*), rather than alone or with only a few others. Part of the pleasure of watching wayang directly, it is emphasized, is talking to people, meeting new friends, and eating or drinking together in the stalls that surround the performance area. These experiences are lost, or altered, when wayang is seen on television. Few people look at the wayang screen and the puppets from beginning to end of the all-night performance. As people watch, their attention fluctuates: when there is an interesting scene, they concentrate more on the action; when they are less interested, they watch other things or talk to people. One interacts with others, but, people say, one also enjoys watching them—as they are served food, as they come and go, as the musicians smoke and talk between playing, and generally, as one spectator put it, one watches "the audience atmosphere" (*suasana penonton*). One puppeteer reflected: "In the case of wayang, what is important is how A meets B and they talk while watching wayang. This is what I don't see on television." And he suggested that to simulate this experience, "the camera should go around and look at the *sate* seller as he fans [the coals under the grill], look at people talking, look at people as they gossip, look at people selling toy-puppets, look at little children ... *that* is wayang, *that*"—but, as he said, at present wayang on television is *not* like that.

The interaction with other people is not talked about as a pleasure separate from watching wayang, but as an integral part of the experience.

3.1 Other plays/shows that are part of wayang: playing chess. (Photo Martin Hatch.)

Altering this aspect of the experience—physically separating myself from others by separating my vision from my body, watching without being bodily present in the midst of what I see, as happens when I watch television—alters the experience of watching wayang.

One viewer said that "watching wayang is not just watching wayang". What does this mean? Watching wayang is not what one may think it is. It is not just looking at the screen, it also involves—among other things—social interaction and watching people. Perception is not just mechanical registering of visual data, but it inheres in my body, it is inseparable from the situation I am in, it is a "communication between me and the world", part of which is being among others.

How is my being-in-the-midst-of-others part of my perception? How is what I see affected by being in the midst of others? Merleau-Ponty:

> My friend Paul and I point out to each other certain details of the landscape; [...] my gestures invade Paul's world and guide his gaze. When I think of Paul, I do not think of a flow of sensations indirectly related to mine through the medium of interposed signs, but of someone who has a living experience of the same world as mine, as well as the same history, and with whom I am in communication through that world and that history.[14]

It is not only others' gestures that invade my world and guide my gaze, but more generally, the other people that I perceive shape my perception of the world and guide me through it with their behaviour, bodily movements and attitudes. Merleau-Ponty emphasizes that

> it is precisely my body which perceives the body of another, and discovers in that other body a miraculous prolongation of my own intentions, a familiar way of dealing with the world. Henceforth, as the parts of my body together comprise a system, so my body and the other's are one whole, two sides of one and the same phenomenon, and the anonymous existence of which my body is the ever-renewed trace henceforth inhabits both bodies simultaneously.[15]

For us, the main implication of this "intercorporeity" is this:

> No sooner has my gaze fallen upon a living body in process of acting than the objects surrounding it immediately take on a fresh layer of significance: they are no longer simply what I myself make of them, they are what this other pattern of behavior is about to make of them.[16]

As I watch wayang, the presence of others and their gestures and behaviour "invades" my way of seeing and "guides" it, and things "take on fresh layer of significance". Perception is a social act, it involves this mutual and mostly preconscious "guiding", it involves interaction with people. Talking to people while watching wayang, and perceiving wayang while being in the midst of people, are of the same nature and are indivisible; they are two aspects of the same experience, of watching wayang with others.

Merleau-Ponty's notion of intercorporeity suggests that the wayang performance "take[s] on a fresh layer of significance" due to the bodily presence of others. This happens on many levels: as I may follow the gaze of another person, as I am affected by the attention of another person to what happens on the screen or somewhere else, as I look at a person eating and I get hungry and go to a food stall, or as I notice people sleeping on the ground and I lay down too. A young spectator said that a big difference between watching wayang on television and directly is that when watching directly, "I can watch the atmosphere of people who are watching, and my emotion can join in [...] Sometimes the dhalang performs something spectacular or displays a skill, and a wave of emotion emerges, '*Wah! Wah!*' [Wow! Wow!]." In contrast, while watching wayang on television, according to him, one tends to be "less focused" and "the emotion is not driven there" because watching wayang on television "tends to be only inner". "Inner" is in Javanese often opposed to "outer" with the connotation of the opposition of the "spiritual" to the "bodily". The statement—"only inner"—thus suggest that there is something "disembodied" about watching wayang on television, when one is not in the midst of a crowd. In contrast, the spectator continued, when watching wayang directly "it's like watching a football game, there are other people, from the beginning one can enter/be involved [*mlebu*], one can chat, one can '*Wah!*'" He said that wayang is "more alive" when watched directly because—and the key word here is "join (in)"—

> whatever we watch directly, our emotion can join in. For instance, when I watch football, and the people are shouting, we can join in feeling it [*bisa ikut merasakan*], because we are at that place. I think in all cases when we are at the place where the thing is happening, our feeling can join in [*isa katut*]. From the beginning we join in enjoying it and from the beginning we enter into the same condition and then [we, our feelings] rise upon [perceiving] the same thing, rise together [*munggahe bareng*].

This, it is said, does not happen to the same extent when one watches wayang on television (even though one may watch television with other people), but it is often suggested that television could, in theory, simulate this, and to a limited extent it does in practice. One viewer said that he would like it if wayang spectators were shown more often on television, so that he "can join in laughing". Another person said that it is good when one can see the audience during a televised wayang because "this way the television viewers at home feel that they are part of the people who watch [at the performance]", but he also said that "some things [about watching wayang directly] can't be replaced". While television may to some extent try to simulate the experience of being in the midst of other viewers—another sign of how important this aspect of wayang is—people generally agree that the particular human interaction and atmosphere that is a part of watching wayang directly, is missing when one watches wayang on television.

To be more precise: the wayang-ly social interaction that is part of wayang experience is missing and imperfectly simulated, but because of its absence—because I am not at the performance—it can be replaced by social behaviour specifically associated with television. I focus on watching television at home, either alone or in a small circle of family and/or friends, because for most of the people to whom I talked, this was the typical context. Other contexts—watching with a number of friends or neighbours, for instance—even though often closer to a communal experience, and thus to watching live wayang, are still very different from the social atmosphere of watching wayang directly. The difference is not just in the number of people, but in atmosphere, in feeling—between a bustling crowd at festive event and a small group of a few acquaintances or neighbours. It is also a matter of separation of the spectators from the performers.

While most people talk about the pleasures of watching wayang directly and being in the midst of many people, a number of viewers also recognize the pleasures of televisual sociality. Only one viewer I talked to, Laksono, preferred the sociality of television, and though his view is not predominant, the advantages of television that he points out can be occasionally felt from other people's comments. Like for most wayang spectators, for Laksono a major difference between watching wayang live and on television—in addition to going there—is that when watching wayang live, one watches with many people. While most people like this, for Laksono the advantage of television is that there are *not* many friends or people. When he watches directly (which he also often does), "there are too many friends/companions" (*kekathahan rencang*), and he cannot see well—he said that in this respect watching wayang directly is more like "watching an [audio] cassette" (*kados nonton tep*), and he cannot listen to the dhalang without being disturbed. (To "see well", clear visibility: is this desire a product of the age of television?) Moreover, for him an advantage of watching wayang on television is that he "can be together with his family" (*isa jagongan kalih keluarga*), and "watching television together is part of having a happy life [*klebet hidup bahagia sejahtera*]". In contrast, "when the father goes here and there, happy family life is not guaranteed". In the middle of the Javanese-language conversation, he said "family" and "happy family life" in Indonesian—a phrase from official Indonesian discourse (birth control propaganda, textbooks, etc.)—which suggests that *this* particular conception of happy family life—watching television together—is not felt to be Javanese in the way that wayang is, but it is something that more recently penetrated into Java, like television. In fact, Laksono explicitly called this advantage of television—the happy family life— "progress" (*kemajengan*)—one can hear here echoes of New Order images of the state as a happy family, as well as early American advertisements for television that emphasized the benefits of television on family life, or the historical roots of modern media in bourgeois society. In any case, it is clear that watching wayang on television is associated with its own way of being-with-others, which at least some people prefer. While few people talk quite like Laksono, several mentioned that when one watches television one can be *sante* (relaxed), in part because one stays home and does not have to be among people. One man said that even though he otherwise prefers watching wayang directly, it is, on the other hand, also nice to be able to watch wayang at home with his wife. Both the advantages and the disadvantages of television derive from the same characteristic of television, not having to be physically there in the midst of many people watching wayang, but rather staying at home.

Performing wayang involves an interaction among the performers, and between the performers and the audience. *Watching* wayang directly involves not only interaction among spectators, but among all the people present, and an important part of this is the interaction between the audience and the performers. One dhalang said:

> Technology can only produce a good product. But a direct performance is alive. So, there is an event/affair between the performer and us [the spectators]. If we are touched, if it is felt, that is life. When we watch a dance, in a palace or somewhere, we can lose ourselves/drift away, directly, because it is direct. [...] When this becomes a TV programme, that is technology—merely good, but not alive.

In contrast to live performance, he said, on television "there is not an affair/phenomenon [*peristiwa*] of *persenyawaan*". The root of the word *persenyawaan* is *nyawa* which means "life" or like the Latin *anima* , "life-soul"; the prefix *se-* signifies a union, here of multiple *nyawa*; and the combination of *per-* and *-an* signifies a process. Thus *persenyawaan* is something like "the process of uniting lives/souls", and it is this that does not happen when one watches television. Another person spoke about wayang performance as the performer's "living interaction with the people who watch", and he contrasted watching wayang live and seen on TV: "This is a person, [whereas] this is a picture; in fact, not a picture, but electron-dots! Hahahahaha ...". Incidentally, if in previous chapters we have seen that television claims to "just bring" wayang to people's homes, to claim that what people see is reality and not simulacra, we see here what is the thoughtful answer of at least some of the viewers to television's self-proclaimed power: "Hahahahaha ...".

Several people compared this to the difference between meeting a person and seeing her photograph. A television producer in charge of wayang who is also a dancer said:

> When the dhalang produces a kind of energy that the Balinese call *taksu*, which is very, very difficult to capture with a camera. But if we look with a naked eye, not with the television medium, the power of this energy of the dhalang whom I consider to have taksu can be captured. But as soon as [wayang] enters television, the power cannot be captured.

Another Javanese dancer explained that taksu is an "inner power", but it is not just "charisma", but "it is more *here*"—and he pointed at his chest, emphasizing the physicality of taksu. He said that when he dances, he absorbs energy from space and from the people who watch, and he showed with one hand the energy from the people present, as constantly moving, swirling around, and with the other hand he showed the performer's energy—first the two were separate, and then the "performer's energy" gradually joined in the movement of the "audience energy", as if letting itself be carried in the whirling movement. In the case of wayang, he explained, the energy comes from "everybody around, including the sellers at food stalls and the people who eat there". This, he said, does not happen when one watches wayang on television.

One thing to note about these descriptions is that the interaction between the performers and the audience is mutual, that the audience's experience of the event is affected by the performers, and the performers' by the audience. The puppeteer Anom Suroto, very frequently featured on Indosiar, told me that even when his performance is televised, he prefers it when there are many spectators physically present,

> because if not, the studio-recording is clean but dead [*resik namung pejah*]. It does not have a feeling of energy. This is what I feel myself ... It is unpleasant [when there are

> not many spectators], because this cannot animate/make alive the dhalang [*mboten saged nggesangaken si dhalang*], because he sees only his musicians, and the musicians are already used to just following him. But it is different when many people watch—that can inspire the performance.

Ki Tristuti, a widely respected dhalang and Anom's mentor, said:

> In the public performance, there is fresh air, many people gather, there is atmosphere, the waiters serve food to the guests—that too is something that is not found when we watch television. On television, we *just* watch *that*—and the electric rays hurt our eyes. So you get sleepy. But in a public place, you can watch the waiters serving food, you can watch a guest leaving, first taking his leave of the sponsor of the performance, so—hahaha. That's pleasant. And when the dhalang is skilful, all this can be brought through jokes onto the screen—yeah, that is nice!

That the dhalang himself is constantly "inspired" by the people present, by the "energy" of their presence and by all that is happening at the performance-event, that he "brings" all this "onto the screen", into play—this shows again how interpersonal interaction is central to the event, and that watching is not separate from the whole of social interaction that is the performance, the state of being together, the "intercorporeity". Merleau-Ponty writes that "[i]t is more accurate to say that I see according to [a painting], or with it, than I see it".[17] Viewers see the screen and the dhalang *according to* or *with* other people, and they see the other people and the whole event, the human interaction, *according to* and *with* the screen and the dhalang, who encourages this perception by bringing the whole social event onto the screen. A viewer prefers watching directly because, unlike on television, "it is as if ... when I join in watching the puppeteer, I join in playing [*sudah ikut main*] when I watch directly". Perception here is a feeling of other people's movements in my body. It is this constant interaction, this process of fusion of the perceived and the perceiving, of what is happening on the screen and what is happening among the people present (performers, audience, others), that is "split" on television when the spectator is no longer in the midst of what is happening, and watching wayang is no longer a direct, living interaction among people physically present at the same place.

My exposition of the experience of watching wayang has broader social implications. Often, a person watches wayang because he is invited to a celebration of which wayang is a part, or he or she may be a family member of one of the sponsors, or one of the many people involved in the organization of the event. A person's presence at the performance event is an affirmation of the person's belongingness to his or her community—status, relationship to the sponsors and other guests, belongingness to the particular village that usually as a whole participates in preparing the event. This is part of the total experience of watching wayang. Wayang is a deeply social experience, in which what happens on the screen and what happens around it reflect each other.[18]

When one watches wayang on television, one participates in society in a different way. The spectator is then an individual whose particular relationship to the sponsor, other guests, the village, and the community, is not reflected in and affirmed by watching wayang. Were one to use Louis Dumont's terms, one could say that one watches live wayang rather as a member of a "holistic society" and television as an "individual".[19] The departure, in the case of watching wayang on television, from social holism and from perceptual holism (perceiving through the whole, situated body) are two aspects of the same process. Watching wayang is a way of being with and relating to other people, a way of being part of a community. This being-with-others is what is affected by television.

Touching-Smelling-Tasting-Eating-Breathing-Seeing Wayang

When Javanese spectators talk about watching wayang directly, they almost always mention the pleasure of drinking and eating at the food stalls at the performance, or being served food and drink when they are present as guests. When they compare the experience to watching wayang on television, they often talk about breathing the fresh air outside, about "night air", or about the pleasant breeze, as well as about unpleasant cold and rain, and the possibility of catching a cold.

But is not this separate from *watching* wayang? But if it is, why do Javanese wayang fans talk about it as something that belongs to watching wayang? We should rather ask: Why and how are these experiences felt as part of watching wayang?

3.2 Drinking and chatting at a coffee shop at a wayang performance. (Photo Martin Hatch.)

Is there a confusion in the way that people talk about sense-perception? I talk about television as a kind of vision—but television involves both seeing and hearing. People talk about watching (*nonton*) wayang, which suggests primarily visual perception—but people talk not only about seeing but also breathing the night air, feeling cold, or eating *sate*. Or does this confusion—this overflowing of the meaning of words relating to vision to include other senses—reveal something important? Is perhaps seeing, watching, vision indivisible from the other senses, is seeing also hearing-touching-breathing-feeling-tasting-etc.?

We need not go into the question why seeing is in many languages, including English and Javanese, privileged as the sense to comprise all other senses as well as knowing (as when I say "I see!" and mean

"I understand", or "*Ayo nonton sekatenan!* ["Let's watch *sekaten* night market!", which means walking, pushing one's way through and being pushed around by crowds, shopping, hearing music, tasting snacks and drinks, smoking, and so on]). In some cases, a reference to an action or sensation other than seeing and watching can similarly imply a broader experience. Think about the implications of statements such as: "Let's have a drink!" or "Will you sleep with me?" In either case, what is meant involves more than drinking and sleeping, and those other things may be in fact more significant than the drinking and sleeping. We need to see how, in yet another way, "watching wayang is not just watching wayang", and how this more-fully-understood watching of wayang directly is different from watching wayang on television.

Perception through the different senses is not separate but originally one, just as my eyes, ears, nose, tongue, and skin are not separable parts of my body. It is with my body that I perceive the night air, not with different parts of my body separately. Oenologists remind us that olfactory perception contributes to what people experience as the taste of wine, and red wine enhances the flavour of red meat in part because of its colour. People do not misinterpret their experience; rather, taste as experienced involves the olfactory as well as visual perception (among many other things: a wine "tastes" good also depending on with what and with whom I drink it, how I feel, etc.). The "watching" of wayang, as Javanese fans talk about it, involves the living body *as a whole*, rather than eyes and ears on one tray and nose and tongue on another. This unity of the body is also the unity of the world I perceive. In my experience, there is not an audible world and a tangible world and a visible world which I consciously combine; rather, there is a single physical, "fleshy" world of which my body is part and which it perceives. This is why Javanese spectators can speak about eating *bakso* or about the night air as an integral part of watching wayang.

Watching television involves seeing and hearing (tastes, smells, and other sensations are evoked indirectly, through sights and sounds). Television involves a degree of separation of eyes and ears from the rest of the body; of seeing-hearing from touching and smelling and other bodily sensations; of the visible-audible from the world wherein I am with my body. Television breaks the unity of the body, and establishes seeing-hearing as separable from the rest of the bodily sensation. This newly separable seeing-hearing is a different seeing-hearing and "television is a new kind of vision"; because the unity of the body is split, watching wayang on television is different from watching wayang live. What I see is a different world.

Watching wayang directly involves perception with one's whole body that is in the midst of what it perceives, and watching wayang on television is a new kind of seeing-hearing wayang during which my fleshy body stays at home. There is an enjoyment in watching with my whole body, in touching-smelling-tasting-eating-breathing-seeing-and-otherwise-sensing wayang. This way of experiencing wayang is described in contrast to the televisual experience of watching, it's something that is missing when I watch wayang on television.

By separating seeing-hearing from the wholeness of the body, the televisual experience not only prevents me, as I sit on the sofa, from certain enjoyments, but it has its advantages as well. Rain and weather are often mentioned as an adversity from which television can save me. The "night air", for many a pleasure of watching wayang, is at other moments or for other people a reason to avoid watching wayang directly. In short, by enabling me to watch wayang without having to be physically present in the midst of what I watch, television protects my body from discomfort, and this protection is an advantage of television. Not-having-to-be-there also means that I can be at home. While most people say it is more fun to eat outside the home and it gives one greater choice, some people also talk about the pleasure of sitting at home and drinking hot coffee, and staying dry and warm when it rains outside. As one person said, "it is a different kind of fun" [*ada keasyikan yang berbeda*]. At home, "I can watch with my wife, while drinking coffee, not having to be cold"; in the village, "there is the atmosphere, people sell *ronde*, and there are all kinds of other food stalls". That he mentions wife and coffee in the same breath reminds us that what we have said about being-there in this section—about touching-smelling-tasting-eating-breathing-seeing-hearing-and-otherwise-sensing—is only one aspect of what we discussed in the previous section—watching wayang as social interaction—only one aspect of (not) being there in the midst of it.

Moving-Perceiving: Human Perception and/or/as the Jumping Squirrel

As I watch wayang on television, I am shown a succession of views—the dhalang from behind and the screen with the puppets, then perhaps a long shot of the gamelan ensemble, then a close up of the face of a female singer, then the hands of a musician, then a close-up of a puppet. Television simulates the way I see. As I watch wayang live, too, I attend to various things, and television tries to select things that would interest the television spectator. Javanese spectators say that "the camera's eye represents the spectator's eyes" (*mata kamera mewakili mata penonton*)—"represent" in the sense of acting as deputy or agent. There are two visions, mine and the camera's, and as I watch television, my eyes are "represented" by the camera's eye. I see through the camera's "eye"—I do not simply look at television; television sees on my behalf as my deputy, my agent. This is its power, but also its problem—because it is *its* power. Javanese spectators also say that "the eye of the camera *should* [*seharusnya*] represent the eyes of the spectator", which implies that in reality the deputy of my eyes does not represent my eyes very well. The problem, one person said, is that "the look of our eyes differs from the look of the camera's eye". A television producer said:

> When we see with the naked eye, we edit it ourselves [*kita edit sendiri*]. ... That way, this way, there, then here—right? *Des*—we want to see that, so we look there, right? At this moment it is *our own* wish [what we choose to see]. ... Oh, I want to look there, because that is interesting for me. But it is different with the television editor. Because his basis is not only his inner vision ... but his basis is the existing norms [of television production].

The problem is that television represents my eyes, but it sees differently than me, it "edits" differently than I "edit" what I see. One reason that television, compared to myself, is a bad "editor", is because it is not me: I choose what I look at on the basis of what I see, while television chooses that for me, as my deputy, and its choices are not always the choices I would make, and more importantly, the whole process of seeing is different, as is my involvement in the process. What is at stake is my attention and my focus, and who or what is in control of what I attend to. Who and what: in the quotation above we see that the producer decides on the basis of "existing norms"—something beyond him that he does not quite control, a larger-than-me, impersonal technological system or culture.

What happens when I attend to something?

> To pay attention is not merely to elucidate pre-existing data, it is to bring about a new articulation of them by taking them as *figures*. They are preformed only as *horizons* [...] Thus attention is [...] the active constitution of a new object which makes explicit and articulates what was until then presented as no more than an indeterminate horizon.[20]

At stake is the "new articulation", the "active constitution" of what I perceive. When I watch television, something or somebody else constitutes my vision for me. I still make sense of the montage of shots, but I am presented with ready-made building blocks produced by an attention that is not my own, rather than with an indeterminate horizon—the "vague beckonings"—to which I reply with my bodily movement, attention, and focus. At stake is the communication between my body and the world—perception itself—because something other than my own body—the television *medium*—is between me and what I perceive, because not my body, but something else, is in the midst of what I see. Television acts as a substitute for me in the process of constituting what I see.

We have seen in Chapter Two that puppeteers complain about how the television editor selects what is seen on television, especially in close-ups. For example, Manteb told me how during the performance of the story *Sugriwa-Subali*, in which the two characters fight, at the climactic moment in the story when Subali is shot dead by a third character, "the arrow was just about to kill Subali when this [television] focused on the gong-player! ... And when the camera returned [to show the screen], he [Subali] was already dead! It all failed! ... [That's what happens] when the one who shoots is an idiot!" Viewers of wayang on television voice the same complaints about close-ups, that is, televisual attention. Even some people who agree that when used in the right way close-ups may be useful, criticize *what* is shown in close-up *when*; they complain that television attends to things that are not important at the moment. One person whispered in my ear during an interview—so that my tape-recorder couldn't capture the dangerous secret: "My feeling is this: *television is a dictator!*" And he explained:

> [Suppose] Mas Jan is [i.e., you are] shown on television, and I am watching. I am interested—if you pardon me—in your glasses. I desire a close up of Mas Jan's glasses—but that is not on the programme of the production director! ... *Lhaa*, my desire is not fulfilled! But if I look at Mas Jan giving a lecture, it is possible [to focus on the glasses]. Well, this is what annoys me [when I watch television]. ... I can't choose! Everything is chosen by the producer! And if the producer does not know, it's a disaster!

I cannot focus on what I wish to see, because television does not know what I want to see (though it may try to guess)—television has a different "programme", and it "dictates" what I see. Normally, as I am about to see something, I bring into my dialogue with the world my own preconscious and conscious understanding of the world and my personal interests, but television prevents me from doing that to some extent, and it constitutes the visible without having *my* understanding of it or *my* interest in it, without knowing me. Moreover, people often complain that "the cameraman doesn't know wayang". In this case it is television's lack of understanding of wayang that makes it "a disaster". In sum, television compels me to see in the way it sees, and thus it is felt to be a "dictator". What's worse, television does not have a good understanding of what it "sees"—so the "dictator" is an "idiot" (Manteb's word).

The metaphor of the dictator, the sense that television controls what and how people see and do not see, how they are in the world and how they are (or not) with other people—these observations reveal a power struggle between television and its audiences. We have seen in previous chapters that in our case television, business and (local and state) politics are indivisibly entangled, and the politics of watching television are a part of a larger complex of political and economic relations and processes. We are getting a glimpse of this here on a level that is particularly close to actual seeing. Also, it is significant that viewers have a degree of critical awareness, they keep trying to see for themselves, and in that sense, to an extent they resist the forces that attempt to control their vision. I will return to this point at the end of this chapter.

A related kind of complaint challenges more generally the dominance of the close-up on television.

> Those who are used to watching wayang in fact don't like too many cameras. ... What's important, they can watch from the front of the screen, or from behind—that's enough. For Javanese like my mother, my uncle, my neighbours, when the camera changes a lot, moves continually, moves here, moves there—oh, they don't like that! They like more static, long shots, [from] afar, but taking in everything. At the most, when the female singer is pretty, *njluuuut* [zooming in], close up—hahahaha ... but if the *kepyak* is taken [i.e., focused on], *gender* is taken, the *gambang, rebab, gong*—hahahaha—an extreme close-up, like if it is this close, huge like this, the picture—they don't like it!

This preference for a "broader view" and a dislike of close-ups hold true for many viewers. One prefers watching directly because he "can see all the activities", while on television "now you see it, now you don't". Watching directly,

> I can see the spreading-out of wayang and the musicians the whole night, but not on television: the dhalang for a moment, the female singer for a moment. It's unpleasant: it's not whole [*utuh*], it's only for a moment, I am not satisfied. ... When the *pesindhen* is shown, I can't see the dhalang.

Another viewer said that on television "[now] the picture is close, [now] the picture is far; the advantage of watching directly is that it can be constant". Another disliked that "on the television, the shooting is back and forth [*wolak-walik*, i.e., from different angles], not in one direction". The word *utuh* (whole, complete), appears frequently: watching directly, "it" can be complete, while on television one gets, in the words of one person, "cut-up pieces" (*sepotong-sepotong*). The "wholeness" that is sacrificed in close-ups is the indeterminate horizon of things, the unseen visible that surrounds everything I see and that invites me to attend to it like "a kind of muddled problem for my body to solve". Instead, television presents me with a world organized and to some extent rid of the mystery of vision, a world that can dispense with the world-constituting power of my body. We can think back to what has been said about clarity and shadows in Chapter One: in this case, what is not fully seen, that on which I do not (yet) focus but which is the ground of everything I see and to which my sight responds, is replaced by television with ready-made, clear, newly ordered sights.

We have discussed the difference between the way that I experience the distance between my home and the place of the performance on the one hand, and how, on the other, television "covers" this distance by being at two places at once. That my seeing-hearing is separated from my bodily position and movement when I watch television, and that this disembodied seeing-hearing—television—does not move through the space the way I do, that it can be at more than one place at a time, is also important for understanding close-ups.

In many descriptions of televisual attention by Javanese spectators, attention is discussed in terms of movement, position, and direction, specifically that of the "camera's eye", the televisual movement of varying perspectives and foci. This kind of movement is contrasted to the movement that is part of the experience of wayang performance. Note that they talk of moving around as part of watching wayang. One spectator said: "I can look for another view—[for example] if I don't like a battle-scene, I can walk away." Another said that when watching directly, "I can change views, I can talk to people"; another: "I can joke with friends, go out for a moment to buy something, return; Limbuk and Cangik [clown-servants] aren't funny so I take a nap—that's a part of the enjoyment of *wayang kulit*." Manteb said that people get more easily bored or sleepy when they watch wayang on television than when they watch directly, because "when viewers watch directly [and], let's say, [they feel:] '*Wah*, this audience-scene is taking a long time!' They can go out to drink, smoke, eat, or watch the female singer." Watching wayang—which also involves socializing, looking at people, eating, and generally being in the midst of it all—involves bodily movement (eye movement, turning of the head, walking to a food stall) that is an aspect of my changing focus. As I move about, I do so in order to have a different view or to attend to another aspect of the wayang experience. Moving about is not merely a means to get from one place to another, but it is inseparable from touching-smelling-tasting-eating-breathing-seeing-and-otherwise-sensing. I perceive only by physically moving in response to what I perceive and what I intend to perceive. Moreover, each perception is framed in a bodily position or movement, it is "made sense of" (on a preconscious level) in the context of my bodily movement or position.

> If I draw the object closer to me or turn it round in my fingers in order "to see it better," this is because each attitude of my body is for me, immediately, the power of achieving a certain spectacle, and because each spectacle is what it is for me in a certain kinesthetic situation. [...] [A]ppearances are always enveloped for me in a certain bodily attitude.[21]

Javanese spectators talk about perception that is bound to a body, and therefore moving about in the performance area, such as going to have a drink or just walking around to stretch one's legs, is part of watching, inseparable from the movement of my eyes and variation in perspective.

When I watch wayang on television, my seeing-hearing no longer inheres in my body. I see the performance as if from different places and different distances, but this variation is not effected by bodily movement, but by television. A curious term, used by Indonesian cameramen, relates to the rapid televisual alternation of attention and perspectives: *bajing loncat*, or "the jumping squirrel". The humorous analogy describes televisual vision in terms of bodily movement, but the body with which I see is no longer a human body. It is as if I had the eyes and body of a squirrel, as if I moved like a squirrel. I would like to ask the honoured reader to take a moment and imagine that he or she has the body of a squirrel rather than a human body, that he or she is jumping like a squirrel from one tree to another, surfing through the air, and looking at the world in this way.[22] Admittedly, watching television is not *precisely* like this, but the analogy points to the heart of the matter: when I watch wayang on television, I don't do it with my own physical human body. My vision is separated from my own body and if this strange vision is felt to be bound to another body—and, as the analogy shows, I tend to envision vision as bound to a body—it must be a body of a quite different nature, infinitely lighter, fleshless body (from a human perspective), a body that is almost a non-body, a body that can leap through space almost as if it were not subject to gravity, and see the world in quite a different way than I do with my fleshy, fatty body, without moving through space the way I have to, without experiencing space the way I do. If "the eye of the camera represents the eyes of the viewer", it is these squirrelesque eyes that are the surrogate of my own eyes.

An Indonesian research report on how wayang should be shown on television discusses the "'TV jumping squirrel' problem" (*masalah "bajing loncat TV"*) and "the 'jumping squirrel' syndrome" (*sindrom "bajing loncat"*).[23] Like Javanese viewers' comments discussed earlier, it compares the visual movement of changing points of view on television to the physical position and movement of viewers watching directly, and it concludes that although typically the viewers are moving about at a performance, it is a different movement, and results in different perception, than the rapid alternation of perspectives on television:

> The viewers are free not to watch from one direction all the time. Changing the direction of viewing, it appears, has become a habit in the wayang kulit performance, although the reasons for this movement of viewing direction need to be further researched. What is certain, the reasons are not the same as the reasons of a production director as he mixes the views from different directions.[24]
>
> Except when the place is extremely crowded, it is still possible for viewers to move from one place to another, because they are bored, want to be closer to the female

> singer, want to pee, etc. [...] In the new place he returns to the state of "*watching from one place/direction/distance*." So the eyes of the viewer still cannot follow the cameras' "numerous eyes" in a TV broadcast. If the camera were to follow this viewer movement, it would mean including also the scene [*adegan*] of places where people eat, the pretty female singers, the comedians, etc.[25]

The phrase "cameras' 'numerous eyes'" is another interesting metaphor. It suggests, not a body with many eyes, but many eyes not bound to a body, floating about in the space. This gives a feeling of the way that televisual perception is not involved in, not bound to my body, the place where I am physically present, my point of view.

The research report's main aim is to address problems of televising wayang, and the problem of the "jumping squirrel", it appears from the report, relates to spatial orientation. As television viewers are shown alternate shots from different perspectives and even from behind the screen, occasionally they are "confused about spatial orientation" and "lose orientation of left and right".[26]

Why is the viewer confused? While normally "each spectacle is what it is for me in a certain kinesthetic situation" and "appearances are always enveloped for me in a certain bodily attitude", this is no longer the case when my eyes are separate from my body. "[C]lear perception and assured action [are] possible only in a phenomenal space which is orientated."[27] When I watch television, too, I look for cues in order to orient myself, and television, as the "deputy" of my eyes, helps me by simulating human orientation—most obviously, it generally retains the horizontal/vertical orientation of space, and it helps me orient by "establishing shots" and organizing the different shots so that the spatial relationships among them are clear—but occasionally it fails, and the viewer "loses" one's orientation, that is, becomes confused about how he is situated in relation to the visible, and the spectacle becomes confusing because it is no longer "in a certain kinesthetic situation" and it is not "enveloped for me in a certain bodily attitude". While normally "there is an immediate equivalence between the orientation of the visual field and the awareness of one's own body as the potentiality of that field",[28] when I watch television I see with a simulated, "virtual body",[29] "the eye of the camera", and I orient in the visual field with that virtual body, simulating embodiment, because it is only with a body that I can orient myself and thus perceive. Hence the physicality of the metaphors like "eye of the camera", "jumping squirrel", and "numerous eyes", that all suggest that I see as if with a non-human body.

The report suggests this cure for disorientation:

> When it is decided that [the camera's point of view] moves from outside to inside [i.e., from the shadow side to the puppeteer's side of the screen], the first scene should be put into [computer] memory [*dimemori*], and then with computer-graphics-TV equipment the scene should be rotated from one point of view to the other, and dissolved into the following point-of-view/scene. So, the viewer will know that the camera "invites/urges" the viewer to move to another place, from the back of the screen to the front or the other way around, so that [the viewer] does not lose orientation of right-left, and the "jumping squirrel" syndrome is reduced.[30]

The manipulation of images envisioned here is a long way from the present way of showing wayang on television, but it shows how the disorientation is thought about as the viewer not being able to follow the camera with his virtual body, his virtual body is lost in space, disoriented, and this has to be prevented by "'inviting/urging' the viewer to move to another place", so that he can make sense of—see—what is shown to him. The "movement" and "place" meant here are of course movement of a virtual body and a virtual place, a virtual "kinesthetic situation", because my fleshy body remains at an actual place, at home in front of the television.

I see and move with a virtual, jumping-squirrel-like body, I see with "the numerous eyes of the camera(s)", or as Dennis Marks of BBC said about televised opera, you get "the equivalent of being in about eight different opera seats at the same time"[31]—it is not important which metaphor or description one uses, as long as one gets a feeling of the difference from normal perception.

Watching Three Wayang Performances at Once, and the Therapeutic Effects of Television on Jumping Squirrel's Nostalgia

One Saturday evening, armed with fried bananas, I joined two volunteer night watchmen at the Neighbourhood Security Post. It was just before eleven, and we were watching the recently popular, weekly *Ketoprak Humor*, an adaptation of a traditional Javanese theatrical form to television. After a while, one of us switched channels to TVRI Surabaya, which was broadcasting wayang. But the puppeteer was not so good, and we switched back to *Ketoprak Humor*. Around midnight, when *Ketoprak Humor* ended, the television was switched to Indosiar to check who was the dhalang in the weekly broadcast of wayang on that station. We watched for some time, and then we switched again to the wayang on TVRI Surabaya, and watched that for about an hour, because the entertaining first clown scene had just started. When the scene was over, we switched to Indosiar again, where the wayang started later and so the first clown scene was still in progress. The rest of the night, we were switching between the two wayangs until about 3 a.m., when it was decided that enough had been done for the security of the neighbourhood and the television was turned off.

A few days later, I found the following text in a Yogyanese newspaper, in the "Reader's Thoughts" section. (In Yogya it is possible to receive the signal from the local TVRI Yogyakarta, unlike in Solo where I was guarding my neighbours.)

> *Watching 3 TV-wayang kulit*
> On Saturday 13 February 1999, after the television Evening News, we watched TVRI Yogya because there was an all-night *wayang kulit* performance. During the audience scene, we switched to TVRI Surabaya, and there was also *wayang kulit*. At 24:00, we tried to switch to Indosiar, and there was also *wayang kulit*. So, we were confused, [because] on one TV there were three *wayang kulit*. However, the fact is that when there is a *wayang kulit*, we are very happy. [We watched] in such a way that when we were not pleased by a scene we switched channels, which we did very often during the night.[32]

This multi-channel manner of watching wayang is another aspect of televisual disembodied seeing-hearing that abolishes distance. One can see-hear without having to move physically. Like when one sees with the cameras' "many eyes" when one watches a montage of shots, when I switch channels I switch between seeing from different places without moving my fleshy body to those places, often far removed—Surabaya, Yogya. However, here we encounter an element of interactivity in which the television spectator can exert some control on what he sees. He has a degree of freedom to choose what he wants to see, freedom to control his virtual seeing-hearing body. In contrast, in the case of the montage of shots, television makes choices for him and he has to follow. One wayang viewer said that when he watches wayang on television, "if it is not exciting, I switch channels; when I watch outside [i.e., directly], when it is not interesting I chat with friends". This suggests that multi-channel television is in a way more like watching wayang live, because on a particular level it lets me choose what I see, although I am restricted to selecting from a small number of options, already pre-constituted, numbered and labelled. (This foreshadows later, more interactive ways of watching wayang on the internet, which we will discuss in Chapter Five.)

One reason why the montage of shots on television discussed in the previous section tends to be criticized whereas the possibility to switch channels is seen as an advantage, may be that in the former case, I feel that my agency and my power to control what I see are taken away from me, while in the latter case I am, to some extent, in control of what I see. We may think back to our discussion of the interaction between puppeteers and producers in Chapter Two, and what has been said earlier in this chapter about the politics of the television-dictator: each party, like the audience, wants to be in control, and dislikes to be controlled by the others. This is taken seriously because what is at stake here is not just the enjoyment of a television programme, but freedom as such, as well as people's vision. While the television spectator's control is partial in comparison to watching wayang directly, its advantage is precisely that his control is "remote". Switching channels allows me to control what I see with minimal physical movement. I am not at a lived distance from what I see, but I am remote, separated from it. Indeed, "remote control", which has become an integral element of multi-channel television and which further reduces the involvement of my fleshy body in what I see, is a good metaphor for watching three wayang at once: the special pleasure of this is that I can be remote from what I see, neither near nor far, and yet I can to some extent control it.

The case of watching "three wayang on one TV" shows another way in which lived distance is abolished, this time not only the distance between home and the place of performance or between the different points of view from which I see a performance on television, but also the distance between, for instance, Yogya and Surabaya. This needs to be seen in a broader context. Many Javanese viewers of wayang on television live away from their homes, either because they work there (in Jakarta, Batam, or elsewhere) or because of transmigration. I talked to Javanese who work in Jakarta, and as some explicitly said, and as was apparent from the way they talked, they watch wayang on television *with nostalgia*. When they talk about wayang, many gradually "broaden" the subject and talk about the experience of which wayang is a part, namely, about home and living in their village. We have seen in Chapter Two that television exploits and stimulates nostalgia through the wayang programmes. Television is said, by both television executives and many viewers, to "cure nostalgia" (*mengobati nostalgia*): as they watch wayang on television, the viewers talk about "my village" or "when I was a little boy living in my village". As they watch wayang, television helps them virtually return "home"— a virtual, simulated home, which works as a painkiller for nostalgia. The same is apparent from letters that the Indosiar television station receives from people who have transmigrated to other parts of Indonesia. This kind of nostalgia is part of the televisual experience—to some extent even in Java, when people find themselves watching television because it is easier than going to a live performance. This suggests that the separation of perception from the physical body that television effects and the abolishment of distance that allows me to perceive from a place without moving my fleshy body—on many levels, from the "jumping squirrel" vision to watching three wayang at once—is rooted in the modern world. In the same way that wayang performance is changing in response to the developments in the present world, including the existence of television, the fact that people watch wayang on television is—among other things—a response to the way that people are increasingly alienated from their homes, roots, surroundings, and communities, and television appears to help them "return home", to (a simulacrum of) the pre-televisual world, a world unaffected by television, paradoxically by separating their perception from their bodies and their present situation.

Concluding Thoughts

The experiences of watching wayang on television and watching it directly are both part of life. I make choices between watching wayang directly or on television, I compare the two and, depending on my particular situation and disposition, see advantages in one or the other. As I watch either a live or televised performance, I see it against the horizon of my experiences of both live and televised performances.

The interaction of wayang with television affects not only how wayang is performed, but how it is experienced. Even when watched "directly", the experience is never pure, it is always haunted and invaded by images, representations, and technologies; and wayang itself is a medium through which people participate at the event. The lived body itself, I have suggested earlier, is something like a medium, in that it is through my body (my lived, situated body: a body with memory, style of being, moving, sense-making powers) that I perceive and am in the world.

Yet, all this does not mean that the experiences of watching wayang on television and watching it while being present at a performance are the same. Levelling out the differences between the two—as has been a strong tendency in some scholarship[33]—blinds us to the multiplicity of experiences of wayang, to how people make choices and orient themselves in the world, to how the two experiences affect and haunt each other, to the tensions between the two. Such levelling out would blind us to how wayang and television are part of people's lives.

Moreover, such levelling out would amount to saying that it is enough to see the world through television, that television "just moves what is there to the viewers' homes—that's all", that the world is a picture, without noting the resistances to images which attempt to substitute for being there. In contrast, the thoughtfulness of the observations made by viewers of wayang on television, and the fact that many people reflect perceptively and critically on what happens, and understand that watching wayang on television is not the same as being there, are signs of a resistance to television's power, a resistance which is saving the experience of being at a wayang performance from entirely dissolving into television. This is resistance to dictatorship, not just television's, but dictatorship as such, to political and commercial forces that attempt to control how and what people see, their position and point of view (literally and figuratively, which are, in this case, not quite separate). "We look into the danger and see the growth of the saving power."[34] Television tries to conceal the difference between being at a wayang performance and watching it on television—in emphasizing that televised wayang is authentic, that "we just move what is there to the viewers' homes", but most importantly through what it does to distance and vision. Yet when one talks to people who watch wayang on television, one gets the sense that they see through, so to speak, and critically perceive the workings of television. This does not mean that wayang fans are not susceptible or open to the powers of television, and many do watch and enjoy televised wayang.

We have seen in previous chapters that puppeteers are sometimes eager to make wayang more like television and collaborate with it, but that there is also a resistance to this process and to being controlled by television. What has been described in this chapter is part of the same process. When the viewers are seduced by television, or choose to take advantage of its powers and pleasures, but at the same time are critical and resist television, in part by understanding what is happening, by "looking into the danger", it is like when puppeteers are seduced by, take advantage of, or resist television. In all cases, television is powerful and it transforms people and the world, yet there is resistance and friction, and all parties try to take advantage of television. Such desires, seductions, frictions, and struggles must have been part of the localization of ideas, technologies, media, religions, and worldviews in Southeast Asia over the past centuries and millenia.

What is it that the viewers are attracted to and that they resist? It is something more than television. In the last section of Chapter One, we reflected on various inheritances which television brings into the present and which affect wayang. Reflecting on the present chapter, we could think about how the viewers are both attracted by and resist a particular philosophy of perception and a particular way of being in the world as embodied in television: a uniquely disembodied, detached, egocentric, and mechanistic model of perception (think of Descartes); in Husserl's words, "a *new sort of attitude* of individuals towards their surrounding world", which grows into "a systematically self-enclosed cultural form", in which "man becomes a nonparticipating spectator, surveyor of the world"; or, in Heidegger's words, "modern kind of representing" in which

> the world [becomes] conceived and grasped as a picture. What is, in its entirety, is now taken in such a way that it first is in being and only in being to the extent that it is set up by man, who represents and sets forth. [...] The Being of whatever is, is sought and found in the representedness of the latter.[35]

When Javanese wayang fans articulate the difference between watching wayang on television and being there, they are doing essentially the same thing as Husserl, Heidegger, and Mearleau-Ponty. Each in his own way points to the danger that the life-world is hidden behind the obviousness of objective, scientific and technological representations, or that being-in-the-world, being-there-in-the-midst-of-it, is replaced by attending to, surveying the world-as-represented, world that has become a picture. ("To be beheld by what is, to be included and maintained within its openness and in that way be borne along by it, to be driven about by its oppositions and marked by its discord"[36]—this is what is replaced by watching television.) They point to the danger that the darkness uncaptured by representation, the "shadow"—that which "extends itself out into a space withdrawn from representation"... "pointing to Being, which remains concealed"—will be forgotten.[37]

As they are attracted to the powers of television that allow them to see regardless of place and distance, regardless of where they physically are, and as, at the same time, they resist the claim that the clear visibility of television is better than watching wayang through the thickness of the social event while being immersed together with others in the wayang celebration, perhaps they are attracted to and resisting, beyond wayang and beyond television, a particular new, disembodied, dislocated way of seeing and being in the world in which the world is a picture that can be instantaneously transmitted; perhaps they are attracted to and resisting a new kind of light and visibility, without shadows, and a world without dark and muddy roads. And if the resistance to television is a matter of saving the experience of being at a wayang performance from entirely dissolving into television, perhaps it is a matter of saving—or a nostalgia for? or perhaps a fantasy of? or all at once?—not just wayang, but a particular way of being in the world: being with others in the midst of what is happening, being bodily immersed in it, seeing-hearing-touching-smelling-feeling it, walking along dark and muddy roads, being free to respond to the world rather than being guided by a "stupid" "dictator".

4

The Diversity of Creatures: Experiments, Disappointments, Dreams (1970s–2005)

So far, I have discussed *wayang* on television without emphasizing differences among various cases. The Indosiar wayang was, for less than a decade after its emergence in 1995, the mainstream form of wayang on television. Its popularity and importance at that time, and the intensity of the encounter at that moment, compelled me to make it central in my discussion in the preceding chapters. Some of the experiments considered in this chapter were conceived as critical responses and alternatives to wayang on Indosiar. Other cases stay closer to the Indosiar version, and more generally to a style (with variations or sub-styles) of presenting wayang on television that could be called mainstream or normal.

In spite of the pervasiveness of this common general style of televising wayang, to disregard the differences between various cases would create a misleadingly homogeneous picture. This chapter begins to show the diversity of creatures in the history of wayang on television. It goes beyond the mainstream and includes a discussion of the experimental, unorthodox moments—ranging from productions of various television stations and other entities, to unrealized plans and unfulfilled dreams. It considers cases from before and during the era of Indosiar wayang. It also briefly considers Indosiar wayang in a different light, focusing on its—and on it *as*—experiments and fantasies. More recent, "post-Indosiar" times, including how wayang, television, and the internet (and radio and cassettes) haunt each other, will be discussed in the last chapter.

One can envision what has been happening as the surface of a young planet marked by several hotspots characterized by a great deal of volcanic activity—at some moments monotonous to watch but from time to time it is interrupted by a sudden change of colour or an individual outburst of energy—in a constantly shifting landscape of many unexpected eruptions of varying sizes and character. The instances of televised wayang are connected by family relationships, although not always loving ones. The chapter also aims to give a sense of the history of wayang on television, not in terms of linear development or intelligent design, but rather through multiple views of and from different moments; through giving a sense of how people thought and worked at different times, and in each case imagined the past and fantasized the future from their particular present.

This is a story midway between reality and imagination, a story of unfinished projects and broken or forgotten promises; a fragmented, non-Aristotelean story without a beginning, "logical" causal progress, and conclusion; a story in which people's actions, ideals, and dreams, formed in the encounters between people and technology and between different media and their cultures, are only imperfectly controlled by consciousness. Thought and fantasy make the future alive in the present, and as one reflects on the various unfinished or unbegun projects, one realizes that all cases of wayang on television, all projects and projections, like all technologies, are fantasized and imagined, whether or not they are "realized".

At the end of Chapter One, we saw that the encounter of wayang and television has a prehistory in the encounters between wayang on the one hand, and radio, cassettes, electric light, and modernity on the other. The cases of wayang on television discussed in this chapter, to the extent that they give glimpses of the history of wayang on television, should be seen as part of that larger temporal constellation or net of technologies and dreams. They should also be seen, cautiously and critically, against the backdrop of larger social and political developments in Indonesia from the 1970s to the present. We can think of President Soeharto's centralized government up to his fall in 1998, his cultural projects through which the unity and success of Indonesia were articulated, his strong, if far from perfect, control of cultural and artistic life, and his support of Central Javanese arts. At the same time, Soeharto supported a "free-market" economy and with it an intensified interaction with global cultural economy and the popular culture of Western capitalist countries. One can imagine how in this situation, foreign and modern commercial culture would fuse and/or clash with local Javanese culture with a new intensity—as exemplified by our case. The government's permission to establish new commercial television stations in the early 1990s, in which Soeharto's family and partners were commercially involved, made Indosiar wayang possible—and with it the most intense conflict of Jakarta-centric commercialism with wayang. As we will see in the next chapter, the political and cultural decentralization after the fall of Soeharto in 1998, alongside the emergence of new technologies such as the internet and smartphones, appear to be reflected, with some delay, in the changing relationship between wayang and television.

However, the strong light and sharp images of a sweeping historical narrative do not always help us to see all the shades of people's lives, or for that matter, the often unpredictable dynamics and multiple forces in the interaction between wayang and television, and the particular ways in which people experience and think about, not only wayang and television, but also their world and times—shades of which can be better sensed when one attends to specific cases and moments.

Wayang on State Television (TVRI)

Indosiar was a dominant landmark in the landscape that I have been sketching only since 1995. Before that, the most significant role was played by wayang on TVRI. Even after 1995, TVRI wayang continued to play an important part.

The gradual creation of a national television network was a project meant to unify the nation, and in various ways TVRI has attempted to project unity and the central government's messages and images of Indonesia—from centrally produced news to emphasis on productions showcasing Indonesian culture. To some extent, the idea of the production of wayang on television can be seen as part of these efforts. And yet, on closer inspection, TVRI wayang is even less a homogeneous project than Indosiar wayang, each local TVRI station has a different approach, and their approaches have been changing. Just like in the case of some other projects which were meant to promote unity and the government's vision, in practice a space is opened that is not entirely coherent and not entirely under control, and that allows for divergent voices. Javanese *wayang kulit* is or was broadcast by TVRI Jakarta, Yogyakarta, Semarang, and Surabaya. TVRI Bandung broadcasts Sundanese *wayang golek* and, exceptionally, wayang kulit.

While I tend to emphasize the year 1995 as a turning point, there was also a continuity between TVRI efforts and the Indosiar project. The director of operations at Indosiar told me: "As soon as we began to broadcast wayang, everybody was saying, 'Wow! This is very TVRI! [*Ini TVRI sekali!*]'" TVRI has been associated with cultural programmes, but "TVRI" as an adjective is hardly positive—it has the connotation (only partly justified) of state-sponsored, underfunded programmes produced by civil servants. While Indosiar was praised for showing the arts in their environment, in an "authentic" situation, TVRI was criticized for lifting traditional arts out of context—to use Supanggah's example again, "a dance from Irian would be performed by a person from Jakarta, the child of a government official", perhaps against the backdrop of a national monument.

The pre-Indosiar history of wayang on television is not well documented. According to a number of informants, wayang was first broadcast in Indonesia by TVRI Yogyakarta. The book *Gamelan, Dance, and Wayang in Jogjakarta* by Wasisto Surjodiningrat, published in 1971, mentions half-hour wayang kulit broadcasts on TVRI.

> Some time ago a foreign corporation I.T.T. placed a fascinating full-page advertisement with pictures of Bima, Gatutkatja, and Hanoman wajang puppets in LIFE magazine. It read that in the near future our country will enter the space communication age and that it will be one among the selected countries with satellite communication making possible the Dalang shadow puppet show to be seen by new audiences around the world. We are sceptical due to the fact that our TV-RI television stations have shown only half hour wajang kulit programs and never an all-night program. Considering the enormous costs of such an undertaking it seems like an illusion that

> someday [*sic*] the wajang shows of Ki Dalang Timbul or Ki Nartosabdo may be seen by new audiences around the world.[1]

The possibility of an all-night wayang performance appears as part of "enter[ing] the space communication age", and feels almost like a technological utopia of science fiction, manifesting the element of fantasy that we find in many, or all, cases of wayang on television. Here it is a fantasy sparked by a foreign corporation's advertisement in an American magazine. The association of televised wayang with the West continues in the next paragraph: "according to the newspapers of June 1, 1970, an all-night wajang-kulit shadow play was shown live [on television] in the United States", at the University of California at Los Angeles, "for the first time in the history of this art".[2] In another chapter, "Radio, Television and Wajang-kulit," the author reiterates that all-night wayang has not been shown on television in Indonesia, but "at most a half hour program has been shown, notably the Ramajana series".[3] Ramayana is conceptualized as "series": from the very outset, television and wayang worlds begin to dissolve into each other, and television projects its concepts onto wayang, or sees wayang through its concepts, its picture. The programme's brevity is not seen as a creative innovation, but a technological and economic necessity—although it involves a major transformation of wayang performance and its experience, and the difference between wayang time and television time has caused friction ever since. The author discusses wayang on television in connection with, or as an improvement on, wayang on radio, which had been commonplace for several decades before the book was published. Surjodiningrat mentions that Jakarta, Semarang, Surakarta, and Yogyakarta all broadcast all-night wayang on radio regularly, "so that practically every Saturday night people can have this favorite entertainment".[4] He opines that "actually a TV wajang-kulit program is more interesting than a radio program".

> Dr. Sularko from Bandung, who won the second prize at the recent Documentary Film contest held by TVRI, proved this with his film, 'From wayang to dance drama.' The film showed the fight between the wicked ogre, Tjakil, in the

> wajang kulit and in the wajang-wong dance drama using leather puppets and human performers alternately.[5]

In Indonesia at this time, television was not widespread, and people's memories of early televised wayang programmes are shadowy. Surjodiningrat's book from which I just quoted mentions wayang on television in 1971 (and 1970 in the USA), and some performers recollect watching wayang on television "around 1972". According to Habib Bari, the head of TVRI Yogyakarta in the 1970s, the first television programme involving wayang was called *Apresiasi Wayang* (Wayang Appreciation). It was not a wayang performance, but a documentary-like educational programme in which a narrator presented information about wayang. Later, TVRI began to broadcast monthly "fragments" (*fragmen*) of wayang live from the studio, each lasting 30 or 45 minutes. Habib Bari emphasized that they need to be seen in the context of early television broadcasting. Then, TVRI Yogyakarta was on air only several hours a week, so even the 30–45 minute programmes were considered quite long. People were not faced with a choice between producing a brief or an all-night wayang—the latter was not an option. Also, all broadcasting was done live at TVRI at that time, so it was not possible to broadcast from recordings.

Habib Bari emphasized the novelty of the idea of showing wayang on television, and the fact that his team knew of no models to follow. However, before moving to TVRI in 1966, Habib Bari worked at the state radio station, RRI Yogyakarta, and he used his experience with radio wayang broadcasts as the basis (*patokan*) for developing the television broadcasts. We have also seen that Surjodiningrat's 1971 book discusses wayang on television and on radio together. I suggested in Chapter One that we need to see television as a member of a larger family of technologies and ways of perceiving and representing the world—the first attempt to put wayang on television was shaped by prior interaction between wayang and radio, a member of television's family.

Compared to the Central TVRI in Jakarta, TVRI Yogyakarta itself was new. Habib Bari emphasized the difference between the national, pan-Indonesian orientation of the first, Central TVRI, and the local orientation of TVRI Yogyakarta. Wayang was introduced on television because "TVRI Yogyakarta had to have specific characteristics of

Yogyakarta" (*TVRI Ngayogyakarta kedah gadah ciri khas Ngayogyakarta*). He said that even though many Javanese worked at Central TVRI in Jakarta, they were afraid to introduce Javanese culture because people might see it as "Javanization", an undesirable image on the national television in a multi-ethnic state where the Javanese are a politically and culturally powerful majority. Even at this time, concern with appearances and image-building were key factors, and wayang was thought of as Javanese in contrast to the national or to Jakarta. Jakarta is a symbol and embodiment of a style of being which supersedes local and ethnic identities and attachments. Jakarta is associated with the national Indonesian, the international, and the modern, and as such it is like television. Introducing Javanese wayang on television was a matter of making television—previously a national, Jakarta phenomenon—more Javanese, more local.

There is one difference between TVRI Yogyakarta and (later) Indosiar, which one may discern even in this early period: the people and institutions at this local television station, and the world they live in, seem to be closer to the world of wayang than in Indosiar's case. (Even Indosiar's Javanese employees are immersed in and marked by the society and culture of Jakarta, just like the Javanese working at TVRI Jakarta.) Habib Bari himself "felt" to me different from most wayang producers in Jakarta. He speaks beautiful Javanese, he loves and understands wayang, he is very good at "reading" (i.e., singing) Javanese poetry. He is not an outsider to the world of wayang. Other people working at TVRI Yogyakarta later, such as the producer Kristiyadi in the 1990s, were similarly deeply involved with Javanese arts and culture. We will see later that this cultural proximity of television and wayang also characterizes the private local television stations that began to emerge around 2005, in the time of political and cultural "regional autonomy". Clearly, even during the New Order, and even at a national institution like TVRI, there was a degree of regional autonomy, even though its dynamics were to some extent different, and there is an interesting continuity with much later developments after the end of the Indosiar era, a continuity across political and technological changes.

In previous chapters, when I discussed the gap between the worlds of wayang and television, I was referring mostly to the dominant Indosiar broadcasts. In Yogyakarta, the distance between the media and their cultures has been there as well, but some Yogyanese television producers, more than those at Indosiar, have been in some way on both sides of the gap. Habib Bari said that "there is difference between television customs and Javanese customs [*adat televisi kaliyan adat Jawi*]" and he had to try to "make nearer" (*nyelaki*) the two.

Habib Bari said that Indosiar producers do not treat the *dhalang* in accordance with Javanese culture:

> The dhalang, of course, has a high status. Javanese people say he has received a boon from the gods [*wahyuning dewa*]. Now, if the young kids [i.e., television producers] who have no manners/etiquette [*kirang tatakramanipun*], [tell the dhalang] directly, just like that, "This must be done like this, this must be like that [*ini nanti harus begini, harus begitu*]"—well, [the dhalang] does not want [to follow]. I never had any problems, but as I said, the manner of approaching [the puppeteer] must use Javanese culture [*cara anggenipun nyelaki kedah ngangge budhaya Jawi*]. The kids today are always in a hurry. [...] In the world of wayang, I consider the dhalang omnipotent [*mahakuwaos*].

He used Indonesian for the phrase "this must be done like this, this must be like that," sounding strikingly coarse in the middle of his refined High Javanese, in the middle of what sounded almost like a puppeteer performing the story of wayang on television. He expressed through his use of language that such direct command is part of the Indonesian (or Jakarta) way, not "Javanese culture" or "the world of wayang". The word that I translated as "approach" is again *nyelaki* in Javanese, "to come nearer," suggesting that there is a distance between wayang and television and between their cultures and "customs" (*adat*). Note also that time, and the difference between Javanese/wayang time and Jakarta/television/"kids'" time, is an issue: "The kids today are always in a hurry."

Nonetheless, Habib Bari would correct performers when they did something that he considered wrong. For example, he forbade the gong player to play with the fist (rather than the mallet); he told musicians how to place the mallets neatly on their instruments when they were not using them; and they were not allowed to smoke. These "corrections" foreshadow problems that would emerge in later years, such as the sense that wayang on television has to be clean and neat, and that television staff have the authority to decide what is correct and what is not and, paradoxically, change and correct wayang to make it more authentic. Habib Bari said that "everything that becomes a show on television must give guidance" (*sadoyo ingkang dados tontonan wonten televisi kedah dados tuntunan*). The sentence paraphrases an oft-repeated saying that wayang is not just a show (*tontonan*) but also gives guidance in life (*tuntunan*). Here, however, television is substituted for wayang in the statement (which makes television into something like wayang). Because television is tuntunan, everything has to be done "correctly". Part of bringing wayang closer to television is "correcting" wayang and Javanese culture. Habib Bari described the cleaning up and correcting of wayang as "culture-ing" of wayang (*kita budhayakaken*). The "culture" of this "culture-ing" is rather like culture represented in a museum, culture that has become a picture, clean, neat and visually appealing.

Abbreviation of performance time has been an issue throughout the history of televised wayang, but television was least flexible in the earliest days, and the temporal frame of wayang had to change most radically. Habib Bari said that the main criticism of the early wayang broadcasts was that they were too short. Later, it has become possible to produce longer programmes, closer to the traditional timing of wayang. Thus, it would not be correct to say simply that wayang has been becoming increasingly more like television, because in its early history it was in some ways radically adjusted for television (extremely abbreviated, performed in a studio without an audience), while in many later versions television has become more flexible and accepted some of the characteristics of wayang that are not television-like.

In the 1980s, not only have longer broadcasts become possible, but the use of video recording allowed post-editing of performances, adjusting their time after the performance, and broadcasting them at a time of the television station's choice. There were different experiments and formats. By the early 1990s, there were two kinds of wayang programmes on TVRI. By then, wayang programmes were produced at TVRI stations in Yogyakarta, Surabaya, Semarang, the Central TVRI Jakarta, and (mostly *wayang golek*) in Bandung.

The first type can be seen as a descendant of the earliest wayang programmes described earlier. It is a short version of wayang, usually one to two hours long, typically recorded in a studio, and either broadcast live or, more commonly, recorded and aired later. These performances were often substantially adjusted to fit the television medium, especially, but not only, in terms of shortening an all-night performance to mere one or two hours, now conceived of as a whole performance rather than a "fragment". In most cases, there was no audience in the studio—the performers performed for the cameras and for television audiences. Sometimes, the conventions of *padhat* (condensed) performances newly developed in the art academies,[6] as well as innovation inspired by modern theatre, were incorporated into these performances. Rather than television covering a live event, in these cases wayang was much more of a television studio production.

In Central and East Java, this type of programme has gotten less popular since the mid-1990s, when Indosiar entered the stage. Kristiyadi, a producer at the TVRI Yogyakarta, where one-hour wayang shows were broadcast monthly in the early and mid-1990s, said that while in the past it was believed that wayang must be radically changed for television, it turned out, remarkably, that—in the station's perception—the short performances were not successful beyond an initial interest, and people actually prefer simple coverage of live all-night performances. Therefore, around the mid-1990s the station discontinued airing the abbreviated studio versions of wayang and decided to focus on the latter type. It is parallel to the philosophy of Indosiar where "authentic" "wayang on television" is preferable to "television wayang" because it exploits people's familiarity with, and nostalgia for, wayang events. Again one may think of this as "localization" of television.

In contrast, TVRI Bandung has been broadcasting wayang twice a week since the late 1980s, and the short studio version of wayang golek has been a creative, locally popular, and widely discussed programme, since long before Indosiar.

At a recording session that I attended at TVRI Bandung in 2000, a stage was set up in the studio with an artificially created setting of palms and a curtain with paper stars. While in wayang kulit the puppets are seen against the white screen, in wayang golek one can see what is behind the puppets. An Indosiar producer told me that this is a problem specific to shooting wayang golek, since under normal circumstances at a live event one can see perhaps a building and people behind the puppets, which doesn't look "clean" on television. In the Bandung studio, not only did the palm leaves and stars serve as a clean and neat backdrop for the puppets, but the camera often moved to the sides of the stage so that the musicians were visible through the artificial palm leaves.

4.1 A wayang golek performance on a decorated stage in the television studio of TVRI Bandung, 2000.

4.2 A wayang golek show shot in the TVRI Bandung studio as seen on television, with artificial palms in the background.

A wayang story was divided into four "episodes", bringing wayang closer to a television series. They were all recorded in one day, with rests between the episodes. Each episode was introduced by a beautiful female announcer in traditional dress standing in front of the puppet stage. All editing was done during the recording and there was no post-production. The performers began on a cue given by the television producer and each episode had to be timed precisely. Yet within this strictly structured temporal frame and highly artificial environment—so unlike a normal event—the performance was lively, in spirit rather close to a regular show, and unlike many of the short performances that I saw on TVRI Yogyakarta. The latter attempted to show a whole wayang story in one or two hours, making the performance much less relaxed and leaving little time for playful innuendos.

Wayang golek on television has been discussed in a rich multi-author volume edited by Goenawan Soebagio, and by Andrew Weintraub in his book.[7] It is interesting to see how the Sundanese discussions are in many ways similar to those concerning Javanese wayang kulit.

Second, a newer type of wayang broadcast, which developed at several TVRI stations in the early 1990s, was a live coverage of an all-night performance. At first, when all-night wayang performances on television were less common, they were customarily broadcast on special occasions such as New Year's Eve. In later years, TVRI stations sometimes aired wayang monthly for a period of time, often in collaboration with a sponsor, such as the influential monthly performances in Semarang supported by the governor and broadcast by the local TVRI. Otherwise, TVRI stations had broadcast wayang irregularly, and still do, on special occasions, or whenever a sponsor is available.

While some people felt that Indosiar was technically better and more glamorous, others like(d) all-night TVRI shows because they were not abbreviated and interrupted by advertisements. However, in part because they have been much less frequent and usually not regular, and because they have been generally broadcast only within a particular region, after 1995 they have become less prominent than Indosiar wayang. During the economic crisis that began in 1997, TVRI wayang broadcasts became even less frequent.

The styles of the TVRI stations differ(ed) somewhat. For example, TVRI Surabaya was known for experimentation with camera angles, or, as one person put it, it was more *artistik* (for instance, a camera was placed under the screen in front of the puppeteer so that his face could be seen from the front when he manipulated the puppets).

The dominant image of TVRI, perhaps especially among younger people, has been that of an underfunded state organization, following and promoting government policies, producing programmes that are out of date, boring, and lacking the aggressive excitement of the fashionable and the trendy that has attracted many people to the commercial stations. Still, some preferred TVRI to Indosiar. TVRI has played an important role in the story of wayang on television, and the negative image of TVRI, while to some extent reflecting reality, also hides some lively creativity and variety. Each TVRI station is to some extent unique and has a unique history and culture, and the diversity of wayang programmes on TVRI has reflected this.

Experimental Aspects of Indosiar Wayang and Special Indosiar Broadcasts

Indosiar wayang, as a kind of mainstream version, was the main point of reference in the previous chapters, and here I will focus instead on certain experimental or innovative moments and tendencies as well as some special productions, to show that even on Indosiar, there was a diversity of wayang programmes.

Indosiar began broadcasting wayang in 1995, in part to distinguish itself from other private television stations which began to emerge beginning in 1989. While Indosiar wayang built on the earlier TVRI broadcasts, the weekly broadcasts have brought television wayang to people's attention. After initial test performances (the first on 1 August 1995, with Manteb Sudarsono as the dhalang), Indosiar, in collaboration with the *bupati* (regent) of Sukohardjo, organized a series of 36 special performances by different puppeteers, and recordings of these (as well as 18 similar performances of wayang golek recorded in Bandung) would form the initial collection, with each performance broadcast one or more times over the following years.[8] Additionally, Indosiar started to record performances organized and sponsored by other people and not meant primarily for television. Thus, Indosiar generally moved towards coverage of "normal" performances.

Indosiar tried to make wayang into a popular, mass entertainment. It went about its business carefully, it tried to lose as little money and take as few risks as possible, and in general it did not value experimentation involving the producer's creativity and co-operation with puppeteers. Indosiar claimed just to "move what is there to people's homes", and I have discussed the ways in which Indosiar profited from presenting wayang as "authentic", aside from the fact that this was a way to keep costs low. Even as television's presence affected wayang, Indosiar retained the basic framework of event coverage and hesitated to get involved with wayang too closely.

The average wayang programme on Indosiar has not changed dramatically over the years. Any sense of linear progress is also negated by the practice of rebroadcasting old performances. Many of the 36 performances recorded in Sukohardjo and all of the 18 performances recorded in Bandung in 1995, for example, were rebroadcast in the following years. A performance recorded in August 1995 was broadcast in December 1996, March 1997 and March 1998. Another performance recorded in 1995 was first broadcast in 2000. These are not exceptions. The historicity of the recorded events was concealed, and no distinction was made between old and new recordings.

Against the background of this overall conservatism, I want to attend to certain experimental moments. The initial conception of Indosiar wayang was the most daring experiment. While wayang had been broadcast on television before, the decision to make wayang a permanent feature, and the organization of more than 60 nights of recording between October and December 1995 was unprecedented. Indosiar was then a young enterprise—it began to broadcast less than a year earlier—and the wayang recordings were in the spirit of adventure. It was an attempt to do something aggressively new. In later years, Indosiar never invested and risked so much in order to open up new ground.

The moments standing out from the continuity of later years were individual special events, and occasional new concepts initiated by a producer, tested and usually soon abandoned. I have mentioned some special performances in the previous chapters. The events usually amplify existing tendencies of mass, popular wayang performances—

as described in Chapter One—rather than moving in a radically different direction. In Chapter Two I have discussed the *Lakon Goro-Goro* programmes that combined the clown scenes from a number of performances, thus taking further the general tendency to emphasize these scenes. Special events are always *kolosal* and *spektakuler*, involve a large stage, many guest stars, many attractions (usually including dance and various kinds of performing arts), and often feature multiple screens and puppeteers. Sometimes, they are recorded in the studio. The wayang screens and puppeteers are on a stage, which recalls variety shows or modern theatre. The programmes use more complex, spectacular lighting and camera techniques, multiple spot lights, coloured lights that go on and off, and so forth. The *Paket Wayang Spesial*, which featured the clown scenes recorded in the Indosiar studio in Jakarta, is one typical example. Here I will comment on two others.

Wayang Kolosal was broadcast in January 1999. It featured three famous puppeteers (Slamet Gundono, Enthus Susmono, and Manteb Sudarsono), each at his own screen, as well as guest stars and dancer/actors. Elements of modern theatre and dance were prominent, and the troupe of Slamet Gundono from the Solonese arts academy brought onto the large stage some of the artistic experiments usually confined to the academy. For example, at one moment near the beginning, a large number of dancers, each holding a *kayon* (tree of life) puppet, performed a modern choreography inspired by the movements of the kayon with which a wayang performance traditionally begins. In this example, as in many other cases, one notices the expansion of the performance space from the wayang screen to a large stage, where people take the roles of puppets. Later in the performance, *Wayang Kolosal* featured actors in the roles of demonstrators, standing and shouting into megaphones on the stage and in the audience space. One of the developments in wayang has been a change in the role of the puppeteer. In *Wayang Kolosal*, the puppeteer Slamet Gundono frequently left his place in front of the screen and joined the dancers or actors, with or without puppets in his hands, or stood on the stage declaiming poetry or singing. There was also a screen above the stage on which documentary coverage was projected as a part of the multimedia show. Indeed, at a show like this, wayang becomes only one of the media, and the wayang screen and the puppeteer lose their centrality.

Another once-in-a-lifetime event was called variously *Wayang Koalisi* and *Wayang Kompilasi*. It featured two puppeteers, one performing wayang kulit predominantly in Javanese and the other wayang golek mostly in Sundanese, with some Indonesian mixed in. There was a stage for dancing and acting, with painted scenery—a palace gate—as the background. There were wayang kulit and wayang golek stages to the right and left of the stage, respectively. During much of the performance, the two kinds of wayang—different theatres, different languages, different musics—alternated, but there was also an interlude with clowns performing on the stage. More unusually, there were actors—representing, for example, the Kurawa king, Duryudana, captured by pro-democracy demonstrators—acting on the stage as well as around it (this was in the era of demonstrations surrounding the end the Soeharto era and the *reformasi*, and demonstrations were seen frequently on television news). In this performance, too, the wayang kulit puppeteer, Enthus Susmono, occasionally stood up and performed as an actor. Several times, the wayang kulit screen was slid aside, revealing actors who suddenly replaced the puppets. Live actors were talking to puppets held in the puppeteer's hands. Dancers and "demonstrators" were throwing garbage at the wayang screen, the puppeteer, and the puppets. The performance combined not only two kinds of wayang, but also—more explicitly than usual—modern theatre. However, it was primarily a television programme. No audience was visible, and the action was taking place against a clean and tidy bright blue background.

While there is much talk about innovation and experimentation at Indosiar, the atmosphere and the system are not always conducive to those initiatives. The sense that the most important measure is the ratings and profit, and the hierarchy in which the people who actually work with wayang are responsible to their bosses who do not necessarily have a special interest in wayang, makes everyone think twice before doing something new. Personal differences sometimes prevent the realization of an idea. Panca, the first producer in charge of wayang, was relatively keen on trying new things. While he had a good connection with the president of Indosiar, apparently his philosophy didn't suit Indosiar's director of operations. He was replaced by another producer, less idealistic and more business-minded, who was especially fond of the idea of "authenticity" of wayang on Indosiar, and his subordinates said that he was interested only in ratings.

Indosiar personnel told me that as soon as a more radical experiment is undertaken, there are complaints from the audience and from certain powerful persons and agencies who prefer more traditional wayang (this was true during the New Order as much as later). This is especially true when Indosiar tries to introduce permanent change, such as in the case of *Lakon Goro-Goro* and *wayang spektakuler*. Experimentation seems to be more easily accepted when it is seen as a one-time event, an exception rather than a new rule—or at least this is how Indosiar perceives its audience views.

Indosiar's dominance has lasted for about ten years. In 2005, new broadcasting regulations prohibited television broadcasts from 1 a.m. to 5 a.m. in order to save electricity, and Indosiar wayang was discontinued. When, in 2006, some television stations recommenced broadcasting beyond 1 a.m., Indosiar began to broadcast wayang again on some nights, but not regularly. In 2007, informants at Indosiar said that one of the reasons was that when wayang was discontinued in 2005, football broadcasts were introduced in the late evening. The ratings were higher than wayang and Indosiar did not want to swap back to wayang permanently, though it still broadcast wayang occasionally in the following years. The new Indosiar producer also mentioned conflicts with two puppeteers whose recordings are most numerous in Indosiar's collections, Anom and Manteb (nothing new, but perhaps an additional consideration for Indosiar). He said that they "cannot be managed" (*tidak boleh diatur*) and they began saying that it is the dhalang who has the copyright on the recordings. The producer said that the wayang programme is not profitable anyway, and it is broadcast as a "charity" (*amal*). We saw in Chapter Two that Indosiar does profit indirectly, and the anthropologist Budi Setyono (personal communication) commented that a reason why Indosiar became well known was because of its wayang broadcasts, but nonetheless, after 2005, one began to feel that there is not much excitement about wayang at Indosiar. As we will see in the next chapter, this was not the end of wayang on television, as private local television stations began to take over with a new enthusiasm.

Arswendo's Telewayang: Too Far but Not Far Enough

Telewayang, broadcast in 1998 but produced several years earlier (in 1995 or 1996), was, at the time, one of the more extreme experiments in the degree it departed from the mainstream version of wayang on television. On Indosiar, wayang is covered as an event and television keeps its distance from it and pretends not to transform wayang. Telewayang, in contrast, went further than most realized versions in its attempt to transform wayang in such a way that it—in the view of the creator—fit television and merged, rather than juxtaposed, the two media.

Produced by Arswendo Atmowiloto, a well-known journalist, television critic, novelist, and entrepreneur, Telewayang developed from traditional wayang kulit via an intermediate step, *wayang kartun* ("cartoon wayang"). Wayang kartun, itself inspired by the mass media, was created by the Yogyanese journalist Bagong Soebardjo and his collaborator Hasmi. Both later participated in the production of Telewayang.[9]

Telewayang tries both to cling and to escape from wayang; to bring it to television and to leave it behind. Telewayang is closer to such televisual genres as the soap opera and television cartoons, and it gets there in part by taking further some of the innovations common in mainstream wayang performances.

Telewayang is not shown as a performance event in a particular place and community. One sees only the cartoonish world of the story. The annihilation of distance and detachment from places has been a characteristic of the developments of wayang on television, and Telewayang takes wayang further in this direction. It is not performed in Javanese, but in simple Indonesian, the language of national television. Less bound to Java, it attempts to belong to everyone and no one, like modern technology. This brings it closer to television, and the modern, super-local, intercultural world of Jakarta. Telewayang's modern electronic music has no local memories either, unlike Javanese gamelan, which evokes and musically embodies the Javanese world and its ways of being.

4.3 Wayang kartun/ telewayang puppet—an army general with bribe money in his pocket.

4.4 A scene from Arswendo Atmowiloto's Telewayang. (Promotional materials courtesy of Arswendo.)

Telewayang's visual style, while still drawing on wayang, is more easily understandable regardless of where one comes from, like Indonesian language compared to theatrical Javanese. It leaves behind much of the complexity and symbolism of wayang representation, and approaches global visual styles, like those of television cartoons. From mainstream performances it borrows new conventions, which are commonly associated with television and film, such as acrobatic "kung fu-like" puppet movements and busy scenes with fast action. There is a new degree of explicitness in the visual representation, also enhanced by painted sets—more is made easily visible and understandable. Given up is the wayang-ly use of space where position subtly expresses the relationships between people and their social roles. Largely given up is the specifically Javanese way wayang puppets and people move in space, as well as the imaginative, theatrical ways of evoking the world. Telewayang does not use the familiar characters and stories from wayang—the Javanese mythology. Yet this "giving up" is not simply a loss. It is also a kind of release from Javanese images, imagination and ways of being.

In wayang, a single light source defines the centre and the spatial order of the screen, it is brightest at the centre and dims as one moves to the sides. In Telewayang, there is no single light source and no centre. The light is equally bright: everything is made more visible, understandable, electric, modern. There is no darkness.

The all-controlling single puppeteer, the awe-inspiring, God-like centre of wayang, is replaced with a number of manipulators who work the puppets from below, hidden from the eyes of the audience. Elsewhere I argued that watching the making of the theatrical performance is essential to its enjoyment and significance.[10] In Telewayang, the work, the medium itself, is hidden, rather like in the case of television, and performers adhere to a script, which is written by Arswendo.

The work of television is not separate from that of the performers, as television techniques—close-ups, editing, special effects—help to tell the story. This is both a technical and social issue: Telewayang has been created by a single team. Still, as Arswendo puts it, "The creative dynamics [or the programme makers] have to compromise with the dynamics of the broadcasting station—SCTV—regarding broadcasting time and day, as well as commercial interests."[11]

Telewayang works with time more like film and television. One scene is immediately followed by a cut to the next. An episode lasts less than 30 minutes. Everything in Telewayang happens and moves fast. While the weekly regularity of wayang on Indosiar has been seen as a contributing factor to Indosiar's success, Telewayang is even more recognizable as a series: the episodes connect to each other, and each is followed by a preview of next week's instalment. Telewayang is also removed from wayang-ly time in that it is broadcast in the afternoon, rather than at night.

Among Telewayang's new features that Arswendo and journalists like to mention are "helicopters with blinking lights and turning propellers" and "cheerleaders—girls screaming happily" ("cheerleaders" is in English in the Indonesian original).[12] If motorcycles and girls in modern dress look strange and funny in mainstream wayang, in Telewayang these signs of modernity, together with "*teknologi televisi*" (television technology: special effects etc.), seem more at home. While Arswendo emphasizes that Bajra, the protagonist, is a new version of the wayang hero Gathotkaca, he also resembles Superman or Batman. More generally, Telewayang has something of television programmes like the *Muppet Show*, which Arswendo, in his newspaper articles, posed as a model for Indonesian children programmes.[13]

Telewayang is clearly and neatly intended for children, a segment of the television audience, whereas wayang is a show for the whole community. Telewayang was closely integrated into the flow of television programming: it was presented as a part of a Saturday afternoon children's programme, *Pesta Anak* (Children's Party). It was punctuated by advertisements, mostly for children's products and programmes. The MC in *Pesta Anak* often referred to it as "film".

A viewer might consider Telewayang just another television programme. Yet for Arswendo, the claim that Telewayang is a form of wayang, is crucial. He describes it as "wayang performance presented by means of television technology,"[14] thus claiming both that it is wayang and that, as a television programme, it retains some of the separation between wayang and television that is characteristic of Indosiar. The intro sequence seen at the outset of every episode consists of shots of the wayang hero Gathotkaca in different forms of wayang, including Javanese wayang kulit, Sundanese wayang golek, *wayang suket* (wayang made from grass), "cartoon wayang from the night market", and finally Telewayang's own version of Gathotkaca, Bajra, making the links explicit. According to Arswendo, it is meant to show that there are many kinds of wayang and Telewayang is just another, as its name also suggests.[15] At the same time, the introduction conforms to televisual rhetoric and frames Telewayang as a television programme.

Arswendo, dhalang, wayang fans, and even people who like neither wayang nor Telewayang, discuss Telewayang in relation to (other forms of) wayang, as well as to existing wayang on television. For example, the newspaper article "The 'Bajra' Telewayang: An Approach to Tradition [or: A Traditional Approach]," states that Telewayang uses the "idiom of wayang";[16] another article reports that the title "Telewayang" describes the "combining of television with wayang".[17]

It is typical of the experiments discussed in this chapter that not all ideas and hopes are realized, including those that are at the heart of the producer's conception. Arswendo told me in a 1999 interview that he was thinking about introducing "guest stars"—characters from traditional wayang—in future episodes of the Bajra story, and about producing Telewayang with a traditional wayang story such as the Ramayana. In spite of the radical changes, Arswendo is attached to wayang, and if Telewayang had a future, it might in fact be drawn back to traditional wayang rather than continue to distance itself from it.

But this attachment is problematic for Telewayang's identity. It is almost as if Telewayang was haunted by its "*identik*" double, the spirit of wayang. Because Telewayang has become so much like a television cartoon, the echoes of traditional wayang often appear like flaws in an unprofessional television programme. For example, occasionally a hand of one of the puppet manipulators hidden below the stage can be seen for an instant. People accustomed to cartoons on television are likely to see this as a flaw in Telewayang, even though, according to Arswendo, the intention was indeed to let the viewers occasionally get a glimpse of the hands, because watching the puppeteer's hands is part of wayang, and he didn't want Telewayang to become entirely like a cartoon or *sinetron* (the Indonesian version of soap opera). More generally, Arswendo kept the puppet manipulation rather simple. When his collaborators suggested that computer animation could be used more often, he refused.

Because of Arswendo's attachment to traditional wayang, because Telewayang is haunted by its double (in a confused multitude of doubles), there remains a split between wayang and television within it. In the introduction to Telewayang published in *Pro-TV*, a tabloid owned by Arswendo, one gets the impression that Telewayang's connection to wayang is a bond or fate rather than a choice: "Wayang kulit, it appears, still 'must' be Javanese [*'harus' Jawa*] in its cultural inspiration. Telewayang Bajra is no exception."[18] The article "Wayang à la Arswendo" presents this idea more forcefully:

> It seems that wayang indeed still must be identical [*identik*] to wayang kulit. Even Wendo is not able to free himself from the heroes of wayang kulit as it is performed in the world of wayang kulit performances. Such as Bajra, for example, who is actually identical [*identik*] to Gatutkaca.[19]

Even if the words "must" or "is not able to" were not used, one feels a kind of hesitation in the movement from wayang toward television. Telewayang is

> made from hide, with the character and accessories which really exist in conventional wayang kulit. [...] Telewayang Bajra, in a simple way, can be said to come closer to the world of television, with an old capital [*modal lama*]. It is a new alternative to products [*produk*] available so far. It is not exclusively a soap opera with human actors [*sinetron orang*], it is not exclusively teaching and words of advice, it is not something that is governed by rules and standards. It does not depend on actors. The new approach is still supported by elements of entertainment: an interesting story, a lot of humour, and characters that evoke many associations. [Traditional] wayang kulit itself is rich with these elements.[20]

Having changed wayang radically, the main point that Arswendo seems to want people to remember is that, in spite of the new appearance, Telewayang is not really that different from its double, good old wayang, that it is essentially *identik*. Arswendo, like others, is torn between two objects of desire, wayang and television; or between making wayang into television and television into wayang.

Telewayang failed to attract much attention. Radical as it was, it provoked no strong emotions, controversies or ongoing discussions. Many considered it a failure. Arswendo partly blamed the SCTV station. He said that the programme had not been given sufficient promotion, its scheduling could have been better, and SCTV allowed him only half an hour for each episode, instead of the planned full hour.

According to the dhalang Slamet Gundono, Telewayang

> failed because it is too far from wayang. Whatever it is like, for Javanese people, if it is called wayang, it must not go too far. There has to be Karno, there has to be Kunthi. [Telewayang] is just wayang-ised soap opera [*sinetron diwayangkan*].

The appeal of wayang on Indosiar is that it is "authentic" Javanese wayang—something out there, beyond television. Yet, this Javanese-ness and wayang-ness are problematic on national television and so wayang tries to be somewhat less Javanese and wayang-like. Telewayang has gone too far. It does not appeal to wayang fans. It lacks (Indosiar-style) authenticity. The Indosiar producer, Didik, in fact used Telewayang as an example of a wayang programme that is different in concept from Indosiar wayang in that "it has been arranged for television" and "has never been performed outside".

Arswendo said that people haven't had the chance to become familiar (*kenal*) with Telewayang. In contrast, the Indosiar executives said that a major factor in the relative success of Indosiar wayang is Javanese viewers' familiarity with wayang (Chapter Two).

Hardja Susilo, in his article on the experimental *wayang ukur*, concludes: "Perhaps the innovations in wayang ukur have gone too far beyond renewal of the audience's experience of the more socially oriented wayang kulit."[21] The same can be said about Telewayang. Indosiar's "authentic" wayang, on the other hand, appeals to people by— to borrow Susilo terms—renewing their experience of traditional wayang.

The well-known Indonesian filmmaker Garin Nugroho told me that the main problem of Telewayang is that it is *tanggung* (gone halfway, half-hearted). Garin said that "if he [Arswendo] wants to enter the pop world, he has to take up pop elements", and that perhaps Telewayang should be more like a cartoon. I asked Garin if that would still be wayang. "That's the dilemma," he said.

Yanusa Nugroho, the producer of a wayang videos (which I will discuss later in the chapter) and a poet sensitive to language, expressed a similar feeling—that wayang has not gone far enough:

> This is the weakness of Mas Wendo's work. For me, if you want to use Indonesian language, well, it has to have Indonesian "voice", and not Javanese language that has been Indonesian-ized [*bahasa Jawa yang di-Indonesiakan*].

Wayang is tied, in all its details, to a sometimes intimidating richness of meanings, associations, resonances, restrictions, rules, etiquette, aesthetics; to theatrical, social, political, lingual norms. Because wayang is at the same time so much alive, this heavy baggage—culture, tradition, rootedness—makes it often powerful and exciting. Every innovation, every divergence from the "rules" is both welcome and criticized, and a discussion of the rules often turns out to be a discussion of morality, ethics, etc.—which makes it only more complicated and interesting. People's comments on Telewayang suggest that its main problem is that it went too far from wayang as people know it, yet not far enough. It is uncomfortably different, yet *identik*. It leaves behind much of the complex appeal of traditional wayang, yet it is not quite free from wayang, it is still weighed down by it, and tanggung—"half-hearted, gone halfway"—in exploiting the appeal of modern television culture. Telewayang seems to appeal to neither cartoon nor wayang audiences.

Sujiwo Tejo's "*Wayang Televisi*": Television Wayang versus Wayang on Television

In October 1996, about a year after Indosiar's first wayang broadcasts, another commercial television station, TPI (Televisi Pendidikan Indonesia), announced plans to develop a wayang programme. The puppeteer Sujiwo Tejo, who was also a journalist and would later become a movie actor and pop music singer, and TPI's public relations officer

Theresia Ellasari emphasized that TPI came up with a new concept, and that TPI's wayang was planned to be very different from the then already popular Indosiar wayang. The newspaper article entitled "TPI packages 'TV Wayang' à la Soap Opera", introduced the project in the context of the increasing competition among television stations and a new "spirit of creativity" at TPI.

> So why is this package called "TV Wayang"? Ella said, this programme is not just a wayang event lifted to the television screen [an allusion to Indosiar], but its packaging is adjusted to the format of television broadcasting. "For instance, this package will be produced in a controlled way, like in the case of production of soap opera," she said. For example, the package will be produced on the basis of a strict scenario. There will be a director, lighting, and editing. "Yeah, basically it will be like producing [television] drama or soap opera," she said.[22]

The puppeteer's view was published in another article, "Wrong, Television's Packaging of Traditional Arts: Typically—Traditional Artistic Aspects Do Not Appear".

> The packaging of the broadcasts of traditional wayang kulit on television is in fact wrong. Because, in general, the production process does not use a television approach, and does nothing more than merely move the stage show—with all its limits—to the television medium.[23]

Central to Tejo's concept is the distinction between "wayang on television" (*wayang di televisi*)—such as Indosiar wayang—and his "television wayang" (*wayang televisi*).

> The making of "television wayang" makes use of the advantages of televisual recording and editing technology. This will result in wayang show that can be enjoyed only on television.[24]

In an interview, Tejo said:

> The difference is that my concept at TPI was television wayang, whereas at Indosiar it is wayang on television. Television wayang is wayang which pays attention to television principles, including the tempo, dramatization—it moves fast—and editing. Indosiar wayang is wayang on television—actually a regular stage wayang, only it is moved to television, on Indosiar.

In an earlier Javanese publication about *kethoprak* on television, Bondan Nusantara makes a distinction between kethoprak for, or on, television (*kethoprak kangge televisi, kethoprak ing televisi*) and "television kethoprak" (*kethoprak televisi*). The former is "staged kethoprak broadcast on television". The latter combines (*nggabung*) norms of television and kethoprak, from plot scenario to lighting.[25] At Indosiar, the producer Didik used the same terms to explain Indosiar's approach to wayang, but while Tejo and Bondan are interested in performances that are integrated with television and for Tejo "wayang on television" is simply "wrong", Didik said that Indosiar sees the "wayang on television" model or concept (*model, konsep*) as preferable to "television wayang" such as Arswendo's Telewayang (Didik's example).

In some respects, Tejo's "television wayang" is like Telewayang: in its short duration, the use of written scenario, the serial form (Tejo's presented the Ramayana as a 13-"episode" series), Indonesian language (in subtitles in Tejo's wayang), and, in Tejo's vision, post-production editing and filmic cutting from one scene to another would be organically integrated into the tele-theatrical technique. While Telewayang used slow motion for dramatic effect as well as some more complex television special effects, Tejo talked about manipulating the electronic image in such a way that the light and the puppets' shadows would appear alive, like when oil lamps used to be employed in unmediated wayang. Tejo also emphasized the need for close co-operation between television people and wayang performers, and the importance of detailed collaborative planning. Like Telewayang, Tejo's television wayang attempts to closely integrate television and wayang techniques, and leave behind the coverage model of Indosiar. But all similarities notwithstanding, the two visions of how to go about this differ sharply.

Perhaps the main difference is that, while Telewayang does away with the audience and the qualities of wayang as a live event and makes performers invisible, Tejo hoped to do the opposite. Tejo explains:

> A television camera has to work in such a way that when people watch [wayang] on television, it is different from when they watch it directly. For example, the camera should be able to show even the fingers of the female singer, the pores on her skin, her hair, how she sweats, or the camera should be able to show the puppeteer's foot which he uses to play the *keprak* [metal plates used for sound effects]. But if I look at television [now], the camera is too limited to the screen. If it's just that, people don't have to watch television, they can watch it live. [...] Actually, wayang in traditional performance is not a performance. In my view, performance is a Western concept. In the case of wayang, what is important is how Person A meets Person B, and they talk while they watch wayang. This is what I don't see on television, including Indosiar. My thinking at TPI was like this: when, for example, the puppeteer sings or narrates, the camera should go around and show the *sate* vendor fanning [the coals under the grill], show people gossiping, show people selling toy puppets, show little children—because *that* is wayang.

Tejo said that the camera should "show the atmosphere, people socializing, people sleeping, a mother carrying her child, a person just coming back from the rice fields", and the "specific sensuality" (*sensualitas tersendiri*) of wayang, because "wayang is not only that which is on the screen".

Whereas Telewayang moved entirely away from presenting wayang as an event and made the television screen replace the wayang screen, Tejo wanted television to better show the whole event. Tejo emphasizes that television viewers would see wayang differently than people present at the performance event, and he sees the emphasis on the event as part of producing a programme which integrates wayang and television. The presumption is that by understanding what wayang is, by sensitivity to its "specific sensuality", and by showing wayang more fully, television producers would make a better television programme. Television could show wayang in a different but no less appealing way than it is seen by audiences present at the performance. Rather like electric light suddenly illuminating something previously hidden, television would show aesthetically appealing aspects of wayang that the regular audience cannot see.

The difference between Tejo's and Arswendo's visions manifest a difference between two ideas of what wayang is, and between two understandings of television. For Arswendo, bringing wayang and television together means changing wayang into something that is close to such programmes as children's cartoons and soap operas. Tejo, on the other, combines this view with an interest in the kind of television that lets viewers see actuality, often in new ways. Unlike Indosiar, Tejo emphasizes the active, even artistic employment of television techniques: wayang is not just brought to the homes of the viewers, as Indosiar would have it, but a programme is created that emphatically presents itself as something distinctly televisual, a "television wayang". While the Indosiar programme pretends not to get involved (*campur tangan*) in the puppeteer's business of performing, Tejo emphasizes that the puppeteer and the television personnel have to work closely together on every detail of the performance. For example, Tejo said that while Indosiar often shows the musicians, it

> does not do so meaningfully, because the cameramen and the producer usually do not understand wayang. For instance, when there is a fighting scene and one wants to focus on something other than the puppets, one could show the drum player as he strikes the drum when one puppet-character strikes another. That would be nice. But when during a battle scene the camera shows the flute, as it happens now, there is no connection.

During battle scenes, the drummer emphasizes puppet movements with drum strokes, and in a live performance, both the sounds and the drum player's movements magnify the energy and violence of the blows seen on the screen during battle scene.[26] The camera could bring this out.

Tejo's is a compelling vision, but it is significant that as far as translating it into practice, to a large extent it failed. Tejo said that it was successful "about 20 percent" of the time. Most of Tejo's ideas were never realized, and the actual programme was much less unique than one might expect from listening to Tejo.

The ideas that failed to be realized were precisely the most unique ones, such as showing the atmosphere and the "specific sensuality" of wayang and the people and activities taking place around it. The actual shooting took place in a studio against the background of uniformly blue décor. There were no *sate* vendors or people gossiping, and no audience at all. The atmosphere of the night and the audience may not be captured on Indosiar very artistically, but one does get occasional glimpses of them, and Tejo's wayang doesn't even manage this.

Some other aspects of the plan were realized to a limited extent, particularly those which make wayang more like a television drama, rather than being inspired by wayang's "specific sensuality": short performance time, planned breaks for commercials, the serialization of the Ramayana story with "cliff hangers" at the end of every episode instead of a conventional ending, and Indonesian subtitles. The performance had the feeling of light entertainment. Camera technique and editing were hardly different from wayang on Indosiar or TVRI.

Tejo's "television wayang" is a case of a defeated "spirit of creativity". In an interview, Tejo spoke about the difficulties of moving "from theory to practice" and the lack of understanding of wayang on the part of the television producers at TPI. He said that "usually the cameramen and the producer have already fixed ideas/expertise [*sudah tahu jadi*], and they are always confused about how to follow the puppets' movements". Several years after the programme had been made, TPI's public relations officer told me how Tejo and the producer were not able to work together and were arguing constantly. Even after several years, when Tejo appeared on television screen starring in a film, the producer angrily left the room so that he would not even have to see Tejo's face. This despite the plans for wayang performers and television producers to work seamlessly together, and even though Tejo is more at home in the world of modern entertainment than most puppeteers—he was a journalist for a major Jakarta newspaper, composer and singer of pop songs, and movie actor.

Just like in Indosiar's case, the distance, mutual misunderstanding, and power struggle between television staff and puppeteers, often resulting in people regarding each other as ignorant and arrogant, was a factor that prevented the implementation of new ideas.

When asked what was the main aim of "television wayang", Tejo said:

> Among other things, to introduce a kind of wayang to those viewers who are not wayang viewers. So, if one looks at Indosiar, there wayang is packaged only for wayang viewers. At TPI, [...] the aim was to reach out to young people with music and humour.

He wished to stress: "I hope that the television wayang production style can become a bridge to young people."

The "80 percent" failure to realize Tejo's plans is a failure to create such wayang that would reach out to people not familiar with wayang. It is a failure to remove the split between wayang audiences and television audiences, to integrate the world of wayang and the world of television; it is a failure to build a "bridge".

Tejo's television envisioned wayang remains "80 percent" unrealized. It remains a dream of a harmonious unity of wayang and television, a harmonious unity of different groups of people who coexist in society (those who love wayang and those who do not), a harmonious unity of cultures. Like other fantasies, it grows from the feeling that the world is torn.

Kalasinema: A Case of Wayang on VCD

Yanusa Nugroho, the producer of Kalasinema, emphasizes in his writing about the "experiment" (on a website and in e-mail correspondence)[27] that his "dream" was "how traditional art can be raised and brought next to other shows of people living in cities. Thus, traditional shows would not be only 'pitied', but people would buy a ticket [for them] because they would be truly good and could be enjoyed." ("Pitied": one may recall Indosiar talk of televising wayang as "charity".)

In his internet article, Yanusa writes that for many people, wayang is

> something very (profoundly) Javanese [*sangat Jawa (njawani)*], local, and the possession of a community from a certain social stratum. The local refers to the culture of a certain region, including the problem of language. The language of wayang is of course Javanese. One cannot ignore this fact, because culture is born from and adheres to people. It is exactly this element that makes an art to be near its community. But if we talk about cultural plurality, the issue will be different: how we are a part of a plural society. Our common duty is to bring local culture to the centre of plural society [*masyarakat plural*].

This problem, if people just argue about it, is "a stale cake that is warmed up repeatedly". However, "culture is something that can be easily shaped, something dynamic. So why not take a practical approach: [to create] something that can bridge the problem?" The "bridging of the {'gap'} between the young generation and our traditional performances"—and between the Javanese village and modern Indonesian city—like putting the local, exemplified by wayang, at the centre of the modern "plural society," is central to Yanusa's thinking behind Kalasinema. In conclusion to his article, he writes:

> The challenges of plural culture, urban society, cultural innovation, and western pop [culture], are the seed from which Kalasinema was born. Gelar Nusantara attempts to bridge [*menjembatani*], to package, to make things easier [*mempermudah*], so that wayang kulit is not only an artefact in a museum. For to adapt/harmonize culture—rather than just placing it in the chair of honour—needs a lot of energy.

In his e-mails, Yanusa was more explicit about the negative associations of wayang.

> In Indonesia, traditional art is marginalized because: (1) It has the image of *low class*; (2) the Javanese language

> [in wayang] is an obstacle because even Javanese people themselves do not fully enjoy it; (3) duration of the performance, which can go for as long as 7 hours.

Yanusa is clearly not thinking about wayang fans who love an all-night wayang. Like Tejo and Arswendo, Yanusa hopes to make wayang that would appeal to people who might not otherwise watch it. The "bridging" (*menjembatani*, Yanusa's favourite word, also used by Tejo) takes place between these people on the one side and the "low class," "Javanese," "local" people on the other. The bridge needs to be built over the gap between two identities, two cultures, of the same people, or even the same person.

A way to bridge the gap is making wayang easier (*mempermudah*) for people who are not used to watching it. Yanusa wrote in an e-mail: "I had a dream to make wayang easy to enjoy and understand." Yanusa used the example of language:

> The obstacle of language is one of the things that makes wayang kulit acceptable only for one ethnic group, whether we admit it or not. Why should this not be bridged with things that make easier [*dijembatani dengan hal yang mempermudah*]: with subtitles in Indonesian.

Another way in which Yanusa made wayang easier was to abbreviate it, as done by Arswendo and Tejo. The fact that Yanusa employed Manteb, one of the most popular puppeteers, and Sunyahni, a superstar singer, both celebrities familiar to television viewers, as well as the use of filmic special effects can be seen as part of the effort to make Kalasinema easily acceptable. The medium of VCD and potentially television allows people to watch wayang at home, without the hassle of having to go to a live performance. The sense that Kalasinema is easy to enjoy for the modern consumer can be felt from the advertisement in Gelar Production's online store (in 2001, the VCD was the only product sold there):

> Packaged in a condensed performance (60 minutes), it nonetheless retains the structure of wayang kulit purwa

> [wayang kulit featuring narratives set in the mythological times of Arjuna Sasrabahu, Mahabharata and Ramayana epics; the most common kind of wayang kulit ...]. The VCD *Dewa Ruci* features cinematographic effects usual in a film. Aside from that, the VCD is complete with Indonesian subtitles, to help those viewers who do not understand wayang language well. With the support of the famous singer, Sunyahni, this VCD presents a quality show and is pleasant to watch with the family.[28]

The new features of Kalasinema are comparable to other experiments and dreams: the short time, the use of Indonesian, filmic special effects, television dramatic techniques, and post-production editing (Yanusa used complete footage from three cameras). In some ways, Kalasinema is close to the mainstream form of wayang on television: in the emphasis on visuality, involvement of celebrities, and openness to the possibility that wayang could be easy, commercial entertainment. In some ways, Kalasinema is quite conservative. It is basically a coverage of a wayang performance that is rather "authentic," in Indosiar's sense. Some characteristics are perceived as the hallmarks of wayang in the past, such as an emphasis on story-telling. Yanusa wrote me that "the strength of the performance in the Kalasinema format is in the shadows", and he explained further: "Since I was little, I often watched wayang from behind the screen [i.e., the shadow side], and the wayang shadows have truly opened my imagination in an extraordinary way. For me, black and white turned out to be far more 'colourful' than the different colours."

While watching wayang from the shadow side associated with the past, Kalasinema's innovative play with shadows and various shadow "special effects" are characteristic of experimental wayang forms, such as those created at the art academies in Solo and Yogyakarta. Future and past fuse in the imagination of the present.

Yanusa emphasizes both Kalasinema's traditional and modern features. For example, he stresses that Kalasinema retains Javanese language, and adds Indonesian subtitles, rather than replacing Javanese with Indonesian. He writes on the website:

> [N]ow, urban society is typically dynamic, modern, and pays attention to packaging. [...] [Kalasinema] flirts [*bergenit-genit*] but retains *pakem* [the traditional rules], essence, and transfers Javanese philosophy to the viewers. [...]
>
> What we present in Kalasinema is truly the essence [of wayang], and of course it abides by the *pakem*: [the division into] *pathet* [part of performance] *nem, songo,* and *manyura*. The plot of the story also does not deviate from the existing pakem. So Kalasinema remains on the same track [*tetap dalam jalur yang sama*], but in a shape that is more acceptable to the broader society.

Similar to other cases, Kalasinema's major concern is the gap between the Javanese culture of wayang, and the culture of the modern, Indonesian world of televisions and VCD players. The producer's main concern is how to bring the two together, to "bridge" the gap, or to integrate one into the other. The aim is not simply to modernize wayang. Yanusa, like others, tries to make wayang different and simultaneously keep it the same; to remain within the tradition and depart from it. This keeps all experiments, with all their innovations, from getting very far. It is striking how all those involved in the experiments constantly refer to memories of traditional wayang performances watched in a village, and it seems that it is these memories that they want to revive on television or VCD.

Yanusa's wayang on VCD successfully attracted the attention of buyers and VCD pirates. Yanusa worked for seven years in an advertising agency, and his approach is relatively pragmatic. Yet, when I asked him to tell me about Kalasinema, the first sentence of his story read: "Kalasinema is my dream" (*KALASINEMA adalah impian saya*) and the word "dream" appears frequently in his writing. The finished product, he emphasizes, is only "an experiment" or an "embryo", with which he "is up to now not yet satisfied". This quality of a personal dream, "not yet" satisfactorily realized, is typical of the attempts to bridge gaps and introduce wayang on television. That Kalasinema was realized on VCD may be a factor why Yanusa was more successful than if he had to collaborate with a television company. But this can also be read as a failure to bring wayang and television together, which is clearly one of Yanusa's aims, and Kalasinema has not become popular as a television programme. Several episodes were shown on RCTI in 2000 as a "test" (*uji coba*)[29]—starting 30 minutes after midnight, which is not exactly prime time, especially if Kalasinema is supposed to attract people other than wayang fans—but it has not developed into a regular programme. As a "television wayang"—Yanusa has borrowed this term from Sujiwo Tejo—Kalasinema remains an experiment and a dream.

Other Experiments and Fantasies

We have encountered Panca in previous chapters in our discussion of Indosiar, where he played a crucial role as the first producer of wayang broadcasts. When I interviewed him in 1999 after he had left the company, he talked about his plans to create televised wayang that would be different from the Indosiar version, of which he had become strongly critical. He said that Indosiar is "too lazy" to spend enough time on wayang on television. "So, it's *instan* [instant, as in instant noodles]. [...] The people are *instan*, the images are *instan*, the images are *flat*, the *lighting* is *flat*, the story is *flat*, including the editing."

His own plans involve a radical departure from Indosiar's framework of "authenticity". Panca emphasized that people would have to work as "one team". "In my concept, the puppeteer is not the most important/eminent [element] [*dalang bukan yang utama*]." There would be different people speaking or "dubbing" the voices of the puppets at different times—some for singing, some for joking, etc. Other people would manipulate the puppets. This dismemberment of the puppeteer's functions is reminiscent of Telewayang and more generally, it is prefigured in the puppeteer's loss of centrality in mainstream performances with guest stars. However, Panca's terms and emphasis also suggest that in this case the envisioned end of the dhalang's sovereignty is a reaction to Panca's own experiences as a former television producer at Indosiar, and specifically his constant struggle with the puppeteers and what he sees as their arrogance. It is as if he were saying that in order to televise wayang, one needs to get rid of the puppeteers. In his vision, the performers "must be willing to agree/give in—today there is no one who is willing".

Like Telewayang, Panca's production would involve painted scenery, newly designed puppets, animation, and special effects. Yet, Panca stressed that certain elements from traditional wayang must be retained, such as gamelan accompaniment, and he objected to the use of keyboards and diatonic music in contemporary performances. Panca's production, then, like Telewayang, would go halfway, being both radically televised yet clinging to certain elements of traditional wayang with an almost moral determination. Panca's vision remains unrealized.

Asep Sunandar is the most popular Sundanese wayang golek puppeteer. When I talked to him in 2000, he told me that he recorded a VCD with three "episodes" which involved some animation effects—the ten heads of a demon become visible, an image of a puppet grows in size—and, like in the production of a film, the "performance" was often interrupted during the shooting and parts were repeated to allow for a variety of shots. He said that on television it should be done in the same way. Asep, too, was critical of existing wayang on television (in which he has been often involved, both at TVRI Bandung and at Indosiar), and like Panca, he complained that neither the producer nor the puppeteer has the will to spend enough time and thought on the production of wayang.

Asep, too, had his dream of a better wayang on television or VCD, a "multimedia, multicultural [*multibudaya*] wayang golek art". He would perform a story taking place after the Great War. Parikesit, the king at that time, would be telling people about the Great War and about his ancestors, and this narrative would be realized with the use of a filmic technique, the flashback (*flesbek*). The present time in the story would be represented with Sundanese wayang golek, and the past with Javanese wayang kulit, "and its culture would differ as well". "But there has not been a producer yet who would think this far—only I have."

In contrast to Panca's vision or Arswendo's Telewayang, Asep stays closer to traditional wayang. He retains the basic performance framework, the centrality of the puppeteer, a traditional story, puppets, and music, but with television's help, the performance would combine Javanese and Sundanese traditions. While these would be combined in a novel way, they have been combined before, for example, in Indosiar's *Wayang Koalisi* discussed above. Moreover, Asep's idea resonates with the tendency to bring together various regional traditions and different media in a single show. In this case, too, we are speaking about an unrealized vision.

In addition to realized and unrealized productions such as those described above, the desires to put wayang on television have resulted in a number of more or less academic seminars, workshops, research projects and associated reports. These discussions, experimentation, and writings are another aspect of the thinking and doing that goes on around the marriage of wayang and television, even as they are often less involved in the real life practicalities of actual performances and television productions.

Beginning in 1996, Studio Audio Visual Puskat (Audio Visual Studio, The Catholic Centre) in Yogyakarta, led by Fred Wibowo, organized a series of workshops combining discussions and practical trials, in an attempt "to find a format for traditional arts on television". They invited dozens of television producers and executives, academics, government officials, and performers. Many kinds of traditional performing arts were included, but wayang kulit, wayang orang, and kethoprak had a unique place in the discussions because they alone were considered to be viable television programmes. In the gathering of these different people, we can discern some of the defining personal and professional tensions involved in the production of wayang, discussed in Chapter Two. Fred Wibowo told me:

> They fought! Indeed, when I first brought together the artists and the television producers, they fought! Really! They discussed to the point of becoming angry! [...] Those on the side of performing arts accused television of excessively exploiting the elements of traditional arts so that the arts lose their form and their soul [...] even though they don't know the stories [*lakon*], and what is the power [*taksu*], soul [*roh*], and the philosophy of wayang. The television side accused the traditional artists of not wanting to understand the television medium, being unwilling to change how things are done,

> always clinging to tradition, [their performances] are not suitable for television, and so on. There was always friction.

One of Fred Wibowo's aims was to help the different parties to communicate: "The friction is still there, surely it is, but at least now they are making friends and do not act as enemies." He believes that he helped to improve the situation, and that his workshops have had an impact on how wayang is broadcast, whereas an Indosiar producer who attended some of the workshops does not speak well of them, suggesting that they have had no influence on how wayang is broadcast.

Fred Wibowo and the Audio Visual Studio have been also involved in other projects. For example, he attempted to create wayang golek in which the manipulating sticks would be blue, as would be the puppeteer's dress and face mask. Using a common cinematic special effect technique, the puppet, moved by the dhalang, would be recorded against a blue background in such a way that only the puppet would be visible, but not the blue sticks and the puppeteer. While this sounds like a radical departure from the mainstream way of televising wayang, when I asked Fred Wibowo if the next step would be computer animation, he said that "it could be done, but the art would be lost, the art of puppet manipulation—that has its own appeal. [....] Wayang has that *something* about it." There is again a sense that one must not go too far.

The programme *Balai Budaya* ("Culture Hall," a community cultural centre) was another project of the Audio Visual Studio. Their website described it as a "series" (*serial*) which is "made in a semi-documentary format. The story is a blend of real experience of the community of Culture Hall in Minomartani, Yogyakarta, and a fictional story."[30] Within the semi-fictional format, each episode introduces one kind of performance and shows parts of performances in the context of the story—including *ruwatan* (ritual wayang), *wayang kancil* (wayang for children, presenting animal stories), kethoprak, and others. The story of each episode illustrates the meaning and function of these performances.

Fred Wibowo said:

> It is actually a *sinetron* [soap opera]. We were trying to make a counter-formula [to standard soap opera].

> Because in soap opera, there is always conflict, violence, weeping, so we made a counter-formula. Is it possible to make a sinetron which has culture, sympathy, caring about people as its background/setting?

Balai Budaya tries to go beyond showing a performance with occasional shots of audience, even beyond Tejo's unrealized ideas of better showing the people present at the event (the *sate* seller and all) and toward showing wayang as it is part of the lives of individuals and a community. This is certainly an interesting idea. Yet, these one-time experiments have never become popular or well-known like the mainstream ways of showing wayang on television. The six episodes of *Balai Budaya* were broadcast on Indosiar on Sunday mornings, and video recordings were also available for purchase.

West Javanese wayang golek, broadcast since the 1980s by TVRI Bandung, which I have already discussed, has been the object of many lively academic and non-academic debates, seminars, and publications. Here I want to focus on a research project, which involved a number of experiments, and which was later continued in collaboration with the Jakarta-based Senawangi (National Secretariat for Indonesian Wayang Kulit), with focus changed to wayang kulit. My account below is based on unpublished research reports and interviews, especially with Professor Dr Primdani Tabrani, a senior member of the research team.

The long-term research started in 1982 with an examination of the visual language of *wayang beber* (narrative picture scrolls). By 1991 a comparative study was finished of "visual language of prehistoric images, children's images, wayang beber, Borobudur reliefs, and modern audiovisual media," culminating in Primdani's doctoral dissertation.[31] Up to this point, the research was mainly "theoretical".[32] The follow-up research that began in 1992 was meant to "apply" (*menerapkan*; interview with Primdani) the theories for more practical purposes, specifically creating a "wayang golek soap opera" (*sinetron wayang golek*) for television, which could then become a model for other local television programmes.

Throughout this long-term project, the main question concerned the difference and incongruity between "Western" and local visual languages, and, in the later stages, the possibility of combining them in the creation of wayang golek soap opera and later televised wayang kulit. The history of the project, as written by the research team, reads like a classic example of Oliver Wolters's localization.

> The theoretical research was spurred by cases in developing countries where media used for campaigns were produced by communication experts from the West with the most sophisticated technology (as a "help" from advanced countries), but sometimes the messages did not get across. Conversely, there were not a few cases when Western experts "were not able to read" traditional images because the traditional visual language differed from Western visual language.[33]

From the start, the research team thought in terms of a dichotomy between "Western" and "local" visual language, and failures of communication. The first years of the research were devoted to understanding the traditional local visual language. The researchers emphasize that the languages are not just different, but the difference may be a source of misunderstanding and conflict. What is "correct" according to one visual language is "wrong" according to the other. The production of the sinetron wayang golek was an attempt to fuse (*memadukan*) two conflicting languages. Television became the representative of the Western visual language, and wayang golek of local visual language. In fusing the two, the aim was to

> create a "new" visual language which is modern and compatible/harmonious [*serasi*] with the Indonesian public. This can strengthen national resistance [*ketahanan nasional*]. If the visual language is compatible/harmonious, it will feel as one's possession based on traditional visual language that lives and flourishes in the present era. So, it will not be just an "import" from the West.[34]

Primdani shared with me what would be his suggestions to Indosiar, and his idea of a wayang on television as a "new art" seems to be an extension of the "new visual language":

> Take a television crew that understands wayang. Then, having that understanding, they will understand that the technologies [*teknologi*] and visual languages [of wayang on the one hand, and television on the other] differ. Then there has to be an effort to merge them. It will be a new art. It's not open-air wayang, and it is not television, but it is actually a new art.

In addition to the more general problem of local and Western visual languages, Primdani described a more specific motivation for producing wayang golek on television in 1991. In the 1980s, TVRI Bandung began to broadcast wayang golek, and to shape wayang so that it would be appealing on television, such as including more realistic and visually explicit representations of actions. This has been criticized by some members of the public as not being in the spirit of wayang.

> We began long-term research because we knew there was a big problem. Wayang has its own technology and visual language which differ from those of television. This is what was happening at that time: TVRI was forcing wayang to follow its own language. So what was correct according to the language of TVRI, was wrong according to wayang golek's language.

A recurrent feature of Primdani's thinking is his characterization of wayang golek's language as *simbolik* or *imajinatif*, and television's language as *realistis*, *naturalis* or *konkrit* (we have encountered similar ideas first in Chapter One). Sinetron wayang golek was a reaction to TVRI's coverage, described as "eye-view reporting" (*laporan pandangan mata*), that is, simple coverage in the "realistic" visual idiom of television. A part of the effort to bring the language of television closer to the language of wayang golek was to make television less *realistis* and more *imajinatif*.

This included especially setting in the form of painted backdrops in an *imajinatif* (non-realistic) style.

The sinetron wayang golek tried to bring wayang and television together in a number of ways, many of which resemble other cases, such as Arswendo's Telewayang. "The puppets became the soap opera actors [*artis*]," said Dr Primdani, and the research report uses the same terms when it asks: "Why not use wayang golek puppets as actors [*artis*] in making golek soap opera [*sinetron golek*]?"[35] There was a script and rehearsals—"just like producing a movie," Primdani said. A continuous video recording was produced, and plans were made about how the recording could be cut into episodes. The sound, including dialogues, was recorded separately. Instead of a single dhalang, there were seven puppet manipulators, and an effort was made that they stay out of the view, unlike the traditional dhalang—the report mentions that this was a difficulty for the puppeteers. The manipulating sticks were extended so that puppets could be handled while the puppeteers were standing and moving around, which created a sense of depth and "an impression of limited three-dimensionality of movement," a compromise between what was seen as the three-dimensionality of television and the two-dimensionality of traditional wayang golek movement. The backdrop "fused the visual language of TV ('real' backdrop) with the language of wayang golek ('empty' backdrop)". [36]

Two sinetron wayang golek were produced, and third one was planned but never realized. The first one, *Lutung Kesarung* (1991), with dialogue in Sundanese (the local language in West Java and the language of wayang golek), was "still local West Javanese" (*masih lokal Jawa Barat*).[37] The second, featuring the wayang story *Gathotkaca Sabda Guru* (1994), was in Indonesian. The unrealized *Kisah Putri Bosu* was planned to be in Indonesian with a story from outside Java, Southern Sulawesi. Notice the gradual movement from local Sundanese language and story, toward a local story in Indonesian (a language less bound to a particular locality), to, finally, a story, adapted from "outside Java [...] in order to feel the challenge"[38] and "to find out to what extent [lit. "how far"] the art form of a particular region, in this case West Java (wayang golek), is able to present [lit. "carry"] a story from a different region in Indonesia".[39] However, a story was chosen that "contains general moral values" and "its regional-ness does not stick [to it] too much" (*kedaerahannya tidak terlalu melekat*).[40] It is a movement from the local to something "general" that is less bound to the local, towards a universal translatability. As wayang golek is gradually delocalized, it becomes more like television in that it can "carry" a story from beyond a particular place, and become detached from a particular local language, as medium becomes detached from content.

The last sinetron wayang golek (1994–95), and with it the research on wayang golek, was left unfinished. Subsequent research, sponsored by Senawangi, involved three members of the earlier wayang golek team. The research focus changed to Javanese wayang kulit, but the theoretical framework and many of the ideas remained the same, except for problems that are specific to wayang kulit, such as the question whether it should be shot from the front or the back of the shadow screen and how to combine these views.

The research report was meant as a prescriptive guide for television stations, from more practical observations on how to improve wayang programmes, to ideas for the future, such as the use of special effects (for example, using digital editing to effect the disappearance or transformation of a wayang character, use of playback as in television coverage of football, etc.). The report also proposed the creation of wayang kulit soap opera (*sinetron wayang kulit*), which would present "children's fairy tales, folk stories, and so on. The hope is that WK [wayang kulit] would widen its popularity and our children would become familiar with our own various fairy tales and folk stories, and not just Batman, Superman, the Kamen Rider, etc."[41] It proposed the use of multiple puppeteers, several screens and lamps, and new forms of lighting. It stated that it is necessary to use script [*skrip*], that there must be "close collaboration between wayang kulit puppeteer(s), the director (*sutradara*), and the writer of the TV script," and that there must be multiple rehearsals involving both the "dalang crew and the TV crew" (*kru dalang dan kru TV*). Finally the research report proposed "Wayang Kulit Shadow Computer Animation", in the form of a television series, using "television animation computer technology".[42]

Primadi and his colleagues emphasize that academic, scientific research is the necessary basis for creating the desired television programme. Primadani said about the famous puppeteer Asep, whose ideas I have discussed above, that he is very creative, but his shortcoming is that he is not scientific (*ilmiah*) and "does not use research" (*tidak pakai riset*). The research reports use phrases such as *mengilmiahkan sinetron*, "to make soap opera scientific" in reference to wayang-sinetron.[43] We see here (yet) another group of people—with their own culture, values, ways of thinking, fantasies—getting involved in televising wayang. The scholars are less directly engaged in the down-to-earth, practically oriented work of regular wayang television programmes. But while their ways of thinking may be more self-consciously "scientific", some of the underlying desires are similar to other cases: people are dissatisfied with the dominant manner of showing wayang on television, they feel that wayang and television differ and conflict (the Western-modern vs. local-traditional dichotomy is evoked), and they try to bring them together.

It is not clear to what extent, if at all, the "guide" that resulted from the research was used by television stations. When I interviewed Primdani in 2000, three years after the research report was completed, he said that there were originally plans to organize a workshop, to which television producers would be invited, and the recommendations of the research team would be presented, but this plan was not realized. He also said that the researchers approached Indosiar with suggestions for improvements, but one of the problems was that the team in charge of wayang production often changes, so even when the producers are willing to try out some of the suggestions, the programme goes back to "normal" when the television team changes. I asked Primdani if TVRI was interested in learning from the research project and he said: "Not yet. But because we involved golek artists, it was the artists who later improvised based on, or, let's say, were influenced by, our research." Later he said:

> So, after the research, we went down when they [TVRI] were shooting wayang, our team went, and we became consultants, and we had a dialogue with them, even though sometimes it was not easy, because they, the TV crew, [were saying/thinking:] "This is my area! What are you trying to

do, meddling with what's not your business?" But they also knew, they admitted, that they are not experts on wayang.

Musings on Imagination and Experimentation in the Age of Indosiar

Before we move on to more recent times, let me pause to reflect briefly on the cases discussed above.

The initiators of the various experiments often criticized Indosiar for not spending enough time, money and thought on adapting wayang for television. They saw Indosiar's wayang as "only" coverage of live performance and an "instant" product. The experiments differed from Indosiar in that they attempted to create something new and spent much time on conceptualizing and planning each broadcast and its specifics—the word *dikonsep* ("conceptualized") was often used. Yet, none of these experiments came anywhere near to challenging the dominance of Indosiar wayang, or to offering what would seem a viable alternative.

The various cases again give a sense of the persistence with which people try to bring wayang and television together. They betray people's profound attachment to wayang and its world, and, at the same time, their sense that modern media like television are inevitably and vigorously part of Indonesian present and future. Even as people see themselves as belonging to a modern world, they are unable or unwilling to give up certain continuity with the past—tradition—and they try to "bring" it with them, not simply as a memory, but as something that should be "at the centre" (in Yanusa's words) of the envisioned modern world.

And this chapter shows again the difficulty of the project. Wayang is felt or feared to be out of place in the modern world, and people feel that it needs to be changed, but when wayang becomes too different from what people know as wayang, it loses its appeal. People are faced with the dilemma of transforming it *and* keeping it *identik*, unsettlingly both other and self-same—I think of the double that haunts the I—so that it could be "at the centre of the modern world", which is itself split, ever self-othering through its fantasies (of the modern and the traditional, of the foreign and of home). The experiments and plans dream to bridge gaps and divisions between people, media, cultures. In contrast, Indosiar's version of wayang on television "covers" the wayang performance as an event, retains the gap between wayang and television, and does not dream of bridges.

In Chapter One, we saw how the living present is infiltrated by the past, and how the interaction between wayang and television is also an encounter between the pasts that wayang and television animate in the present. At the same time that televising wayang is lived, it is (also) a dream, a desire, sometimes more or less realized. While it is commonly said that a single experiment has failed or that a vision was not fully realized, more experiments and more dreams of success follow. Existing failures appear like footnotes to passionate descriptions of fantasized wayang on television, and reality like a footnote to tales of mystery and imagination. Failures, or dissatisfaction with actuality, are the ground from which imagination and fantasies grow, which in turn shape how people see and what they do in the living present.

Even in the cases of "realized" forms of wayang on television, puppeteers and television executives get involved in the process because of their desires—for fame, money, power, image, creative possibilities—and dreams of reliving childhood or "putting wayang at the centre of the modern world". Imagination and dreams motivate and pervade even the most "realized" performances and television programmes.

In his book *Technoromanticism*, which focuses on IT technology, Richard Coyne writes:

> The unity of which digital narratives speak (harmonious digital communities, immersion in space, holistic lifelike systems, the unity of the animate and the inanimate) reside in the future. Digital narratives commonly emphasize what will be accomplished while downplaying current achievements, which are inevitably more modest than the predictions. [...] The message is of a future rather than of an actuality. [...] The difference between description and prediction is ambiguous.[44]

Much the same could be said about televising wayang, as well as television and modern technology generally. Something like Coyne's "technoromanticism" is crucial to television—seeing regardless of place and distance, something that has a curiously close relation to fantasizing—and to modern Western technology—dominated as it is by imagining the future, by looking forward beyond the present time, by desires to transform the world.

There are traditions of fantasizing about the future of technology: pasts and futures haunt the living present together. In the last section of Chapter One, we were talking about the historical traditions of fantasized futures; both Siegel and Mrázek describe modern technology in the late colonial East Indies primarily as figures of far-reaching and obsessive imagination and objects of desire (Siegel: "...use it or, more importantly for us, fantasize about it ...").[45] In this light, the dreams of the marriage of wayang and television are part of the culture of television, and they are stimulated by television. Always in part: one could look into the past of wayang's own fantasizing about the future and find that when puppeteers and television producers dream about a perfect television programme, they are continuing a wayang tradition, a tradition of openness to new narratives, religions, media, and a flexibility of form and identity. In a later era, speaking of his experimental wayang that incorporates the latest audio-visual technologies and sounds and images from the internet, the Yogyanese puppeteer, Aneng Kiawantoro said that wayang needs to be *elastis* (elastic) if it is to survive. Perhaps it always needed to be elastis.

Fantasies of a perfect marriage and dissatisfaction with existing reality generate each other. Thinking back to the idea that this "marriage" of wayang and television is a "collision" between Javanese and "modern-global" cultures, and considering that "dominant technologies feature in our narratives to reinforce the aspirations and the obsessions of our age,"[46] we can ask whether the (hi)story of wayang and television may be about something more than the two media, and about more than the clash of Javanese and modern-global cultures. Perhaps this is a story of something—is it still possible to use these words?—more universally human. (*My thoughts continue, but only because we are sitting in a coffee shop, more asleep that awake, it is 3 a.m. already, a time when thoughts lightly come and lightly disappear, like the puppets and shadows that rush across the screen, and we can think what we would not want to write in a book.*) Perhaps the story of wayang and television, puppeteers and producers, is but a drop in a sea of (hi)stories, told and lived, each a variation of all others, about an endless search for the fulfilment of the dream of harmony, unity, peace, Perfect Marriage ... the passionate fantasy of a world where people work and create together, where Past, Present and Future converse attentively, with affection and humility, like three old friends sitting together in a coffee shop ... a search that is a never-ending journey through battles and divisions, a story in which dissatisfaction and fantasies nurture each other, a story of bridges, built and destroyed ... the search a Sisyphean task, the story without a happy end, or any end, without conclusion. Also because—why do I always have to talk back at myself?—it is not just a story, but life.

(And therefore never a single story, but a sea of stories.)

5

Decentralization, Diffusion, Infusion: *Wayang*, Television and the Net (2005–2017)

From the distance of time, and if one were to describe only the main outlines of the picture, the history of Indonesian television—with the internet figuring in the latest episodes of the story—appears to be characterized by a gradual decentralization. After the early sole, national TVRI Jakarta, an increasing number of regional TVRI were established, which were still under the control of the central National TVRI (TVRI Nasional) and the Ministry of Information, and broadcast within a framework emphasizing the unity of the nation, but also had a strong local character (which, as we have seen in the discussion of the early years of TVRI Yogyakarta, was also manifested through wayang programmes). Mainly in the first half of the 1990s, several Jakarta-based private television stations were established, which overshadowed TVRI and introduced new ideas and programmes, including the weekly *wayang* broadcasts on Indosiar as well as various wayang programmes and experiments on other channels. However, these private television stations were to a great extent controlled by the centralized government and owned by President Soeharto's relatives and close business associates. After the fall of Soeharto and the subsequent "liberalization", these channels have continued to play a prominent role, but an increasing number of Jakarta-based private television stations were set up, followed by the emergence of dozens of local private television stations in many cities across Indonesia in the first decade of this century. Jakarta remains the most influential source of television programming, but, in

Java at least, since about 2005, local stations have formed an important and lively part of the landscape. This protracted decentralization is also a localization of television, as local television stations appeal to local audiences and sponsors, and typically emphasize their local character and programmes, including wayang. In many cases, here, in the margins, wayang and local programming are at the centre. The introduction of the internet (especially YouTube and social media) can be thought of as further decentralization and diffusion of production and control, as just about any netizen can in some way participate, in striking new ways, in the "production" (in a broader, diffused sense) of wayang on the internet. Especially in the age of the internet, in the apparently decentralized and (as the saying goes) increasingly interconnected world, one feels more and more often a shared sense of disconnection and loneliness.

This schematic account, even as it vastly understates the complexity of the story (such as the strong local character of early TVRI, in Yogyakarta for example), still leads to an ambiguous and untidy picture. It describes a path from a centralized system to chaotic multiplicity, where television is "produced" locally. Television may be becoming localized, more Javanese. Yet as this happens, Java is more profoundly pervaded by television, it is touched more intimately.

This narrative also suggests a great degree of continuity, close kinship and interpenetration, even a sense of identity, between what are in some ways very different media: television and the internet. Doubles again: essentially both identical and simultaneously other. An examination of how the Net functions in Java suggests *both* that it is in some ways a radically new medium, enabling and seducing people to mediate, perform and watch wayang differently, *and*—especially in the particular ways it interpenetrates television and wayang (as one watches old television recordings of wayang on YouTube, as television stations use the internet to distribute televised wayang, but most importantly as one talks to people about issues, preferences, feelings, pleasures, and irritations, as they perform or watch wayang on television and the internet)—the Net is merely the latest development in a long history of media in Java, one is even tempted to say it is the latest face of television, and certainly a part of the same net that extends across media and across time. At several points in the previous chapters, I suggested that the Net and its involvement with wayang was foreshadowed by media interaction in the past, by older media and older "nets". The later part of this chapter offers a more concrete exploration of diffusion and infusion, continuities and change, as well as the net of multiple/linked media, in the age of the Net.

The diffusion and infusion of television and the internet into life in the post-Indosiar era explored in this chapter, is continuous with the developments in the age of Indosiar that we have examined in Chapter One: television and wayang pervading and haunting each other, the "dissolution of TV in life, dissolution of life in TV". Yet we now see their interaction in a different tonality, different mood. There seems to be less friction, less resistance, less clashing between wayang and television, perhaps in part because one important factor, the association of television with "Jakarta" (and all that means culturally, politically and economically), has become less dominant or less visible, perhaps because the cultures/worlds of wayang and television—as a result of the dissolution—have become less distinct, and the newness and otherness somewhat faded. From this position, we also see the Indosiar age in a different light.

If one looks only at a brief period in this history, particularly the years after the resignation of Soeharto, the above narrative appears to be part of political and economic decentralization and a movement toward "regional autonomy" (*otonomi daerah*) at that time. Drawing on the more general political and economic analysis by Robison and Hadiz, Rachmah Ida has described the post-Soeharto developments in the media industry.[1] To the extent that the development of wayang on television can be seen as part of larger political processes, it seems to fit better, but also complicate, representations of the period that emphasize a degree of continuity between the New Order and the (post-Soeharto) new New Order as well as the complexity of the processes, rather than accounts that represent the period primarily as a transition from "dictatorship" and "democracy". Ida writes in 2011, more than a decade after Soeharto's abdication:

> Large corporations, particularly those privileged by the New Order regime, continue to control private national TV broadcasting services and to expand their media business at the national and regional levels. [...] After Suharto's

> resignation, there has been little significant change among the players in the television business. On the face of things, people like Suharto's second son Bambang Trihatmojo and Sudono Salim (also known as Liem Sioe Liong, a close Suharto crony [and owner of Indosiar from 1995 to 2004]) are no longer major media owners in Indonesia, but they appear to have maintained effective control. [...] These tangled webs of media ownership which began to emerge in the last decade of the New Order have come to dominate and shape the entertainment industry in the post-Suharto era.[2]

Significantly for our case, a major development has been the "diffusion"—Hadiz uses this word in reference to political and economic power—from Jakarta to more regional and local levels. Ida writes: "The expansion of regional autonomy has opened up the possibility for development of more local commercial media. Local and community newspapers, radio stations and television channels competing for local audiences with local content have been established by both local governments and local media business groups."[3]

However, this is not necessarily a matter of "democratization": "The initiative to establish local media institutions is supported by major private (mostly oil) companies located in provincial areas, and by individuals, especially those with prior interest in local media and other business."[4] Ida concludes that her "discussion bears further witness to Robison and Hadiz's argument that 'There now appear to be great opportunities for the emergence of local oligarchies fusing local business, bureaucratic and business interests in diffuse, predatory networks of patronage.'"[5]

This chapter, too, "bears witness" to the arguments above. However, the political and economic decentralization and diffusion, and the continuities that Robson, Hadiz and Ida reveal, are seen in a somewhat different light. Television as a kind of culture, vision, or a way of being is diffused: the process involves not only the appearance of multiple new centres of agency and creativity, but also the regeneration of the (almost) "same old" television.

For most ordinary wayang viewers and even participants in media production, the "predatory networks of patronage" and "tangled webs of media ownership" are largely hidden, or at least partly obscured. That is one of the reasons why my study shows these times in a particular way, somewhat different from the surveying eye of a political scientist. Yet this view from below, while limited, also shows what sometimes disappears in a view from above. A cultural production exploited by business and political powers may at the same time be a space of genuine creativity, pleasure, openness and communication. As Els Bogaerts writes in her examination of local television in post-Soeharto Yogyakarta, "[I]t is important not to shut our eyes to the artistic input that has managed to escape the generalising idea, or to the more varied and pluriform content that has been the positive result of the birth of new local broadcasting industry."[6]

Taking into account the whole period of the history of television in Indonesia, the schematic decentralization narrative with which I began this chapter also brings out a long-term continuity, a very gradual diffusion of television, beginning from its introduction to Indonesia in 1962. Granted that the context and significance of this diffusion varied over time, our particular story nonetheless cautions us against putting too much emphasis on the end of the New Order as a historical break—such as "from dictatorship to democracy"—at least for people such as performers or wayang and television audiences.

Not only television and related media, but also wayang has changed since the age of Indosiar. Two recent dissertations provide rich pictures of some of the developments. Miguel Escobar Vallera's dissertation on *wayang kontemporer* (contemporary wayang) examines the latest incarnations in a tradition of radically innovative, experimental performances, revealing a whole world of creativity, as well as abundant continuity with the past, in the margins of what might be called the mainstreams of wayang.[7] Kathryn Emerson's work on the "all-night contemporary-interpretative style", with focus on performances of Ki Purbo Asmoro, analyses an influential trend that in some ways moves away from what previously seemed to be the direction of wayang development, in particular in its emphasis on presenting the story, with less time given to the entertainment in the comic interludes. Emerson writes that the era of wayang that emphasized comic interludes and entertainment "is now referred to in the past tense. ... Some dhalang returned to more classical practice, some simply softened the frenzy and extremity of their hura-hura-ness [rah-rah-ness, or strong emphasis on comedy, entertainment, and shocking, "crazy" innovation, especially but not only in the comic interludes], and some, Purbo Asmoro in particular, began developing in other directions entirely."[8] I share the impression that there are multiple directions that characterize the wayang world today. However, while it is true that among some people (some: here we come back to the multiplicity of divergent perspectives that we have already encountered in the 1990s) "the dominance of hura-hura performances in wayang is considered primarily over",[9] others disagree, and around 2016–2018 I have seen many performances that are little different from what I saw in the age of Indosiar—with extremely long interludes, stand-up comedians, often similar participation of audiences and local politicians, and sometimes a prominent presence of video or television cameras and monitors or projection screens. The difference in views, and the coexistence of multiple styles, may be in part a factor of cultural geography, as some puppeteers and observers in Yogyakarta and Semarang suggested to me (to oversimplify shamelessly: Semarang seems happy to continue its tradition of long comic interludes; in Yogyakarta I find the greatest diversity, from traditional performances to the "craziest" ones, to what Emerson calls the "all-night contemporary-interpretative style"; while Solo may fit best Emerson's description). Not

5.1 A 2016 colossal wayang performance with three puppeteers and three screens (two wayang kulit and one wayang golek) and a large stage for guest stars in Jakarta, uploaded on YouTube.

unlike in the case of television, the situation is complex, characterized by many directions, returns, and a diversity of points of view, and perhaps there is even something like the decentralization, even (paradoxically in the interconnectedness of the internet age) disconnection between places, that we find in the media industry.

Wayang and the localisation of television since 2004

In the age of Indosiar, wayang broadcasts on that television station were felt to be the mainstream, the various TVRI all-night performances were also important, and the various experiments were perceived as interesting but marginal. Since about 2004, the landscape has gradually changed. Indosiar wayang became less prominent and eventually turned into a memory—although the same programmes would be watched again on YouTube. People's perspectives on wayang on television have changed with the emergence of new television stations, expansion of the broadcasting coverage of existing ones, and other changes, including, in more recent years, the internet. The local private television stations, which have emerged since 2004, combine the commercial agility of the Jakarta-based private companies with an interest, in some cases at least, in exploring local material and commitment to local audiences and sponsors. A number of these new local television stations, in Yogyakarta, Solo, Surabaya, and elsewhere, have begun broadcasting wayang in ways that build on the wayang programmes on Indosiar and TVRI, but explore new possibilities as well.

Each case is different. Let us take Jogja TV as an example.[10] Established in September 2004, it is often said to have been founded and owned by the younger brother of the sultan of Yogyakarta. One may think of both the continuity with and the difference from Jakarta-based commercial stations established in the Soeharto era, which were owned by Soeharto's children and business partners: the (perceived) owner is again a person of power, but this time from the family of a local ruler (although one integrated into the Indonesian state as provincial governor), rather than the nation's president. However, this emphasis on the originary connection with the court of Yogyakarta seems to be itself part of a business strategy—image making—related to the television's focus on local culture, including wayang. Jogja TV, along with Bali TV, Aceh TV, Bandung TV, among others, is in fact a part of the nationwide Indonesia Network, a group of local commercial television stations, owned by yet larger Bali Post Media Group, developed and owned by the Balinese media baron Satria Naradha, who has expanded the media empire of his father, Ketut Nadha, the founder and former owner of the newspaper *Bali Post*. Ida writes about Naradha:

> His idealism in promoting the importance of local identity, especially for the Balinese, and their culture has been remarkable. For Naradha, the success of local TV stations like Bali TV (and his other local TV stations outside Bali) depends on their capacity to bring the richness of local cultural sites and practices to the screen and to mobilise local cultural products to challenge the dominance of centralised (Jakarta-based) "national" television stations. Naradha was the main proponent of the notion of Ajeg Bali (roughly translated as "Bali standing strong"), a cultural and economic movement aimed at creating a Balinese cultural renaissance that he popularised through his media. His critics regarded his popularisation of Ajeg Bali as merely a sales pitch of Bali Post Media Group.[11]

Ajeg Bali, "a moral movement that claimed to protect and strengthen Balinese culture"[12] was proclaimed in 2002 at the launching of the first of Satria Naradha's TV Stations, Bali TV. "With the backing of the provincial authorities, religious institutions and community leaders, this private channel, owned by the proprietors of the Bali Post Media Group, has been given the mission to foster Balinese cultural and religious identity, with a view to promoting the development of tourism."[13] The strong focus on Javanese culture and the "local" on Jogja TV is in some ways, paradoxically, a product of a nationwide business strategy designed by a Balinese, and the "local" on Jogja TV is on some level an extension of the "local" on Bali TV and even "Balinese nationalism". The discussion that follows further complicates this picture, by showing that even as nationwide television and business interests produce and frame "the local", nonetheless local producers, wayang performers and others in Yogyakarta creatively frame, shape or exploit the possibilities of local television. This is reminiscent of the creative, hilarious ways in which wayang puppeteers manipulate puppets representing television celebrities.

Since the channel went on air in 2004, Jogja TV has shown wayang every day in a number of programmes, from daily hour-long wayang broadcasts, to the use of the wayang medium in evening news, to prominent images of wayang in their jingle and logo. Related traditional performing arts are also broadcast.

Wayang can be watched on Jogja TV daily from 11 p.m. to midnight. Faizal Noor Singgih, the producer in charge, introduced it to me thus: "We make wayang into a series. Not only soap opera can be a series. [...] It is a normal wayang performance, only we cut it into pieces." Jogja TV records all-night wayang performances sponsored by others as part of celebrations—rather like Indosiar—but rather than cutting each performance down to about four hours and presenting the performance in one night, each performance is shown in one-hour instalments broadcast over several nights (usually 6–8). I discussed in Chapter Two how wayang on Indosiar was somewhat like a television series (in terms of audience familiarity, expectations and loyalty), but Jogja TV goes much further in this respect, because on Indosiar there was a different story each Saturday (although like in soap opera, many wayang characters reappear in every "episode" of the epics), whereas on Jogja TV one wayang performance is presented in a number of instalments. Wayang is thus closely incorporated into the temporal structure of television programming, with the hope that the regularity of broadcasting, and the continuity connecting the instalments, will make viewers watch every night. This programme, thanks to its frequency and regularity, has been for well over a decade the most prominent wayang programme in the Yogyakarta area, and it has attracted the attention of some puppeteers and wayang fans in Solo and elsewhere. Faizal said that a puppeteer in Solo told him that "Jogja TV is the second Indosiar", and I have heard similar statements to that effect from others, implying both that it took over Indosiar's role as the television station most associated with wayang—although on a local scale—and a certain continuity with Indosiar wayang.

The daily wayang on Jogja TV shares with Indosiar the idea of presenting wayang as an "authentic" live performance, as well as the general style of broadcasting wayang. When I asked Faizal about what he considers the ideal wayang programme, he said that the wayang performance in its traditional (*tradisi*) form should be "presented as well as possible using our television technology". At the same time, just like Indosiar, Jogja TV selects "good" performances (though perhaps less aggressively, and with a different concept of what is good), it influences to some extent what is happening in front of cameras, and it "censors" (Faizal: *kita sensor*) performances by cutting out what is considered inappropriate, such as bawdy jokes and behaviour. Faizal: "We choose good [performances]. By 'good' I mean, not that the puppeteer must be famous, but his performance has to be nice, and if he deviates, we cut [parts of the recording]." At another time, he told me that what is common in wayang—sexually explicit jokes and horseplay, for example—is not acceptable on television, and viewers complain. I asked him if Jogja TV influences the appearance of the stage and the performance. "Yes! We meddle with it [*cawe-cawe*]. It may be about the soundman, about sweeping the floor clean, about cleanliness." Modern cleanliness was also a desired quality on Indosiar wayang. At a performance covered by Jogja TV that I attended, the television crew asked for the stage to be rearranged, and when a musician began reading a newspaper during the performance (normal in the relaxed atmosphere of a village wayang), he was asked to put it away. Thus, broadcasting "authentic" wayang does involve "meddling" with the performance.

In these ways, Jogja TV's coverage of wayang shares much with Indosiar. In addition to the differences already mentioned—the daily schedule and the serialization of wayang—the most important difference has to do with the relationship between Jogja TV and the world of wayang. Even as Jogja TV is part of Indonesian and global television culture, it feels to be local Javanese and Yogyanese, and it is much closer to the world of Javanese wayang, or is a part of the same world. In this sense, the interaction between wayang and television to some extent reflects the increasing political and cultural regional autonomy in the post-Soeharto era—while retaining elements of the

Indosiar heritage, it is made by and for the people in Yogyakarta, with substantial involvement of local government, rather than broadcast from the centre, Jakarta.

This local character is manifested in many ways. The performances seen on Jogja TV feature numerous local puppeteers, rather than the small number of superstars that dominated Indosiar. Indosiar performances tended to be spectacular, mass events, often sponsored by large businesses and institutions, government agencies (national and local), or government or army officials, and they tended to take place quite often in cities. Jogja TV shows tend to have a more local feel, be more modest and smaller in scale, and while some take place in urban Yogyakarta, and some are sponsored by local government officials or branches of government, many are recorded in villages as part of village or private celebrations, sponsored by private parties, village committees and village heads.

For example, one wayang performance covered by Jogja TV that I attended was sponsored on the occasion of a village blessing/cleansing ritual by the local villagers under the leadership of the sub-district head living in the village. While the village was near Yogyakarta, it was a world apart. We drove through rice fields on a narrow, very muddy road, the only access to the village. The performance was held in a simple village house, everyone seemed to know everyone else, and everyone participated in making the event happen. The TV crew set up their cameras and lights, but their presence, too, was less glamorous than when the Indosiar crew arrives at a performance. The *dhalang* was good but not famous.

Jogja TV and its employees are in various ways nearer wayang—geographically, culturally, personally—than Indosiar. Faizal, the main producer in charge of wayang, is a dhalang who studied at the dhalang school at the Yogyakarta court. He is on friendly terms with puppeteers (he often refers to puppeteers as *kanca-kanca dhalang*, "dhalang friends" or "fellow dhalang") and obviously has a good understanding of wayang. I have not heard from him the kind of condescending or critical views of puppeteers that I had often heard from Indosiar producers. More generally, most of the people working at Jogja TV tend to be more familiar with the world of wayang. When I was talking to some Jogja TV employees, with a television set tuned to Jogja TV audible from another room, they were suddenly startled and one exclaimed: "Why, they cut it just before the gong!" Gamelan was used as background music on a TV programme, and they noticed the sudden ending. This showed their familiarity with gamelan, and for me it was a startling reminder that even though I was at a TV station, I was not in Jakarta, but very much in Yogyakarta.

Jogja TV station is itself a local Yogyanese institution, with buildings set among rice fields, close to villages where many puppeteers and musicians live. Many performances take place nearby. In the case of the wayang performance covered by Jogja TV that I described above, a number of the villagers knew some of the Jogja TV employees, and they interacted with them like they would with their neighbours. Another time I talked to Faizal, he was planning a wayang shoot even closer to Jogja TV, in a village where many of the employees lived. He said that they would be involved both in helping to organize the wayang performance, in their capacity as members of the local community, and they would be involved in shooting the show for Jogja TV, in their capacity as the television company employees. Jogja TV and its employees are in some ways a part of the local community, which makes their attitude to wayang quite different from that of Indosiar. If previously I suggested that Indosiar is more like the subject who is in control of its object of vision, in the case of Jogja TV the subject and object are not clearly separate, and Jogja TV sees wayang less from above or from a distance and more from inside.

I speak of a sense of community and old-fashioned neighbourliness at Jogja TV, and that is what I found most striking, but another point could be made: in some ways, this opening to the participation of local people and the informal, neighbourly interaction among people involved with television, wayang and the celebration, is not only a kind of return, a kind of homecoming of televised wayang, but it foreshadows the interactive possibilities of the internet, particularly as they would be realized in the case of wayang on the internet, as we will discuss in the later part of this chapter. I say foreshadows, but the timeline is shadowy, and the interactivity of the internet appears as a kind of double, or shadow, of the neighbourly interactivity: we are talking about times when the internet was already in use, and YouTube started to become part of the wayang world, and gradually, over the years, became an increasingly lively wayang space; and social media was used as part of the Javanese socialization around wayang and television at this time.

In addition to the programme described above, wayang appears on Jogja TV in the daily prime time evening news (*Pawartos Ngayogyakarto*). There are two segments that involve wayang. One, lasting three minutes, is called "Pitutur" (advice, especially traditional wisdom). In it, as Faizal described it, "we use the wayang media [*media wayang*] to communicate an advice". The wayang screen is shot from the back so that one can see the shadows of the puppets arranged on the screen, in a suitable traditional scene, such as when a hero visits the hermit and receives advice from him, or when Semar, the wise clown-servant, gives advice to his master or his children. With gamelan music in the background, wisdom is communicated through a short dialogue between the characters. Before I saw "Pitutur", I asked Faizal:

Jan: "So, you have a dhalang?"
Faizal: "Yes!"
Jan: "Who is the dhalang?"
Faizal: "I am!"

It was another revelatory moment reminding me that we were in Yogyakarta, where the television producer is also the dhalang. The wayang screen and puppets, as well as a few musical instruments used in this programme, are borrowed from people in the neighbourhood—"around here there are of course many people who have wayang puppets, and they say, 'Sure, if you want to use them, please do!'"

Another brief segment during the evening news is the "Awicarito", which Faizal translates as "biography". It introduces specific wayang characters—"for example, who is Dasamuka, what is his country, who is his wife, and so on". On a less regular basis, wayang appears in other programmes. For example, the daily programme *Langenlaras* features traditional arts performed by children, including occasionally child and teenage puppeteers.

Wayang is not a stranger to Jogja TV. Compared to Indosiar, it is more at home on television, and not just because it is a regular and frequent feature of daily programming. On Indosiar, wayang appears in the midst of programmes such as international sports, American, Chinese and Indian movies, and soap operas showing people in luxurious houses in Jakarta, Mexico and America. On Jogja TV, wayang is part of programming that shows its local world—in the news, one sees the streets of Yogyakarta and nearby villages, many programmes concern local issues and present local people—in this sense, it is rather like a wayang performance—and many programmes are in Javanese. The presenters of Javanese-language news speak using a formal, rather theatrical voice and language resembling that used in wayang, and they dress in traditional Javanese formal attire, like the dhalang. The talkshow programmes, too, resemble Javanese theatre, and, rather like wayang, showcase stylized, aestheticized images of formal Javanese etiquette, social interaction, and intellectual discussions. There are weekly programmes featuring Javanese arts related to wayang, such as *kethoprak, macapat* (poetry reading/singing), and gamelan. In the midst of these programmes, wayang is quite at home, because television in Yogyakarta has evolved to be a bit more like wayang.

5.2 At a Jogja TV studio during the shooting of a Javanese programme.

Faizal said: "I stopped performing as a dhalang when I began working here [Jogja TV]. Now I am not a dhalang in front of the wayang screen, but a dhalang behind the cameras." He called himself "the second dhalang" at televised wayang performances, and as he was directing the shooting of a wayang performance, he joked: "There is the dhalang, and then there is dhalang Faizal." These playful self-representations suggest something about what is happening between wayang and television in Yogyakarta. When the TV producer in charge of shooting wayang is a dhalang, when he brings his knowledge and the culture of wayang into his work with television, when he equates himself with the dhalang and television with wayang, television becomes a bit more like wayang.

I will return later to the question of how wayang simultaneously becomes more like television, perhaps in a different, less spectacular and less questioned way than in the age of Indosiar. But first, I would like to say more about Faizal, the protagonist in my story about wayang on Jogja TV, because his background suggests, in a subtle way, the interpenetration of the cultures of wayang and television, or more generally modern media and forms of storytelling.

Not all, but most puppeteers are from lineages of wayang performers. Faizal's parents, however, had no professional connection to traditional performing arts. Still, Faizal said that he "was introduced to wayang by [his] father", who liked to listen to wayang on the radio. Faizal said that his performing style is closest to Ki Timbul, because he heard his performances most often on the radio, when his father was listening. Another childhood experience which lead Faizal to wayang was a visit to the house of his father's friend, who was subscribed to the Javanese-language weekly *Joko Lodhang*, which has a regular wayang (*pedhalangan*) section. This was when Faizal was about four years old, and before he could read. He told me:

> I opened the magazine, and there was a picture of a wayang, if I am not mistaken Bathara Narada [a god—not the Balinese media baron]. And that made me somehow interested. So I asked, who is this and who is that, and my father's friend explained in his own way. And then he showed me, "This is how you make wayang." He made a photocopy [of the picture of wayang in the magazine], had it enlarged, glued it

> to cardboard, cut it out using scissors, added bamboo sticks. So, the first wayang [puppet] I knew was from a magazine.

Later, he would see a performance on television, and only after that, when he was in second grade, did he have a chance to attend a live performance—he remembered that the dhalang was Ki Suparman—but he was taken home well before the end, and, as he noted (one can sense a dhalang's perspective), he just watched and was not able to hold the puppets. In the coming years, his father brought him borrowed comics featuring wayang stories by R.A. Kosasih. He learned the "flow of the stories" from them, noting that the comics are based on Sundanese versions of the epics. He would also go to bookshops and look for books about wayang, noting that these were mostly about Solonese stories and puppets, and there was very little about Yogyakarta. Let me stop the narrative here, as this is enough to illustrate my point: the man who would become a dhalang and later a producer—the "dhalang behind the cameras"—came to like wayang through other media in the first place: radio, a magazine, photocopies of wayang images, television, comics, books. I am not concerned here with how Faizal's childhood influenced his later life, but rather I feel that the story of his early years gives a sense of how people involved with wayang and television today have grown up in a world in which wayang is inextricably entangled with a variety of modern media, including radio and television, and today, the internet. This interpenetration of wayang and other media has a long history; what may be new is that its novelty has worn off.

Another local private television station in the "post-Indosiar" era is TATV in Solo, also founded in 2004. When I visited there in 2007, wayang was shown in a similar fashion to Jogja TV, in that a live performance was recorded at a celebration and cut into one-hour "episodes", but at TATV these episodes were broadcast weekly, rather than daily. In other ways as well, wayang, and Javanese arts generally, were, as one observer put it at the time, somewhat "less thick" (*kurang tebal*) than in the case of Jogja TV, and would get thinner still in following years; a decade later, at the time of writing, there are no regular wayang programmes on TATV, only occasional live broadcasts. Still, around 2007, wayang, gamelan, kethoprak, and other arts were broadcast on a weekly basis, many programmes, including news, were in the Javanese language, and there was an emphasis on local issues. Some of the programmes, like in the case of Jogja TV, evoked Javanese theatre and life, from the very formal Javanese news, to the informal and relaxed *Obrolan Sar Gedhe*, a localized talk show in which the host and a few guests sat on the ground at a traditional food stall, drinking tea or coffee and eating snacks (a very Solonese form of socializing), against the painted setting of a popular Solonese market. The music for this programme was provided by a *gender* player (a *gender* is a gamelan instrument), who also sang and joked with the other people on the programme. The *gender* player employed for the show was a dhalang.

As in the case of Jogja TV, I was impressed by how "local" TATV was, and TATV employees repeatedly emphasized this quality as something that distinguished it from national television stations. While Jogja TV is located in the middle of rice fields, TATV occupies a large shophouse, a former bakery (TATV's owner also operates a bakery), in a Solonese neighbourhood. The building does not look different from the other shophouses. Looking out the windows of TATV, one sees the backyards of kampung houses, where women are hanging laundry out to dry, and chickens, dogs, cats, and rats cohabit. In TATV's own backyard, there is a food cart used in the *Obrolan Sar Gedhe* programme mentioned above, an older *gender*, and a heap of objects, which are used as props for television programmes, but could also be found in many other backyards in Solo. TATV is part of a neighbourhood. For example, I was told that there had been recently a celebration involving wayang just a couple of houses away from the TATV building, so the crew was able to simply extend cables from the studio when they were shooting the wayang performance. I had a strange feeling when I was watching the streets and people of Solo on TATV, in news, advertisements (so slow, subdued and relaxed, with nothing of the aggressive volume and speed typical of television commercials), and other programmes. The way of moving and talking, the rhythm of life, the atmosphere and feeling of a place that are the raw material and the inspiration of wayang and gamelan, the world represented and dramatized by wayang, were here seen on television. When wayang appears on TATV, it is seen against the background of—or in the middle of programmes representing—this local life-world.

On TATV, gamelan is often used as background music in the local news. It is curious to see the local news—the visit by a politician to

5.3 The backyard of TATV Solo, with a hawker stall, pots, a gamelan instrument, and other real objects used as props in TATV's programmes.

Solo, the visit by a Czech scholar interested in wayang and television to the TATV studio, the police investigating a crime—set against the background of gamelan music: again, it feels like watching wayang. In some cases, the result is a strange juxtaposition, such as when, during the concluding segment of the news, one can see the images of a pop music concert in Solo, with singers, guitarists and a drummer in action, but hear "background" gamelan music. In Solo and Yogyakarta, it seems, the separation of television and wayang is less under control than ever, as television is wayang-ized, and, to a greater extent, comes to share and reflect the same world.

Yet things are not that simple or uniform. Wayang and the Javanese world shape television to their image, but conversely television continues to shape the Javanese world and people's way of seeing in its image. Let us consider another wayang performance covered by Jogja TV. It was different from most of the other cases of wayang on the station. It was broadcast live, which required more manpower, equipment, care, and "meddling" than recording a performance to be broadcast later. Held at the courtyard of a local government office, it was more glamorous than the village performances typically covered by Jogja TV. The presence of television was much more strongly felt than in other cases. Being present at the event was like attending the shooting in a television studio, where everything is designed to fit television. Wayang was preceded by live *campursari* music, a few Javanese dances performed by children, and a (television) interview about the wayang performance. There was a large screen on which the Jogja TV broadcast was projected. The loudspeakers sometimes blasted the sound from the location, at other times the voice of the television anchor, and at other times the soundtrack of television advertisements. The events taking place were structured as television programming, and ordered by the television producer. For example, one would hear the television anchor (in the amplified television broadcast) announcing a children's dance, which would be the cue for the dancers to begin to perform. At the end of the dance, one would hear (and see on the projection screen) a series of television commercials, at the end of which the anchor would announce the next item on the programme, such as an interview. The interviewee was seated near the wayang screen in the far corner of the stage, mostly hidden behind gamelan instruments, cameras and cameramen, so it was easier to watch the interview on the projection screen. In other words, everything was arranged in such a way that it could be captured by television cameras. Thus rather than a wayang performance at which television cameras would be discretely present, here one had the feeling that everything was primarily a television programme, and only secondarily a real world and live performance—being present at the performance was like watching television, with commercials and TV jingles punctuating time. There were strong lights set up by the television crew, and directed at the wayang stage, sharply separating it from the surrounding darkness, so that looking at the stage felt almost like watching a bright television screen in a darkened room. The four cameras and cameramen were situated conspicuously on high platforms in a large open space between the wayang stage and the audience, further strengthening the sense that the stage is the object of television's gaze. One saw the cameras "looking" at the stage, and one's own seeing was influenced by them.

While this performance was not the most typical for Jogja TV, it would be too simplistic to dismiss it. Rather, it shows that multiple forces are at work, and the relationship of wayang and television continues to be unpredictable, different from one performance to another, and

5.4 A wayang performance covered live by Jogja TV in 2007. The stage is strongly lighted, and cameras, set on office desks and a ping pong table, are prominently visible. The space of this live, outdoor performance "feels" rather like a television studio.

5.5 A television interview on the wayang stage preceding the same performance.

5.6 A projection screen at the same performance, on which people watch the televised interview taking place on the nearby wayang stage. Later, on the same screen, people will watch a simulcast of the performance.

defying any simple conclusion. If the earlier examples seemed to suggest that television is becoming more localized and is closer to wayang because it is more intimately part of the Javanese world, the last example highlights that, for the same reason, Java and wayang are becoming more like television.

In this context, I should mention that the practice of simulcasting live performances, already occasionally occurring in the late 1990s, has gradually become very common. For example, at a performance in Solo in 2007, two large projection screens were positioned so that the masses of people watching the performance who couldn't find seats near the stage, could watch on the two screens, which were much nearer to them than the wayang screen, which was only visible to them in the distance. Even though the performance was not broadcast on television, there were several cameras and a switchboard for instant editing, and the projected images were similar to wayang as it is normally seen on television. After the performance ended, the hundreds of people who stayed until the end were not getting ready to leave. The MC, visible in close up on the screens, was heard saying that the winners of the lucky draw would now be announced, which indeed happened, as we could all

5.7 One of several projection screens for simulcast at a wayang performance that was not covered by television. The actual wayang screen is (barely) visible on the left side of the photo. Solo, 2007.

see on the huge television-like screens. Somehow it all felt like being on television—even at a wayang event not broadcast on television.

In the case of Jogja TV, the localization of television and the televisation of the wayang world is further complicated when one takes into account that on the level of ownership (from where influence is diffused to other levels), the Yogyanese "local"—and the emphasis on local culture, traditional performances, and so on, with the involvement, agency, indeed genuine love of local arts and culture of people like Faizal and many others—is an image produced in the framework and (in part at least) for the profit of a pan-Indonesian conglomerate, a nationwide network of local televisions, owned by a Balinese media baron.

The case of Semarang TV, another television station under the Bali Post Media Group, enables us to see another fragment of the larger picture. Established in May 1995, less than a year after Jogja TV, its programme *Langen Budaya*, broadcast every evening except Sunday and running continuously from 2005 till present, closely resembles Jogja TV's hour-long wayang. Here too, it was described to me as a "series", produced by cutting an all-night performance into segments. In fact, for the first broadcasts, the recordings were borrowed from Jogja TV, and in the early years, the two stations occasionally exchanged recordings. *Langen Budaya* features *wayang kulit* most often by far, although (especially in the early years) occasionally kethoprak or *wayang orang* were broadcast. In addition to these near-daily programmes, an all-night performance is shown regularly once a month, either live or previously recorded. Wayang or its elements also occasionally appear in other programmes, as do other Javanese performing arts, some of which have their own programming slots (e.g., *Macapat* for Javanese sung poetry, *Gendhing Jawa* for gamelan music, scheduled just before *Langen Budaya*). While Yogyakarta's (self-)image is that of a centre of Javanese art and culture, Semarang is known more as a hub of commerce and modern industry. While this is to some extent reflected in the self-representation and programming of the two television stations, and perhaps in the greater "thickness" of cultural programmes in Yogyakarta, there are also many similarities, and various local Javanese programmes do have a strong presence on Semarang TV. When I first asked about wayang broadcasts, I was told that "that is indeed our flagship programme [*program unggulan*]", and when I checked the company's YouTube channel, two out of the three "popular uploads" there were wayang performances, one of them with 21,000 views. I was told at Semarang TV that one difference is that while Yogyanese wayang is *full klasik*, in Semarang there tend to be long comic interludes and generally more entertainment. While this is not a black and white contrast, and performances on Jogja TV can have extended *gara-gara*, it is true that Jogja TV tends toward the "classic" style, to the point that it does not represent—or presents an "edited" representation—the variety of performances in the Yogyakarta area, many of which have long interludes, pop music, singing and dancing guest starts, and so on. The later kind of wayang, with more emphasis on light entertainment, has a long tradition in the Semarang area. In fact, since the 1990s, it has been often identified as *pantura* (north coast), and wayang on Semarang TV keeps this tradition alive. In this sense, the programme has its own strong local character, in addition to being most often performed in the Semarang/pantura area, and reflecting local issues.

While in Yogyakarta, the television company's association with the royal court and the strength of local cultural tradition dominate both the public images and informal conversations, and one does not immediately hear about the Balinese connection, at Semarang TV the association with Bali Post Media Group is readily talked about, as are the business practices of the television station (all this seems to go hand in hand with a more matter-of-fact, business-like attitude, as well as a less heavy emphasis on Javanese identity). The chief of Semarang TV, from its founding till the present (2017) is a Balinese man, formerly a journalist of *Bali Post* (the original media outlet from which the Bali Post Media Group developed). At the beginning of Semarang TV (then Cakra TV), 50 employees were invited from Semarang to Bali for two months training at Bali TV, which, like other television stations that are part of its Indonesia Network, place a strong emphasis on local culture and identity. In the following years, there were more meetings and training sessions for employees from the various stations of the media conglomerate.

Another side of Semarang TV being local—as it was presented to me in conversations with the employees—is connected to the business workings of television.

> We, as a local TV station, are different from TV stations in Jakarta, because they get advertisements easily, because they broadcast to the whole of Indonesia. But we are local, and in local [TV] it is more difficult, so we sell hours and we sell programmes ... for example, programmes to the government, [such as] a dialogue on a certain theme.

Wayang broadcasts work on the same model, in that the sponsor pays for the performance as well as for the television coverage—a practice very similar to that of Indosiar in the past (except that Indosiar interrupted the broadcasting with various other advertisements), and no doubt to many local television stations today, including Jogja TV. As we were talking about other programmes sponsored by government or commercial sponsors, a recurring word was "dialogue": it was through "dialogue" that government or commercial messages were communicated. In the simplest form, a programme consisted of a conversation on a particular "theme", with the aim to promote a particular message. Many wayang broadcasts function as such "dialogues": a certain "theme" is promoted by the sponsor, most directly when a local government official comes on the stage during an interlude, and has a "dialogue" with the puppeteer, or, as it often turns out, gives a speech, directed at both people present at the event and television audiences. Additionally, the puppeteer usually introduces the theme or message into the discussion among the clowns on the screen, and the stand-up comedians may also discuss it. There may be additional strategies for the government officials to attract attention, such as the frequent lucky draw—in one performance on Semarang TV, for example, several new bicycles were prominently displayed on the stage next to the gamelan, to be given out by the official to the lucky winners, of course with more conversations promoting the "theme". All this, in 2017, is strongly reminiscent of the spectacular performances in the 1990s, in the era of Indosiar.

A commercial company also frequently sponsors a wayang performance and its shooting. In addition to the promotion of its products in the performance, the televised programme may include advertisements for that company's products, such as—the example I was given is telling—the services of a mobile network provider.

Not all wayang broadcasts are sponsored by government or corporations. Among the most frequent sponsors are villages, where wayang is part of ceremonies (such as village cleansing), and individuals sponsor wayang on occasions such as marriages. Here again the sponsor pays for both wayang and television, and while the feeling of these events is different from performances promoting messages of the government and of large corporations, there is a curious continuity between, or interpenetration, of what appear to be different worlds, for example, between village rituals, the advertising campaign of a mobile network provider, and government propaganda. And somehow all of this, including the television stations' links to the nationwide conglomerate Bali Post Media Group, is part of how these television stations, wayang broadcasts, and wayang performances taking place before the cameras, are "local" and not; or perhaps one could say, to bring out the contradiction in the term "local television": tele-local.

New Wayang Programmes on Older Television Stations: Snapshots from 2007

To get a wider picture of the overall situation in the era of local private television stations, let us consider some other wayang programmes. I offer merely a few glimpses, a few close-ups, a few examples from a multitude of cases.

In the 1990s, the signal of the Jakarta-based TPI station could not be received in Central Java, but TPI produced some interesting wayang programmes, such as wayang kulit with the dhalang Sujiwo Tejo that I discussed earlier, and the *Asep Show*, featuring the Sundanese *wayang golek* puppeteer Asep Sunandar with the puppet of Cepot, a popular clown-servant, in hour-long talk show-like programmes, broadcast daily during Ramadan. The *Asep Show* was more a talk show than wayang. There was no wayang story, and it was recorded in a studio, with the scenery changing with each episode. For example, in the episode "Cepot Korban Mode", or "Cepot, the Victim of Fashion", the puppet of the clown Cepot appeared from behind the counter in what appeared like a high-class boutique, with a poster of the Eiffel Tower in the background. Still, a dhalang, a puppet and Sundanese gamelan music were at the centre of this television programme. In 2007, when TPI could be watched in Central Java, on Saturday nights the station was broadcasting a new wayang golek programme, *Ngedate Sareng Cepot*, "Dating Cepot". The programme builds on the *Asep Show*, especially in that it moves wayang performance to the studio and makes an extensive use of the studio setting, atmosphere and technology. It is quite different from mainstream wayang programmes. At the same time, *Ngedate Sareng Cepot* departs from the *Asep Show* in that the former presents a complete wayang performance (complete plot, presented primarily in the wayang medium). If one sees it as a development of the *Asep Show*, it returns to traditional wayang and brings much more of it onto television.

The setting of *Ngedate Sareng Cepot* is the semi-virtual world of modern television studio, dominated by luminescent blues—largely a typical television talk show setting. The background is decorated with two large props shaped like giant *kayon* (tree-of-life puppet), and in the centre of the back wall is a decoratively framed screen for the projection of slides. The wayang golek stage is placed just in front of that screen, in the centre, so that, when the cameras shoot the puppets from the front, the puppets are seen against the background of the projected images—a village street, rice fields, a temple, a palace gate. The gamelan set is not placed behind the puppeteer as usual, but it is split into two halves that are placed to the sides in the foreground, so that there is stage-like space in the centre foreground for guest stars (comedians, singers, etc.). Within this radically transformed arrangement, the wayang performance is otherwise quite traditional, but it is interrupted by a comic interlude, which, in the new space, places the guest stars neatly in the centre foreground, with the wayang stage in the background. The guest performers interact with each other as well as with the clown puppets, but the space (and perhaps the cultural setting) enables them to go further than usual. For example, sometimes the actors/comedians stage a comic scene reminiscent of folk theatre in which puppets are not involved. When the comedians talk to the puppets, sometimes they stand next to the puppet stage and lean on it like on a counter in a bar. In one episode, at one point in the clown scene, the dhalang put on a monstrous fake moustache and wig, stood up, and began to dance; at another time, one of the comedians took a puppet and began to manipulate it, in effect replacing the dhalang. The very risqué clown scenes, the rearrangement of the stage, the studio setting, and the slides in the background aside, much of the performance is quite conventional. On the whole, the programme gives the impression, not so much of an experiment or of stumbling attempts to show traditional arts on television, but of a professionally made, well-polished television programme, in which wayang becomes rather smoothly and effortlessly an effective part of television entertainment, even as the wayang performance retains much of its liveliness.

What is there to say about the smooth professionalism of the programme? Has a successful marriage been achieved? Or is it a sign of wayang dissolving in television, becoming so much part of its culture that television does not have to worry about wayang being different, about wayang challenging television by showing the world differently? Is this also the moment when one suddenly realizes that what used to be only a harmless dream may now be coming true, and one is surprised to find something frightening about it? Similar to the image of a Huxley-esque, perfectly happy, carefree future? What would it mean if the dream was realized, if wayang and television were really happily married and there would be no conflict, no tension? (Note, however, that we are talking here about wayang golek, which, I get the impression, has been often happier or somewhat more comfortable on television than wayang kulit.)

Another programme, popular in East Java in 2007, was *Elizabeth Nyindhen*, produced by TVRI Surabaya. This show took the controversial relationship between dhalang/wayang and *pesindhen* (female singer) to a caricature-like extreme. The pesindhen, as we have seen in Chapter One, has become very prominent in wayang performances. The main criticism of this fact has been that she or they (together with guest stars) overshadow the dhalang and thus destroy the structure of wayang, when during the interludes the dhalang functions more like an MC. In *Elizabeth Nyindhen*, the American pesindhen, Elizabeth, is the undisputed centre of attention whereas the dhalang and wayang are in all ways in the background, merely creating a setting for the star to shine. The American pesindhen functions as the talk-show host and the main guest at the same time, and she alternately sings and talks to the dhalang. There is no story, and not even much talk between the clowns—they only complement Elizabeth. The small gamelan is arranged so that it is convenient to play music independent of wayang, rather than to accompany it—the instruments are not behind the dhalang, but to one side. The gamelan is of the type and size today associated with relaxed music making (*gadhon*), rather than wayang. The gamelan's primary function here is not to accompany wayang (and there is no wayang play to accompany) but the pesindhen. If in the past there were complaints about the pesindhen standing up, because this was considered impolite next to the sitting puppeteer, Elizabeth towers confidently high above the puppeteer and the musicians. The main attraction of this programme is of course the fact that an American woman can sing as a pesindhen and speak Javanese. One may be reminded of what we have discussed in Chapter One about the foreign, strange and funny in wayang as an attraction in itself (from strange and new kinds of music to the comic character "Landa", or Dutchwoman/Foreigner). In *Elizabeth Nyindhen*, the *landa* pesindhen combines the double threat to the sovereignty of the dhalang and the traditional structure of the wayang medium: the new prominence of the pesindhen (and by extension the guest stars) and the appeal of the foreign and the new—all in the realm and under the control of television. For the traditionalist dhalang, this programme may be a nightmare coming true, as wayang, perhaps more than ever before, becomes more a toy than an equal partner of television; on the other hand, many people find it entertaining. In any case, it is one of the fascinating culminations of the trends apparent in wayang for several decades, and its existence suggests quite a different conclusion about what is happening than possible conclusions suggested by other cases.

The last programme that I will mention is a cartoon version of the *Mahabharata*, the epic that is the most common source of wayang stories. It was produced in 2007 by a group of independent artists in Yogyakarta, and sold to a Jakarta-based private television station, RCTI, where it was broadcast for several months as a weekly cartoon series. The iconography of wayang orang (wayang with human actors instead of puppets) is translated into the Japanese-style cartoon. When I was watching the cartoon with the makers in their little studio in Yogyakarta, I pointed out to them that the voices of the characters closely follow wayang conventions (for example, a very big, low voice for Bima, a particular colour of high-pitched voice for Durna, and so on), and more generally, the characters or personalities of the heroes resemble wayang more than anything else. The makers said that they had realized this, and that this had happened unconsciously, *automatis* (automatically). They tried to distance the wayang cartoon from traditional wayang in order to make it more appealing to the "younger generation", yet they found it difficult to free the stories and characters from wayang. As the young cartoon makers were trying to escape from wayang, the wayang imagination crept back into the television programme from inside the makers' experiences and imagination, against their will. (Recall how a newspaper commented on Telewayang: "Even Wendo is not able to free himself from the heroes of wayang kulit as it is performed in the world of wayang kulit performances.")

Wayang and the Internet

When wayang was first shown on Indosiar, sparking the debates that are at the core of this book, and even for a few years afterwards, the internet played practically no role in the world of wayang. My own dissertation, finished three years after the first Indosiar wayang, was completed without using the internet at all. Around 2018, "the time of writing": the internet and the various gadgets on which it is accessed seem indispensable to doing research, and for many people, in many places, they sometimes appear to have replaced other media, including television, as the dominant form of entertainment and information. The research for this section involved much more internet browsing, searching, and online eavesdropping than other parts of this book. And yet, without chatting (in the old, pre-internet, prehistoric sense) about the internet with people over coffee in Java and physically attending performances (especially in 2016–2017), my understanding would be entirely different and, I believe, much more limited. The limits of perceiving and living through the internet is itself a recurring motif in this and the next sections, as are limits, borders, walls, frames, and screens more generally.

As we perceive and inhabit the world through the Net, and as we (in Singapore at least, the "future city") are inculcated with an ideology of technological progress and inevitable global spread of technology (when it does not spread, it is a sign of backwardness), one might assume that the internet has displaced television in Indonesian towns and villages in the same ways and to the same degree as in other places, or that it inevitably will. To what extent and in what particular ways has the reality-fantasy of the internet penetrated (the reality-fantasy of) the wayang world, and in what ways has it become a part of the story of wayang's interaction with television, are some of the questions in this section, which again offers glimpses rather than a comprehensive survey.

One has to think anew about the historicity and temporality of this brave new world—but perhaps that thought emerges with every new medium and every new frame. The internet and the ways in which we inhabit the world through it, are often surreally new and strangely familiar, even ancient, prehistoric, at the same time. The internet involves time travel to various futures and pasts, sometimes in the same movement.

The visual language in wayang videos available on the internet remains largely the same—and it *is* the same in the many YouTube videos that originated as television programmes. Visibility, promotion, framing and cutting are still key issues, although they figure in new incarnations. With respect to distance and place, too, the internet seems to have inherited some of the ways and powers of television—distance-seeing—that we have explored in this book. When people talk about watching wayang on the internet today, they tend to bring up similar issues as in the case of television, with some differences. Being and not being physically present at the performance, is still a central theme, and they still talk about the atmosphere and sociability of wayang. Still, most people say that "of course" watching wayang on YouTube does not come anywhere close to the direct experience of a wayang event. Among the appeals of the internet, like those of television, is that one does not need to be physically present at the performance, and this is still discussed in the context of how people's lives have changed, and in particular their busy-ness (*kesibukan*).

Alongside these continuities, there is change. Some of the traits of television wayang seem to be further developed in the world of the internet, as if the internet was the next stage in an evolution. In the case of television, and especially a large, national network like Indosiar, the sense that a wayang performance can be seen "anywhere" was already important, and it shaped the performances before the cameras. Then, "anywhere" meant vaguely "Indonesia" (to the extent that anyone thought about what it meant, as this anywhere was not contrasted to any other anywhere). However, already in 1971, in the earliest years of imagining wayang on television, the possibility of global reach was mentioned, albeit as something incredible, in a passage I have quoted in the previous chapter: "We are sceptical ... it seems like an illusion that someday [*sic*] the wajang shows of Ki Dalang Timbul or Ki Nartosabdo may be seen by new audiences around the world." Today, the global reach of the internet has become a prominent theme in Javanese discourse, and it is one of the first things that puppeteers point out when asked about the difference between wayang on television and on the internet: a distinction has emerged between the more limited "anywhere" of television and the global "anywhere" of the internet.

One puppeteer, Sri Mulyono, said that the internet "is able to make it easier to make [puppeteers] known by many people, not only the local people here, but people in other provinces, abroad, and in the whole world [*sadonya*] .... This is good ... because the world community [*masyarakat donya*] can watch thanks to the internet. Even you in Bohemia, when you return, or in Singapore, if you want to watch wayang, you just click [*namung klik*] and all the wayang emerges." This puppeteer has never been to Bohemia or Singapore, he is known for his conservative traditional performances, and like me, he doesn't use Facebook or other "social media". As we were sitting on the floor of his small, village-style *pendhapa* in his house outside the city of Yogyakarta, I sensed that for both of us, speaking of the internet and of clicking in Bohemia was in the realm of fantasy or freely travelling imagination—somehow I think of Jules Verne's *Extraordinary Voyages*.

Ki Purbo Asmoro, one of the best known Solonese puppeteers in the age of the Net, speaks from a somewhat different position. He has performed in different parts of the world and his performances had, for some time, a strong presence in the world of online wayang, and were among the most often live-streamed and promoted for international audience, thanks in part to Kathryn Emerson, an American musician and scholar who often sponsored the live stream. However, when Purbo speaks of "the whole world", as he often does when he mentions the Net in his performances, we are again drawn into a realm of lively imagination—if anything, the contact with reality (his travels, the frequent live-streaming of his performances) intensifies the desire for the "whole world" and brings it deeper into his thought. When I talked to him, his first statement about wayang on the internet was that "the positive [aspect] is that it can be accessed by the whole world", and this motif was repeated, in various variations, throughout our conversation. In one performance, live-streamed to the whole world, Purbo spoke through two puppets, Cangik and her daughter Limbuk. As part of a scene where the dhalang, through these characters, commonly thanks the sponsors and special guests (including foreigners, whenever one is present), Cangik noted that "Dr Kitsie Emerson from America" came, and she explained that thanks to her, the performance

> Cangik: ... is live-streamed [*di-live-streaming*], broadcast, directly through the internet. So don't think that only this many people [i.e., the ones you can see] came here.
> Limbuk: Well, this is already a lot.
> C: But more numerous than these are the ones watching [the performance on] the internet.
> L: Wow! As far as where, mother?
> C: Around the world! [*Saimbenging jagad!*]
> L: So, as far as America, as far as Japan, as far as Australia, and other places, they watch?
> C: They do!
> L: So the celebration of [the sponsor] Mr Sumadi and his wife and family—people around the world can access [*meng-akses*] it this evening? .... Wow, thank you!

Only a few dozens of people were watching the performance at that moment (the number is visible on the webpage), while Purbo's performances regularly attract hundreds and sometimes thousands of spectators. The way he brings the internet into wayang is quite typical, as are pronouncements made by puppeteers during the interludes that "this performance is watched not only by people here, not just in the whole Indonesia, but in the whole world!" The question of how wayang is watched abroad aside, the internet stirs puppeteers' imagination in old and new ways, and they bring these new motions of the mind—those fantasized distances, those uncounted people on all continents—onto the screen, into the play, just like traditionally and still today, they bring onto the screen everything happening among musicians, spectators, sponsors, and waiters in the performance space; or for that matter, in the same way they brought Indosiar into the performances through comments and otherwise.

Another way in which the "anywhere" of television has been taken further by the internet, in this further de-localization of wayang: very commonly (most commonly, I am told), viewers watch on mobile phones. If in the case of wayang on television, people didn't have to travel to a wayang performance and could watch wayang wherever the television set was located—which, by the time of Indosiar wayang and thereafter, was most commonly at home, or less often in another fixed location. Now people can, but do not have to, stay home or near the television. The screen on which they watch can be held in their hand, allowing them to watch, to a new degree, wherever they are, even "on the go". A couple of decades ago, television seemed to liberate people from having to be in a particular place; now, to watch wayang on television seems like a comparatively settled, place-bound manner of enjoying wayang. (Although—my cranky prehistoric cave-dwelling double interrupts—as I see people's worlds shrink into the space between their eyes and the screens of their phones, as I see them stoop as they watch within the tiny frames of their "smartphones", I wonder whether such mobility is not an even smaller cave dwelling.)

We seem to be talking about a kind of historical evolution, from television wayang to internet wayang. In Java, too, sometimes this becomes one of the narratives of technological modernization, kept

5.8 One way to watch a live stream of wayang on a smartphone. A photo made public on Facebook, with the note, "watching streaming of [the puppeteer] Bayu Aji".

alive by constant "upgrading" of commodified technologies, such as the allegedly ever-smarter versions of smartphones. This evolutionary narrative is amplified by the common perception that the internet is used by younger people in urban areas, while older people, especially in villages, are more likely to enjoy wayang on television. However, this point also suggests that the "past" that is television—as well as other technologies, such as radio—is well and alive in the present (in the villages and among older people—although certainly not exclusively). In fact, rather than discounting television (and radio) as media of the past, their importance today is asserted by puppeteers, often to the point of suggesting that in some ways, for certain viewers, perhaps most, especially in Java, television is more important than the internet. Aneng Kiswantoro, a dhalang and a lecturer at the Indonesian Art Institute in Yogyakarta, said: "Common people [*orang biasa*] rarely watch wayang on YouTube. On TV, it's easier, because it's free. But as complete enjoyment, that too—it's still halfway [*setengah-setengah*]. Watching directly will be different. As a tendency among the public, 'I want to watch wayang on YouTube'—that is very very minimal [*sangat minim sekali*]." Sri Mulyono also said that people prefer watching directly, whenever possible, but that "many viewers of traditional arts still do not understand the internet—the public, or the farmers [don't]", and would rather watch television—"I don't have to go into any trouble, I don't have to pay, turn on TV—*ceklek* [the sound of turning on TV]—done!" When I asked about radio broadcasts of wayang, he said: "People in villages who love culture are not sophisticated in watching the internet—he [such a villager] does not want it, he does not want the hassle, he just wants to enjoy, so he just turns on the radio. Radio still has its consumers. ... [And] at night, still, among wayang fans, Jogja TV has many viewers, all the way to Solo. [In villages] TV is more popular [than the internet]." I heard these sentiments in many other conversations with puppeteers and wayang spectators. It needs to be remembered that the puppeteers who express these views live and mostly perform in rural areas, so when they speak of villages, they speak of their own world, the present world, and not—as it may appear, for example, from distant, "future"-oriented Singapore—an Other world, soon a matter of the past.

These are views from Yogyakarta, where, as of 2017, wayang is broadcast daily on Jogja TV. The situation is somewhat different in Solo.

Although it is possible to tune in to Jogja TV in Solo, there seem to be much less interest in the very Yogyanese TV station there. In Solo, one more often gets the sense that television "failed", as one local village puppeteer put it categorically ("*Gagal!*"—"Failed!"). But this, too, is just one view. Purbo, whose performances have been featured on various television stations as well as on YouTube, believes that in Indonesia, television has greater potential to reach Indonesian audiences than internet. "Indonesians work in front of the TV. ... More people access [wayang] on TV. Only, as I said earlier about area coverage, internet is international, and television only national. ... Many people are *kaptek* [*kapok teknologi*, "hopeless with technology"] ... [people who use the internet in Indonesia] are not as many as abroad; but many watch television, it is still the favourite dish." These statements are made with the knowledge that the "booming" (Purbo's word) of wayang on television, the age of Indosiar, is over, but when I suggested that wayang on television today is not as prominent as it was in the past, Purbo resisted the idea that it is gone for good or that this is somehow an inevitable progress, but simply a wrong decision on the part of Indosiar to stop, and on the part of other television stations not to try. Rather than focusing on the failure of Indosiar to continue its broadcasts, he presented the Indosiar case as evidence that wayang *can* "boom" on television, "if only the broadcasts were continued and if they were conceived in an even better way". He turned to the future of wayang on television, clearly feeling that television offers some possibilities that the internet does not. He referred to a recent showing of an Indian-made *Mahabharata* series on a private Indonesian television station, which, according to him, was done very well and which was very popular (*meledak*, "exploded") in Indonesia, "and children got to know wayang" (i.e., wayang characters and stories). He said how once, when he was about to start a performance,

> the gamelan was already playing, [but] everyone was waiting in front of the television [for the beginning of the Indian series]. Why is it that an Indian movie can do this, why not our own wayang kulit? ... Actually it could—with a powerful wayang performance. It's OK to use Indonesian, with one-hour episodes. ... Why do Indonesians not make it like that [the Indian series], so that people

> would be drawn to wayang? It would be possible... If only it were broadcast on television, it could boom again.

Evidently, the idea of wayang on television still stirs the imagination, as it has for decades—perhaps even more than the internet? At the end of our interview—mainly about the internet—Purbo wished to reiterate: "It is my hope that there would be a regulation in this republic that, like it or not, television [companies] must do it [broadcast wayang and other traditional arts]. Why is it that in the 24 hours, there are no traditional programmes? That is strange. In the whole world people take care of culture." (As is often the case with Purbo's thought, an image of the "whole world" permeates his views and fantasies of Javanese wayang, and a global vision supports caring for local world.)

The linear, evolutionary narrative coexists with these views, in which television is not a technology on the verge of extinction, destined to be superseded by the internet. These views are close to the ground of contemporary reality, and are at the same time infused with imagination about the future possibilities of television. No one denies the importance of the internet, but many people do seem to resist the particular mode of linear technological fantasizing, in which older media, such as television and perhaps wayang itself, become necessarily obsolete because of new media. With respect to puppeteers' imagination, television and the internet spark different fantasies, even as they overlap: fantasies of wayang on television concern the future of wayang specifically in Java and the actors are the Javanese people, whereas the internet, while certainly also involved in imagining about wayang in Java, often leads people to fantasize about "the whole world", such as clicking on "wayang" in Bohemia.

The powerful evolutionary narrative is further complicated by what happens with wayang online. The net-like interconnectedness of various modes in which wayang is entangled with the Net involves not only knot-like intersections with older and newer online genres (such as YouTube, and indivisibly, social media, websites, various forms of messaging and chatting), but it extends to older media, including television, radio, audio- and video-recording, as well as writing, including scholarship. The media appear within other media, like frames within frames that enframe each other (wayang frame within television frame seems like

5.9 The photo of an old radio on the website for fans of streaming of radio wayang.

the simplest, almost prehistoric scenario), where what one sees overflows across the frames' borders, or where the frames merge at one moment and become distinct at another. Many Indonesian television stations, including those that broadcast wayang, live-stream their programmes on the internet; as do some radio stations. Some Facebook pages collect links to these stations, such as one called "Streaming Wayang Kulit", which has a photo of an old transistor radio on its main page, along with this statement: "All-night wayang kulit broadcasts on radio are the soundscape of Javanese people every time the night arrives. All-night broadcasts of wayang kulit are its indivisible part in food stalls, in houses, in community security posts, in places of work." Many wayang videos on YouTube were originally broadcast on television and/or sold on VCDs and DVDs. This is often clear in the video itself (for example, the Indosiar or other logo is visible in the corner of the "screen" throughout the performance) and sometimes mentioned in a note by the person who uploaded the recording. In one case, for example, a YouTube viewer comments on a video labelled as a 2001 Indosiar wayang: "Why is the Indosiar logo intentionally covered?" Answer: "Sorry, Pak, I just copied the video from a VCD cassette." (The common use of *kaset*, "cassette", to refer to newer technologies, helps to further collapse time.) Other wayang videos online were privately recorded or commissioned, often by sponsors of wayang events, such as weddings, and later uploaded on

YouTube. Audio recordings of wayang uploaded on YouTube include those originally published on cassette tapes decades ago, from at least as early as the 1970s (such as those of Ki Nartosabdo, who passed away in 1985). For example, a note on a video states: "I acquired this Wayang Kulit performance of Ki Nartosabdo from a wayang kulit collector. This is the product of a cassette recording that was digitized, and made into a video version, so that it can be enjoyed by everyone [*sedulur semua*, lit. "all relatives"]."

The Javanese word *sedulur*, denoting relatives, or cousins, introduces a touch of warmth, of Javanese sociability, into the statement that frames the online video. Some wayang videos on YouTube generate comments and discussion, which anyone can read. People often thank the person who uploaded the video, praise the performance and the puppeteer, ask for more recordings to be uploaded, and share their thoughts, in which they often travel, not to the technological future, but home and to the past. For example, for one YouTube video of Nartosabdo, one person writes: "I got reminded of the past when I was in primary school. Every eve of Thursday and Friday a radio was readied (the battery had to be full because it was for a whole evening) to listen to the broadcast from a radio station in Ponorogo, East Java. Of course the favourite puppeteer was Ki Narto Sabdo." In the same discussion, another netizen explains, after expressing his gratitude (I am translating here Javanese terms of address, to evoke the sense of the homely, traditional familiarity): "I am in kalimantan can be a medicine when I miss *kahanan* [being/situation/circumstances] in Java and listening to the late grandpa narto's wayang kulit......I am originally from surokarto brother [*sic*]." The viewer's online name is "Borneo law office" (*kantor hukum Borneo*), with a map of Borneo for the profile picture. The netizen who uploaded the video, responded to this Javanese Almayer, sending his greetings to "you and all beloved kinfolk [*kadang kinasih*] in Kalimantan". Yet another viewer, after adding his thanks, recognizes the mythological past floating in the present: "The Baratayuda [Final Battle] story indeed mirrors the conditions of the world in our times. Grandpa Narto performs it with true perfection." And like a refrain of a song, or like the gongs marking with perfection the cyclical time of Javanese music, where the cycle's end and its beginning coincide, people repeat that till today, no one can compare to the late grandpa Narto.

Another YouTube video, an Indosiar recording of Ki Manteb's performance, was uploaded in 2014 but "recorded from TV Indosiar on Saturday, 21 December 1996", as is stated below the video, in which the Indosiar logo is visible. The first viewer to comment states, in 2015:

> I miss [*kangen*] the Indosiar broadcasts of wayang kulit. They were my favourite, for the time before sleeping. But now they are no more ... So that when I am about to sleep, I must open YouTube ☹ I hope national TV can return to broadcasting wayang kulit programmes ☺

Another netizen posted a "reply", in 2016: "That's very true, Mas." And third one wrote in 2017: "nostalgia ... they used to play until dawn". Indosiar wayang is missed (*kangen*), as one misses a lover or home, or a dhalang like "grandpa" Narto, or wayang on radio—but it has also gained another life on YouTube, rather like wayang itself. Like television, Indosiar wayang is still around, in people's minds and on the internet. So is nostalgia (much talked about by Indosiar men: see Chapter Two), although now, ironically and tellingly, it is television and Indosiar broadcasts that are its objects, that evoke home and the past, rather than (or in addition to, at other times) wayang performances watched directly at celebrations. This particular segment has 40,621 views, as of October 2017, not an unusual number for wayang videos on YouTube (the number of views ranges from hundreds to hundreds of thousands).

The comments on YouTube videos accumulate over weeks, months, and years, in a conversation with an otherworldly tempo, like John Cage's composition "As Slow As Possible", one version of which is planned to last for 639 years. A conversation with a different tempo, closer to ordinary exchanges among viewers at a wayang performance, although still not the same, is part of live-streaming wayang. In Chapter Three, we have seen that one of the main attractions of watching a performance directly is being among people: chatting with others, listening to other people's comments, cheers, and laughter; togetherness of which the puppeteer, the puppets and the action on the screen were organically a part. Javanese wayang fans, we have seen, often felt that this was missing when one watched wayang on television. In the case of live-streaming wayang, next to the frame with the live video stream, there is a frame for online chat. Even more than the comments on YouTube video recordings, this enables people to "chat" while they watch the live broadcast. People comment on the puppeteer's skills, on the beauty of the female singer's voice, on funny or interesting things happening at the performance (a toddler sitting on stage and listening attentively), on weather (heavy rain!), they ask about the story and the characters, about the sponsor and occasion, and about future performances. People introduce themselves, greet each other, and sometimes longer conversations ensue. Many of the interlocutors obviously know each other, either only from these online encounters or they have met in person, so online watching wayang is also a virtual reunion. The atmosphere varies: sometimes there are only a few dozen people watching, and a comment appears or a dialogue is started only now and then. In other cases, there are commonly over a thousand people watching "live", and the fast-running chat reflects the noisier atmosphere, as people talk and sometimes seem to shout, as if at the same time. For example, the shows of the Yogyanese dhalang Ki Seno Nugroho typically have 1,000–1,500 people watching live online, and the YouTube channel PWKS Live has over 8,000 subscribers at the time of writing (PWKS stands for *Penggemar Wayang Ki Seno Nugroho*, "Fans of wayang of Ki Seno Nugroho").

In the simultaneous chats, people commonly ask for the phone or WhatsApp number of the puppeteer, and are often provided with it, usually by the operator of the live stream. This enables them to send a message to the dhalang, normally a request for a song, standard practice in wayang for decades (in the past, written notes were used, later replaced by text messages). WhatsApp groups are formed or joined through the chat.

Especially at these livelier events, and especially during upbeat songs during the comic interludes, people may join in the music by writing out words from the lyrics of the song performed at the moment, or the familiar stylized calls and "shouts" that are part of Javanese music (*alok, senggakan*), with YouTube viewers responding to each other and the music, as in this case (I copy from the chat; A, B, C and D indicate four people in the chatroom):

A: *hookya*
B: *haaa..eeee..hhaaa...eeee*
C: *hokya*
D: *...e...e ... yak.e......yak.eeee hokyaaaaa*

This is interspersed with chatting by others ("she is dancing well"... "anyone knows the puppeteer's phone number?" ... "I want to order the song 'Mendem Wedokan'").

Drinks and food are often mentioned in the chats. At the beginning of a performance, a person might say, "I am getting ready, preparing coffee", and during the performance, people often mention what they are drinking, or joke that they are off to a food stall. Sometimes, as in the example that follows, talk of drinks and snacks develops into a playful re-enactment of what commonly happens during live wayang performance:

A: Mbak @Esti, where is the coffee I ordered?
B: I would like ice tea, no sugar @esti [B seems to be playing with the similarity between the sound of Esti and *es teh*, "ice tea"]
Esti: It's sold out, all we have is tea. Hot ice tea [*es teh*], you want?
B: Do you still have salted fish, @esti?
C: Esti, good evening, I would like hot water.
Esti: All we have left are intestines.
B: Am I crazy or the seller is? Hot ice tea?
D: I ASKED FOR HOT SAUCE A WHILE AGO AND NEVER GOT IT. Whatever, I just sauce myself.
E: One gingery drink, Mbak Esti.
B: Please wrap it for me, I will bring it all the way to the front @esti.
Esti: I apologize, everything is sold out.
All we are left with are prayers.

One netizen likes to jokingly evoke the sellers who often walk among the audience, writing in the chat: "coffee coffee coffee coffee tea tea tea tea tissue tissue tissue".

Eavesdropping on these conversations, watching wayang on YouTube through them, I am surprised that I feel like I am at a wayang performance, I feel the social, familial atmosphere and hear the conversations, through which one enjoys the performance; that particular mode of being among people that is so essential to wayang, and that wayang viewers miss when they watch wayang on television—that "being there in the midst of it" we have discussed in Chapter Three; wayang as a multisensory social experience, in which drinking, talking and laughing with others is indivisibly part of the experience, and in which spectators can "join in playing", as a television viewer put it (quoted in Chapter Three), and as the examples above demonstrate in different ways (joining in the music, the re-enactment of a food stall scene).

If one feels that this online space allows for what television has taken away (or controlled like a dictator), that this is a return of sorts, or a step back from television; if, while watching wayang this way, one feels more deeply in touch with the past as something that lasts, then chatting on the internet while watching wayang involves a sensed movement back in time, into a time before television, even as the internet allows people to return to television (like when people watch Indosiar wayang on YouTube). Or, better: when one feels that a movement forward is a movement back, the sense of linear time, progress and evolution is put in doubt.

The movement back to television's prehistory creates a counterpoint to the more obviously new capabilities of live-streaming, especially the fact that people in many places, on different continents even, watch wayang together and chat about it. While in some ways the conversations resemble those at an ordinary performance, they also reflect this new way of being and not being at a place—here the internet furthers the displaced perception, discussed in Chapter Three, characteristic of television (and radio). While people take pleasure in chatting as if they were together at a wayang performance, they also readily bring into the exchanges, often with certain playfulness or sense of marvel, the fact that they are physically dispersed all over Indonesia and the world.

The fun of re-enacting the coffee-shop scene in the chat room, or joining in the music from different parts of the world, draws on the pleasure of sitting in the coffee shop and the pleasure of music, but part of the fun derives from the fact that the people both are and are not together, and from the play-acting. One can of course even think of watching wayang directly as a performance, one that interacts and interpenetrates with what happens on the wayang screen;[14] and we spoke of wayang performance covered by television as two interpenetrating performances, wayang and television. Similarly and differently, the performance that is part of chatting on internet interacts and interpenetrates the complexity of live performance(s) of puppets and people that go on at the physical location of the event. All this is brought out by Javanese viewers and performers, as can be seen in some of the anecdotes or examples above, as well as in another interesting phenomenon: some people who take part in the chatting that is part of a wayang live stream, adopt the names of wayang characters as their "usernames" or "online identities": Bima, Raden Setyaki, Wara Srikandi, and so on. Other people use "portraits" of wayang puppets as their profile photo. Both usernames and the profile pictures appear before every statement the person makes in the chatroom, rather like in the script of a play. Sometimes, the people playfully bring out the theatricality of wayang names by using wayang language to address others (such as when at one point Raden Setyaki asked Wara Srikandi, "do you still remember when we were on chat last time, *kakang mbok* Wara Srikandi?"). One of the live stream companies is called Punakawan—the collective name for the clown-servants in wayang, characters who have played a central role in the modernization of wayang, as we have seen in Chapter One. During the performances streamed live by Punakawan, the operators often join the online chat, under the username Punakawan. Even traditionally, offline, people's "real" names are from wayang (Soekarno is one example of this very common practice), as are sometimes their nicknames; and it is common to talk about one's character and identity in terms of wayang characters.[15] All this delightfully confounds the already confounded online and offline realms, life and theatre, playing with these oppositions rather than simply erasing them, in a multi-layered, multi-frame online-offline performance-life.

That people sometimes watch live streams and join in the chat while being at a live performance—either the same as the one online, or another one—and mention this in the chat, further adds to the confusion. A photographic collage of sorts, posted on Facebook, shows a performance of the play *Petruk Triplets* (Petruk Kembar Tiga), as watched

5.10 Twin triplets: watching a live performance along with two other performances "live" on the internet. The title of the performance in the top photo is "Petruk Triplets". Posted on a public Facebook page with information about wayang performances and live-streaming.

online (with titles showing the name of the play and the performer), and another photograph, taken at a live wayang performance in Jakarta, with two smartphone screens visible, each showing a different online performance. And so, the Petruk Triplets story (Petruk is one of the *punakawan*, the clown-servants) intersects another "triplet" phenomenon: the three wayang performances (one live and two online) watched at the same time. In between the two images is a fragment of the "live chat" screen, where the two sets of triplets are mentioned. The photos framing what we see in them, the "live" wayang screen frame and smartphones screens within the frames that are the photos, the wayang screens within the frames of the smartphone screens, the "live chat" where this play of frames was introduced, and the Facebook page where it was reframed and rescreened: all this presents us with a haunting representation of the play of multiple frames and screens, a whole crowd of spectres, which is an important part of what happens with wayang today, even as it is also reminiscent of older times, such as the interplay of the frames and screens of television and wayang (we may recall the case of "Watching 3 TV-wayangkulit", from Chapter Two).

Part of the pleasure, play, or marvel of online chatting comes from the curious clashing and mixing of the homely and the global. Place names figure prominently in the online chats. Many of these chats begin by playful reporting: Depok [in Jakarta], present [*hadir*]! Mecca, present! Osaka, present, it's loud and clear! Nusa Tenggara, present! Papua, present! Bojonegoro [in East Java], present! The Hague, present, crystal-clear from here! Yugoslavia [in a 2017 performance!] monitors! People present at the performance, as well as people watching other performances, may also join in the conversation. Especially from the more distant locations, people talk about towns and villages in Central Java, places where they come from. Often, they mention their hometown when they introduce themselves, and others may ask for exact directions (a favourite topic of ordinary Javanese conversations as well). For example, in one case, a Javanese viewer from The Hague and another one from Mecca began to chat, and, as they went through the routine of ascertaining where exactly their homes are, soon they realized they both come from the Boyolali area, and, in fact, from nearby villages. "God, we are neighbours! (*alah tasih tangga piyambak*)... Hopefully another time we can meet and watch wayang together." This thread in their conversation was interwoven with questions about their work abroad. One of them directed the other to google his website, "if you want to know my history (*sejarah kula*)".

Watching and chatting online sometimes overflows into the live performance—especially into the clown scenes, not surprisingly. Earlier, I have quoted an excerpt in which Limbuk and Cangik talk about live streaming and how it enables people in the whole world to watch this event. In another live-streamed performance by the same dhalang, Purbo, Cangik mentions people watching in America, England, India and Arabia, she says that it is all "extraordinary", and thanks the American sponsor and asks the audience to clap hands. The dhalang then dedicates a song to the Javanese musician "Pak Harjito, who lives in America" and who, Cangik asserts, is certainly watching, to the puppeteer Joko Susilo in Australia, and, in a joke that brings out the play-acting element in all this, to the former Indonesian president Ibu Megawati Sukarnoputri.

Limbuk asks: "Is she also listening?"—"Maybe!" answers Cangik. A few minutes later in the performance, the dhalang, through these character, has a long discussion about live-streaming with the sponsor of the live stream, Kitsie Emerson, and at one point mentions that he would like to send a recording of the wayang to a dhalang living abroad, and Emerson says that she will email the file for him. This whole conversation—about live-streaming, about people watching abroad, and about emailing a video recording—is part of the performance, watched by people physically present at the event as well as people around the world, myself included. Not only does wayang become part of the internet, but the internet becomes part of wayang.

As people chat while watching wayang online, and as puppeteers bring people watching from distant places into the performance, there are moments when wayang seems to return to itself, to its particular Javanese sociability, and, as if in the same gesture, it opens itself to the new internet-ly being and not being at a place. At the same time, there is also something "virtual", perhaps illusory, about wayang's smooth collaboration with the internet (I am thinking about the wayang-ly word for "illusory", *maya-maya*, whose root implies that the world itself is an illusion). In one wayang performance, streamed live, Semar announced: "I am watching wayang on YouTube." One of Semar's sons, Gareng, took the opportunity to tease his brother: "Bagong opens YouTube only for sex education." Semar and Bagong may seem like opposites—Semar is caring and wise, Bagong always talks back, misunderstands, mispronounces and misbehaves. Yet, it is said that Bagong originated from Semar's shadow, Semar's image—he is his double. Showing Semar as watching YouTube is already a joke, and in that dialogue, this ridiculous image is further developed by connecting it to Bagong watching internet porn. Porn becomes the image (*bayangan*) through which we see something of wayang on the internet.

As viewers, sitting in front of the screen somewhere in the Hague, Kalimantan, Osaka, Mecca, Jakarta, or "Yugoslavia" try to create a homely, Javanese atmosphere and talk about their home villages and towns, one is reminded of what that man watching in Kalimantan said, and what one hears often online in various variations: that online wayang is for him "a medicine when I miss being in Java"; it is a substitute for the real thing. We may sense here a continuity between television and the Net: we hear echoes of much earlier comments about wayang on television, as a drug for nostalgia/homesickness, and of the television business supporting the addiction for its own ends (Chapters Two and Three)—this is a continuation of that story, and it is not simply a happy ending. The dhalang Catur told me that one reason people might watch wayang on the internet is because of the kind of life they lead today. To illustrate his point, he said he has a friend, a manager at an oil drilling platform in the middle of the sea, where the man spends at least nine months every year. He watches wayang every day, because, in his words, "otherwise [he] would go mad". Sometimes he calls Catur and they chat about wayang, and only on his rare days back on land, they watch wayang together. Catur used this case to explain why people, even those in less extreme situations, might watch wayang on the internet, as if suggesting that we all dwell today on little artificial islands. One feels, sometimes at least, loneliness of oceanic magnitude and depth, that underlies wayang on the internet and the jolly chatting online. Perhaps in this, Semar and Bagong watch YouTube—wayang/porn—for similar reasons.

Catur repeatedly used the word *kesibukan* in his explanation why and how people watch wayang today, including on the internet. Kesibukan (from the word *sibuk*, "busy, lively") is Google-translated by a busy crowd of words: occupation, activity, bustle, racket, rush. Catur's anecdote, about watching wayang on an oil rig, was one illustration of kesibukan. The dispersion of people, mostly due to their work, is also part of what Catur means by kesibukan. Another side of kesibukan is that the majority of wayang spectators today, puppeteers say, want entertainment and fun, and they do not watch the full performance, but "only cuts/pieces" (*namung potong-potong*), such as the comic scenes and lively battles. Aneng said that young people are "bored" at a "conventional performance" because it is "too long" and "it is not their aesthetic", so they choose to watch a movie; "because what they encounter every day is like that, like on TV and on the internet: like it for a moment—done; know it for a moment—done [*seneng sesaat ya sudah, tahu sesaat ya sudah*]". Moreover, Aneng said, most people use their mobile phones and have to pay for data: it is too expensive to watch a whole performance (this is also clear from online comments—the lucky ones who can afford to watch for a long time sometimes boast that they have Wi-Fi). More generally, "if one watches on the internet, a laptop, or a mobile phone, the empirical experience becomes not whole [*tidak utuh*]". Somehow, the medium and culture of Indonesian internet compels a particular, quick way of watching: *potong-potong*, "cut-cut".

Cutting has been a longstanding issue in debates about wayang on television, including wayang on Indosiar: cutting the performance time, cutting whatever is not profitable or desirable on television, cutting from one shot to another. In Chapter One, I have quoted the first Indosiar wayang producer Panca emphasizing that audiences are interested not in the whole, but in the "sexiness" of the parts. Combining "cuts"—such as interludes from several performances to form a new programme—is another practice central to television. In Chapter Three, we have heard viewers of television wayang that on television they see only *sepotong-sepotong*, "cut up pieces" and we talked about the disorienting "jumping squirrel syndrome"; and in Chapter Four we saw that when wayang was first shown on television, at TVRI Yogyakarta, it was as "fragments" (*fragmen*). But cutting, on television and on the internet, is and is not the same. In the past, puppeteers and spectators have complained because the television producer is a "dictator" who controls the process and the cut-up pieces that people see. In the case of the internet, much of the cutting, much of the "production", is done by internet users, both wayang spectators and puppeteers. Production and reception blend. While in some ways this may be, as suggested earlier, a step back away from television and closer to live performance—where viewers choose what to look at or when to walk away—nonetheless the speed and ease of cutting with a single touch of the smartphone screen or a click, and the kind of choices (which part of a performance to watch, what performance to watch, skipping forward or backwards) make for a new experience. And perhaps a new technology of control, too: if television is no longer the dictator controlling the "jumping squirrel" of camera movement and thus our (the spectators') eyes, we may ponder on our new Power, our great new Independence, our Vision—of a gloriously free jumping squirrel, caught in the Net.

(We may recall, from Chapter Two, how Indosiar broadcasts were recorded from television and the videos were shown, for a fee, at village celebrations, or sold on VCDs. Through these various forms of "pirating", people outside the television companies were taking control of video-recorded wayang, blending reception and production—in ways like and unlike in the case of the internet.)

When one cuts the performance and selects what to watch, one leaves a mark. The numbers of "views" and "likes" are carefully observed by puppeteers, to see which cuts are popular and which are not. Internet users leave comments ("very funny!"), which, Aneng says, can help to promote the puppeteer. The performers cut their performances and upload what they think will advertise them best—"no need to upload the whole performance, but one can cut, cutting the interesting parts", Catur said, echoing the Indosiar producer Panca. Cutting, sampling and a particular kind of watching is characterized by a rushing, jumping rhythm of like-done-like-done and cut-cut-cut, against the backdrop of kesibukan and boredom. Like in music, it exerts power over minds and bodies, compelling people to follow and to continue: like-done-like-done-like-done-like-done ... jump-jump-jump-jump-jump.... If, in the age of Indosiar, we have heard a whisper that television is the dictator, one wonders—whispers a dissident squirrel—whether this power of the Net is not a kind of decentralized, diffused Huxley-esque totalitarianism ("a population of slaves who do not have to be coerced, because they love their servitude").

I have begun this chapter with a story of the decentralization of wayang on television, which resonates with political and economic decentralization—diffusion and reorganization of power—especially after the fall of Soeharto. Political scientists speak of "predatory networks". I write about the Net. The dispersion of people, the lonely artificial islands where we would go mad without the Net, the absorbing rhythm of sampling and of like-done-like-done, when everyone feels he is the producer (or: everyone is the "dictator", to follow the logic of that whisper from the television age), all seem to be the other side of internet-ly connectivity, the other side of the Net, the other side of that online chatting that is so full of life and playfulness. It is a curious, complicated continuation of the story of decentralization and diffusion.

Rather than trying to speak generally to the larger question of how the rhythm and culture of the internet pervade mainstream wayang performances, I would like to offer a glimpse of this process by looking at Aneng's experimental work, which also manifests how wayang is infused with digital media, including the internet: talking to him in his studio (in 2017) inspired the excitement of observing a laboratory experiment, as if he was injecting wayang with IT to produce a new organism.

Aneng told me about the origins of his experimental wayang. Only a short time ahead of an event organized by his institution, the arts academy in Yogyakarta, he was asked to prepare a 20-minute performance. Students were all too busy to attend rehearsals. (Note how the new wayang originates in kesibukan: quick, 20-minute performance, short time to prepare, everyone too busy.) So, Aneng decided to do much of the preparatory work himself, aided by electronic technology. (Leitmotif: *alone with wayang, like on an oil rig.*) He recorded sound samples of individual gamelan instruments and male and female voices, downloaded audio and video clips, and digitally remixed everything. Pre-recorded or downloaded melodies, voices, sound effects and projected images (videos, computer-generated colour patterns, etc.) were controlled by pressing keys on a keyboard. It "sounded like radio drama [*sandiwara radio*]", Aneng said. "All that was left for the puppets/wayang to do was to follow [*wayangnya tinggal mengikuti*]."

The internet pervades Aneng's wayang. His work with fragments or samples—recording, downloading, and pressing keys to play them—mirrors the activity, rush, kesibukan of internet users, puppeteers and spectators, as they busily upload and download samples of wayang, watch a this-is-funny! moment, then with a click stop the recording, jump forward or back, or cut to another show, wayang or not. The editing and cutting of sound and video samples, the incessant squirrelish jumping, seems to be another manifestation of the multiplicity of frames and the play of frames and screens.

"We have already calculated its economic value: only 15 people; no need for gamelan, singers, and so on." Halfway between performance and recording, this wayang is labour-efficient. Aneng has been invited to perform in Padang in Sumatra, with airfare paid. How to bring the large, heavy screen usually employed for wayang? He made a small, light-weight, collapsible version—"one just checks it in". His wayang is portable and mobile, like a smartphone, almost like a video file.

But if IT is at the heart of Aneng's wayang, his performances and ideas also manifest something like the longing for an absent home, like when people scattered over the whole world virtually chat during a live stream as if they were at a wayang performance. Aneng emphasizes that "we still hold wayang high [*menjunjung*], we still hold onto it [*memegang*]. The story is also a pure [*murni*] wayang story, only we conceptualized it [*membuat konsepsi*] for young people." With sponsorship from the BCA bank, he has performed his wayang in schools for children of different ages. While, according to him, they are "apathetic [*apatis*] regarding wayang" and would be "bored" watching a conventional performance because it is too long and because "it is not their aesthetic", the new form of wayang kept their attention. Aneng says that because the world has changed, "because our culture now is the culture of the internet, technology, gadgets, global culture ... puppeteers have to accept it even if they do not like mass media and so on, they have to reconcile themselves to it [*rekonsiliasi*]", and wayang needs to be *elastis* (elastic) if it is to survive. Aneng insists that all the technological innovation is really a way of "holding onto" wayang, it is done for the sake of wayang's survival, it is, paradoxically, a kind of clinging to something of the past, an heirloom. It is a bit like a Javanese watching wayang on YouTube, from 2017 "Yugoslavia".

When I talked with puppeteers about wayang and television, they discussed commercialization and publicity, but more often than not, the topic also sparked their artistic creativity and fantasy, as they would imagine how wayang could be shown on television in a better way. When I talked with puppeteers about wayang on the internet, the emphasis was somewhat different. While, as Aneng's case shows, some dhalang creatively appropriate IT, most talk about, above all, good and bad business. While this is continuous with older views about the promotional potential of television, in the case of the internet the focus feels much sharper. The majority of younger puppeteers (including Aneng) say that the internet can be good for wayang, because it can help in advertising and promotion. They talk, in unison, about being noticed, as people watch wayang on YouTube, and about promotion through social media. Clearly, the fantasy of "going viral" is infectious.

Some puppeteers feel differently, but business-related concerns are still important. The case of Purbo Asmoro may not exemplify the collective imagination of any group of dhalang either, but, like Aneng's work, Purbo's "mixed feelings" mirror, in an idiosyncratic way, present-day fantasies, fears, and confusions. When I asked Purbo, in October

2016, about his views of wayang on the internet, and especially live-streaming, he said that "there are positive and negative aspects. It is positive that [wayang performances] can be accessed form anywhere in the world ... at that very moment." After this one quick point about the positive aspect—one which clearly does matter to him, and which he repeatedly brought out in his performances—the rest of the interview turned out to be about what he saw as the problems and dangers of streaming wayang live, in particular for "a puppeteer who always searches or is creative or always shows something new". This was his first illustration of the problem:

> For instance, when I create or compose a *lakon* in a particular way, it becomes public on the internet, and is accessed by all kinds of people, it is also downloaded and disseminated. Now the challenge is when I perform the same lakon, with that creative work [*kreasi*], I think again, "Oh no, I have performed like this already on live streaming, on the internet, and now I am performing like this again, but what can I do, I haven't had a chance to change to a new version of that lakon."

While the challenges take different forms, in all cases they concern the newness of the performance. Purbo feels that his performances have to be new for people, and with live streaming, dissemination of video recordings on YouTube and on VCDs, and other puppeteers copying his versions of particular stories or the texts (which they transcribe from YouTube), he fears that he cannot create fast enough and that he will repeat himself.

Purbo's presumption that he has to be always "new" evokes the world of commerce as well as contemporary art and in particular the mentality of the art academies, with their interest in new experiments. Purbo is closely connected to the Solonese art academy, and is sometime referred to as *dalang akademis*, with a variable mixture of appreciation and criticism. He spoke of "creating or composing a new lakon", suggesting that for him the lakon is something like an artwork, in the modern sense, and a product. At the same time, and this is not unique to Purbo, such artistic values are difficult to separate from the commercial appeal of novelty in today's world of entertainment. Purbo certainly seems to fear that if he can't be constantly new, his audiences might lose interest in his performances. As one listens to his complaints, one senses that he is struggling to stay ahead, never jumping quite fast enough, in a world rushing forward—overwhelmed by existential kesibukan.

Purbo's work, as I mentioned, was frequently live-streamed, and especially for the international community of scholars and students of Javanese performing art, he was the most visible puppeteer online, thanks in part to Emerson's help. A few months after my interview, he decided he would no longer allow his performances to be live-streamed, except in exceptional cases. This decision had no doubt complex reasons, some of which are suggested by his previous complaints about live-streaming. Emerson told me about how once, when Purbo performed without live-streaming, he particularly enjoyed performing, because he felt that people would see a wonderful performance but then it would dissolve into the air like it should, like in the old days.[16] One may sense how the puppeteer feels about the kesibukan of constant live-streaming, incessant recording and replaying, and perhaps his refusal to live-stream is an attempt, a fantasy too, to go back to the particular pleasure, simplicity, settled calm, and analogue togetherness of a live performance.

In mid-2018, Purbo's official website www.purboasmoro.com, managed with Emerson's help, was deactivated, with a message signed by the latter: "DEACTIVATED. Deepest apologies, but due to his ever-growing dislike of an internet presence, Ki Purbo Asmoro has asked me to deactivate this site."[17] (The Indonesian version reads "*atas perintah langsung dari Ki Purbo Asmoro*", "on the direct order of Ki Purbo Asmoro.") In a play of doubles and shadows across time and media, in a present enthusing about future and technology, one may hear echoes from the boom years of television wayang: "Puppeteers are sick of Indosiar broadcasts."[18]

The Scholar and the Net

> *Like their European prehistoric counterparts, the stone-age inhabitants of Indonesia's* Eastern Islands and New Guinea left to posterity pale shadows of their hands long since turned

> into dust. They pressed their outstretched fingers against the surface of the rock, daubed red paint around them, and thus produced lasting stencilled images. The wild array of hand silhouettes on the Abba cave wall appears today like a flaming clamor *across the ages. Somehow they are reminiscent* of the outstretched hands of Bali *ketjak* dancers which, illuminated by the flickering flame of an oil lamp, are thrust upward into the blackness of the night to the upsurge of humming or rhythmically chattering voices [emphasis added].
>
> – Claire Holt, "Some Prehistoric Roots",
> *Art in Indonesia: Continuities and Change*[19]

Global interconnectedness is a fantasy of the Net, a fantasy overflowing into reality. Trying to resist, I have been exploring the particular: the ways in which the reality-fantasy of the internet seeps into the wayang world; how wayang, as well as television and other older media, penetrate the Net, and have gained a new life there without necessarily giving up the old, like when *lingga* merged with/into prehistoric menhirs in the story of localization of Hindu art in Indonesia. There is much "flaming clamor across the ages", much in one age that is "somehow ... reminiscent" of other ages.

But as I write yet again about the particular and about localization, I am "online", I am distracted, in a particularly internet-ly way, as a part of my research, I am caught in the immense net like a fish, like a squirrel, one among millions. I go to YouTube to look for a wayang recording, I email a puppeteer in Yogya, I look for wayang websites, I can't concentrate on writing because last night I watched wayang live-streamed from Java, enjoying people's "live" conversations. Here, too, we talk about increased visibility, increased exposure, like when we reflected on the strong television lights at wayang performances, and about new forms of exposure, like the "indirect light" of television that makes things visible regardless of place, when the "real time of the image prevails over the real space of vision, and instantly transmitted appearances supersede the usual illumination of places". It is not all about connectivity: since I do not use "social media", I am barred from certain current ways of scholarly sociability and visibility and, equally, by the same wall, the same frame border, from certain Javanese framed online spaces, certain online caves, where people talk about wayang. This disconnection, these caves, walls, and frame borders, paradoxically link me, intimately even, with some other people who feel like me, including some Javanese puppeteers. Yet as I talk to puppeteers in this age of decentralized interconnectivity, even the more digitally active ones, I find their views and experiences more disconnected than ever, and they seem to have less understanding, for example, of who watches wayang on the internet and how. And so, my insistence on the particular and on slowness of thought, seems to bounce back at me and hurl me into a new, busy, jumpy electronic interconnectedness of Javanese wayang with the world of international (wayang) scholarship, which is also an interconnectedness of new walls, frames, and the enclosing of new caves. Homesick, I crawl to my own Facebookless cave, which feels increasingly prehistoric, as I try not to be swept by the powerful current of like-done-like-done, and the viral, "chronoscopic system of under-exposed, exposed, and overexposed".[20] Yet this sense of omnipotence and omnipresence of the Net, even as it might be my end, is not my conclusion, but rather I feel scattered between internet connectivity, and what, not just remains, but thrives beyond or despite or within the Net.

I may be an example of a scholar who is helplessly struggling with the Net, in which he is caught. I am not the only one, but not everyone is like me. The Mexican performer, hacker and wayang scholar Miguel Escobar Vallera wrote and programmed his dissertation in the form of a website, focusing, appropriately, on "new versions" of wayang, *wayang kontemporer*—many of these forms of wayang actively engage digital technology and the internet, as well as video and audio recording (Aneng's work is an example).[21] The web-based dissertation takes advantage of the medium's possibilities, indeed adopts the structure of the internet, with numerous photographs and videos embedded in the text and a net of hyperlinks—all of which makes for a non-linear, net-like, multimedia exploration, with cartoon-like figures of *punakawan* appearing as helpful guides. In conjunction with his dissertation, Escobar worked with Javanese puppeteers and scholars to create the online Contemporary Wayang Archive, where one can watch 24 wayang performances, with optional searchable Javanese, Indonesian and English subtitles, and explanatory notes.

Rather than building walls, the Mexican scholar is tying performance, writing, programming and archiving into a net. In his reflections, these threads (performance, writing, programming) become metaphors of each other, metaphors that cross borders, of places and screens, and reveal affinities—metaphors "somehow reminiscent" of Holt writing about prehistoric images being somehow reminiscent to Balinese dance, or being "[l]ike their European counterparts", in the motto to this section. One essay by Escobar shows the similarity between hacking, in the original sense of "creative tinkering", and contemporary performance; another reflects on the possibilities and impossibilities of archiving performances, and juxtaposes the idea of more conventional archives to that of internet-based collections of recording, from his own online wayang archive to YouTube.[22] His discussion of online security is characteristic. He refers to the film *Samsara*, where "a character is puzzled by the question 'how do you prevent a drop of water from drying up?' ... 'By throwing it into the sea.'" This attitude to so-called intellectual property is "somehow reminiscent" of what I hear these days from many puppeteers. What others (especially some foreigners) see as pirating or as something immoral, the puppeteers welcome with a smile as "free promotion", and talk about it in terms of learning and helping each other. This is "somehow reminiscent" of traditional attitudes to creative imitation in Javanese performing arts—which is itself "somehow reminiscent" of localization, the selective adoption of motifs from distant cultures and their merging with local or previously localized motifs.

Escobar's work opens border-crossings not only between different spheres of creativity, but also between Javanese performers and non-Javanese scholars: not only through collaborations, but especially through being drawn, like them and with them, into a sphere of creativity, a sphere of risk, that crosses the borders between performance and IT. Certain phenomena and structures are prominent equally in his work and in wayang kontemporer, as well as, in less choreographed ways, in mainstream wayang performances, interlinked as they are with multiple media, including the Net. I am haunted by the image of multiple frames and screens, next to and within each other: I have commented on the phenomenon earlier, in talking about watching wayang on television, the internet and smartphones (remember that Facebook image of smartphone-wayang "triplets"), and one sees multiple frames on Escobar's websites as well as in wayang kontemporer performances; the multiple frames are also "somehow ... reminiscent" of wayang seen on the multiple television screens in the mobile studios at wayang performances, and recall, moreover, that precursor of smartphone-wayang triplets, "watching three wayang at once" on television, narrated in Chapter Three, as well as mainstream colossal, spectacular performances with multiple wayang screens in the Indosiar era. Many of the wayang kontemporer performances in Escobar's archive employ multiple wayang screens, in various configurations, typically with images and characters crossing across the screens, and often with digital imagery projected onto them. In some cases, the creators foreground television—and we again note that the medium is far from being a matter of the past: for example, in one case, "at the beginning of the performance, the video projected on the screen represents a TV broadcast, where a *wayang* character [the goddess of wisdom and art, Dewi Saraswati, with four arms, in full *wayang wong* costume] played by an actress becomes a television presenter, reporting on the news of the wayang world, which will lead to the development of the plot of *Jabang Tetuka* (Baby Tetuka)."[23] Another performance, *Bungkusan Hati*

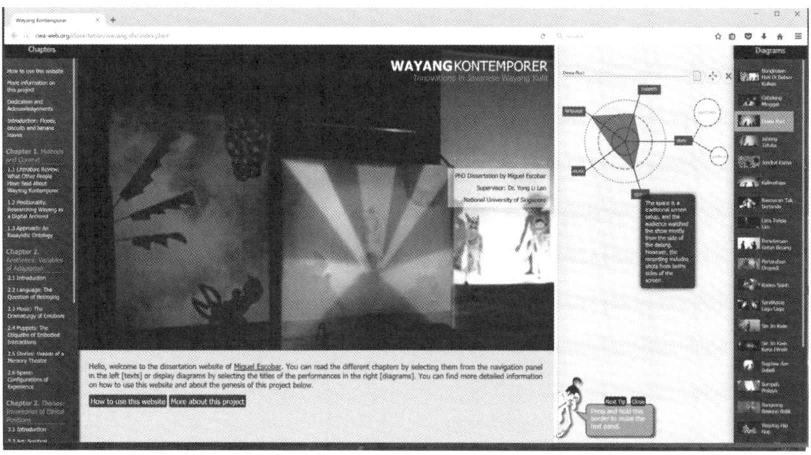

5.11 Miguel Escobar's online dissertation "*Wayang Kontemporer*: Innovations in Javanese *Wayang Kulit*". The performance in the main frame/window shows a wayang with multiple frames/screens, on which digital images are projected. The clown servants (*punakawan*) provide guidance.

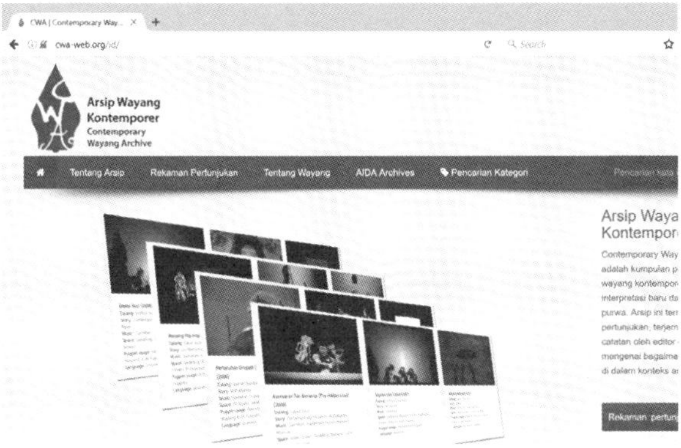

5.12 The welcome page of online *Arsip Wayang Kontemporer*/ Contemporary Wayang Archive, directed by Miguel Escobar. Note the multiple screens/ frames/windows. <http://cwa-web.org>.

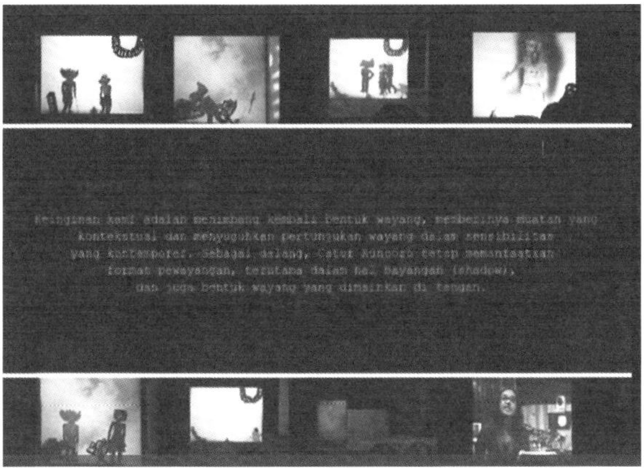

5.13 The initial sequence with multiple screens/frames/ monitors in the contemporary wayang performance *Bungkusan Hati di Dalam Kulkas* (A Heart Package Inside the Refrigerator) by Eko Nugroho and Catur Kuncoro, on the Contemporary Wayang Archive.

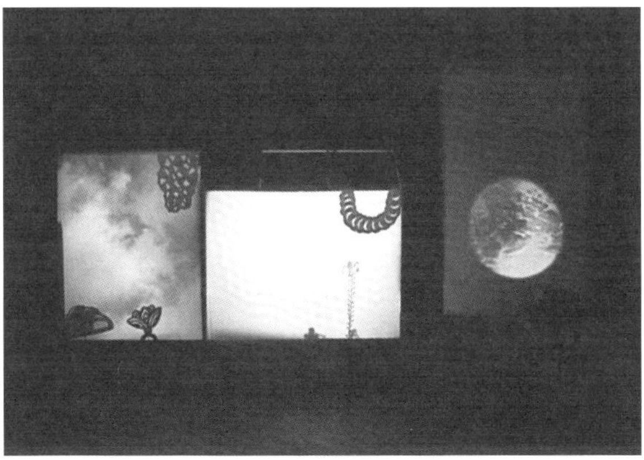

5.14 Multiple screens/ frames with projected digital imagery, on a proscenium stage, in the contemporary wayang performance *Bungkusan Hati di Dalam Kulkas* by Eko Nugroho and Catur Kuncoro, on the Contemporary Wayang Archive.

di Dalam Kulkas (A Heart Package Inside the Refrigerator), begins with a video of what appears like multiple television monitors, after which, still in a video projected on the wayang screen, an old television set is visible, with an anchor reporting on a crime. The events surrounding this crime are then represented with puppets moved against the backdrop of projected digital imagery. Escobar said about this performance that here "wayang appropriates television". In these and some other cases, there is additional framing, as wayang is performed on theatre stage, as "wayang within the play"[24]. These three luminous, digital, coloured wayang screens on a dark stage particularly remind me of the multiple lighted smartphone screens that—I am tempted to say "traditionally"—luminesce at Javanese wayang nights, as well as, again, the multiple screen in a television mobile studio, but I think also of that old radio on the Facebook page dedicated to wayang audio recordings. I see all this within the frames of Escobar's archive and dissertation, on the bright screen of my laptop.

There is of course the other, shadow side to all this border crossing in a play of multiple screens, frames and projections: it is also all "somehow reminiscent" of, it is not entirely separate from, the Javanese fantasy of, yes, clicking on wayang in Bohemia, or the lonely watching of wayang on an oil rig.

Escobar's most recent project (at the time of writing), too, exemplifies the border crossings and how online socialization and loneliness permeate wayang scholarship. Extending his focus beyond (digital) archives, Escobar is now interested in wayang encyclopaedias, a genre particularly popular in Indonesian wayang scholarship over the last half century. Into the online world he brings a scholarly tradition that may feel old-fashioned, almost like bicycles or wayang, clinging to some old principles and aims of encyclopaedias, but using IT and "quantitative data analysis" to expose wayang characters and their relationship in a new light. For example, based on calculating how many times a particular character appears together in a scene with other characters, the encyclopaedia reader/clicker can see each character's "centrality" and "degree", and this is illustrated by an interactive, web-like graph, where one can see and compare the relative centrality of many characters. Each character is represented by a "node", and the higher number of "connections" a character has, the larger the node (this is the character's "degree"). When

I told Escobar that this seems to bring the culture and values of Facebook to the wayang world, he said that indeed the concept and the algorithm he used is the same kind as Facebook. It is as if all the characters had Facebook, and one could see how many "friends" each had, and thus judge their popularity, centrality or importance. This thought titillates me rather like when I hear Indonesians using television terms (dhalang's *crew*, etc.) to refer to wayang, or analysing magical powers in terms of radio waves, broadcasters and receivers. In wayang, like on Facebook, high value is put on interpersonal interaction and relationships: in some ways, the Facebook algorithm fits wayang uncannily well, just as radio waves fit the workings of magic. At the same time, to calculate "friends", "likes", or popularity as the valuation of a person's place in society, or to calculate the degree or strength of his or her human relationships, brings modern modes of socializing, loneliness, desires and fears into wayang in ways that are rather frightening. What about Facebookless shadow characters like me, in this value system, in the "chronoscopic system of under-exposed, exposed, and overexposed"? What about some very significant characters in wayang who wouldn't fare well in terms of Facebook "friends"? Dewa Ruci, in some ways an extremely important character, central in discourse about wayang and the central character of a famous play, is an unpopular, insignificant loner in Escobar's scheme. Far from criticizing Escobar's thought-stimulating, revelatory IT/wayang/scholarship performance, I suggest that what he does is reminiscent of, and is part of the same net/Net of practices, ideas and fantasies, as what happens between wayang and the internet in Java, when Javanese puppeteers and audiences use, think, and fantasize wayang and the Net.

Beyond Facebook, I think further of "citation metrics" and "impact factor", which have, in the age of the Net, begun to play a dominant role in how scholars and their work are seen and valued, influencing who makes it as a scholar and how scholars work—who becomes (metaphorically speaking, thinking back to Chapter One) the superstar puppeteer in academia, and who remains a village dhalang, with increasingly limited performance opportunities as people are trained to see and value according to television. Universalistic, scientific, technological, objectivistic, panoptic system, producing clear and neat images: it is "somewhat reminiscent" of tele-vision, as the metaphorical cameras selectively shoot scholars, who scramble to "look good" (recall Chapter One) under their panoptic gaze and do anything to attract masses of spectators/citations/views/likes, as they fantasize that they would be "lifted" into a placeless sphere of success, or just struggle and jump for survival (and I think, with deep sympathy, of Ki Purbo Asmoro and "his ever-growing dislike of an internet presence"). The "universal" value systems of citation metrics and impact factor are not simply deficient in how they screen and (en)frame scholarship, but have become efficient destructive weapons of academic imperialisms (like other "universal" ideologies in the past and present), as is certainly felt locally, in Southeast Asian academia. If there is indeed a paradoxical, unsettling resemblance ("somewhat reminiscent") between what is so dissimilar, between Escobar's creative, norm-breaking, provocative wayang encyclopaedia (particularly the quantitative analysis of character centrality) and its destructive double, the current academic norm-imposing systems of disciplining and punishing, we are getting another glimpse of how scholarship and wayang are caught in the same net. But perhaps this is

5.15 The stage, with laptop and microphone puppets, of *wayang hip hop* with the dhalang Ki Catur Kuncoro at the launch of the Contemporary Wayang Archive at the National University of Singapore, organized by Miguel Escobar, with the author as an invited speaker and drummer. (Photo courtesy of Miguel Escobar.)

my pessimistic, technophobic double speaking; perhaps they—we—are not merely caught in the net, but the border crossings to which we have been led by Escobar's work, and the play of resemblance and otherness with which we have been faced, can allow us to think about and even hack the net, or play with IT as if it were a puppet.

Escobar said that the ideas behind the Contemporary Wayang Archive are similar to wayang kontemporer performances, in that, like the performers, he is drawn to both digital technology and traditional performance, and because of this commonality, this doubleness, he feels at home among puppeteers of wayang kontemporer. He said about his dissertation that even though the online medium has certain strengths, particularly for writing about performance, it does not supersede (book) writing. The occasionally busy (*sibuk*) like-done-like-done rhythm of hyperlinks and clickable images notwithstanding, reading the chapters of the online dissertation feels to me like reading a book, more so than in the case of many academic books today—the writer takes the time to dwell and slowly explore thoughts, details, or the atmosphere of a performance. His work on the online wayang encyclopaedia—which he understands as an Indonesian tradition—bridges the old and the new in a similar way. It is as if Escobar, especially online, is "holding high" and "holding onto" book writing, *menjunjung* and *memegang*, rather like Aneng and other young puppeteers do with wayang in their experimental performances. Escobar told me that because he spends much of the day in front of the computer, he feels a greater need to read and surround himself with books. He talked about their physical, tactile qualities. Again I find this "somehow reminiscent" of Javanese puppeteers who incorporate computer technology into their performance, while holding high, holding onto, material technologies and old values. For example, in one performance in Escobar's online archive, puppets are made of old bicycle parts, in a story where the bicycle becomes a symbol of a particular, treasured life philosophy, morality and slower speed. The screen frame for this performance is made of plain bamboo sticks, noticeably simpler than the usual carved and painted wayang frame, like simple bamboo village hut instead of a palace—I see it in the frame of my laptop as I watch it online, the "screen capture" of which I frame in the old-fashioned medium that is this book.

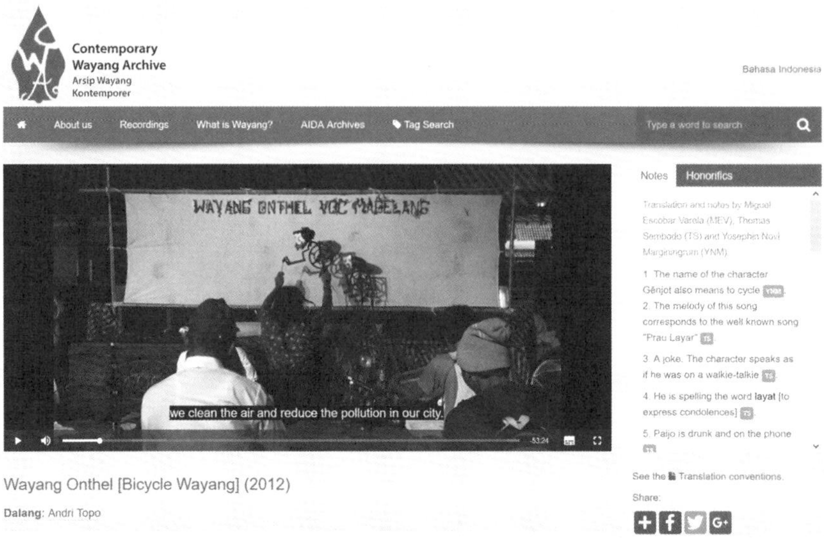

5.16 Another performance in the framework of the online Contemporary Wayang Archive, Andri Topo's *Wayang Onthel* (Bicycle Wayang), with bicycle parts for puppets, seen in a simple bamboo frame.

In 1988, soon after I had come with my parents from Prague to Ithaca, Martin Hatch gave me a copy of Claire Holt's *Art in Indonesia: Continuities and Change*. Like some other books, the volume has become one of my heirlooms, "a minor sphinx adrift in time", in Holt's words.[25] Wayang, television, and the internet likewise drift and surf across times, as well as across spaces and imageries where past and present overflow into each other, as do inheritance and desire, home and the faraway, actuality and imagination.

The feeling is not that of looking at a map. As I read Holt's book, I slowly sail across ages through an archipelago of images. "The contours of the distant past slowly emerge.... On the historical horizons now are ranged peaks of power ... not unlike mountaintops whose lower slopes are enveloped in mist."[26] Holt speaks of "a mosaic of Indonesian history": the desire for an image is there, but multiplicity persists. In the subtitle of her book, "continuities" are plural, discontinuous, while change is an uncountable noun, like air or water, like that which we breathe or within which we drown. "[F]actors have always precluded the development of a homogeneous art with a single line of evolution. Today a multitude of cultural phenomena coexist in the archipelago at quite different stages of their life cycles."[27] The cyclical temporality and the absence of "a single line" makes me think of Indonesian music and dance, but also of the temporality of the interaction of wayang, television, internet, and other media, where "past", "present", and "future" are like the multiple intertwined voices in the cycles of Javanese music. The continuities of the book's choreography are those of returns or recurrences: "Certain significant motifs recur in Indonesian art throughout the ages."[28] The logic of these continuities is not primarily that of art historical influences, historical causality, archaeological stratification, or a "national character"; they are plural continuities revealed by the powers of metaphors and free association, which allow us to glimpse images and media "adrift in time", in a sea of change, crossing borders of historical periodization, moving through their walls like spectres.

Just as she crosses borders in time, Holt moves across conceptual spatial borders: Indonesian cave art has "many aspects in common" with that in Europe, but "instead of bison, mammoth, deer and horses", one finds "lizards, fish, turtles, birds, and boats".[29] The whole world becomes Noah's Ark. The localization of foreign motifs—in the age of the internet it tends to be called globalization—takes place against the background of, as a part of, an underlying play of commonality and a softer otherness, one permeated by affinity.

Holt writes that "the idea of [her] book originated" with a question about the "effects" of recent political developments on Indonesian arts.[30] A question centred on the present—not so different from asking about the effects of television or the internet on wayang—propels us back to prehistory, and away from the logic of effects. Chapter One begins with the earliest surviving images in what is today Indonesia, images on the walls of caves, images of hands, spectres from a distant past visible in the present: "pale shadows of their hands long since turned into dust". But in the next sentence, they become flesh and blood like room painters in blue overalls or preschool children on an excursion: "They pressed their outstretched fingers against the surface of the rock, daubed red paint around them, and thus produced lasting stenciled images." As Holt continues, everyone is drawn into the same dance of bodies and shadows, prehistoric and insistently, physically alive in the present: "Somehow they are reminiscent of the outstretched hands of Bali *ketjak* dancers which, illuminated by the flickering flame of an oil lamp, are thrust upward into the blackness of the night to the upsurge of humming or rhythmically chattering voices."[31]

Metaphor is a revelatory recognition of the kinship of previously seemingly unrelated images, across times and oceans, across borders, across frames, alive with the tension between affinity and distance, blending and dissonance, love and violence. Holt's method mirrors the poetics of localization, and the merging and clashing of the local and the foreign, and the old and the new in Indonesian arts. Her "somehow they are reminiscent" is somehow reminiscent of how people in ancient Indonesia poetically recognized foreign motifs and felt that "somehow they are reminiscent" of familiar ones. She, too, is caught in the net. This is not all about shadows from the past: somehow it leads back to those room painters in overalls.

The internet is a new style of being and fantasizing in space and time; it is a relatively new player in the history of wayang's flirting with other media (although the fantasy is not that new, as suggested, for example, by the subtitle of a 1989 article, "Why Shouldn't Wayang Golek Use Computer?").[32] Thinking about the internet, I feel I am lagging behind as the world escapes toward a shadowy future; I feel the shadow of my own deactivation. And yet, what happens today—as people today "miss" Indosiar wayang on the internet, as they listen to old cassettes and VCDs online, and remember listening to wayang on radio in their youth, as they playfully recreate the atmosphere and even the drink stalls of a wayang performance in the chatting that is part of a live stream, or as many find the internet too much hassle and prefer enjoying wayang on television, radio, and, whenever possible, directly—is "somehow reminiscent" of the encounters between the familiar and the foreign, the old and the new, and the cyclical, musical, dance-like structure of time, as they are revealed in Holt's book about the history of Indonesian arts. It is as if the pale shadows of people long since turned into dust, gained flesh-and-blood presence—and virtual online shadow-presence.

Writes Merleau-Ponty in an essay—another heirloom—that Professor O'Connor gave me to read when I was a student: "The very first of paintings in some sense went to the farthest reach [or, less optimistically translated: 'to the bottom': *jusqu'au fond*] of the future."[33] Like a metaphor, the boats, fish, and sun in that prehistoric painting do and do not transform the enclosing cave walls into an opening onto the world, virtually, magically transporting us from a dark cave out to the sea on a sunny day, the most open of spaces, even as the painting thus detains us in the cave. In going to the bottom of the future, does not that prehistoric painted cave wall, which encloses even as it opens, also foreshadow the internet?

Another heirloom: I realize that my latest reflections on the latest developments were foreshadowed by my teacher almost a quarter of a century ago when he wrote of multiple screens:

> Almost everywhere today television images and computer screens are present.... Increasingly the perceptual field of widely scattered populations is saturated with a play of shimmering, fluid, weightless images that are the similar, if not identical, shadows of the lightness of being. And since artists live in, and are at home in, this specular reality, it may offer one clue as to why there is an increasing convergence of world art. The main thing to grasp is that we are all wandering in the same storm. A new visual realm is being forged, one imposing new disciplines and requiring new skills. Students in New York or Berkeley will find that the ungraspable, confusing and hopeful world in which they are immersed is also recognizable in works of art being made today in Bangkok, Singapore, and Hanoi.[34]

While Miguel Escobar has gone further than most non-Javanese scholars in bringing the internet and performance together, all scholars today are "somehow reminiscent" of wayang puppeteers, in that we are all caught in the net, all immersed in the same "ungraspable, confusing and hopeful world". In an article on "contemporary wayang in global context," the wayang scholar and practitioner Matthew Cohen writes with an optimism "somehow reminiscent" of avant-garde manifestos from the 1920s: "Today the lines separating academic experimentalism and the popular, the foreign, and the local in Indonesia and abroad are increasingly blurred. The future of *wayang* is now."[35] (The 1920s: should one reminisce deeper, how that inter-war sunny optimism was growing from deep darkness, of its immediate past and foreshadowed future?

In 2018: "... due to his ever-growing dislike of an internet presence, Ki Purbo Asmoro has asked me to deactivate this site.") In Bohemia or in Singapore, I click and "all the wayang emerges". I don't regret that I was first learning about wayang at a different time and situation, when I had to travel to the other side of the world to watch it, when such a journey was the fulfilment of a dream and work of imagination, and when it was clear that one had to struggle and probably fail to translate one's experiences across distance. I do not regret that in order to converse with people, I had to meet them, sit next to them at performances and in coffee shops, vulnerable to their questioning, drink sweet coffee with them or visit their homes, rather than being able to electronically eavesdrop on a constant stream of Javanese spectators' self-transcribed conversations, as in the case of the chatting that accompanies a wayang live stream, as I sit "anywhere in the world": the cave of my Singapore flat, my Little Bohemia. I do not regret all that, but I think that there is an opportunity now "to grasp ... that we are all wandering in the same storm"; to grasp anew at the ungraspable, grasp anew at how we are (and are not) all somehow reminiscent of each other, doubles of each other, as we keep getting lost in our dreams and screens, as we live through new media yet hold onto and hold high older ones, like wayang and books, as we are alone in our digital togetherness and together in being alone, dreaming of going viral and dreaming of deactivation, sinking together and alone to the bottom of the future; how we are all wandering in a storm that is new and extraordinary, yet "somehow reminiscent" of all past storms, also those in the Indonesian history of imagination and engagement with the new and foreign, with "the world". We—puppeteers, scholars, and puppets, in our respective caves and frames—make those shadowy border crossings, across times and spaces, and have to deal with walls built by others and ourselves: attack, paint, protect them—also walls between older media like wayang and books—the heirlooms—and their doubles, like television and the Net.

Endnotes

Introduction

1. In my past life, I argued for this kind of scholarship in, and through, Jan Mrázek, ed., *Puppet Theater in Contemporary Indonesia: New Approaches to Performance Events* (Ann Arbor: Center for South and Southeast Asian Studies, The University of Michigan, 2002).
2. In Indonesia, most written discourse on television has taken the form of newspaper and magazine articles, and some important books on television are collections of such texts. Examples include Arswendo Atmowiloto, *Telaah tentang televisi* [*Research on Television*] (Jakarta: Gramedia, 1986) and Veven Sp. Wardhana, *Televisi dan prasangka budaya massa* [*Television and the Prejudices of Mass Culture*](Jakarta: Institut Studi Arus Informasi, 2001). Many articles in the press deal with wayang on television, and I often refer to them in this work. In English, the first book-length study of Indonesian television is Phillip Kitley's *Television, Nation and Culture in Indonesia* (Athens, OH: Ohio University Center for International Studies, 2000), to which I refer the reader both for the history of Indonesian television, including case studies of programmes, and for a survey (on pp. 10–2) of pre-2000 studies on the subject. In Kitley's work, the emphasis is on television as a tool of state control and its role in the promotion of unifying national culture as envisioned by the state. Works on Indonesian media by David Hill and Krishna Sen, *Media, Culture, and Politics in Indonesia* (Melbourne; New York: Oxford University Press, 2000) and *Politics and the Media in Twenty-First Century Indonesia* (New York: Routledge, 2010) also focus on media in the context on state politics, which is indeed a dominant trend in Indonesian media studies. Edwin Jurriëns's *Cultural Travel and Migrancy: The Artistic Representation*

of Globalization in the Electronic Media of West Java (Leiden: KITLV Press, 2004) and Klarijn Loven's *Watching Si Doel, Imagining the Nation: Television, Language and Identity in Contemporary Indonesia* (Leiden: KITLV Press, 2007), share with my book an interest in television in relation to local culture. The chapter "Televisual Mediations" in Andrew Weintraub's *Power Plays: Wayang Golek Puppet Theatre of West Java* (Center for International Studies, Ohio University: Athens, 2004) focuses on Sundanese *wayang golek* on television. Miguel Escobar Valera's recent work, including his web-based doctoral dissertation, "Wayang Kontemporer: Innovations in Javanese Wayang Kulit" (National University of Singapore, 2015), bring wayang scholarship into the internet era—I discuss his work in the last chapter.

3. Stanley O'Connor, "Humane Literacy and Southeast Asian Art, *Journal of Southeast Asian Studies* 26,1 (1995): 155.
4. Jan Mrázek, "Ways of Experiencing Art: Javanese Shadow Puppets in Art History, in Performance, and on Television," in What's the Use of Art? Asian Art and Material Culture in Contetx, ed. Jan Mrázek and Morgan Pitelka (Honolulu: Hawai'i University Press, 2008), pp.272–304.
5. Sarworo Sp, "Pergelaran Wayang Kulit di Televisi: Dalang Ditantang, Dalang Bisa 'Kelimpungan'" [Wayang Kulit Performance on Television: When Dalang is Challenged, Dalang Can be "Confused/In Trouble"], *Kedaulatan Rakyat*, 15 Sept. 1996.
6. Words that appear in braces were originally spoken in English in speech that was otherwise in Bahasa Indonesia.
7. Pamudji, "Ketika Panggung Ketoprak dan Wayang Diusung ke Televisi" [When Ketoprak and Wayang Stage Are Moved to Television], *Suara Merdeka*, 9 Aug. 1997.
8. Ibid.
9. Arie Sudibyo, "Biarkan Gamelan Alternatif Berkembang" [Let Alternative Gamelan Flourish], *Kedaulatan Rakyat*, 22 Aug. 1996.
10. Stanley O'Connor, "Memory and Discovery in Southeast Asian Art", *Asian Art and Culture* 8,1 (1995): 4.
11. Val Dusek, *Philosophy of Technology* (Blackwell: Malden, MA 2006), p. 35.
12. Neil Postman, *Amusing Ourselves to Death* (New York: Penguin, 1985), p. 79.
13. Salman Rushdie, *The Enchantress of Florence* (London: Jonathan Cape, 2008), p. 83.

14. Harsrinuksmo, *Mengungkap Rahasia Isi Keris* [*Revealing the Secret of the Content of the Keris*] (Jakarta: Pustakakarya Grafikatama, 1990), pp. 64–5.
15. "Grandfather"; Javanese term of address for an older man.
16. Hardjowirogo, quoted in Becker, *Beyond Translation*, p. 53.
17. Martin Heidegger, *The Question Concerning Technology and Other Essays* (New York: Harper & Row, 1977), p. 154.
18. Martin Heidegger, *Poetry, Language, Thought*, trans, Albert Hofstadter (New York: Harper & Row, 1971), p. 55.
19. Kitley, *Television, Nation and Culture*, p. 333.
20. Benedict R. O'G. Anderson, *Mythology and the Tolerance of the Javanese* (Ithaca: Cornell Modern Indonesia Project, 1965).
21. Ward Keeler, *Javanese Shadow Plays, Javanese Selves* (Princeton: Princeton University Press, 1987).
22. Elsewhere, I have explored the family resemblances between television and art history. Jan Mrázek, "Ways of Experiencing Art: Javanese Shadow Puppets in Art History, in Performance, and on Television," in *What's the Use of Art? Asian Art and Material Culture in Context*, ed. Jan Mrázek and Morgan Pitelka (Honolulu: Hawai'i University Press, 2008), pp. 272–304.
23. Raymond Williams, *Television: Technology and Cultural Form* (Hanover and London: University Press of New England, 1974).
24. Oliver Wolters, *History, Culture, and Region in Southeast Asian Perspectives* (Singapore: Institute of Southeast Asian Studies, 1982).
25. Wolters, *History, Culture, and Region*, pp. 41–5.
26. James Siegel, *Fetish, Recognition, Revolution* (Princeton: Princeton University Press 1997).
27. Kitley, *Television, Nation and Culture*, p. 330.
28. John M. Echols and Hassan Shadily, *An Indonesian-English Dictionary*, rev. and ed. by John U. Wolff and James T. Collins (Ithaca, NY: Cornell University Press, 1989), p. 557.
29. Maurice Merleau-Ponty, *Phenomenology of Perception*, trans. C. Smith (London and New York: Routledge 1962), pp. 362–3.
30. Merleau-Ponty, *Phenomenology*, p. 363.
31. Paul Ricoeur, *Time and Narrative*, (Chicago and London: Chicago University Press, 1992), vol. 1, p. xi.
32. Ricoeur, *Time and Narrative*, p. 3.
33. Merleau-Ponty, *Phenomenology*, p. 346.
34. Bernard Arps, "The Sound of Space: How to Hear the Mise en Scène

in Audio Wayang", in *Puppet Theater in Contemporary Indonesia: New Approaches to Performance Events*, ed. Jan Mrázek (Ann Arbor: Center for South and Southeast Asian Studies, The University of Michigan, 2002), pp. 315–6.

35. For a history of Indonesian television, see Kitley, *Television, Nation and Culture*.
36. Rachmad Ida, "Reorganization of Media Power in Post-Authoritarian Indonesia: Ownership, Power and Influence of Local Media Enterpreneurs", in *Politics and the Media in Twenty-First Century Indonesia: Decade of Democracy*, ed. Krishna Sen and David T. Hill (London and New York: Routledge, 2011), pp. 13–25.
37. For a (hi)story of wayang on television, see Chapters Four and Five.

Chapter 1

1. Jean Baudrillard, *Simulacra and Simulation* (Ann Arbor: The University of Michigan, 1994), p. 30.
2. Baudrillard, *Simulacra and Simulation*, pp. 1–42.
3. Jacques Derrida and Bernard Stiegler, *Echographies of Television* (Cambridge: Polity, 2002) and Jacques Derrida, *The Specters of Marx* (New York: Routledge, 2006).
4. Philip Auslander, *Liveness: Performance in a Mediatized Culture* (New York: Routledge, 1999). See also Miguel Escobar Vallera, "The Archive as Repertoire: Transience and Sustainability in Digital Archives", *Digital Humanities Quarterly*, 10, 4 (2016): 15–7.
5. E.T.A. Hoffmann, Die Elixiere des Teufels [Devil's Elixir] (Munich: SWAN, 1993), pp. 79–80.
6. Derrida and Stiegler, *Echographies*, p. 3.
7. Derrida and Stiegler, *Echographies*, p. 38
8. Marshall McLuhan, *Understanding Media* (Cambridge: MIT Press, 1999), p. 8.
9. Derrida, *The Specters of Marx*.
10. Derrida and Stiegler, *Echographies*, pp. 24–5.
11. Alton Becker, *Beyond Translation: Essays Toward a Modern Philology* (Ann Arbor: University of Michigan Pres, 2000), pp. 48–58.
12. Jan Mrázek, *Phenomenology of a Puppet Theatre* (Leiden: KITLV Press,

2005), Chapter 8.

13. "Limbukan Pun Diprotes" [Limbukan, Too, is Protested Against], *Kedaulatan Rakyat*, 7 Sept. 1996.
14. Amien Nugroho, "Pagelaran Wayang Kulit Perlu Pembaharuan?" [Does Wayang Kulit Need Renewal?] *Kedaulatan Rakyat*, 29 Sept. 1991.
15. Ki Manteb Soedharsono, quoted in Joko Dwi Hastanto, "Dari Sarasehan Wayang: Menggugat Kreativitas Dalang" [From Wayang Workshop: Contesting Puppeteers' Creativity], *Suara Merdeka*, 12 Oct. 1996.
16. A. Komar Abbas and Seno Subro, *Ki Manteb "Dalang Setan": Sebuah Tantangan* [Ki Manteb, "Devil Puppeteer": A Challenge] (Surakarta: Yayasan Resi Tujuh Satu, 1995), p. 148.
17. Kicuk Parta, "Nggugat Dhalang Setan: Daniwara 'Oye...eee!'" [Contesting the Devil Puppeteer: Daniwara "Oye...eee!"] *Jaya Baya*, 27 Aug. 1995.
18. "Ki Manteb Sudharsono: 'Gendheng nek aku nglecehne wayang!'" [Ki Manteb Sudharsono: "It's Crazy That I Would Insult Wayang"], *Jaya Baya*, 27 Aug. 1995.
19. TPI featured Sujiwo Tejo for a wayang series, TVRI Jakarta featured Manteb, and at TVRI Bandung wayang golek story may be broadcast as a kind of "serial" in several instalments performed by a single dhalang.
20. Suratno, "Ki Slenk (Saya Lebih Enak Nonton Kamu): The Tactics of a Best Selling Puppeteer", in *Puppet Theater in Contemporary Indonesia: New Approaches to Performance Events*, ed. Jan Mrázek (Centers for South and Southeast Asian Studies, University of Michigan: Ann Arbor 2002), p. 161.
21. Raymond Williams, *Television: Technology and Cultural Form* (Hanover and London: University Press of New England, 1974), p. 99.
22. Mrázek, *Phenomenology*, Chapter 6.
23. The next few paragraphs summarize some points, with special focus on the questions at hand, of my extended discussion of innovations in wayang in Mrázek, *Phenomenology*, Chapter 8. As elsewhere in this chapter, the discussion focuses on the "Indosiar" years, the later 1990s. In subsequent years, developments in wayang performances that react to or resist the tendencies described here have gained greater prominence, yet even at the time of writing (2017), it is common to hear people speaking rather like they did in the 1990s, for example, complaining about the focus on clowning, clown scenes, commercialization, etc.; and many performances still fit well the description given here.
24. Suratno et. al., *Limbukan Pada Pakeliran Wayang Purwa Gaya Surakarta*

Dalam Lima Tahun Terakhir [Limbukan in the Surakarta Style Wayang Purwa Performance over the Last Five Years] (Surakarta: STSI, 1996).

25. René Lysloff, "A Wrinkle in Time: The Shadow Puppet Theater of Banyumas (West Central Java)", *Asian Theater Journal* 10, 1 (Spring 1993): 60.
26. A. L. Becker, *Beyond Translation: Essays toward a Modern Philology* (Ann Arbor: The University of Michigan Press, 1995), pp. 39–40.
27. On kethoprak's adventures in the modern world, including its adaptations for electronic media, see Judith Ernestine Bosnak, "Shaping the Javanese Play: Improvisation of the Script in Theatre Performance", PhD dissertation, Universiteit Leiden, 2006.
28. For a discussion of abbreviated or condensed performances, see Kathryn Emerson, "Transforming Wayang for Contemporary Audiences: Dramatic Expression in Purbo Asmoro's Style, 1989–2015", PhD dissertation (Leiden: Leiden University, 2016), pp. 59–91.
29. Paul Virilio, *The Paul Virilio Reader* (New York: Columbia University Press, 2004), p. 136.
30. Ibid., p. 139.
31. Ibid., p. 142.
32. "Ki Manteb Soedarsono: Film Kungfu" [Ki Manteb Soedarsono: Kung Fu Films], *Suara Merdeka*, 6 Oct. 1996.
33. Abbas and Subro, *Ki Manteb*, p. 142.
34. Nugroho, "Pagelaran Wayang."
35. Heryus Saputro, "Ade Kosasih Sunarya: Wayang Golek Pakai Komputer Mengapa Tidak?", *Femina* 17, 6 (1989): 65.
36. Ibid., p. 65.
37. This is especially true about the early parts of the performance; later, the structure is freer and depends more on the particular lakon.
38. Hardja Susilo, "The Personalization of Tradition: The Case of Sukasman's Wayang Ukur", in *Puppet Theater in Contemporary Indonesia: New Approaches to Performance Events,* ed. Jan Mrázek, (Centers for South and Southeast Asian Studies, University of Michigan: Ann Arbor 2002).
39. Manteb was not the first dhalang to use flashback, but he has popularized it.
40. See Mrázek, *Phenomenology,* pp. 226–68.
41. Sri Hastanto, "Sapa Sira Sapa Ingsun" [Who Are You, Who Am I], *Kedaulatan Rakyat*, 27 Oct. 1991.

42. Virilio, *The Paul Virilio Reader,* p. 138.
43. McLuhan, *Understanding Media,* p. 8.
44. Quoted in "Pedhalangan Wis Rusak" [Puppeteering is Kaput], *Mekar Sari,* 6 Sept. 1996.
45. Bambang Sadono, *Apa & Siapa Orang Jawa, Edisi 1995–1996* [Javanese People, What & Who, 1995–1996 Edition] (Semarang: Citra, 1995), p. 52.
46. Herry Gendut Janarto and Arswendo Atmowiloto, *Teguh Srimulat* (Jakarta: Gramedia, 1990), p. 159.
47. Becker, *Beyond Translation,* pp. 48–58.
48. Derrida, *The Specters of Marx,* p. 48.
49. Derrida, *The Specters of Marx,* p. xviii.
50. Bernard Arps, "The Sound of Space: How to Hear the Mise en Scene in Audio Wayang", in *Puppet Theater in Contemporary Indonesia: New Approaches to Performance Events,* ed. Jan Mrázek (Centers for South and Southeast Asian Studies, University of Michigan: Ann Arbor 2002), p. 316.
51. I am grateful to Philip Yampolsky for this information. Email, 28 Apr. 2005.
52. Arps, "The Sound of Space."
53. See Suratno, "Ki Slenk", p. 163.
54. Mrázek, *Phenomenology,* Chapter 8.
55. Y.B. Mangunwijaya's novel *Durga Umayi* (Jakarta: Pustaka Utama Grafiti, 1994) shows the microphone in interesting ways: the "[Independence] Proclamation Microphone" is "magically powerful" (*sakti*), it comes alive, talks, and "replaces" the boyfriend of the female protagonist (it cannot be hugged but can be kissed). It is "able to stir hearts without the need for electric current or a generator, because it has special wavelengths generated by the vibration of the longing of millions poor and powerless people" (pp. 70–71). The novel appeared in English under the same title in Ward Keeler's translation: *Durga/Umayi* (Seattle: University of Washington Press, 2004).
56. Ward Keeler, *Javanese Shadows, Javanese Selves* (Princeton: Princeton University Press, 1987).
57. McLuhan, *Understanding Media,* p. 9.
58. James Siegel, *Fetish, Recognition, Revolution* (Princeton: Princeton University Press, 1997), pp. 8–9.
59. Ibid., p.6.
60. Ibid., p.19.

61. Ibid., p.13.
62. Ibid, p.15.
63. Ibid., p. 158.
64. Ibid., pp. 61–2.
65. Ibid., p. 74.
66. Ibid., pp. 69–70.
67. Ibid., p. 62.
68. Ibid., p. 85.
69. Ibid., p. 70.
70. Ibid., p. 18
71. Ibid., p. 36.
72. Ibid., p. 17.
73. Ibid., pp. 85–6.
74. Ibid., p. 5.
75. Ibid., p. 252.
76. Ibid., p. 254.
77. Ibid., p. 3.
78. Rudolf Mrázek, *Engineers of Happy Land: Technology and Nationalism in a Colony* (Princeton: Princeton University Press, 2002), p. xvi.
79. Ibid., pp. xvi–xvii.
80. Ibid., p. 8.
81. Ibid., p. 22.
82. Ibid., p. 8.
83. Ibid., p. 24.
84. Ibid., p. 11.
85. Siegel, *Fetish*, p. 8.
86. Mrázek, *Engineers*, p. 31.
87. Ibid., p. 31.
88. Ibid., p. 32.
89. Ibid., p. 35.
90. Ibid., p. 35.
91. Kartini, quoted in Mrázek, *Engineers*, p. 91.
92. Mrázek, *Engineers*, p. 113.
93. Ibid., p. 113.
94. Ibid., p. 116.
95. For a history of Indonesian theatre in the colonial period, see Matthew Isaac Cohen, Inventing the Performing Arts: Modernity and Tradition

in Colonial Indonesia (Honolulu: University of Hawai'i Press, 2016).

96. Edmund Husserl, *The Crisis of European Sciences and Transcendental Phenomenology* (Evanston: Northwestern University Press, 1970), p. 276.
97. Ibid., p. 283.
98. Ibid., p. 285.
99. Ibid., pp. 285–6.
100. Ibid., p. 286.
101. Ibid., p. 286.
102. Ibid., p. 22.
103. Ibid., pp. 48–9.
104. Ibid., p. 48.
105. Ibid., p. 49.
106. Martin Heidegger, *The Question Concerning Technology and Other Essays* (New York: Harper & Row,1977), p. 127.
107. Ibid., pp. 129–30.
108. Ibid., p. 134.
109. Ibid., p. 135.
110. Ibid., p. 134.
111. Ibid., p. 135.
112. Ibid., p. 135.
113. Ibid., p. 136.
114. Ibid., p. 154.
115. Erwin Panofsky, *Perspective as Symbolic Form* (New York: Zone Books, 1997), pp. 28–9.
116. Panofsky, *Perspective*, p. 34.

Chapter 2

1. Stanley J. O'Connor, "Art Critics, Connoisseurs, and Collectors in the Southeast Asian Rain Forest: A Study in Cross-Cultural Art Theory," *Journal of Southeast Asian Studies* Vol. 14, No. 2 (Sep. 1983), pp. 400–408.
2. James Siegel, *Fetish, Recognition, Revolution* (Princeton: Princeton University Press, 1997), p. 5.
3. Siegel, *Fetish*, p. 4.
4. Siegel, *Fetish*, p. 5.
5. Edward M. Bruner, Culture on Tour: Ethnographies of Travel (Chicago:

Chicago University Press, 2005), p. 211. Bruner also provides a good critical survey of literature on Taman Mini.

6. Jacques Derrida and Berbard Stiegler, *Echographies of Television* (Cambridge: Polity, 2002), p. 79.
7. Germain Bazin, *The Museum Age* (Brussels: Desoer, 1967), p.7.
8. Martin Heidegger, *The Question Concerning Technology and Other Essays* (New York: Harper & Row, 1977), p. 14.
9. "Kisah Sukses Petruk di Indosiar" [The Tale of Petruk's Success on Indosiar], *Forum Keadilan* 4, 16 (20 Nov. 1995): 68.
10. Philip Kitley, *Television, Nation and Culture in Indonesia* (Athens, OH: Ohio University Center for International Studies, 2000), pp. 288–95.
11. Kitley, *Television*, p. 291.
12. Kitley, *Television*, p. 292.
13. David Hill and Krishna Sen, *Media, Culture, and Politics in Indonesia* (Melbourne and New York: Oxford University Press, 2000), p. 120.
14. Hill and Sen, pp. 120–1.
15. Kicuk Parta, "Wayang Indosiar: 'Kesandhung Ki Anom Suroto'" [Indosiar Wayang: "Stumbled Over Ki Anom Suroto"], *Jaya Baya*, 24 Mar. 1996.
16. Ibid.
17. Sarworo Sp, "Pergelaran Wayang Kulit di Televisi: Dalang Ditantang, Dalang Bisa 'Kelimpungan'" [Wayang Kulit Performance on Television: When the Dalang is Challenged, the Dalang Can be "Confused/In Trouble"], *Kedaulatan Rakyat*, 15 Sept. 1996.
18. "Oye" is a reference to the advertisement for painkiller in which Manteb acted, and with which he is associated.
19. Kicuk Parta, "Geger wayang Indosiar: Kasus Anggada Balik" [Wayang Indosiar Tumult: The Case of Anggada Balik], *Jaya Baya* 38 (20 May 2001): 30. I am indebted to Ben Arps who called my attention to this article.
20. Ibid., p. 31.
21. Ibid., p. 31.
22. Ibid., p. 31.
23. "Para dalang gerah tayangan Indosiar" [Puppeteers are Sick of Indosiar Broadcasts], *Suara Merdeka*, 1 June 2001.
24. "Ki Enthus Susmono: Yen dhalang mudha Solo ora 'melu' aku, bakal mati sandhang pangane" [Ki Enthus Susmono: If Young Puppeteers Don't "Follow"

Me, They Will Have No Livelihood], Jaya Baya 42 (17 July 2001): 37–8.

25. Parta, "Geger," p. 31.
26. Thanks for this e-mail (18 May 2001) go to Yayank Naza of Indosiar.
27. E-mail from Yayang Naza, 6 Aug. 2001.
28. Joko Dwi Hastanto, "Rekaman Lagi, Ki Manteb Rujuk dengan Indosiar" [Recording Again, Ki Manteb Reconciles with Indosiar], *Suara Merdeka*, 22 Oct. 2001.
29. I take this idea from Edwin Jurriëns.
30. The shooting took place on 3 Jan. 1999. The broadcasts of the two parts took place on 9 and 16 Jan 1999.
31. Jan Mrázek, *Phenomenology of a Puppet Theatre* (Leiden: KITLV Press, 2005).
32. Karl Marx, "Capital" in *The Marx-Engels Reader*, ed. Robert C. Tucker, 2nd ed. (New York: Norton, 1978), p. 347.
33. Marx, "Capital", p. 350.
34. Heidegger, *The Question Concerning Technology*, p. 17.
35. Heidegger, *The Question Concerning Technology*, p. 16.
36. Heidegger, *The Question Concerning Technology*, p. 16.
37. Heidegger, *The Question Concerning Technology*, p. 15.
38. Marx, "Capital", p. 334.
39. Marx, "Capital", p. 334.
40. "Peredaran CD Empat Lakon Ki Manteb Ditangguhkan" [Distribution of CDs with Four Plays by Ki Manteb Suspended], *Suara Merdeka*, 19 Apr. 2001.
41. Won Poerwono, "Pentas Wayang 10 Malam Dibiayai UNDP" [Ten-Night Wayang Performance Financed by UNDP], *Suara Merdeka*, 8 Aug. 2001.
42. In the discussions, CD and VCD are used interchangeably, both referring to VCD. That it is VCD that is meant here is also suggested by the context of the message, and by the fact that items one and two mentioned in the message also appear in other reports of performances available on VCDs.
43. Won Poerwono, "CD Bajakan Pergelaran Wayang Laris di Pasaran" [Pirated CDs with Wayang Performances Sell Well in the Market], *Suara Merdeka*, 18 Apr. 2001.
44. Ibid.
45. Poerwono, "CD Bajakan".
46. Poerwono, "CD Bajakan".
47. I am grateful to Ben Arps for this point.

Chapter 3

1. An earlier, shorter version of this chapter appeared in Jan Mrázek, ed. *Puppet Theater in Contemporary Indonesia: New Approaches to Performance Events* (Ann Arbor: Centers for South and Southeast Asian Studies, University of Michigan, 2002), pp. 333–61.
2. Maurice Merleau-Ponty, *The Visible and the Invisible*, trans. A. Lingis (Evanston: Northwestern University Press, 1968), p. 131.
3. Merleau-Ponty, *The Visible*, pp. 130–1.
4. Merleau-Ponty, *Phenomenology of Perception*, trans. C. Smith (London and New York: Routledge 1962), p. 214.
5. Merleau-Ponty, *Phenomenology*, p. 216
6. Merleau-Ponty, *The Visible*, p. 135
7. Merleau-Ponty, *The Visible*, pp. 134–5.
8. Merleau-Ponty, *Phenomenology*, p. 111.
9. Samuel Weber, *Mass Mediauras: Form Technics Media* (Stanford: Stanford University Press, 1996), p. 114
10. Weber, *Mass Mediauras*, p. 115
11. Weber, *Mass Mediauras*, p. 116.
12. Weber, *Mass Mediauras*, p. 116.
13. Weber, *Mass Mediauras*, pp. 116–7.
14. Merleau-Ponty, *Phenomenology*, p. 405.
15. Merleau-Ponty, *Phenomenology*, p. 354.
16. Merleau-Ponty, *Phenomenology*, p. 353.
17. Merleau-Ponty, *The Primacy of Perception* (Evanston: Northwestern University Press, 1964), p. 164. I have discussed how "those who watch [wayang] join in being watched" at a wayang performance and how people see themselves through the wayang medium, in Jan Mrázek, *Phenomenology*, Chapter 7.
18. Mrázek, *Phenomenology*, Chapter 7.
19. Louis Dumont, *Essais sur l'individualisme: une perspective anthropologique sur l'ideologie moderne* [Essays on Individualism: An Anthropological Perspective on The Modern Ideology] (Paris: Seuil, 1983).
20. Merleau-Ponty, *Phenomenology*, p. 30.
21. Merleau-Ponty, *Phenomenology*, p. 303.
22. I assume here that the reader is a human being rather than a squirrel.
23. Drs H. Wiyoso Yudoseputro, et.al., *Penayangan Pergelaran Wayang Kulit*

Di Televisi [Broadcasting Wayang Kulit Performances on Television], unpublished research report (Proyek Penelitian Yayasan Senawangi [Jakarta], 1997–98), especially pp. 55–58. I am grateful to the project members and especially Pak Sumari for making this report available to me.

24. Yudoseputro, *Penayangan*, p. 55
25. Yudoseputro, *Penayangan*, p. 60.
26. Yudoseputro, *Penayangan*, especially p. 68 and pp. 73–4.
27. Merleau-Ponty, *Phenomenology*, p.251.
28. Merleau-Ponty, *Phenomenology*, p. 206.
29. Merleau-Ponty uses the term "virtual body" in discussions of psychological experiments that artificially disturb perceptual orientation by manipulation of bodily position. See esp. *Phenomenology*, p. 250.
30. Yudoseputro, *Penayangan*, p. 74.
31. Brooks Riley, "Camera Angles", *Opera News* 54 (June 1990): 14.
32. "Nonton 3 Wayangkulit" [Watching 3 Wayangkulit] signed Wirjosuparto, *Kedaulatan Rakyat*, 24 Feb. 1999.
33. See Miguel Escobar Valera's critical commentary on this tendency in "The Archive as Repertoire: Transience and Sustainability in Digital Archives", Digital Humanities Quarterly, 10, 4 (2016), pp. 15–7.
34. Heidegger, *The Question Concerning Technology*, p. 33.
35. Heidegger, *The Question*, pp. 129–30.
36. Heidegger, *The Question*, p. 131.
37. All quotations in this paragraph, unless otherwise indicated, are cited in Chapter One.

Chapter 4

1. R.M. Wasisto Surjodiningrat, *Gamelan, Dance, and Wayang in Jogjakarta* (Jogjakarta: Gadjah Mada University Press, 1971), p. 60.
2. Ibid.
3. Surjodiningrat, *Gamelan, Dance, and Wayang*, p. 63.
4. Ibid, p. 62
5. Ibid, p. 63
6. For a discussion of *padhat* performances in the 1980s, see Laurie Sears, *Shadows of Empire: Colonial Discourse and Javanese Tales* (Durham, NC:

Duke University Press, 1996), pp. 244–51; for a more detailed history of "condensed style", including latest developments, see Kathryn Emerson, "Transforming Wayang for Contemporary Audiences: Dramatic Expression in Purbo Asmoro's Style, 1989–2015", PhD dissertation (Leiden University, 2016), pp. 59–91.

7. Gunawan Soebagio, ed., *Wayang Sebagai Pinisinetron* (Bandung: Citra Aditya Bakti, 1989); Andrew Weintraub, *Power Plays: Wayang Golek Puppet Theater in West Java* (Athens: Center for International Studies, Ohio University, 2004).
8. I am indebted to Indosiar producers for providing a list of recorded performances, with recording and broadcast dates.
9. See especially Bagong Soebardjo, "Dari Wayang Kartun ke Telewayang Bajra Bagaskara" [From Cartoon Wayang to Telewayang Bajra Bagaskara] (unpublished). I am indebted to Arswendo Atmowiloto for giving me a photocopy of this and other materials. See also "Wayang Kartun, Kenapa Tidak?" [Cartoon Wayang, Why Not?] *Jaya Karta*, 2 Aug. 1992.
10. Jan Mrázek, *Phenomenology of a Puppet Theatre* (Leiden: KITLV Press, 2005).
11. "Telewayang Bajra", *Pro-TV*, 1, 1 (February 1999), p. 8.
12. Promotional materials given to me by Arswendo, no date, no page numbers.
13. See the collection of his newspaper articles, *Telaah Tentang Televisi* [Research On Television] (Jakarta: Gramedia 1986).
14. "Kamus Kecil Telewayang Bajra: Apa & Siapa & Kenapa" [A Little Dictionary of Telewayang Bajra: What & Who & Why], *Pro-TV* 1, 1 (February 1999), p. 8.
15. Interview with Arswendo Atmowiloto, Jakarta, February 1999.
16. "Telewayang 'Bajra,' Sebuah Pendekatan Tradisi", ["Telewayang Bajra": An Approach to Tradition], *Suara Merdeka*, 22 Jan. 1999.
17. "Telewayang 'Bajra,' Sederhana Penuh Makna" [Telewayang "Bajra", Plain, Meaningful] *Kedaulatan Rakyat*, 5 Feb. 1999.
18. "Kamus kecil Telewayang Bajra."
19. "Wayang Ala Arswendo" [Wayang à la Arswendo] *Suara Merdeka*, 15 Jan. 1999.
20. Ibid.
21. Hardja Susilo, "The Personalization of Tradition: The Case of Sukasman's Wayang Ukur", in Jan Mrázek, ed., *Puppet Theater in Contemporary*

Indonesia: New Approaches to Performance Events (Ann Arbor: Center for South and Southeast Asian Studies, The University of Michigan, 2002).

22. "TPI Kemas 'Wayang TV' ala Sinetron' [TPI Packages "Television Wayang" à la Soap Opera], *Jawa Pos*, 20 Nov. 1996.
23. Unfortunately the details of this newspaper clipping have been lost.
24. Ibid.
25. Bondan Nusantara, "Kethoprak ing Televisi" [Kethoprak On Television], in *Unggah-ungguhing Basa ing Kethoprak lan Kethoprak ing Televisi,* ed. Handung Kus Sudyarsana and Bondan Nusantara (Yogyakarta: Taman Budaya Yogyakarta, 1990), pp. 39–57.
26. See Mrázek, *Phenomenology*, chapter 4.
27. The website address, in 2001, was www.panggung.net, and the main article on Kalasinema was on www.panggung.net/kalasinema.html, but already in 2007 it was not accessible. The e-mail correspondence took place in October 2001. I am grateful to Yanusa Nugroho for his help.
28. From http://www.panggung.net/toko/vcddewaruci.html , accessed in 2001 but alive no more.
29. From http://www.panggung.net/panggung.net/pustaka/kalasinema.htm.
30. From http://www.savpuskat.or.id/katalog2.php?ver=ina&id=138&idNya=34, last accessed 22 Oct. 2007.
31. The history of the project is summarized in Yardini Yumarta et. al., "Efektivitas Komunikasi Audio Visual Melalui Sinetron Modifikasi Wayang Golek Tradisionil" [Effectiveness of Audio-Visual Communication Through Soap Opera Modifying Traditional Wayang Golek] (unpublished research report, Fakultas Seni Rupa Dan Desain, Institut Teknologi Bandung, 1995), pp. vi, 13.
32. Ibid., p.167.
33. Ibid., p.167
34. Ibid., p.4.
35. Ibid., p. v.
36. Ibid., p. viii.
37 Ibid., p. 14.
38 Ibid., p. ix.
39. Ibid., p. 52.
40 Ibid., p. 52.
41. Drs H. Wiyoso Yudoseputro, "Penayangan Pergelaran Wayang Kulit di Televisi" [Broadcasting/Screening of Wayang Kulit Performance on

Television] (unpublished research report, Proyek Penelitian Yayasan Senawangi, 1997–1998), p. 75.

42. Yudoseputro, “Penayangan Pergelaran”, p. 75.
43. Yumarta, “Efektivitas Komunikasi”, p. 17.
44. Richard Coyne, *Technoromanticism* (Cambridge: The MIT Press, 1999), pp. 19–20.
45. Siegel, *Fetish, Recognition, Revolution* (Princeton: Princeton University Press,1997), p. 8. I have discussed Siegel’s and Rudolf Mrázek’s books in Chapter One.
46. Coyne, *Technoronmanticism*, p. 20.

Chapter 5

1. Rachmah Ida, “Reorganisation of media power in post-authoritarian Indonesia: Ownership, power and influence of local media entrepreneurs”, in Krishna Sen and David T. Hill, eds., *Politics and the Media in Twenty-First Century Indonesia* (New York: Routledge 2001), pp. 13–25.
2. Ibid., pp. 13–5.
3. Ibid., p. 17.
4. Ibid., p. 17.
5. Ibid., p. 22.
6. Els Bogaerts, “Mediating the local: Representing Javanese cultures on local television in Indonesia”, *Journal of Southeast Asian Studies*, 48(2): 215.
7. Miguel Escobar Vallera, “Wayang Kontemporer: Innovations in Javanese Wayang Kulit”, PhD dissertation in website format, National University of Singapore, 2015; Kathryn Emerson, “Transforming Wayang for Contemporary Audiences: Dramatic Expression in Purbo Asmoro’s Style, 1989–2015”, PhD dissertation, Leiden University, 2016.
8. Emerson, “Transforming Wayang”, p. 3.
9. Ibid., p.3.
10. For an excellent discussion of this television station, see Els Bogaerts, “Mediating the Local.” My own observations are based primarily on research in 2007, 2016, and 2017, with a focus on wayang broadcasts.
11. Ida, “Reorganisation of media”, p. 21.

12. Henk Schulte Nordholt and Gerry van Klinken, eds. *Renegotiating Boundaries: Local Politics in Post-Soeharto Indonesia* (Leiden: KITLV Press, 2007), p. 410.
13. Michel Picard, "*Otonomi Daerah* in Bali: The Call for Special Autonomy Status in the Name of *Kebalian*", in *Regionalism in Post-Suharto* Indonesia, ed. Maribeth Erb, Priyambudi Sulistiyanto and Carole Faucher (London and New York: Routledge, 2005), p. 129, n.6.
14. Ward Keeler, *Javanese Shadow Plays, Javanese Selves* (Princeton: Princeton University Press, 1987); Jan Mrázek, *Phenomenology of a Puppet Theatre* (KITLV Press: Leiden, 2005), Chapter 7.
15 Recently, after presenting my paper at a conference about maritime history in Semarang, unrelated to wayang, the first question I was asked was: "Who is your favourite wayang character?" I realized that the question was equivalent to the standard questions about methodology and researcher's positionality one gets asked at less authentic conferences.
16. I am grateful to Kathryn Emerson for this anecdote, and for arranging an interview for me with the dhalang.
17. http://www.purboasmoro.com/. Accessed 17 Aug. 2018.
18. "Para Dalang Gerah Tayangan Indosiar" [Puppeteers are Sick of Indosiar Broadcasts], *Suara Merdeka* 1 June 2001. Quoted and discussed in Chapter Two.
19. Claire Holt, *Art in Indonesia: Continuities and Change* (Cornell University Press: Ithaca and London, 1967), p.11. My emphasis.
20. Paul Virilio, *The Paul Virilio Reader* (New York: Columbia University Press, 2004), p. 142.
21. Escobar Vallera, "Wayang Kontemporer".
22. "Hacking and Rehearsing, Experiments in Creative Tinkering", *New Theatre Quarterly*, 32, 1 (2016): 68–77; "The Archive as Repertoire: Transience and Sustainability in Digital Archives", *Digital Humanities Quarterly*, 10, 4 (2016), < http://www.digitalhumanities.org/dhq/vol/10/4/000269/000269.html>.
23. Escobar, "Wayang Kontemporer", Chapter/Section 2.6 (no page numbers, but searchable).
24. Ibid.
25. Holt, *Art in Indonesia*, p. 22.
26. Ibid., pp. 3, 5.
27. Ibid., p. 3.

28. Ibid., p. 7.
29. Ibid., pp. 11–2.
30. Ibid., p. v.
31. Ibid., p. 11.
32. Heryus Saputro, "Ade Kosasih Sunarya: Wayang Golek Pakai Komputer Mengapa Tidak?", *Femina* 17, 6 (1989): 64.
33. Maurice Merleau-Ponty, *L'Oeil et l'Esprit* (Paris: Gallimard, 2005), p. 92. English version: Galen A. Johnson, ed., *The Merleau-Ponty Aesthetics Reader: Philosophy and Painting* (Evanston: Northwestern University Press, 1993), p. 149.
34 Stanley J. O'Connor, "Humane Literacy and Southeast Asian Art", *Journal of Southeast Asian Studies* 26, 1 (1995): 151.
35. Matthew Isaac Cohen, "Contemporary *Wayang* in Global Contexts", *Asian Theatre Journal*, 24, 2 (Fall 2007): 338–69.

Bibliography

Abbas, A. Komar and Seno Subro. *Ki Manteb "Dalang Setan": Sebuah Tantangan* [Ki Manteb, "Devil Puppeteer": A Challenge]. Surakarta: Yayasan Resi Tujuh Satu, 1995.

Anderson, Benedict R. O'G. *Mythology and the Tolerance of the Javanese*. Ithaca: Cornell Modern Indonesia Project, 1965.

Arps, Bernard, "The Sound of Space: How to Hear the Mise en Scène in Audio Wayang", in *Puppet Theater in Contemporary Indonesia: New Approaches to Performance Events*, ed. Jan Mrázek. Ann Arbor: Center for South and Southeast Asian Studies, The University of Michigan, 2002, pp. 315-32.

Atmowiloto, Arswendo. *Telaah tentang Televisi* [Research on Television]. Jakarta: Gramedia, 1986.

Auslander, Philip. *Liveness: Performance in a Mediatized Culture*. New York: Routledge, 1999.

Baudrillard, Jean. *Simulacra and Simulation*, trans. Sheila Glaser. Ann Arbor: The University of Michigan, 1994.

Bazin, Germain. *The Museum Age*. Brussels: Desoer, 1967.

Becker, Alton. *Beyond Translation: Essays Toward a Modern Philology*. Ann Arbor: University of Michigan Press, 2000.

Bogaerts, Els, "Mediating the local: Representing Javanese cultures on local television in Indonesia", *Journal of Southeast Asian Studies*, 48(2): 196–218.

Cohen, Matthew Isaac, "Contemporary *Wayang* in Global Contexts", *Asian Theatre Journal*, 24, 2 (Fall 2007): 338–69.

Coyne, Richard. *Technoromanticism*. Cambridge: The MIT Press, 1999.

Derrida, Jacques and Bernard Stiegler, *Echographies of Television*, trans. Jennifer Bajorek. Cambridge: Polity, 2002.

Derrida, Jacques. *The Specters of Marx*, trans. Peggy Kamuf. New York: Routledge, 2006.

Dumont, Louis. *Essais sur l'individualisme: une perspective anthropologique sur l'ideologie moderne* [Essays on Individualism: An Anthropological Perspective on Modern Ideology]. Paris: Seuil, 1983.

Dusek, Val. *Philosophy of Technology*. Blackwell: Malden, 2006.

Echols, John M. and Hassan Shadily, *An Indonesian-English Dictionary*, rev. and ed. by John U. Wolff and James T. Collins. Ithaca, NY: Cornell University Press, 1989.

Emerson, Kathryn, "Transforming Wayang for Contemporary Audiences: Dramatic Expression in Purbo Asmoro's Style, 1989–2015", PhD dissertation, Leiden: Leiden University, 2016.

Escobar Vallera, Miguel, "The Archive as Repertoire: Transience and Sustainability in Digital Archives", *Digital Humanities Quarterly*, 10, 4 (2016). Online at http://www.digitalhumanities.org/dhq/vol/10/4/000269/000269.html.

---, "Hacking and Rehearsing, Experiments in Creative Tinkering", *New Theatre Quarterly*, 32, 1 (2016): 68–77.

---, "Wayang Kontemporer: Innovations in Javanese Wayang Kulit", PhD dissertation in website format, National University of Singapore, 2015, http://cwa-web.org/dissertation/wayang-dis/index.php.

Harsrinuksmo. *Mengungkap Rahasia Isi Keris* [Revealing the Secret of the Content of the Keris]. Jakarta: Pustakakarya Grafikatama, 1990.

Hastanto, Joko Dwi, "Dari Sarasehan Wayang: Menggugat Kreativitas Dalang" [From Wayang Workshop: Contesting Puppeteers' Creativity], *Suara Merdeka*, 12 Oct. 1996.

---, "Rekaman Lagi, Ki Manteb Rujuk dengan Indosiar" [Recording Again, Ki Manteb Reconciles With Indosiar], *Suara Merdeka*, 22 Oct. 2001.

Hastanto, Sri, "Sapa Sira Sapa Ingsun?" [Who Are You, Who Am I?], *Kedaulatan Rakyat*, 27 Oct. 1991.

Heidegger, Martin. *The Question Concerning Technology and Other Essays*, trans. William Lovitt. New York: Harper & Row, 1977.

Hill, David and Krishna Sen. *Media, Culture, and Politics in Indonesia*. Melbourne; New York: Oxford University Press, 2000.

---, *Politics and the Media in Twenty-First Century Indonesia*. New York: Routledge, 2010.

Holt, Claire. *Art in Indonesia: Continuities and Change*. Ithaca and London: Cornell University Press, 1967.

Husserl, Edmund. *The Crisis of European Sciences and Transcendental Phenomenology*, trans. David Carr. Evanston: Northwestern University Press, 1970.

Ida, Rachmad, "Reorganization of Media Power in Post-Authoritarian Indonesia: Ownership, Power and Influence of Local Media Entrepreneurs", in *Politics and the Media in Twenty-First Century Indonesia: Decade of Democracy*, ed. Krishna Sen and David T. Hill, London and New York: Routledge, 2011, pp. 13–25.

Janarto, Herry Gendut and Arswendo Atmowiloto, *Teguh Srimulat*. Jakarta: Gramedia, 1990.

Jurriëns, Edwin. *Cultural Travel and Migrancy: The Artistic Representation of Globalization in the Electronic Media of West Java*. Leiden: KITLV Press, 2004.

"Kamus Kecil Telewayang Bajra: Apa & Siapa & Kenapa" [A Little Dictionary of Telewayang Bajra: What & Who & Why], *Pro-TV* 1, 1 (Feb. 1999), p. 8.

Keeler, Ward. *Javanese Shadow Plays, Javanese Selves*. Princeton: Princeton University Press, 1987.

"Ki Enthus Susmono: Yen dhalang mudha Solo ora 'melu' aku, bakal mati sandhang pangane" [Ki Enthus Susmono: If Young Puppeteers Don't "Follow", They Will Have No Livelihood"], *Jaya Baya* 17 July 2001.

"Ki Manteb Sudharsono: 'Gendheng nek aku nglecehne wayang!'" [Ki Manteb Sudharsono: "It's Crazy That I Would Insult Wayang!"], *Jaya Baya* 27 Aug. 1995.

"Ki Manteb Soedarsono: Film Kungfu" [Ki Manteb Soedarsono: Kung Fu Films], *Suara Merdeka*, 6 Oct. 6, 1996.

"Kisah Sukses Petruk di Indosiar" [The Tale of Petruk's Success On Indosiar], *Forum Keadilan* 4, 16 (20 Nov. 1995): 68.

Kitley, Phillip. *Television, Nation and Culture in Indonesia*. Athens, OH: Ohio University Center for International Studies, 2000.

"Limbukan Pun Diprotes" [Limbukan, Too, is Protested Against], *Kedaulatan Rakyat*, 7 Sept. 1996.

Loven, Klarijn. *Watching Si Doel, Imagining the Nation: Television, Language and Identity in Contemporary Indonesia*. Leiden: KITLV Press, 2007.

Lysloff, René. "A Wrinkle in Time: The Shadow Puppet Theater of Banyumas (West Central Java)", *Asian Theater Journal* 10,1 (Spring 1993): 49–80.

Mangunwijaya, Y.B., *Durga Umayi* [Witch Goddess]. Jakarta: Pustaka Utama Grafiti, 1994.

---. *Durga/Umayi* [Witch/Goddess], trans. Ward Keeler. Seattle: University of Washington Press 2004.

Marx, Karl. *The Marx-Engels Reader*, ed. Robert C. Tucker, 2nd ed. New York: Norton, 1978.

McLuhan, Marshall. *Understanding Media*. Cambridge: MIT Press, 1999.

Merleau-Ponty, Maurice. *The Merleau-Ponty Aesthetics Reader: Philosophy and Painting*, ed. Galen A. Johnson. Evanston: Northwestern University Press,1993.

---. *L'Oeil et l'Esprit* [The Eye and the Spirit]. Paris: Gallimard, 2005.

---. *Phenomenology of Perception*, trans. C. Smith. London and New York: Routledge, 1962.

---. *The Primacy of Perception*, trans. James Eddie. Evanston: Northwestern University Press, 1964.

---. *The Visible and the Invisible*, trans. A. Lingis. Evanston: Northwestern University Press, 1968.

Mrázek, Jan. *Phenomenology of a Puppet Theatre: Contemplations on the Art of Javanese Wayang Kulit*. Leiden: KITLV Press, 2005.

---, ed. *Puppet Theater in Contemporary Indonesia: New Approaches to Performance Events*. Ann Arbor: Center for South and Southeast Asian Studies, The University of Michigan, 2002.

---, "Ways of Experiencing Art: Javanese Shadow Puppets in Art History, in Performance, and on Television," in *What's the Use of Art? Asian Art and Material Culture in Context*, ed. Jan Mrázek and Morgan Pitelka (Honolulu: Hawai'i University Press, 2008), pp. 272–304.

Mrázek, Rudolf. *Engineers of Happy Land: Technology and Nationalism in a Colony*. Princeton: Princeton University Press, 2002.

Nugroho, Amien, "Pagelaran Wayang Kulit Perlu Pembaharuan?" [Does Wayang Kulit Need Renewal?], *Kedaulatan Rakyat*, 29 Sept. 1991.

Nusantara, Bondan. "Kethoprak ing Televisi" [Kethoprak on Television], in *Unggah-ungguhing Basa ing Kethoprak lan Kethoprak ing Televisi* [Language Levels in Kethoprak and Kethoprak on Television], ed. Handung Kus Sudyarsana and Bondan Nusantara, Yogyakarta: Taman Budaya Yogyakarta, 1990, pp. 39–57.

O'Connor, Stanley J. "Art Critics, Connoisseurs, and Collectors in the Southeast Asian Rain Forest: A Study in Cross-Cultural Art Theory,"

Journal of Southeast Asian Studies, vol.14, no. 2 (Sep. 1983): 400–8.

---. "Humane Literacy and Southeast Asian Art," *Journal of Southeast Asian Studies* 26,1 (1995): 147–58.

---. "Memory and Discovery in Southeast Asian Art", *Asian Art and Culture* 8,1 (1995): 3–6.

Pamudji, "Ketika Panggung Ketoprak dan Wayang Diusung ke Televisi" [When Ketoprak and Wayang Stage are Moved to Television], *Suara Merdeka*, 9 Aug. 1997.

Panofsky, Erwin. *Perspective as Symbolic Form*. New York: Zone Books, 1997.

"Para dalang gerah tayangan Indosiar" [Puppeteers Are Sick of Indosiar Broadcasts], *Suara Merdeka*, 1 June 2001.

Parta, Kicuk, "Geger wayang Indosiar: Kasus Anggada Balik" [Wayang Indosiar Tumult: The Case of Anggada Balik], *Jaya Baya*, 20 May 2001.

---, "Nggugat Dhalang Setan: Daniwara 'Oye ... eee!'" [Contesting the Devil Puppeteer: Daniwara "Oye ... eee!"] *Jaya Baya*, 27 Aug. 1995.

---, "Wayang Indosiar: 'Kesandhung Ki Anom Suroto'" [Indosiar Wayang: "Tripped Over Ki Anom Suroto"], *Jaya Baya*, 24 Mar. 1996.

"Pedhalangan Wis Rusak" [Puppeteering is Kaput], *Mekar Sari*, 6 Sept. 1996.

"Peredaran CD Empat Lakon Ki Manteb Ditangguhkan" [Distribution of CDs with Four Plays by Ki Manteb Suspended], *Suara Merdeka*, 19 Apr. 2001.

Picard, Michel, "*Otonomi Daerah* in Bali: The Call for Special Autonomy Status in the Name of *Kebalian*", in *Regionalism in Post-Suharto Indonesia*, ed. Maribeth Erb, Priyambudi Sulistiyanto and Carole Faucher, London and New York: Routledge, 2005, pp.116–31.

Poerwono, Won, "Pentas Wayang 10 Malam Dibiayai UNDP" [Ten-Night Wayang Performance Financed by UNDP], *Suara Merdeka*, 8 Aug. 2001.

Postman, Neil. *Amusing Ourselves to Death*. New York: Penguin, 1985.

Ricoeur, Paul. *Time and Narrative*, trans. Kathleen McLaughlin and David Pellauer. Chicago and London: Chicago University Press, 1992.

Riley, Brooks, "Camera Angles", *Opera News* 54 (June 1990): 14.

Rushdie, Salman. *The Enchantress of Florence*. London: Jonathan Cape, 2008.

Sadono, Bambang. *Apa & Siapa Orang Jawa, Edisi 1995–1996* [Javanese People, What & Who, 1995–1996 Edition] (Semarang: Citra, 1995).

Saputro, Heryus, "Ade Kosasih Sunarya: Wayang Golek Pakai Komputer Mengapa Tidak?" [Ade Kosasih Sunarya: Why Shouldn't Wayang Golek Use a Computer?], *Femina* 17, 6 (1989): 64–6, 86.

Sarworo Sp, "Pergelaran Wayang Kulit di Televisi: Dalang Ditantang, Dalang

Bisa 'Kelimpungan'" [Wayang Kulit Performance on Television: When Dalang is Challenged, Dalang Can be "Confused/In Trouble"], *Kedaulatan Rakyat*, 15 Sept. 1996.

Schulte Nordholt, Henk and Gerry van Klinken, ed. *Renegotiating Boundaries: Local Politics in Post-Soeharto Indonesia*. Leiden: KITLV Press, 2007.

Sears, Laurie. *Shadows of Empire: Colonial Discourse and Javanese Tales*. Durham, NC: Duke University Press, 1996.

Siegel, James. *Fetish, Recognition, Revolution*. Princeton University Press: Princeton, 1997.

Soebagio, Gunawan, ed. *Wayang Sebagai Pinisinetron* [Wayang as Pinisinetron]. Bandung: Citra Aditya Bakti, 1989.

Soebardjo, Bagong. "Dari Wayang Kartun ke Telewayang Bajra Bagaskara" [From Cartoon Wayang to Telewayang Bajra Bagaskara]. Unpublished.

Sudibyo, Arie, "Biarkan Gamelan Alternatif Berkembang" [Let Alternative Gamelan Flourish], *Kedaulatan Rakyat*, 22 Aug. 1996.

Suratno, "Ki Slenk (Saya Lebih Enak Nonton Kamu): The Tactics of a Best Selling Puppeteer", in *Puppet Theater in Contemporary Indonesia: New Approaches to Performance Events*, ed. Jan Mrázek, Centers for South and Southeast Asian Studies, University of Michigan: Ann Arbor 2002, pp.153–68.

Suratno et. al. *Limbukan Pada Pakeliran Wayang Purwa Gaya Surakarta Dalam Lima Tahun Terakhir* [Limbukan in the Surakarta Style Wayang Purwa Performance over the Last Five Years]. Surakarta: STSI, 1996.

Surjodiningrat, R.M.Wasisto. *Gamelan, Dance, and Wayang in Jogjakarta*. Jogjakarta: Gadjah Mada University Press, 1971.

Susilo, Hardja, "The Personalization of Tradition: The Case of Sukasman's Wayang Ukur", in *Puppet Theater in Contemporary Indonesia: New Approaches to Performance Events*, ed. Jan Mrázek, Centers for South and Southeast Asian Studies, University of Michigan: Ann Arbor, 2002, pp. 179–88.

"Telewayang 'Bajra, Sebuah Pendekatan Tradisi", ["Telewayang Bajra", An Approach to Tradition], *Suara Merdeka*, 22 Jan. 1999.

"TPI Kemas 'Wayang TV' ala Sinetron' [TPI Packages "Television Wayang" à la Soap Opera], *Jawa Pos*, 20 Nov. 1996.

Virilio, Paul. *The Paul Virilio Reader*, ed. Steve Redhead. New York: Columbia University Press, 2004.

Wardhana, Veven Sp. *Televisi dan Prasangka Budaya Massa* [Television and the

Prejudices of Mass Culture]. Jakarta: Institut Studi Arus Informasi, 2001.
Weber, Samuel. *Mass Mediauras: Form Technics Media*. Stanford: Stanford University Press, 1996.
"Wayang Ala Arswendo" [Wayang à la Arswendo], *Suara Merdeka*, 15 Jan. 1999.
"Wayang Kartun, Kenapa Tidak?" [Cartoon Wayang, Why Not?] *Jaya Karta*, 2 Aug. 1992.
Weintraub, Andrew. *Power Plays: Wayang Golek Puppet Theatre of West Java*. Athens: Center for International Studies, Ohio University, 2004.
Williams, Raymond. *Television: Technology and Cultural Form*. Hanover and London: University Press of New England, 1974.
Wirjosuparto, "Nonton 3 Wayang Kulit" [Watching 3 Wayang Kulit], *Kedaulatan Rakyat*, 24 Feb. 1999.
Wolters, Oliver. *History, Culture, and Region in Southeast Asian Perspectives*. Singapore: Institute of Southeast Asian Studies, 1982.
Yudoseputro, Drs. H. Wiyoso, et.al., *Penayangan Pergelaran* Wayang *Kulit di Televisi* [Broadcasting Wayang Kulit Performances on Television], unpublished research report, Proyek Penelitian Yayasan Senawangi [Jakarta], 1997–98.
Yumarta, Yardini, et. al., "Efektivitas Komunikasi Audio Visual Melalui Sinetron Modifikasi Wayang Golek Tradisionil" [Effectiveness of Audio-Visual Communication Through Soap Opera Modifying Traditional Wayang Golek], unpublished research report, Fakultas Seni Rupa dan Desain, Institut Teknologi Bandung, 1995.

Index